Integrated Marketing Communication

Now in its second edition, this textbook explores the continuing transformation of advertising, sales promotion, and public relations functions within the marketing discipline. The content focuses on emerging new technologies, as well as established digital and legacy media, as the reader is guided through the process of developing and implementing a comprehensive Integrated Marketing Communication plan for companies, organizations, and brands.

Clear, concise, and practical, the book takes the reader through consumer, market, and competitive research; creative conceptualization; market segmentation, identification of a target audience, and brand positioning; as well as strategic decisions involving the timing, placement, and intensity of advertising, sales promotion, public relations, and brand visibility. The new edition emphasizes the importance of social media, website development, search engine optimization, mobile marketing, brand promotion events, and retail store connectivity. Updated to include more digital content with detailed international examples, this new edition adds four new chapters including Integrated Marketing Communication objectives, budgets, and metrics, legacy media planning, business-to-business marketing strategies, and innovative technologies with topics such as artificial intelligence, predictive analytics, synthetic media, virtual reality, and voice marketing.

Upper-level undergraduate and postgraduate students will appreciate this lucid, up-to-date text, as will business professionals in executive education and certificate programs. Experiential learning is provided with chapter assignments and a continuity case study woven into the textbook.

The second edition is also accompanied by robust online resources, including PowerPoint slides, chapter videos, lecture notes, classroom exercises, digital flash cards, test banks, an instructor resource book, and interactive templates for preparing an Integrated Marketing Communication Plan.

Jerome M. Juska is an Adjunct Professor at Seminole State University. Dr. Juska has taught advertising management at the University of Illinois, Northwestern University, and Franklin College in Lugano, Switzerland. He is also a consultant for agencies, media, and advertisers.

Integrated Marketing Communication

Advertising and Promotion in a Digital World

Second Edition

Jerome M. Juska

Routledge
Taylor & Francis Group

NEW YORK AND LONDON

Cover image: © Getty Images

Second edition published 2022
by Routledge
605 Third Avenue, New York, NY 10158

and by Routledge
4 Park Square, Milton Park, Abingdon, Oxon, OX14 4RN

Routledge is an imprint of the Taylor & Francis Group, an informa business

© 2022 Taylor & Francis

First edition published by Routledge 2018

Library of Congress Cataloging-in-Publication Data
Names: Juska, Jerome M., author.
Title: Integrated marketing communication : advertising and promotion in a
    digital world / Jerome M. Juska.
Description: Second Edition. | New York, NY : Routledge, 2022. | Revised
    edition of the author's Integrated marketing communication, 2017. |
    Includes bibliographical references and index.
Identifiers: LCCN 2021028814 (print) | LCCN 2021028815 (ebook) | ISBN
    9780367443368 (hardback) | ISBN 9780367436230 (paperback) | ISBN
    9780367443382 (ebook)
Subjects: LCSH: Internet advertising. | Internet marketing.
Classification: LCC HF6146.I58 J87 2022 (print) | LCC HF6146.I58 (ebook)
    | DDC 658.8/72--dc23
LC record available at https://lccn.loc.gov/2021028814
LC ebook record available at https://lccn.loc.gov/2021028815

ISBN: 978-0-367-44336-8 (hbk)
ISBN: 978-0-367-43623-0 (pbk)
ISBN: 978-0-367-44338-2 (ebk)

DOI: 10.4324/9780367443382

Typeset in Sabon-Roman
by Deanta Global Publishing Services, Chennai, India

Access the Support Material: www.routledge.com/9780367436230

Contents

Detailed Contents

Dedication

When my entire life has revolved around advertising and marketing communication, it is very difficult to thank everyone who has helped and supported me during my professional and academic career. My long list would include so many professors and administrators along with corporate managers and executives. And, there is a multitude of long-time friends, family members, neighbors, and casual acquaintances. So many people were important and valued!

Let me begin with the primary reasons for writing this textbook. At the top of my list are my parents, Tony and Felicia Juska, who always provided me with inspiration, guidance, and tremendous support. It was my mother's creative spirit, enthusiasm, and compassion plus my father's determination, persistence, and motivation that forged my perspective and personality.

Northwestern University enabled me to discover the world of advertising. I was inspired by legendary professors, including the father of modern marketing, Dr. Philip Kotler, as well as Dr. Steuart Henderson Britt and Dr. Vernon Fryburger, Chairman of the Advertising Department.

And, to my Northwestern classmates, thank you for the memories and friendships over the years.

My first note of appreciation is directed toward Alexandro Moneta, former Dean of the MBA program at St. Xavier University in Milan, Italy. Alex encouraged me to write a concise, easy-to-read, and practical textbook for international students who wanted to learn more about the American style of advertising and sales promotion. His insistence propelled me into the challenging task of preparing my first manuscript and constructing details for every chapter.

My next thank you is given to Dr. Greg Marshall, the distinguished marketing professor and former editor of the *Journal of Marketing*. As an experienced and successful textbook author, Greg gave me insights on the publishing process and challenges involved with preparing a manuscript. Knowing what to expect next was an important part of completing the project.

Another expression of gratitude is reserved for Dr. Deborah Goldring, a professor of marketing at Stetson University. She has been an academic colleague, associate in the American Marketing Association, private advisor, and personal friend for many years in Central Florida. Deborah has always unselfishly connected me to the right people at the right time at multiple universities.

I also want to thank Dr. Tulay Girard, a talented marketing professor at Penn State University. Tulay and I have continually shared academic thoughts and theories of advertising, social media, and marketing communication since our days together at Nova Southeastern University. Over many years, we have built a lasting friendship together, along with her husband, Bill.

I also have deep respect and admiration for Professor Yasuhiko Kobayashi at Aoyama Gakuin University in Tokyo, Japan. During the years, I enjoyed many visits and experiences, especially involving Dentsu, the largest advertising agency in Japan, and Nihon Keizai Shimbun, publisher of the *Japan Economic Journal*. I also have many friends at academic institutions in Europe, including: Franklin University in Lugano, Switzerland, the American University in Paris, Passau University in Germany, Bocconi University in Milan, and Jyvaskyla University in Finland.

There are also thanks and gratitude for the wisdom of many other people, such as Joe Cappo, retired editor of *Advertising Age*, and Dan O'Brien, former Director of Advertising at Accenture.

Plus, great friends from San Francisco to New York and from Chicago to Miami, including Jack Minkow, Dor Novak, Ron Krisik, Brent Kubasta, Rafael Martinez-Pratts, Dr. Julia Maskivker, Dr. Kent Williams, and Dr. Arnold Harrison, who have helped me in so many different ways over the years by reminding me to count my blessings and good fortune.

And finally, I want to acknowledge the love and affection of my wonderful wife, Adriana Schiavon. During all the long hours of writing a textbook and computer-filled weekends of writing, she was always patient and understanding. The challenge of completing this textbook was met during the dark specter of the pandemic, which interrupted our lives and made everything more difficult, especially while teaching several courses online during the process. Without Adriana, I am not sure if I could have endured the barriers and limited resources.

My final dedication is to everyone who will be reading this textbook. I may never meet you, know your name, or contact you, but my desire is to inspire you by sharing this information and learning experience. Please use it, apply it, and grow with knowledge and exciting new insights!

Author

Dr. Jerome M. Juska is an author, entrepreneur, business executive, international marketing consultant, and academic professor. His diversified career began after graduating from Northwestern University with a Bachelor's degree in marketing and a Master's degree in advertising management. Juska's business career included executive advertising positions at several global corporations, such as the Jeep Corporation in Detroit and International Harvester in Chicago. As the Global Advertising Manager for the Truck Division of International Harvester, he supervised a staff of six and a budget of $17 million dollars. During this time, he earned two CLIO awards for creative advertising excellence. He was frequently asked to be a speaker at conferences and workshops as an active member of multiple advertising and marketing associations. After being the Advertising Manager at U.S. Telephone in Dallas, Juska returned to Northwestern University to earn his doctorate degree in communication.

Dr. Juska's academic career included teaching at Northwestern University, Evanston, Illinois; St. Xavier University, Kolkata, India; University of Illinois at Urbana-Champaign, Illinois; Florida Atlantic University, Boca Raton, Florida; Nova Southeastern University, Broward County, Florida; Seminole State University, Sanford, Florida; and Rollins College, Orlando, Florida. He also spent three years at Franklin College in Lugano, Switzerland as the Chair of the International Management Division. He has taught undergraduate and graduate courses in advertising, sales promotion, consumer research, public relations, international business, creative planning, digital media, and brand marketing. He was also invited to be part of the Advisory Board for the International Advertising Association, Chicago, as well as a creative judge for a competition sponsored by *Advertising Age* magazine.

In 2017, the first edition of *Integrated Marketing Communication* was published. The textbook was developed using a concise, easy-to-read format for MBA students and executives as well as international students who wanted to learn the basics of advertising and sales promotion. Dr. Juska introduced a new framework with his second edition, which emphasized the importance of applying artificial intelligence for creating and delivering brand messages. His commitment to new technologies and advanced methods of communication has been internationally recognized.

Foreword

In Chapter 1, the textbook begins with a glimpse of the future. The author has taken the position that artificial intelligence and machine/human interactions will precipitate another transformation of the marketing communication industry. The introduction of digital media and mobile apps was only the beginning of a new landscape for delivering brand messages and building relationships with consumers. New technologies, such as facial recognition and seamless voice commerce, have the potential to reach and respond to potential buyers in remarkably innovative ways.

While there are many concerns about privacy and surveillance, technology is moving faster than our ability to adapt to it. The increased use of synthetic media and computer-created avatars, along with the brave new world of artificial reality with social media, is offering new communication opportunities for advertisers. The most amazing vision of the future is exemplified by entrepreneurs like Elon Musk, who is disrupting the communication industry by launching thousands of Earth-orbiting satellites with SpaceX to create a private Internet system.

In Chapter 2, the concept of Integrated Marketing Communication (IMC) is introduced and discussed. This provides the framework for delivering brand content and persuasive messages through six functional pathways: advertising, sales promotion, public relations, brand visibility, digital media platforms, and personal contact. The structure of the IMC industry is outlined, based on the collaboration among four separate groups: advertisers, agencies, media, and suppliers. The chapter continues with the review of three models that illustrate the marketing approach to a customer's journey: the classical AIDA model, the digitally oriented funnel model, and the complex attribution model. This leads into the preparation of an IMC Plan, which is the blueprint for combining all the elements required for strategic brand communication.

In Chapter 3, the foundation of the Integrated Marketing Communication plan is built using the information and insights gathered from marketing research. This includes both primary and secondary research. Four marketing research categories are reviewed: industry, product, communication, and consumer research. The importance of quantitative and qualitative research is emphasized, as well as the need for competitive information. Understanding the mind and mood of existing customers and potential buyers is essential for making creative advertising and effective media decisions. The focus is on the consumer's needs and wants, not just a product.

In Chapter 4, the importance of communication objectives is discussed with a direct connection to performance measurements. However, this is preceded by the generation of budgets and calculating the amounts of financial resources needed. The multiple methods of funding and estimating advertising costs and other IMC expenses are explained. After a budget is determined, then the allocation process begins, with different amounts of money based on IMC pathway categories, product life cycle, calendar time periods, target audiences, and geographic sales potential. Anticipating budget changes and flexible adjustments is also part of budgeting activities.

In Chapter 5, segmentation, targeting, and brand positioning are the primary topics. Four traditional segmentation categories are introduced: demographic, psychographic, geographic, and behavioral. Segmentation must be extremely specific when identifying existing customers and approaching potential new buyers. Since the cost of advertising is directly proportionate to the number of people exposed to a medium, the essential need for specific targeting and consumer personas becomes more apparent. The chapter ends with the differentiation of primary and secondary target audiences as an effective method of utilizing limited financial resources.

In Chapter 6, the process of creativity and the application of creative thinking for advertising are revealed. The chapter defines creativity and identifies the personality characteristics that are most responsible for stimulating original and innovative thinking. The physiology of the brain is used to demonstrate the development of emotional and rational brand message strategies. Multiple storytelling frameworks are introduced with a long list of creative tactical applications.

The organization of a creative department at a large agency is described, along with the planning tools used to create advertisements. These include the presentation formats for both legacy and digital media along with the development of creative concepts based on a compression of the most essential marketing research information contained in a brand brief for the agency team.

In Chapter 7, the connection between creative brand messages and media delivery platforms begins to unfold. An introduction is made using a comparison of digital and legacy media. The difference between paid, owned, and shared media is also explained with connections to other platforms. A web-centric approach is presented, based on driving traffic to a landing page or brand website. This reinforces the purchase funnel model adopted by digital media marketing agencies as well as supporting the attribution model for marketing performance measurements. Website design and navigation is discussed, along with simple dashboard metrics. The balance of the chapter focuses on other important forms of digital media, such as email marketing and the basic requirements to open business accounts and effectively advertise on social media platforms.

In Chapter 8, the complexity of legacy media is discussed with a review of basic terminology, including reach, frequency, duplication, rating points, and gross points. The importance of establishing media objectives for evaluating the effectiveness of the advertising is emphasized.

This reverts to the application of the AIDA (awareness, interest, desire, action) model for legacy advertising and includes the full spectrum of Integrated Marketing Communication. The chapter continues with a detailed outline of the requirements for advertising in television, radio, newspapers, magazines, outdoors, and transit media. This information can be summarized in a media spreadsheet with the planned financial expenditures, advertising units, consumer impressions, and media placement calendar.

In Chapter 9, the concept of sales promotion is defined along with the importance of formulating specific promotional objectives. Multiple sales promotion strategies are reviewed and organized according to four categories: price reduction, value invitation, psychological rewards, and targeted interactions. The utilization of both paper and digital coupons is emphasized, along with the most popular forms of promotions, such as buy-one get-one (BOGO), cash back, free trial, gift merchandise, brand sampling, games and puzzles, contests, and sweepstakes. The importance of measurement is also discussed and related to specific objectives for each individual sales promotion program.

In Chapter 10, the value of public relations is presented within the framework of stakeholder relationships. Since publicity is considered to be a form of earned media, the basic method of calculating its financial value is demonstrated. The chapter continues with a review of the functions of a public relations department, or agency, followed by recommendations for how these activities can support a marketing communication plan. This includes mutual collaboration for new product introductions, trade shows, and brand-sponsored activities and events.

In Chapter 11, brand visibility is defined with a list categories, including product placement, venue identification, brand packaging, licensing rights, retail displays, and logo merchandise. Brand visibility is considered to be different from sales promotion since it involves a longer time frame, greater permanence, and a more substantial impact on consumer awareness of a brand. The financial value of brand visibility can be calculated based on a media exposure model or by estimating its contribution to image and desirability. Brand visibility extends into retail store locations and selling environments through packaging, signage, and portable aisle displays.

In Chapter 12, business-to-business (B2B) marketing communication strategies are introduced. The emphasis is placed on inbound marketing as the most cost-effective method but also as part of a balanced approach that includes vertical and horizontal media. Trade shows have traditionally been the most important way to interact with thousands of potential buyers in a single location during a three or four-day period. But, digital technology has been introduced for virtual online trade shows. This not only saves time and money but enables a greater amount of connectivity among buyers and sellers. B2B activities revolve around the channel of distribution, or marketing intermediaries, such as wholesalers, retailers, dealers, distributors, and brokers. Marketing and merchandising support is offered through a diverse assortment of financial and psychological incentives, including volume discounts, price concessions, co-op advertising, and product information training for sales people.

Preface

Technology is changing the world faster than our ability to adjust. The impact on marketing communication industry during the past 20 years was nothing less than a seismic shift in the way that brand messages had been created, delivered, and measured. And now, artificial reality is rapidly emerging as it promises to launch another wave of digital transformations.

That is why the first chapter of this textbook begins which a brief perspective of the future, including such topics as facial recognition, seamless voice marketing, synthetic media, predictive analytics, and competitive Internet systems developed from Spacex satellites and the vision of Elon Musk. While everything is becoming more sophisticated and complex, there is no doubt about the growing importance of artificial intelligence and human-to-machine interactions.

The dynamics of the marketplace has already adjusted. Everyone is simultaneously competing for customers and opportunities. Enormous amounts of data and information are collected, analyzed, and utilized in a real-time marketing environment. So, it is essential for MBA students, corporate managers, and entrepreneurs to have a basic and practical understanding of Integrated Marketing Communication. This includes knowledge of legacy media as well as digital media, along with the process for researching, planning, and implementing brand content and advertising messages.

Where do we go from here? That's the next challenge that we need to prepare for today.

— a voice from the future.

Chapter 1

Artificial Intelligence

Another Digital Transformation for the Future of Marketing

Learning Objectives

1. Understand the significance of artificial intelligence for marketing communication
2. Explore the emerging new technologies for advertising, promotion, and public relations
3. Imagine the possibilities of voice-only product purchasing and synthetic media
4. Investigate the potential of facial recognition and virtual reality for social media
5. Consider the impact of multiple Internet systems and global brand channels

Introduction

While the future is always filled with new innovations, artificial intelligence is promising to accelerate that trend and to inject even more disruptive business models and digital media transformations. So, what is the emerging technological environment for Integrated Marketing Communication? And, how will it influence the way brands and companies interact with existing customers and potential buyers? This chapter begins with a discussion of artificial intelligence and then moves into an exploration of the most important new technologies shaping the future.

DOI: 10.4324/9780367443382-1

In this chapter, we will briefly explore several of the most influential emerging technologies. Most of these technologies are still evolving with plenty of obstacles, problems, and challenges. Some might fail. And no doubt, many more will be added. New approaches, innovations, and companies will appear with amazing successes and disastrous collapses. But that isn't so important. The critical challenge for corporations, small business owners, and entrepreneurs is to learn how to incorporate these technologies into advertising, promotion, public relations, and brand communication. It might be a lot to ask, but why not? There are only three ways to get ready for the future: avoid it, create it, or quickly adapt to it. So, let's get started!

What Is Artificial Intelligence?

We are beginning this textbook by imagining the world of tomorrow. That is the only way to really understand what could be happening next. By anticipating, expecting, projecting, and wondering, managers and companies become more prepared for change and even more ready to adapt when it arrives. If we maintain a flexible, open-minded, and visionary perspective, then our world becomes less frightening and more predictable. As we progress deeper into the 21st century, a multitude of innovative technologies will emerge. They are already beginning to happen. Some are disruptive, while others are just improvements over previous systems. Still, technology influences our world, how we live, and especially, how we communicate with others.

During the past 20 years, digital media have transformed everything. Remember, only 10 years ago, there was no such thing as an iPhone or an Android system. And, just look at what has happened since the appearance of that super smartphone, which was really a computer, a phone, and the essential center of our daily life in disguise. Now, we are at the beginning of a much more dramatic and encompassing phenomenon: artificial intelligence. This word is relatively new in our vocabulary with a meaning that is perceived differently by many people. To some, it is about faster and more powerful computers, cloud storage capabilities, and advanced software programs. But to others, artificial intelligence is when machines can think and act like humans.

Definition of Artificial Intelligence

There are plenty of textbooks, lectures, videos, and white papers on artificial intelligence, along with a long history of science fiction books, television programs, and movies about the topic. The most relevant example is *2001: A Space Odyssey*, where the visionary director Stanley Kubrick introduced HAL. Without needing to give a spoiler alert, HAL was a sophisticated computer that assisted the crew of a space ship as it was making its initial journey to Mars. The HAL computer performed a variety of operation functions and complex tasks, which included the ability to think independently and make critical decisions for the astronauts. Ironically, this first-class movie was made way back in 1968, but finally on August 6, 2012 for NASA (National Aeronautics and Space Administration) succeed in

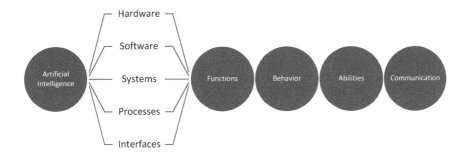

Figure 1.1 Interacting with Artificial Intelligence

placing a remote-controlled vehicle the size of car, called Curiosity, on the surface of Mars.

Elon Musk, the CEO of SpaceX, has an ambitious plan to get human to Mars by 2026. The vehicle that will transport them to the Red Planet is the SpaceX Starship, the largest rocket ever constructed at nearly 400 feet high or 120 meters high, was put into orbital flight during 2021. Ultimately, Musk plans to schedule multiple flights and even create a Mars Colony with its own rules, government, and culture. But then, who can doubt the man who successfully created the Tesla electric automobile?

So, what is artificial intelligence, and why is it important to marketing communication? Let's begin with an original, non-technical definition. Artificial intelligence is "the interaction of computer hardware, software, systems, processes, and interfaces that replicate human functions, behavior, abilities, and communication." As shown in Figure 1.1, artificial intelligence has multiple connecting points and interaction pathways with humans. As a result, artificial intelligence is already performing many complex tasks and activities, such as facial recognition, speech simulation, mood detection, physical mobility, and yes, even independent decision-making.

Threats to Privacy

On a more philosophical level, artificial intelligence is also a threat. First, our privacy is no longer as free and unrestricted as in previous years. Cameras are everywhere. They are located in stores, office buildings, street corners, parking lots, restaurants, and even in our own homes. Plus, nearly everyone is walking, talking, or looking into a small camera in their smartphone. Second, data about you, and everyone else, is continually being collected, analyzed, stored, and in some cases, illegally shared with others. And many times, this personal data is sold to third parties without controls or restrictions. This includes the search results from our computers, the products and services we purchase, the pets we own, the photos we share on social media, and probably even the things we did last summer. And finally, intelligent machines in the form of autonomous robots are replacing humans at an alarming rate. No one is exempt. Nothing is impossible. Machines that think can quickly and efficiently complete physical work, solve the most complex mathematical problems, design a building, and even predict our behavior. The advantages and disadvantages of artificial intelligence will continue to be discussed with greater intensity and concern. Yet, humans created all the hardware, software, systems, processes, and interfaces for artificial intelligence. Is it possible that machines will eventually become inorganic duplicates of humans? It's more than just a science fiction story. It just might be a future reality.

Human and Machine Communication

The interaction between machines and humans involves a classical model of the two-way flow of communication. It's pretty simple. There is the sender and the receiver. No need for a quiz on this topic. The sender, or receiver, can be a computer, smartphone, digital appliance, virtual assistant, digital avatar, or physical robot. Surprisingly, every type of machine speaks the same type of language: binary. It is amazingly simple but profoundly complex. It is the language that every computer and electronic device knows and understands with the proper programming and software instructions. There are only two numbers involved: zero and one. What magic and power are bestowed on these numbers! But, we are just learning how to become more fluent in the language of artificial intelligence.

Let's take it one step further. What happens when the communication is a continuous flow involving nanoseconds? Or, how can data be processed when it is being created faster than it can be absorbed? Let's look at the process this way. The machine–human interaction has four basic parts: questions, refinements, recommendations, and commands. Ironically, the action can be initiated in any one of the four parts. A single question can lead to a refinement or a command. A recommendation can lead to a question, then a refinement, and finally, a command. Or, a concise command can be provided by a human at any time. For example, you ask Siri a question, and you immediately get a specific answer. If you are not satisfied with the response, the question is revised, and you proceed to ask Siri once again. Another example is a command asking Alexa to play some jazz music, but Alexa might respond by offering specific information involving an the artist, style, or specific title.

Data-Driven Marketing

We are also experiencing an increase in data-driven marketing. This can be anything from predictive analytics to programmatic media buying. The foundation of this process is displayed in Figure 1.2. This is a simplification of the activity,

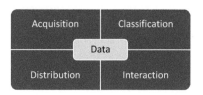

Figure 1.2 Phases of Data-Driven Marketing

but it does provide a framework. These are the four pillars of data-driven marketing: acquisition, classification, delegation, and interaction. The acquisition of data is really a combination of the production or generation of data along with a simultaneous ability to retain large volumes of data. The Apple iPhone, which was introduced way back in 2007, was the initial force behind the accelerating curve of data. The iPhone has continued to evolve and every year offers new features, options, and models. The capability to share photos and videos contributed to the data explosion. And, there was also the ability to share and distribute user-generated video content on YouTube. The final ingredient was the growth of cloud computing, especially Amazon Web Services (AWS), which has silently dominated the market for storage of data with millions of interconnected servers and complex data networks.

The other phases of data-driven marketing are most frequently associated with the decision sciences, along with knowledge management, while marketing is dependent on management information systems. That is where classification and delegation originate, especially when there is any interaction between humans and machines. Social media is the primary data-generating activity involved with consumer communication, while brand marketing focuses on increasing website traffic.

In the next 10 years, our personal communication with artificial intelligence will dramatically change. It will be faster and more complex but will gradually blend into a more natural style. The millions of algorithms that digital scientists and engineers will be creating will go much further, probably well beyond our comprehension. Machines will sense, understand, and react to our moods, our behavior, and even our thoughts. This concept should be no surprise to anyone in the field of marketing communication, since we have all viewed many different visions of the future from movies, films, television programs, digital media, streaming content, and video games. Our journey to the future has begun; now we just have to get there.

Marketing Technology's Digital Landscape

There is an unprecedented number of new technologies restructuring the digital marketing landscape. They have emerged from entrepreneurs, small businesses, and large corporations. They could have been developed most anywhere in the world. While you are aware of some, others will be completely new to you. It is difficult to determine which will succeed or fail, or which will have the applications of greatest impact involving advertising, promotion, and public relations.

Figure lists 12 technologies that will provide you with a visual perspective of the future digital landscape for marketing and Integrated Marketing Communications. The fascinating technologies that have been selected include facial recognition, interactive voice commerce, synthetic media, social virtual and artificial reality, holographic television, retail store beacons, personal identity chips, proximity marketing, programmatic media, and finally, the alternative Internet.

This chapter will concentrate on the three most important applications of artificial intelligence for Integrated Marketing Communication: facial recognition, voice commerce, and synthetic media. These technologies are expanding so rapidly that it is nearly impossible to keep up to date. So, what you are reading right

Data Visualization	Synthetic Media	Virtual Reality Platforms	Facial Recognition
Store Beacons	Proximity Marketing	Programmatic Media Buying	Interactive Voice Commerce
Personal Identity Chips	Predictive Analytics	Holographic Television	Private Internet Systems

Figure 1.3 Marketing Technology's Future Landscape

now has already changed. And by the time you finish this textbook, there will be another series of improvements, enhancements, and practical applications.

Facial Recognition

Have you ever watched Tom Cruise in the science fiction movie *Minority Report*? There was a great scene when his character, walking through a large transportation center, was continually being confronted by video screens promoting different consumer brands. The facial recognition system was not only identifying him but using his first name in every simulated commercial. Not a good situation when you are trying to hide from everyone who has been chasing you.

The most powerful, yet controversial, technology of the 21st century is now facial recognition. However, many companies and organizations have already developed and effectively utilized facial recognition software in their market products and services. While praised for its ability to provide safety and security, this aspect of artificial intelligence has also been criticized for its intrusiveness. Often, facial recognition is associated with discrimination or exclusion. This is a perplexing situation for management and marketing communication. Do consumers have the right to privacy? And, is there an obligation to inform people that facial recognition is being used for business purposes? That is a philosophical, ethical, and cultural debate that is beyond the scope and purpose of this textbook. But, it is a very serious and important issue for a global society.

Definition of Facial Recognition

Let's start with a more complete definition of facial recognition: "a biometric software application that identifies, verifies, classifies, compares, and stores digital data about a person's facial features, contours, and individual characteristics using complex algorithms." If you have a recent model of an Apple iPhone or Samsung, then you are experiencing facial recognition each and every day. Recognizing and validating your identity is always required to physically activate your mobile device. But, have you ever wondered how this technology works? Or where facial recognition is being used for marketing and brand communication? That is where our exploration of artificial intelligence will begin, but from the perspective of the future and how it can affect us.

There are four basic steps in facial recognition: virtual measurements, application of algorithms, database matching, and accuracy estimation. The physical characteristics of the human face can include many features, but the most important physiological variables for measurements include the size, location, and spatial distances between distinct human parts, such as the eyes, nose, and ears, and basic head geometry. Individual differences in the overall structure, and even particular idiosyncratic motions, such as head movements, mouth shapes, and eye blinking, can be incorporated into the algorithm. Unique items, such as moles, freckles, discolorations, and scars, are other characteristics that can be utilized for identification. The most sophisticated facial level of recognition systems can detect and record the expression of moods and reactions to situations.

The use of other biometric measurements, such as thermal heat cameras, is another part of the complex spectrum of facial recognition. As shown in Figure 1.4, there are multiple aspects to the acquisition of data involving people, classifying that information, then distributing the results, and eventually, interacting with the users of this technology. As you can imagine, the same process can be applied to voice characteristics and speaking patterns. And finally, the information obtained from facial recognition can be compared with images on private files and public records, including finger prints and several other biometric identification measurements.

There are many questions about the reliability and accuracy of facial recognition. Depending on the algorithm, and the individual who designed it, results can often be inconclusive. This means that a certain amount of error always occurs, but is it significant, and can it be trusted? If the situation is a shopper in a store, a misidentification would only be an embarrassment, but using this same technology for law enforcement, security surveillance, or private protection might have other, more severe consequences. So, there is plenty of room for improvement in facial recognition technology, but as artificial intelligence continues to observe and learn from the process, the degree of accuracy and reliability will dramatically improve. Until then, marketing communication can only use what is available and recognize that errors will always be possible.

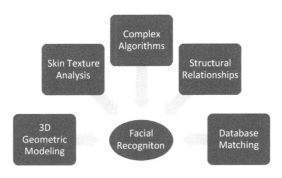

Figure 1.4 Biometrics and Facial Recognition

Surveillance Environments

Nearly all of us are exposed to facial recognition cameras, as well as other biometric detection devices, several hundred times a week, or even more. That alone is a significant amount of information about us. The data collected provides an accurate record of our mobility, including the time, place, and duration of activities. For example, facial recognition compiles information from many different locations, but the most important input sources are public places, homes and apartments, business locations, retail stores, transportation, and social media.

This situation has often been described as a surveillance environment. But, it is part of the world that we now live in. The challenge for marketing management is to learn how to leverage this technology for brand communication, sales promotional activities, and relationship building.

Let's begin by developing a perspective of a surveillance environment, especially with the locations that are shown in Figure 1.5, along with the benefits that might emerge from different methods of data collection.

Public Places   Yes, cameras are everywhere. Some you see, but most of them are hidden. Small video cameras are placed on street corners, buildings, bus stops, road signs, traffic signals, and many other locations. While most cameras are strategically arranged and used for specific purposes, such as the monitoring of automotive traffic, crime prevention, or crowd control, others are for private purposes. Do you have any idea how many cameras are located in your city or neighborhood?

In New York City alone, there are 18,000 surveillance cameras used by the Police Department to monitor the movement of people and activities around this large metropolis. The entire city has a recorded number of 31,900 cameras, compared with Los Angeles with 22,675, Paris with 26,835, Tokyo with 39,500, and Hong Kong with about 50,000. London was ranked as the third most intensely surveilled city in the world in 2020 with an astonishing total of 627,000 cameras. This means that a density of 67 cameras per 1000 people is used for observing, monitoring, and recording the population of London. While the safety and security of its citizens are very important, England has taken extraordinary precautions to maintain a network of social media connections, or digital eyes, to identify problems and then take action immediately.

But, the utilization of facial recognition in Europe and the United States is extremely low compared with China. Now, are you ready for this number? The capital of China, Beijing, has over 1,150,000 cameras monitoring its population.

Figure 1.5 Video Surveillance Locations

Shanghai has an equally high number of more than 1 million cameras. In fact, nearly 100 cities in China also have intense surveillance and video observation environments. Even though it is the most populated country in the world, China has more than 200 million video cameras installed. That's right, 200 million!

Homes and Apartments When you are looking at your computer, is your computer looking back at you? It can, if programmed correctly. That small red dot at the top of your laptop or desktop that indicates when your camera is turned on could be activated remotely by a hacker. Many people are already concerned about the possibility, and that is why tech experts recommend putting a piece of tape over your camera viewing port at the top of your computer. Yes, that solves the problem fast.

But facial recognition in home environments is all about those other video cameras. While very small and inexpensive recording devices can be placed in any room of a house or apartment, the most dramatic location is a different location. How about outside your entrance door? About 10 years ago, Doorbot was introduced to the home security market. From virtual obscurity as a start-up, this little product would begin a whole new chapter in surveillance. The original device was simple, at first, with a camera inside a doorbell to enable viewing who was outside your entranceway. It also included a mobile app that enabled you to see a visitor or guest on your cellphone. Later, the product was rebranded with a new name, Ring. This version featured a high-definition camera, a microphone, and a small speaker for two-way audio communication. So, when a person comes to the entrance doorway, the owner or resident can silently view the person in real time, record their appearance, and even have a short conversation or provide instructions. As the technology improved, Ring was capable of playing a pre-recorded message, musical song, or special sound effects, or remotely performing other functions, such as activating exterior lights.

During its early development, it was known to share crime-related video incidents with local governments and police departments. This was perceived as a positive activity. But, the other opinion is that while you are protecting your home, you are also contributing to the global network of surveillance. Suddenly, this became both an ethical and a personal issue, especially when it was discovered that data from these devices was being sold to several digital marketing companies, including Facebook. This raised an increasing number of questions about its usage.

There is one final fact about Ring that you need to know. In 2018, Ring was purchased by Amazon. And, it provided an entirely new data collection resource for marketing purposes.

Then, there are apartments. You go out. You come in. And you go out again. And you return. If you live in a large apartment building, these events are repeated many times. But as you exit, or enter, the cameras are silently watching and recording. The data collected is enormous. Just imagine! Who has left? What time? How long were they gone? While most of the video cameras in apartment buildings are used for live surveillance and security, the potential exists for sharing this information with other data storage systems. It can be connected with movements around the city or just down the block. And if social media is involved, the power of social media and facial recognition are combined to match who you are, where you are, and when you were there.

Offices and Warehouses   The need for security and surveillance becomes the most important motivating factor for using facial recognition in work locations. This is primarily used for accessing both private and government locations. These include more than just office buildings and warehouses. There are manufacturing plants, transportation centers, storage facilities, and the list goes on. For many years, a security guard was the only gatekeeper and guardian of a work location. The primary responsibility of these security guards was to check the identity of employees, suppliers, or visitors to a work location. Then, technology intervened with magnetic access cards, digital key fobs, and most recently, mobile apps, but now, cameras have taken over by providing the same essential service of identity verification using facial recognition technology. Smile, please!

Retail Stores   In many large retail stores, there is a person at the main entrance who gives you a friendly greeting or welcoming hello. But very soon, you might begin interacting with a different personality, a digital avatar. Since this experience will be a shopper's first point of contact, the avatar has the opportunity to direct a personalized message that is meaningful and relevant. This technological form of engagement has the potential for interactive communication using artificial intelligence.

Here's how it works. As you walk through the entranceway, a facial recognition system is activated. It scans your face, searches the store's internal database, and attempts to identify you. If there is a match, the computer instantaneously knows the answer to three important questions: Has this person ever visited this store before? What did they purchase during their last visit? Is this individual a member of the company's brand loyalty program? There are thousands of different pieces of information about you, and your shopping behavior, that are immediately available for a sophisticated software program to analyze, interpret, and utilize as the store prepares to interact with you. Depending on the technology, you will automatically become part of the process.

That's right. The computer, using artificial intelligence, is going to communicate with you. First, since it already knows your name, it can welcome you on a digital screen. Nothing fancy, just your first name displayed in bright bold letters. Or, the computer can select a voice greeting. Synthesized speech is an easy-to-use technology today. Imagine, "Hello, Martin. Welcome to Harrah's." And, after you walk a few more steps, a video message from a friendly avatar: "Is there anything we can help you with today?" As you can tell, the computer is trying to establish, or maintain, a human-like relationship. This entire scenario might be vaguely familiar. And, it should be. Remember the movie *Minority Report* with Tom Cruise? If you recall that scene, then you fully understand the potential for bombarding a person who is entering a retail store.

In the future, facial recognition can be used to monitor a customer's shopping behavior with the installation of "aisle-cams." These strategically located cameras could be a valuable source of observational research or a tremendous invasion of privacy. Let's begin with an exploration of the first application. The cameras would be using facial recognition to identify individual shoppers and then, begin collecting data that is specifically associated with that person. For example, the purchase of a breakfast cereal. How long did they spend in this section of the grocery store? Which packages did they look at first? Did they check prices online with their smartphone? Which brand did they finally put in their shopping cart?

There is a sizable amount of information about an individual shopper at a particular store at an exact day and time. This is precisely the type of qualitative and quantitative data that can be used for predictive analytics.

There is another reason why retail stores want more cameras installed. Shoplifting. It has always been a big problem. The financial losses from illegally taken merchandise historically run into billions per year. While people who steal are difficult to catch, they are even more of a nuisance to prosecute. There are thrill-seeking teenagers, people in economic difficulties, and others who just enjoy the thrill of not being discovered. Unfortunately, there are also very experienced professional shoplifters who make a career from their deceptive skills and techniques. Facial recognition will identify most of them immediately as they are entering the store. Perhaps, it's time for their early retirement? This is certainly a big plus for the loss prevention department.

Transportation   Most any public vehicle can have a surveillance camera inside, on top, or mounted in a receptive position. This includes trains, buses, taxis, and even trucks. Millions and millions of them are moving around out there right now. Many of them have already been equipped with a camera for security purposes, and even more will be installed tomorrow. The ride sharing services Uber and Lyft immediately installed more cameras and in some cases, facial recognition systems during the Covid-19 crisis. No mask, no ride. And if the company wants to subtly identify and notify drivers of any previous customers who have been uncooperative or caused problems, the same facial recognition technology can be used. Also, there is another consideration: the physical area around transportation locations, where people are either congregating or passing by the vehicles, such as bus stops, train stations, or waiting shelters. Transportation locations provide an excellent opportunity to use artificial intelligence to know who is going where and when. Fortunately, there is no way to know why these people are traveling, unless Alexa or Siri is involved in the process. Then, it morphs into a gigantic surveillance network.

Social Media   Find your friends, follow your family, and become fans of your favorite celebrities, local personalities, and nearly anyone else with a Facebook or Instagram page. But, wait. Do you know those other people in the photos or posts? Not everyone has been tagged or identified, but now you can do this with your very own social media software. There are plenty of free versions available for download, as well as more sophisticated platforms for business enterprises, non-profit organizations, and government units. During the past few years, as facial recognition has become more popular, a barrage of new apps has emerged in the marketplace. Some are good; others are not. One caution. Be sure you know the reputation of the company and its privacy policy as well as the actual costs of using or downloading the software. Here are a few suggestions that you might want to consider and try out with social media.

Blippar is a face recognition app that can identify over 370,000 celebrity faces for a quick search on their life, work, and other details. FacePhi is dedicated to the financial sector, allowing banks to recognize their customers in order to enhance the mobile experience with an added level of security. Luxand can recognize faces in live video footage, along with an estimate of their age. This company also aggressively markets itself on multiple social media platforms by offering the consumer version of its software, called FaceSKD, which appears to be more focused on collecting visual data from individuals than effectively using it to enhance online experiences.

Face2Gene is a facial recognition app for the medical industry, which has been used to help doctors perform genetic evaluations. FaceFirst uses facial recognition software to identify individuals from a distance, making it ideal for law enforcement, military, and other organizations. Log Me uses helps users find people from any part of the world. Like a social networking platform, it enables users to search for old friends and distant relatives from old photographs and compares the image to find the best matches. If it is successful, you are provided with enough information to contact them. Hopefully, the technology has worked correctly, or you might just be reaching out to the wrong person. Want to see what you will look like in the future? Then, try this "aging" and "feature modification" app. It is appropriately called FaceApp and was launched in 2017 for iPhone users. FaceApp filters include changing the smile, hairstyle, skin tone, age, and even gender of your own image or the image of anyone else that you want to upload. Looks like part of a digital playground, using technology to change reality, but then, what is real and what is not?

Companies Using Facial Recognition

It's not in the news, but many companies are experimenting with facial recognition for a multitude of purposes. These include a "contactless" payment system, customer service improvements, employee performance evaluation, management negotiations, political gatherings, marketing research, music concert audience feedback, and virtual "product trial" experiences. Here are just a few examples of how facial recognition is being used for many purposes other than policing, security, general surveillance, and in-store marketing activities.

Disney Theme Parks   In March, 2021, the Disney Company announced that visitors to its theme parks and entertainment centers had the option to use a "facial recognition" system for the entrance pass. No more printed tickets, no more digital bar codes, and no more QR codes on cellphones. While this was presented as a test program, it is inevitable that the utilization of facial recognition by Disney is a significant advancement in marketing technology. This method serves not only as an admission control procedure but also as a continual monitoring and surveillance system. Just think about it—Disney will know exactly where you are in the theme park, how long you are spending in each location, and your physical movement pattern through your entire visit!

Is this an invasion of privacy? Probably not. Because this is private property, Disney has the right to make certain requirements for entering and utilizing its facilities. This is like a contact and not very different from all the legal statements involved in using any product or services.

Just read the statements and disclaimers when you sign up for any social media platform. If you don't agree to the conditions and regulations, then you cannot use the service.

Disney's expansion and implementation of a facial recognition for its theme parks will be carefully observed by competitors. Other companies that interact with large numbers of people in a single location, such as sports stadiums, outdoor concert venues, shopping malls, and even community events, will also be very interested in the application of facial recognition.

So, this is the just the beginning of the utilization of facial recognition for marketing and the application of artificial intelligence to monitor, interact, analyze, and interpret customer behavior. Let's see what happens next and which other companies follow Disney's lead.

McDonald's When you purchase a Big Mac, large fries, or just a small cheeseburger, facial recognition is working hard to provide you with the best customer service. Surprisingly, the cameras are not looking at you but at the McDonald's employees. The company is using facial recognition to monitor and evaluate the facial expressions of its staff when they are waiting to take your order, making a payment, or delivering the food to you. This is only being used in a few select stores, but the technology could easily be expanded to include customers. Then, in the future, when you are trying to decide between a Big Mac and a salad, the facial recognition technology will be capturing information about your reactions before, during, and after your purchase decision process. And, artificial intelligence might be used to predict what you will buy in the next few seconds based on your previous history. Maybe a large order of fries, again?

Walmart How you shop is even more important than what you buy. That's the approach taken by Walmart when using facial recognition to scan the aisles. What is it searching for with those cameras? Walmart is gathering data about your physical shopping behavior. It wants to know your movements around the display racks, which packages are picked up from shelves, which ones are passed by, and the walking pattern that you have taken while you were in the store.

This is marketing research about in-store shopping patterns. While Walmart wants to study the flow of people going up and down the aisles, there are national manufacturers who want to know more about how shoppers interacted with their brands, specifically the packaging. But, Walmart owns and controls this information. Should it be collaborating with the manufacturers? Or, can this provide Walmart with another source of income from its retail operations? If facial recognition is being used, the technology can identify the person who is shopping and send text notifications to them with coupons, special sale prices, or other promotional incentives.

Chevron Can you buy gasoline just by showing your face? Yes. Chevron is using facial recognition that allows truck drivers to purchase its fuel products at selected service stations along motorways and highways. Will they expand it to include the average motorist? Imagine pulling into a gas or petrol station and then looking into a camera to get authorization and to make a payment. And, that's not all. In some countries, Chevron is using the same facial recognition technology with gasoline delivery trucks to recognize fatigue, distractions, and other safety-related factors among truck drivers. Is it possible that this application will also be used in automobiles in the future?

MAC Cosmetics Imagine being able to try 800 shades of lipstick without leaving your home or apartment? Well, you can. MAC Cosmetics has an interactive online experience on its website that does just that. It uses the camera in your mobile device or desktop for an image of your face. Then, you swipe as many different shades as you want from its vast selections of colors and styles. Whatever you want, from glossy to vibrant shades and from classic to modern, it's on the screen. You can even upload a photo of yourself in your new dress or fashionable clothing. Perfect for going out to a party or clubbing, then match the shade of lipstick to your mood. How cool is that?

But, consider what else might be going on during this virtual experience. Biometric data is being collected about you. This includes not only your facial expressions but also a potential scan of your eyes. It is possible to gather research data about how you reacted to each shade of lipstick after you put it on your lips, or the popularity of different choices of lipstick, ranked by the order of selection, the number of product purchases, and the estimated demographics of the user. But, the same facial recognition technology can be used at cosmetic counters with retail stores. In those cases, the social interaction with a sales representative, or a few of your friends who decided to shop with you, will enhance your shopping experience.

MasterCard Here is a potential industry disruptor. MasterCard has facial recognition software that enables customers to pay for purchases by holding their mobile device, such as an iPhone, and pointing it at an optical scanner at special check-out locations. Just blink twice. Yes, blink! Your eyelids are now acting as keys on a computer or a mouse with a pointer. In those microseconds while you are waiting, the camera is scanning your face, and a computer is using Master Card's facial recognition algorithms to identify, verify, and authorize your purchase. Smiling is not required, but it does make the entire process more enjoyable.

Privacy Rights and Laws

Who said you had a right to privacy? Or, does anyone actually guarantee that right? The answer to these questions has changed during the Digital Age. Technologies have expanded our ability to view, listen, and interact with other in both face-to-face and artificial environments. The most important change is that the process of viewing, listening, and interacting can be initiated without our knowledge. This process can also be completed using machines and artificial intelligence, which gathers data, analyzes and processes the data, and finally, uses the results to accomplish a task.

Biometric Privacy Act Consumers are becoming increasingly concerned about their own privacy. The collection of data by social media without consumers' knowledge has raised awareness of this important issue. After it was discovered that Facebook was selling personal data or collaborating with third-party users, a movement to restrict or limit the power of social media companies was initiated with the introduction of several bills and laws that attempted to solve or alleviate the problem.

In the United States, the first Biometric Privacy Act was passed and approved by the State of Illinois in 2008. Its purpose is to guard and protect against the unlawful collection, storage, and usage of individual biometric information. This was followed by a series of similar laws and legislation introduced into other areas of the country. In 2020, a court in the United Kingdom ruled against the police in New South Wales, Australia, who had collected facial recognition data from a mobile van that was parked outside a football stadium. This ruling is the latest in a growing movement against facial recognition technology on the grounds that it violates personal freedoms, invades privacy, and is discriminatory.

Twenty lawsuits alleging biometric data privacy violations by TikTok have also been filed in federal court in the United States. Eventually, they were combined into a single legal case, which alleged that TikTok facial biometrics and other data were collected from minors by the app and ultimately sent to China. This included claims that TikTok was also securing user data from smartphones that were using the app for social media. Microsoft, which was in the process of purchasing TikTok, stated that it would ensure that all data would remain in the United States but did not indicate whether it would follow the guidelines of the California Consumer Privacy Act.

Consumer Concerns   Expect more legislations and controls in the future. The European Union has already taken strong action, and further debate is anticipated. What this will mean for the future of social media is unclear, but the problem of privacy is much larger and more insidious, especially regarding video surveillance with algorithms for tracking and recording the movement of people. In China, the process of monitoring people even includes rewarding individuals for positive public behavior, such as crossing roads in the correct place, or punishing them for unwanted actions. There is actually a score associated with your observable behavior. There was once a phrase: "The whole world is watching." Well, guess what? Today, the whole world is "being watched!"

Interactive Voice Commerce

Speech recognition software is nothing new. Just pick up a telephone and call a company, office, store, or organization. You will be asked questions by an automatic system and routed to the correct place. Software programs were able to understand the words spoken by a human and respond based on key words and phrases with the help of artificial intelligence. Most of the time, it worked pretty well. However, many other times, it did not. Eventually, you could get help from a live customer service representative. Still, there was plenty of human-to-machine interaction, but the problem was the amount of time involved in the communication process.

Text-to-voice software packages are also available for your computer or mobile device. These allow the user to speak in a conversational tone, with the result of a continuous flow of typed communication. The reverse process, text-to-voice, is also part of different software packages. For example, Dragon speech recognition software is a pioneer and leader in conversational artificial intelligence. Offered by Nuance Communication, Dragon software is easily compatible with either Apple or Android phones. But, there was still something missing. It was the transition from dictation and transcription systems toward live, real-time interactions with customers and retail businesses.

Voice Assistants and Smart Speakers

Siri was introduced in 2011 as an advanced feature with the Apple iPhone 4S. Alexa was launched in November, 2014 along with a black cylindrical speaker, the Amazon Echo. This was another quantum leap for human-to-machine communication. Initial sales were slow, but the Christmas holiday season propelled Amazon Alexa sales to 12 million units, and the following year, sales reached 20 million units. By the time Amazon had reached 60 million units, Google finally entered the market with its Google Assistant smart speaker, followed by Samsung's Galaxy S8 with Bixby. By the end of 2020, more than 100 million smart speakers had been sold to customers.

The smart speaker market evolved and expanded into a new classification of products, which included smaller viewing pieces of technology along with viewing screens that could display the actual products and services being requested. This became the foundation for seamless voice commerce, because physically seeing an object is easier than just talking about it. So, the next level of interaction went beyond asking for music, weather reports, or movie recommendations.

Definition of Voice Commerce

In this textbook, voice commerce is defined as a "seamless customer experience from online search to physical delivery." Now, this is much more than just asking a question and waiting for Siri, Alexa, or Google to respond. Originally, those devices could only provide information and nothing more. Until now. Voice commerce has taken several giant leaps forward. The difference is that Siri, Alexa, and Google now have a new function. They are intermediaries that now have the ability to connect and leverage their voice technology with retail locations.

What Is an API?

Without getting into the technological details, a software program that involves detailed coding, called an API or Application Program Interface, is needed to send actionable instructions to a computer or mobile device. Many of these APIs are simple, routine processes that can be combined and incorporated into larger, more sophisticated programs. Perhaps, a good analogy is Lego building blocks, which become useful only when they are assembled according to a creative design or pre-determined structure. Each one fits into the others and contributes to the final end product. So, APIs can be used to develop interactive voice commerce programs.

Voice responders and personal assistants are providing APIs to software development companies and individuals for building systems involving voice commerce. For example, the Alexa Developer Package has the codes needed to transform a human voice command into a performance task to be completed. These building software building blocks are called "skills" that can be used independently or combined in sequences. Currently, there are more than 100,000 skills offered by Alexa as part of its integration package for intelligent voice control.

Seamless Voice Purchasing

The four sequential stages of a seamless voice commerce experience are shown in Figure 1.6. While the process involves multiple decisions and options, the basic sequence includes search, selection, purchase, and delivery. The search part of the process is initiated through a voice command to a smart speaker, or cellphone, in the form of a request to find a product, service, company, location, or brand name. We have all done that for music, sports scores, or shopping. But, here is where the API takes over. If a retailer has installed a voice purchasing system, then the process goes beyond the traditional search and selection process. Once this request has been identified and confirmed, the user communicates a command to Siri, Alexa, or Google Assistant to run a special program related to a retail location. The command must be short, specific, and use the most appropriate words for speech recognition. Plus, the command must also include the identification name of the retail store or company. For example, a command to Alexa could be: "Start McDonald's" followed by the spoken words "display food menu" and then "show lunch specials." The entire selection process continues down, including the most detailed items or extras, like extra ketchup or mustard. Perhaps some fries? And, don't forget the Diet Coke!

What happens next is achieved by incorporating the API codes that have been previously created for a business by a voice software system supplier. This is not as hard as you think. The software supplier has written instructional computer "code" for specific industries, such as fast food restaurants, hotels, and recreational facilities. Want to reserve a tennis course or golf starting time? There are pre-packaged programs for those functions. Want to book a room for a vacation trip? Or, a dinner reservation for Saturday night? No problem. There are packages of code already complete. What you do need is a dependable voice commerce company to provide the APIs.

The third stage of a seamless voice commerce experience is the purchase. This requires a secure financial transaction involving a bank credit card or debit card, PayPal, or any other form of payment exchange that is approved safe for online transactions. This process is incorporated into the store's proprietary app and activated during the checking-out part of the transaction. The payment sequence is activated immediately after a final check-out is desired. And then, the fourth stage of the seamless voice commerce experience is delivery, which can include bringing the food or merchandise to a private home, apartment, or office location as well as specifying either in-store pick-up or a drive-through arrangement. This

Figure 1.6 Voice Commerce Seamless Experience

is where a voice commerce company is needed to complete the seamless process. Once again, the APIs are there to facilitate the flow. There are dependable service delivery operations in every city, from large national companies to smaller local entrepreneurial start-ups. They just need to be plugged into the voice commerce equation through a voice commerce service company.

Jetson is an example of a typical company involved in the voice commerce industry. Based in New York, it provides retail establishments with the API codes needed to complete seamless transactions. This enables larger corporations, as well as local businesses, to interact with their customers using user-friendly software. It is just another demonstration of how artificial intelligence is shaping the future of communication and brand management.

And finally, a word about the future of voice marketing. What will it become? Expect that brand name recognition, and especially brand name recall, will be the single most important factor that determines success in voice commerce. If a consumer cannot remember the brand, how can they ever order it? There might be room for micro-video advertising here to stimulate or prompt consumers. Let's call it video "blips," which just communicate a brand's position or image. However, the challenge is to demonstrate that voice commerce is viable by providing consumers with a seamless experience, with rapid completion times and accurate delivery arrangements.

Synthetic Media

Not everything is what it appears to be. Not in the world of synthetic media, especially with video. The person you are watching is not there, and the words you are hearing are not coming from a human. That's right! You guessed it. The video was a computer-generated replication using a complex text-to-video software program. Imagine the possibilities. A realistic-looking human avatar is speaking the exact words that you have just written. However, there is a growing danger for misusing synthetic media, called the "deep fake," when a video is created and produced using an authorized image of an actual person along with a manipulated voice to imitate the real one.

Definition of Synthetic Media

Synthetic media can be defined as "the creation, production, and distribution of video messages, programs, and brand communication using complex algorithms that modify, manipulate, and combine user-generated text, images, and digitally stored content." Humanized avatars are used to create messages by transforming the text content into an auditory and visual message. How is this possible? Because synthetic media are based on complex "text-to-video" software, artificial intelligence can realistically replicate human speech patterns. This process is achieved through the subtle manipulations of facial features, especially the lips and mouth, along with body movements, hand gestures, and other forms of non-verbal communication. The artificial intelligence software is still learning to speak and understand the many complexities of a "human" language with all its nuisances, idioms, inflections, and inferences; however, at the same time, we are still trying to communicate effectively with machines.

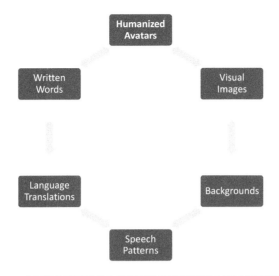

Figure 1.7 Text-to-Voice Synthetic Media

There are four basic parts involved in the creation of a synthetic media video: the digital avatar, the background image, compatible music, and a written script, which is entered as text (see Figure 1.7). The software program combines these four parts using artificial intelligence and generates a finished video product, usually in an MP3 file. It's that simple and easy, but it does require technical or computer programming experience. Fortunately, there are several platforms that provide user-friendly instruction to facilitate the process. The most versatile application technology is by the award-winning London-based company, Synthesia (www.synthesia.com).

Here is a description of how a synthetic media video is produced and the challenges involved.

Digital Avatars

First, the digital avatar who will be featured in your video is selected from a collection of different personalities. These are real people who have been previously recorded and through the power of artificial intelligence, speak the words and phrases that you have entered into a written script. These avatars include men and women from different age groups, physical appearances, ethnic backgrounds, and perceived social orientations. While each one has a distinct speech pattern, accent, and in some cases, even a regional dialect, they are automatically programmed to convert your text words into a spoken language. In fact, there are more than 30 different languages currently being used with digital avatars. This means that you can immediately translate your words into French, German, Italian, Spanish, and even Mandarin Chinese. Just imagine the cost savings, as well as time, when a single written script for a video commercial or short form content can be utilized to generate videos for Europe, South America, and Asia.

Want to become an avatar? You can. Just upload several images of yourself. The software will automatically create a digital version of you. So, after you write a script, your "digital self" will actually be speaking those same words for you in the video. Pretty cool technology! It's a perfect alternative for everyone who gets nervous when they have to make a live presentation.

Text-to-Speech Video Technology

The only major challenges for text-to-video messaging are the rate of speaking, inflection, and pauses. There are options for speeding up or slowing down the number of words spoken. Also, the software program enables the artificial intelligence within its design to recognize and to place inflection points at the beginning of sentences as well as other critical points in the texted script. But, the pauses are a real problem. Fortunately, the insertion of a small piece of code that is generic to the system can immediately correct the issue. It takes practice to establish the correct timing and length of a pause, but the results ensure smooth and realistic communication. As this technology improves, it will be an increasingly easy and fast process for converting text to speech.

Virtual Backgrounds

The background image for a synthetic video is selected from a series of images, which can include uploaded photos from your photo or computer. This is identical to the technology of Zoom and other video meeting services. So, your possibilities are endless. Different scenes, locations, and designs along with a gallery filled with royalty-free pictures are immediately available. This not only makes the video more interesting but provides a much better visual environment for the avatar. And if you are a small or large business, the background image could also be a prominently displayed brand or corporate logo. There are no limitations on the type of image you can include in the background, as long as it can be uploaded properly.

Music Tracks

What to use music with your video? It's as easy as selecting pre-recorded "instrumental only" versions that have been electronically created for synthetic media. Since there are royalty and licensing restrictions on copyrights for musical performances, the music that is currently available will be provided only for enhancing the video production. Since the spoken words and images are more important, the music provided is primarily an enhancement of the final video.

Applications for Integrated Marketing Communications

So, what are the advantages of using synthetic media for IMC?

Let's just go down the list. For advertising, video commercials can be produced in minutes for a fraction of the cost of the traditional method. This represents a significant saving in time and money. The commercials can range from a simplistic announcer-style presentation to a more complex integration of people, objects, and locations. The voice selected can also reflect or represent the mind and mood of potential buyers. But, there is another important distinction. With advanced features and artificial intelligence, the digital avatar can be selected to reflect specific demographic characteristics, such as male or female and young or older individuals. This is an excellent way to create resonance with the viewer, who can relate to a virtual avatar that looks, sounds, and acts just like they do. For example, the avatar might be a 25-year-old Hispanic female, a 35-year-old African-American man, or a 50-year-old white male.

Sales promotion events and activities have a great need for synthetic media. This is because nearly every promotion is short-term and depends on the immediate response of consumers. The availability of a low-cost method of video production provides a manufacturer, or local retailer, with the technology needed for the changing marketplace. Coupon offers, special discounts, flash sales, and other promotional incentives can be created and launched weekly on social media. For public relations, a digital avatar can perform the function of being the spokesperson for a brand or company. These video replications can be a faster and more cost-efficient method for creating and distributing public relations messages, especially for important news announcements or sending messages to journalists during crisis management situations.

For business-to-business marketing, advanced versions of synthetic media have the capability of adding a split screen option for PowerPoint or Keynote presentations. The same technique can be used for sales training purposes involving products and services. Another important utilization is for inbound marketing, where the videos are posted for website visitors to watch.

Dangers of Deep Fakes

Now that you know what synthetic media can do, here is the dark side of the technology. Deep fakes are videos with avatars that appear to be famous celebrities in sports, movies, or cultural popularity. This deception can include people who are trending in social media with a large number of followers. The deep fake might even be extended to use images and videos from members of their own family or close friends. All this is done without their knowledge or permission. Not only is this practice against the law, but it is also extremely harmful to society. It destroys trust as well as distorting the truth. So, synthetic media will be used illegally by some people, especially for posting on social media, until adequate protection measures are provided.

Three-Dimensional Social Media

This is not the social media you are using now. In the near future, there will be plenty of changes. While we all know something about artificial and virtual reality, most of us would not expect that it could be connected to social media. The transformation would be astonishing and revolutionary. Just imagine if your Instagram image or Twitter or Facebook posts also included an interactive, three-dimensional visual component. This could open up new possibilities for personal communication as well as opportunities for advertising. For example, displaying an image of a new automobile using artificial and virtual reality could enable you to walk around the outside of the vehicle and get inside by opening the door, or let you experience features such as the car's navigational map system or music activation panel. Yes, three-dimensional interactions!

Artificial Reality

Sometimes, there is confusion when using the terms *artificial reality*, *augmented reality*, *enhanced reality*, *virtual reality*, and *physical reality*. It is important to understand the descriptive distinctions and the basic functions of the digital technologies involved. So, each of these terms will be discussed and compared. Hopefully, there are no questions about the concept of reality.

The first three terms are essentially referring to the same process. Artificial reality, or augmented reality, involves modifying or changing the visual appearance of an existing environment by projecting images, videos, and other digital information onto the screen of a phone. The result is a merger of the real world with the artificially created images and enhanced visual activity. The user of artificial reality experiences a single vision of the same physical space. Perhaps the best example is the world-famous game Pokemon Go. Introduced in 2016 by Nintendo, this popular augmented reality platform uses the global positioning system (GPS) technology on your smartphone to locate your position and then superimpose images and digital creations. Reality and fantasy become one. If you have seen groups of people intensely looking down at their phone screens while walking around parks, down streets, or gathering in other public places, then they are probably playing Pokemon Go. It's a captivating game with more than 600 different species in 2020 to interact with during the process. If you have played Pokemon Go, then no further details or explanations are needed. But, you might need to demonstrate this by sharing this experience and free-to-play game with some of your friends who have never engaged with it or experienced dealing with these imaginary creatures.

Virtual Reality

Virtual reality is a simulated experience created with a three-dimensional computer-generated environment. This is not exactly the same as Star Trek's fictional Holodeck, but it certainly is moving in that direction. The user is immersed in fantasy worlds and situations involving people, places, and activities. While most of the virtual reality experiences are game-based for consumers, there is growing acceptance of the technology for training programs, academic courses, medical simulations, and an endless list of possibilities. This definitely includes advertising, sales promotions, and public relations for brand communication, but where does artificial intelligence come into the process? Let's find out more.

Oculus Headset Equipment   In 2010, the prototype of a virtual reality headset was completed. Two years later, the Oculus Rift was introduced to the game show market at an industry trade show attended by game designers, software suppliers, technology developers, and many other interested corporations. Apparently, the Oculus Rift was so impressive that in 2014, it was acquired by Facebook for a substantial amount of money. By 2016, more than 230 companies were designing artificial reality products and services. This powerful list included Amazon Apple, Facebook, Google, Microsoft, Sony, and Samsung. Just imagine what things are being planned for consumers.

Since virtual reality requires headsets or goggles, there is sophisticated hardware involved, too. Fortunately, those large goggles have decreased in size. Also, they have become more stylish. Gone are the days of wearing a gigantic apparatus on your head or attaching a cellphone for viewing. Oculus remains the leader in virtual reality, with many different models and options. The product offerings are changing constantly: new updates, operating features, and options.

While there are a few competitors who will be challenging, there is an overwhelming obstacle. Oculus is owned by Facebook. This relationship will result in virtual reality experiences that defy your imagination, excite your senses, and thrust you into a new world of fantasy.

What can you expect in the future? Figure 1.8 provides several categories that will continue to be prominent in the development of virtual reality, including locations, people, experience, sports, activities, immersion, learning, and simulations. While brands are now experimenting with this technology for marketing communication, it has not yet been introduced. Expect rapid development, especially after the transformation of social media platforms with virtual reality.

Facebook Horizon It's time to experience a new Horizon. This is Facebook's attempt to attract a new global user community with a blended application of virtual reality software and hardware featuring selected models of Oculus, a company that produces and sells virtual reality viewing equipment. While Horizon is still evolving in its format, it begins with a simple login that takes you to a digital location, originally named the Plaza, which is a public gathering place. From there, the user can proceed to customize their own avatar and begin to hang out with a small group of friends. But, there is much more to Horizon than just social chat and visual experiences. Facebook is planning to offer a mixture of experiences and environments. So, expect a real surprise with the platform.

Have you ever heard the expression that everything old is new again? It's very true with the launch of Horizon. About 20 years ago, way back in 2013, there was a virtual world created for the purpose of digital interaction experiences, called Second Life. There were over a million regular users just in the first year. After registering at the website, people could create their own avatars, who were able to

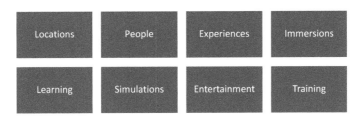

Figure 1.8 Virtual Reality and Social Media

move around on the screen as well as interact with places and objects and communicate with other avatars. Physical motions, such as walking, talking, sitting, jumping, running, and nearly every other conceivable human activity, had been replicated and visually reproduced in a semi-smooth animated form. It wasn't always perfect. But, the intention of Second Life was to let your imagination fill in the details. So, it wasn't a game but rather, a digital adventure that the user controlled through decisions and encounters with other avatars.

One surprising and astonishing twist with Second Life was that it had created its own currency. The Linden dollar was bought and sold with real money from all over the world. The Linden currency was actually traded on several online financial exchanges and had a high positive value; however, actually using the money was exclusively restricted to Second Life. What could you buy with the Linden dollar? Absolutely anything imaginable from other avatars who had set up their own retail stores, manufacturing facilities, recreation parks, luxury hotels, car dealerships, and thousands of other locations to spend time and money. It was exactly like the "real" world!

Second Life was a time vampire. Those who engaged with the platform spent hours on it. And, too, many began to enjoy being in this reality more than being in real life. For example, you could get in your virtual automobile, drive to a sandwich show for lunch, and drink a Coke on the way to meet a friend. Or later, go to the grocery store and purchase an assortment of brand name foods. Maybe, go home and watch a comedy show on television, or call a friend to discuss the latest football games. And finally, spend a few minutes deciding which pub or bar you will go to later in the evening. So, get ready for Horizon and the many experiences and adventures that it will offer.

Personal Identity Chips

You have read about them and talked about them, but would you ever want to get one? The specter of being followed, monitored, or observed on a 24-hour basis is a frightening possibility.

Perhaps, we may not have a choice. The process of individual surveillance is already happening with facial recognition, selling of personal data by social media companies, and the ability of Alexa to listen, record, and analyze every word that is spoken in our homes or apartments.

Orwellian Images

In his famous science fiction novel, *1984*, George Orwell depicted life in a state-controlled society that was constantly monitoring individual activities and rewriting history. Although his book was published way back in June, 1949, the projections of a surveillance society were more than accurate. Today's technology has exceeded Orwell's wildest imagination. But one thing that Orwell did not describe was a personal identity chip. This is basically a microscopic computer component that is embedded under the skin of an individual person. It is completely feasible and actually used today. But, what if the Covid pandemic precipitated a need to have one for tracking, monitoring, and managing populations? In the future, personal identity chips might be our passports or involve different methods of communication or interaction. While it appears to be science fiction, anything is possible.

Radio-Frequency Identification (RFID) Technology

Identity chips have already been used hundreds of thousands of times on animals. Just ask a few pet owners if a veterinarian has ever implanted a microchip in their dog or cat. It is a good way to find lost pets. It is also useful for ranchers who want to know the exact location of their cattle. In business, microchips have been pasted or attached to products to determine their exact location in warehouses, in retail stores, or even on trucks. This is just one more example of the application of identity chips.

How does it work? Whether the method is an implant or a tag pasted on a package, the process depends on a combination of a transponder with a low-frequency radio transmitter and receiver. The technical name is Radio-Frequency Identification (RFID). If you've ever driven down a tollway, motorway, or Interstate Highway and made a cashless payment without even slowing down, you used a small device or sticker with RFID technology. Yes, this was just another form of "near field" communication, which is growing in popularity for many home appliances and personal services, along with GPS navigation systems for geographic locations.

Now, we come to humans. The first successful RFID implant in a person was done way back in 1998 by British scientist Kevin Warwick. Known as a sub-dermal implantation, it has been repeated many times and has slowly increased in popularity. Today, individuals who choose to get one have many options for the location and method of implantation. While this type of device makes sense for medical purposes, such as storing essential information about an individual's health condition, it can also be used for security purposes. Implants have been used for accessing buildings, opening doors in restricted areas, monitoring prisoners, unlocking private phones, and even storing Bitcoin cryptocurrency. Surprisingly, it is a simple, painless, and easy procedure. Plus, the cost can be anywhere from $75 to $300 for the entire implant. While it is not commonly known, a few companies have adopted limited usage of ID chips for employees in specialized jobs.

Starlink: The Alternative Internet

Who Owns the Internet?

No one. That's right, there is no company, government, or organization that actually owns the Internet. Remember, the Internet is a vast collection of communication systems, technological equipment, and sophisticated software that

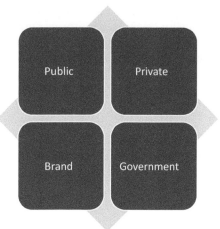

Figure 1.9 Starlink Satellite-Enabled Internets

enables users to create, send, store, and access digital information instantaneously on a global scale. The Internet is a complex collaboration of companies and organizations around the world that share this network without ownership.

However, there are big changes already happening, which will disrupt the Internet that we are using today. How? Because there will be more than one Internet system in the next few years. Yes, competitive systems that can provide the same streaming video and data services that we now enjoy but delivered to us through a different process. This will all be possible because Elon Musk has created Starlink, the new global satellite communication system (Figure 1.9). This is not surprising from the person who created and introduced the world to Tesla, the first completely electric automobile. This enormous demonstration of innovation is just the beginning of new products.

Elon Musk and Starlink

The visionary entrepreneur has been launching satellites from NASA's space flight facilities at Cape Canaveral, Florida. The first batch of these satellites was launched by his own company, SpaceX, in May, 2019. The initial payload was a total of 50 satellites. Then, another group of 60 communication satellites followed several months later. And, the pace of these launches has not slowed down, with the large Falcon 9 rocket propelling hundreds of satellites into space every month.

Now, it's time for the shocker. The vision of Elon Musk is to have at least 42,000 new satellites orbiting the Earth, which can provide everyone on the planet with high-speed Internet access!

But, what does this mean? First, security. Since this is a private network, there is a reduced risk, because the transmission of information will not be shared with any external users. Data will be encrypted and secure. While hacking can still exist, it will be extremely difficult with a private channel. Ironically, many governments of the world are attempting to build their own Internet systems, but Musk is ahead of them. Second, efficiency. The pathways for connectivity will not be competing with other carriers and delivery systems. Less competition avoids delays, and even in microseconds, that is a very important difference. Third, profitability. Starlink will become a digital toll road in the sky. Pay to get in. Pay as you use it. Pay according to your speed. And, pay when you download. There are so many ways to generate revenue, including the ability to stream original content. Netflix has already demonstrated that it can compete, outmaneuver, and innovate more than its competitors. No wonder the traditional broadcasting networks and digital cable systems are scrambling to adapt to new models. Sustainability or obsolescence?

But, the real question is: how will Starlink change global communications? Absolutely! As shown in Figure 1.9, the Starlink system will enable new global Internet for public, private, government, and brand usage. And, why is this so important for marketing and business management? The answer is cost reduction in communication and an entirely new way to reach and form relationships with customers and clients.

The number of satellites being launched is enormous according to any previous standard. This means that the communication carrying capacity will be extraordinarily large, like a gigantic server in the sky with plenty of available unused digital space. So, if you want to have your own private Internet system, Starlink can make it happen. Other entrepreneurial companies and existing global corporations might well take advantage of this opportunity from Elon Musk. The result could be the creation of a series of very competitive, or complementary, Internets that are delivering their own content, storing their own data, and providing global communication services to their clients and customers.

Private Internet Systems

This is already happening. Late in 2020, Starlink began testing its new Internet service in selected areas of the United States using previously launched satellites. Early subscribers to the Starlink service paid a one-time equipment fee of $499 and a monthly service cost of $99 per month. This trial was named "Something Is Better than Nothing" because users were warned to expect periodic outages and interruptions due to the continuing development and refinement of the system. Perhaps more remarkable are the company's plans to open up high-speed satellite Internet connection to rural and underserved areas around the world. Elon Musk announced that the initial demonstration of widespread adoption would be in India during the year 2021.

There is another possibility and opportunity for marketing communication: corporate-owned brand channels with exclusive content. This could emerge as another highly disruptive situation with an alternative media model. The need to use traditional media distribution channels, such as NBC, CBS, and ABC, would be reduced. Brands might actually be competing for viewers with quality programming and entertaining live events. Netflix would be challenged. And, even the movie production studios would be negotiating with brands to purchase their original films and digital content. Also, there is no need to pay for external advertising, because a brand is both the content distributor and the originator of its targeted persuasive communication messages.

Tonight, the evening sky over England, Italy, Japan, Germany, Argentina, India, and the United States, as well as nearly everywhere else in the world, is already filled with a glowing array of small shiny objects. They circle the Earth-like invisible moons and are sending signals from strategically positioned satellites for companies, governments, and ventures. Ironically, many of those satellites can be seen from the ground with binoculars or extremely good eyesight. While changes have been made to reduce their orbital reflection, it still serves as a reminder that we, as humans, have only recently begun to explore the universe. It's time to be adventurers!

Summary

In this chapter, we explored several of the most influential emerging technologies. Most of these technologies are still evolving with plenty of obstacles, problems, and challenges. Some might fail. And no doubt, many more will be added. New approaches, innovations, and companies will appear with amazing successes and disastrous collapses. Artificial intelligence has already begun to reshape our world. The challenge for marketing communication is to understand and utilize the power of artificial intelligence for advertising, sales promotion, and public relations.

While there are many different possibilities and applications, we have focused on the three most important: facial recognition, voice commerce, and synthetic media. Facial recognition software has already been used to identify loyal customers in retail stores and provide them with an expanded shopping experience, including a welcome greeting, department specials, and instant discounts. Voice commerce is still evolving with the technological ability to connect Siri, Alexa, and Google Assistant with local retail stores. This is achieved by using intermediary software that allows customers to interact directly with individual stores using a seamless process of search, selection, payment, and delivery. Synthetic media are slowly gaining momentum. Their user-friendly instructions provide a fast, easy, and low-cost alternative to normal video production. The avatars can be selected to represent different demographic groups, genders, and geographic areas as well as the capability to deliver text-to-video messages in more than 30 languages.

Finally, there are always things just over the Horizon: Google's Horizon, the artificial and virtual video viewing experience that is more like a shared social media adventure. Plus, there are things far above the horizon, like Starlink, the constellation of satellites launched by one of visionary Elon Musk's famous companies, SpaceX. It could very well revolutionize the Internet by creating several hundred new versions of interconnected global communication and information exchange networks. Yes, stay tuned for more to come, because tomorrow is already happening.

There are three ways to respond to the future: avoid it, create it, or adapt to it. Are you ready?

Discussion Questions

1. What is the value of artificial intelligence for marketing communication?
2. Should there be laws and restrictions about facial recognition and video surveillance?
3. How likely would you be to use facial recognition to identify people in social media posts?
4. Which voice assistant is better for providing useful information: Siri, Alexa, or Google?
5. Why is a seamless experience necessary for effective voice commerce with mobile apps?
6. Will supermarkets and department stores begin to use store beacons for text notifications?
7. Do you think that Facebook's virtual reality with Oculus will be a success on social media?
8. What are the advantages and disadvantages of using synthetic media for advertising?
9. What would be the impact and consequences of having more than one global Internet system?
10. Which of the technologies explained in this chapter will be the most useful for marketing?

Chapter Assignments

1. Explore the Consumer Electronics Show featuring the latest new technology (www.ces.org).
2. Look at the future of virtual reality with equipment for Facebook Horizon (www.Oculus.com).
3. Discover the seamless process of voice commerce from a service provider (www.Jetson.ai).
4. Learn more about avatars and the process of text-to-video production (www.Synthesia.com).
5. Find out what is happening with Elon Musk and his alternative Internet (www.Starlink.com).

Chapter 2

Integrated Marketing Communication

Pathways for Brand Messages and Content

Learning Objectives

1. To understand the purpose and value of Integrated Marketing Communication (IMC)
2. To recognize, explain, and apply the six communication pathways of IMC
3. To examine the organizational structure and functions within the IMC industry
4. To utilize and apply the AIDA, sales funnel, and attribution model
5. To know how to develop the most important section of an IMC Plan

---

Introduction

Marketing has changed. Today, there are multiple digital options with a unified system for planning, implementing, and measuring advertising and sales promotion for brands. This system is called Integrated Marketing Communication, or IMC, which ensures consistent consumer brand messages and coordinated media content. This textbook is designed to help you prepare an IMC Plan. There is information in each chapter that can be used to organize and develop each section of an IMC Plan. As you proceed, important decisions are made about strategies, options, costs, and consequences. Programs, activities, events, and creative

DOI: 10.4324/9780367443382-2

materials are developed. Brand messages are prepared for digital and traditional media, as well as public relations and sales promotion proposals. When you have arrived at the end of this textbook, you will have a much better understanding of the basic functions of IMC and what is required for preparing an IMC Plan. This includes learning about the procedures to implement successful advertising, sales promotion, brand visibility, public relations, digital media, and personal contact campaigns. When finished, you will have a valuable IMC Plan for a brand, small business, community project, or organization.

Definition of IMC

The American Marketing Association defines IMC as a concept that "recognizes the added value of a comprehensive plan that evaluates the strategic roles of a variety of communication disciplines … and that combines these disciplines to provide clarity, consistency, and maximum communication impact." The original idea and foundations of IMC were pioneered by Dr. Donald Schulz, a professor at Northwestern University, who introduced consumer "touch points" and the complex interrelationship of opportunities used to influence the perception of brands. The list was long and included almost everything imaginable. Essentially, every place, person, and medium had the potential to shape and build consumer expectations.

Many different definitions of IMC have evolved over the years. The most useful description has been advocated by Shultz—IMC is

> a strategic business process used to plan, develop, execute, and evaluate a series of coordinated, measurable, persuasive brand communication programs over a period of time with consumers, customers, prospects, as well as other targeted and relevant external or internal audiences.

Regardless of definitions or interpretations, every IMC program and activity must focus on delivering concise, consistent, and clear brand messages across different media and within every piece of communication. Reflecting the marketing philosophy of the legendary Dr. Philip Kotler, these messages must also support the approved product positioning, value proposition, and marketing strategies of a brand. The mantra of IMC is to send the right message to the right people at the right time in the right place for the right reason. Anything less is not true IMC.

Here is another approach. IMC has four functions: to inform, persuade, entertain, and motivate. Since the information function is about the actual and perceived characteristics of a brand, such as its features, benefits, and competitive advantages, these IMC messages take a very rational and logical approach. This represents a very logical approach to communication and corresponds to the theories of left-brain thinking from neuro-scientists and psycho-linguists. The persuasive function is similar. Reasons, factual statements, and reasonable proof are required for IMC messages. Entertainment and motivation functions are completely different. They support the theories of right-brain thinking that depend on visual images and emotion for effectively communicating messages.

What does this have to do with IMCs? The selection of the communication function for a brand is a very important decision. While the choice appears to be easy, the process is not. There is no single solution and no best way. Thousands of options and combinations are involved. The result is a series of subjective opinions, based on a large collection of objective facts. So, the challenge is learning as much as possible about customers, then applying the most appropriate IMC strategies, methods, and programs for brand messages.

Communication Pathways

There are six major categories of IMC: advertising, sales promotion, brand visibility, public relations, digital platforms, and personal contact (see Figure 2.1). Each category has its own purpose and advantages for marketing products and services. They are frequently, and effectively, used in combinations to maximize the delivery of brand messages. Most recently, there has been an increased overlap with their ability to communicate, interact, and form relationships with customers and potential buyers.

This section begins by providing a quick overview of the IMC categories. In later chapters, each category will be explored in greater detail, along with examples, illustrations, and many practical applications. The goal is to improve your understanding of communication concepts, strategies, and planning methodology. This can be used to prepare your IMC Plan by the end of the course.

Advertising

We see it. Read it. Watch it. Hear it. Experience it. Believe it. And also, hate it. There is no other form of communication that tries harder to capture our attention, generate interest, and change our perceptions. Advertising is all about selling brands or promoting causes, but it also informs, educates, and motivates. Today's

Advertising	Television	Radio	Magazine	Newspapers	Outdoor/Transit
Sales Promotion	Discounts	Coupons	BOGO	Free Samples	Loyalty Programs
Public Relations	Media Conference	Press Kit	Content Distribution	Community Relationships	Brand Awareness
Brand Visibility	Product Placement	Venue Identification	Event Sponsorship	Licensing Opportunities	Brand Logo Merchandise
Digital Platforms	Websites	Social Media	E-Mails	Search Optimization	Mobile Apps
Personal Contact	Salespeople	Contact Centers	Customer Service	Store Greeters	Influencers

Figure 2.1 Interactive Pathways for IMC

problem is that there is too much competition. How many advertising messages have you been exposed to today? Take a guess. Or, try to add up all the different forms of media communication that reach you during an average day. It's possible that hundreds, perhaps even thousands, of brand messages have reached and influenced you today.

So, how do we define advertising? As part of the entire spectrum of IMC, "advertising is a form of persuasive communication created for a specific purpose, targeted at a particular audience, requiring payment for messages delivered through a proprietary medium." That definition takes a few seconds to absorb. Maybe even more. There are several different ways to look at this, but the primary purpose is creating and delivering "persuasive messages" that influence perception and behavior. These messages are all about brands or companies but can also include services, locations, causes, or important topics.

Sales Promotion

Sales promotion is a strategic method for motivating potential buyers to immediately purchase a product or service. But, the reasons for purchasing have nothing to do with the brand's benefits or characteristics. What is being offered to customers or potential buyers is financial incentives or extra rewards, available only within a limited time period. The offer might be good for only a few hours, days, or weeks, but it has a clear and unmistakable ending date. For example, a weekend only coupon at a grocery store, or four tires for the price of three, are based on saving money. Other examples of sales promotions are when stores give free movie tickets with any purchase over $25 or enter your name in a sweepstake with a trip to Hollywood as a first prize. Here is a list of the most popular sales promotion strategies used to promote both national and local brands: coupons, buy one get one (BOGO), cashback, free samples, sweepstakes, contests, free gifts, low interest rates, bonus rewards, new experiences, and owner loyalty programs.

The most valuable part of a sales promotion program is its measurability. Most of the methods are directly connected to a quantitative result based on a consumer's response to the promotional offer: for example, the number of coupons redeemed, sweepstake entries, gifts awarded, or points earned. However, promotional offers can be expensive, not for consumers but for the brand or company. The total cost of running a promotion must be compared with the value of increased sales or profits.

One of the hidden costs is advertising. This IMC method is almost always needed to inform people about a promotional offer. The details, including time limits, must be communicated in an appropriate and easy-to-understand way. And, the message must be directed to the best target audience. The advertising can focus only on the promotion or be incorporated into existing material. Either way, this is an expense and part of the IMC budget for the brand or company.

The coordination of multiple IMC activities also has to be considered when planning a sales promotion program. There are also digital media, such as websites, email messages, and social media, which often lead the promotion or even replace traditional advertising methods. They are certainly less costly, easier to control, and definitely measurable. Taken together, planning and timing are essential.

Public Relations

The function of public relations is to develop, maintain, protect, and improve the perception of a brand, company, organization, or individual among a diverse group of separate audiences. This can include anyone from stakeholders in a corporation, media reporters, and elected government officials to the local high school, citizen action groups, church leaders, foreign business travelers, or retired military.

There are several different categories of public relations, such as media relations, community relations, government relations, and employee relations. The primary responsibility for managing public relations lies with the corporate communications department of a large company. In smaller businesses, a public relations agency is usually hired to provide these professional services, but in many situations, this function is handled by the company owner or senior executive.

Media relations continually interacts with representatives from television, radio, magazine, newspaper, and other media companies. Publicity from mass media is very important for brands and companies because it shapes consumer opinions and images. The information from news sources and popular publications is always perceived to be more believable and honest than advertising. So, any favorable exposure, especially for brands, is extremely valuable.

Community relations is a company's commitment to interact with people who are influenced or impacted by business decisions. These activities are very important for businesses that operate manufacturing or distribution facilities. While this public relations function is dedicated to improving relationships, solving problems, or providing relevant information, it can quickly become a focal point during a crisis or emergency situation in a local community.

Government relations is lobbying at the federal, state, and city government level for laws and regulations that are in the best interests of the company. Anything that is unfavorable is not supported, and actions are taken to discourage government officials from approving them. Lobbyists use financial incentives, as well as the threat of informing voters about the actions of their representatives, especially in geographic areas that depend heavily on trade, taxes, and industrial growth.

Employee relations involve different methods and strategies for distributing information about activities and decisions within a company to its employees. These include newsletters, publications, digital media, and videos produced by the corporate communications department.

It is especially important that people working for any company understand its mission, purpose, and management decisions that occur on a regular basis. Earning the respect, pride, and loyalty of employees is an essential ingredient for maintaining and sustaining a business.

Brand Visibility

Brand visibility comprises situations when companies or organizations involve their products or services with audiences and consumers in indirect or subtle ways.

It is not advertising, but costs are involved. It is not sales promotion, since there are no incentives offered or suggested. It is similar to public relations, but in this case, the brand controls the content and environment for exposure.

Here are a few examples of brand visibility opportunities: product placement, naming rights, sponsorships, featured prizes, street teams, and philanthropy. These four categories always include the brand name and logo as well as a visually attractive image or appearance of the product or service. While the amount of time, or the space involved, might be limited, the value of a brand visibility strategy is the amount of brand exposure at a very reasonable price.

What was the last movie you saw? No matter which one, the images of brands were everywhere. The popularity of product placement, whereby companies pay to have their brands included in entertainment media, continues to grow.

Brands are in movies, television shows, musical performances, social media, and especially video games. Why? Marketing managers want to encourage people to include their brands as part of their life style, while entertainment producers eagerly welcome an influx of money for their business model.

Naming rights is a relatively new phenomenon. Corporations are paying millions of dollars to have their name prominently displayed on a stadium, theatre, building, or venue. But, it goes beyond that. In news and media coverage of athletic events, entertainment, or any public usage of the facility, the reference for the location is the company name. For example, the American Airlines Arena in Miami, or the Amway Center in Orlando. Good value for the investment? It must be working with all the exposure.

Sponsorship of national, regional, or local events is an excellent way to promote a positive brand or business image. But, the value of sponsorship depends on the composition of those attending and the marketing objectives of the brand. Reaching the right group of consumers makes sense, but too often, event organizers just go after the money. The amount invested by companies in any sponsorship must be compared with other brand visibility alternatives.

Featured prizes, where products and services are given away free, are also a popular method of brand visibility. This occurs every day on television game shows as well as radio stations and other media. The lucky winner receives brand items at their suggested retail selling price, but the actual expense for participating companies is limited to the manufacturing costs. Thus, the media exposure received should be a pretty good bargain for the brand.

Street teams are rampant in today's promotional environment. They are a very low-cost but highly effective form of guerrilla marketing, which can be scaled up or down quickly. Consisting of small groups of paid promoters, street teams go anywhere and do anything required to get a brand noticed. This can involve anything from giving away free samples, hats, and posters to just talking to people at events, perhaps with unusual costumes or props. For example, Red Bull is always around a college campus or popular club.

Philanthropy is corporate generosity at its best. Very little is expected in return and no attempts are made to commercialize donations or support. Although underwriting expenses for cultural and arts are part of brand visibility, there is always an intangible benefit involved. For example, the name of a company sponsoring an educational or a non-commercial program will have its name silently displayed at either the beginning or the end of the video content.

Digital Platforms

There is a parallel world of advertising now. Every form of traditional media has a website, not just for information but for promoting products and services. These websites have the capabilities to play video commercials and stream live messages for brands. But, the influence of digital media does not stop there. Social media, the force that transformed communications in our daily lives, has the same potential to display advertising messages in a number of different ways. There are exciting opportunities for brands to explore these new options and experiment with innovative content and delivery strategies. These developments will be discussed more in the next chapter.

IMC is still evolving. Technology continues to disrupt and change the media environment. Most recently, mobile marketing has emerged as a new force with applications that facilitate almost every imaginable process and business interaction.

Then, there is the digitization of retail marketing strategies with search engine optimization, text notifications, and software to identify and profile customers before they even enter a store.

Personal Contact

The last of the six categories is not as impressive or innovative as digital media, but it remains an important component for implementing every communication program. Personal contact is the human dimension that transcends marketing and connects people in normal and more comfortable ways. Interpersonal relationships involve listening, understanding, interacting, observing, and feeling the needs of other people. This is an underappreciated portion of the brand message experience with a high potential for supporting other IMC activities and programs.

Personal contact includes word of mouth, opinion leaders, store greeters, sales force, and direct sellers. While some are informal and unstructured, others are directly involved with selling products and services. The common denominator is their ability to quickly form, maintain, and improve long-lasting relationships between brands and customers. Personal contact is a powerful force that complements and amplifies persuasive advertising messages as well as brand content.

Message Consistency

IMC must always provide a uniform delivery of brand content and persuasive messages. This includes every form of paid, earned, or owned media within the full spectrum of IMC activities. Paid media are any form of communication that requires an advertiser to purchase access to a method of message or content delivery. Earned media consist of the estimated value of media coverage or exposure that is received free from a communication channel or pathway. Owned media include any communication pathway that is the exclusive property or digital asset of a company or organization. It is essential that brand messages are delivered consistently in each of these three classifications of communication media.

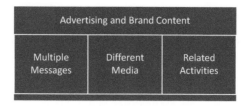

Figure 2.2 Consistency of IMC Messages

As illustrated in Figure 2.2, the consistency of a brand message has to be achieved across different forms of media and among the full spectrum of IMC events, activities, programs, and platforms. This means that a brand message must always communicate the same information in the same way, regardless of the media selected. The requirement is the same for legacy advertising, such as television, radio, newspapers, and magazines, as well as digital pathways, such as social media, email marketing, and mobile apps. So, the message in a television commercial should reflect the same communication concept that appears in a magazine advertisement or a social media post. Every brand message in every media must be consistent.

This basic tenet of IMC must also accommodate multiple variations of the same brand messages over extended periods of time. For example, there might be 7 different television commercials along with 3 magazine advertisements, or 15 posts on Instagram with 7 videos on YouTube and 3 radio commercials. The goal to achieve consistency must be maintained even with modifications in the images, text, audio, and video content. It is a difficult challenge but one that advertisers know how to accomplish.

IMC Industry Structure

The industry structure for IMC can be divided into four distinct groups: the advertiser, the agency, the media, and suppliers. As shown in Figure 2.3, these are separate but interrelated functions. The advertiser has the money and makes the final decision on how it will be spent. The media provide opportunities for delivering brand messages through many different consumer and business communication channels and pathways. The agency works closely with the advertiser and makes its recommendations for IMC campaigns, programs, events, and activities. This includes the creation and implementation of brand messages as well as the selection of specific media purchases. The suppliers support both the advertiser and the agency with a wide range of services, such as marketing research, video production, and digital technology. Now, let's take a closer look at each of these four groups and learn more about their functions, responsibilities, and purpose.

Figure 2.3 Communication Industry Structure

Advertisers

Who is an advertiser? Anyone who has a marketing budget, or money to spend, can be an advertiser. Whether the funds are spent on digital media, social media, television, radio, magazines, newspaper, or any other form of communication, the advertiser is responsible for authorizing all the expenses. Certainly, large corporations qualify. But, many smaller businesses, organizations, and even governments are advertisers. How much money do advertisers spend in the United States? In 2020, it was estimated that paid advertising for brand messages and marketing communication exceeded $240 billion. That's right, billion! It's an amazing number. And, guess what? The United States accounts for more than half of all global advertising expenditures. The single best source to find out more about the companies who spend all this money is Advertising Age publications. In their annual report, *Leading National Advertisers*, corporations are ranked by the amount of their expenditures, the type of media used, and other information about their advertising programs. These companies are primarily involved with consumer advertising, but there are four other categories: business-to-business advertising, government advertising, non-profit advertising, and advocacy advertising.

Consumer Advertising   These are the advertisements that we see every day. And, every night. Plus, all the other moments.

Persuasive messages are targeted at selected groups of people who can purchase products or services at retail locations or online. While there are thousands of different industries and market segments involved, the advertising is focused on brand image and user benefits for individual buyers. But, there is an important distinction between advertisers who are manufacturers and those classified as retailers. The price of a product is rarely displayed when the manufacturer is paying for the advertisement, while in the case of the retail advertiser, it almost always is. And when it comes to media, manufacturers can afford extensive television advertising, but local retailers are more limited to radio and newspapers.

B2B Advertising Business-to-business, or B2B, advertisers concentrate on selling to companies, not consumers. This is also called industrial advertising because it involves the advertising of components, raw materials, and equipment to businesses that are manufacturing other products and services. For example, IBM sells computers to insurance companies, banks, auto repair stores, restaurants, and hospitals but uses business-oriented magazines for its advertising messages. Another part of B2B advertising is trade advertising. This specifically targets wholesalers and retailers that are potential buyers for the B2B advertiser's products and services. Each market segment of an industry has many different publications and other media advertising resources, such as *Chain Store Age*, *Retail Tire Wholesaler*, *Grocery Store News*, and *Fast Food Weekly*.

Agricultural Advertising While you don't usually think about farms and ranches as advertisers, agriculture is an extremely large area of business. This includes hundreds of specializations from beef producers to corn harvesters and from tractors, trucks, and electrical generators to seed distributors, grain storage locations, and even software for agricultural management. All these components involve advertising in magazines, newspapers, and other forms of legacy media, as well as extensive utilization of digital marketing platforms.

Government Advertising Most people do not realize that government organizations are also advertisers. The United States government spends over $1.1 billion per year on advertising campaigns. In 2020, this number placed the government in the position of the 44th largest advertiser in the entire country. How could they be spending that amount of money? There are hundreds of different departments, agencies, and bureaus that have separate budgets for their areas of responsibility. For example, the military spends millions of dollars in recruiting people to join the Army, Navy, Air Force, Marines, Coast Guard, or the new Space Force, which was established in 2019. And most recently, the U.S. Census Bureau launched an event that takes place once every 10 years. During the year 2020, this single government organization spent more than $371 million dollars in paid advertising.

There are also many different states and local governments that spend millions of dollars to promote tourism, economic development, lotteries, and other relevant activities. While their budgets are smaller, these advertisers are still very important. Often, state governments use a variety of promotional methods in the areas of public relations, brand visibility, and personal contact. Local governments tend to use a combination of legacy media and digital communication depending on their available financial resources.

The government is also a customer. It buys most of its products and services from corporations, just like any other business customer. Examples include computers, furniture, accounting software systems, heavy-duty trucks, and the list continues, except for the military, which needs uniforms, combat equipment, and the occasional weapon. However, the buying process for government is different, with requirements in their request for proposals and decisions that favor the lowest price. Companies that want to sell their products and services to the government advertise in special publications, as well as legacy media, including targeted television advertising.

Non-Profit Advertising Non-profit advertisers include charities, educational institutions, religious bodies, hospitals, and cultural organizations. Charities have the largest budgets. No doubt you can name quite a few, such as the Red Cross, the American Cancer Society, and many others. Educational institutions are active advertisers, but their main thrust is using digital media. Is that why you are taking this course? And finally, another important category of non-profit advertiser is the thousands of cultural and arts organizations.

Advocacy Advertising The purpose of an advocacy advertiser is to influence or modify existing attitudes and beliefs of individuals and groups by either stimulating an immediate action or precipitating a long-term change in behavior. At the top of the list are politically funded groups, especially during election periods. Other examples of advocacy advertisers with powerful and effective messages include the Greenpeace Society, Mothers Against Drunk Driving, and local groups supporting controversial issues.

Agencies

The word *agency* is frequently associated with advertising, but it can be used for any company that provides IMC services. Today, there are 10 different types: full service, creative focus, media buying, promotional, public relations, digital marketing, branding, industry specialist, demographic, and internal (in-house) agencies. Their size and expertise are very different across the country, but most major metropolitan areas have a large selection of possibilities. Even in the smallest town, there are IMC agencies. Let's take a quick look at what each type of agency does and how they help advertisers achieve success in the marketplace.

Types of Agency As the name implies, full-service agencies are capable of offering a complete spectrum of IMC services. Their clients are usually large corporations with millions of dollars to spend on advertising. Full-service agencies are very sophisticated and knowledgeable but usually charge high prices to justify their reputation for success. While full-service agencies have been around for a long time, most are now in global networks, controlled by powerful holding companies.

An exception to this category is small, local agencies that provide multiple IMC services to local companies, organizations, and individuals. Their budgets might be limited but their creativity is not. Small agencies' services can include anything from producing a brochure or newspaper advertisement to designing a website.

In another category, the creative focus agency specializes only in the graphics, illustrations, and copywriting for advertising and other IMC materials. As the name implies, these agencies are hired for what they do best. No research. No media. No planning. But, they have plenty of imagination and come up with amazing ideas instantaneously. A creative focus agency could be one person, a group of talented people with different creative skills, or an organized company with management. Typically, a creative-based agency handles projects or assignments for many different clients. And, they frequently accept work with other agencies as a supplier or resource for the development of creative IMC materials.

A media buying service uses its analytical abilities to recommend the most cost-efficient combination of programs, publications, and content channels for clients. Like the previous category, it does not create any advertisements or promotions. Since its purpose is to evaluate different media choices, combinations, and cost-efficient alternatives, this agency focuses on the demographic profiles of brands and potential buyers. Once it has developed a spreadsheet, the buying service can begin to negotiate the lowest possible prices. By leveraging its knowledge of media and business relationships, a media buying service can provide a valuable service to companies and agencies.

The promotional agency develops IMC programs that motivate consumers and businesses to respond to incentives and special offers. The agency searches among hundreds of promotional products and recommends the right priced item for the client. This type of agency also produces creative materials for sales promotion programs in both printed and digital forms. It rarely handles media placements and does not get involved in any other types of advertising creative development.

Public relations agencies have grown in size and importance. While their primary purpose is distributing press releases, interacting with representatives of mass media, and managing a client's image, these agencies can provide other valuable services that complement and support advertising and sales promotion programs.

Digital marketing agencies have emerged as the most recent category of agency. They are composed of a mixture of tech-oriented individuals and creative advertising professionals. Digital agencies employ not only traditional artists and designers but also a growing number of young employees who are proficient in the application of technology for advertising. Digital agencies do everything from building websites and improving search engine optimization (SEO) ranking to organizing and managing social media campaigns, as well as creating mobile apps, bidding for keywords, or using Google Analytics.

Branding agencies are hired to assist a corporation, organization, or individual to develop a name, logo, visual appearance, and psychological image for a new product or service. Creating this complete branding package is only the beginning, since most branding agencies work closely with an advertising company, or their own talented employees, during the introductory phase of the brand. The agency has completed its assignment after participating in a successful launch.

Industry specialists concentrate on a single area of business or market expertise. For example, the agency only accepts clients that are in medical care, automotive, physical fitness, legal services, or the restaurant industry. These agencies always enjoy a very strong advantage against competitors because of in-depth knowledge of a particular industry. There is no need for clients to educate them, and no time or energy is wasted in preparing the most relevant and appropriate IMC programs.

A demographic agency is one that concentrates on a particular life style, age group, or gender. For example, a demographic agency might specialize in developing advertising for young working women, single parent households, or older retired adults who like to travel. There are also agencies in the United States that specialize in preparing creative and media advertising that is designed to reach Hispanics, African-Americans, or Asians, who share the same cultural heritage, background, language, or life style values.

Mid-size corporations and family businesses often form their own advertising or promotion agency, called "in-house" or internal company agencies. Typically, internal agencies focus on the writing, design, and production of creative materials, especially brochures, direct mail pieces, catalogs, and newspaper advertisements. Since the employees already work for the parent company, they are very familiar with the products and services being advertised. And, there is no pressure to make a profit, because the internal agency is also a functioning part of the company itself.

Methods of Compensation   If you are going to hire any IMC agency, prepare to negotiate prices with them. Although there are several methods of compensation, the actual costs involved depend on the budget, type of work required, and level of sophistication needed. There are five methods of compensation used to pay for agency services: hourly rates, project fees, annual retainers, commissions, and performance incentives.

The most frequently used method is the hourly rate. This method is very similar to that used by other professional services, such as accountants, attorneys, or consultants, who also charge by the hour. It is a very fair method that involves paying only for the work that is done. When an initial contact is signed with the agency, a fixed cost per hour for services is established as well as an annual budget. The client is then billed for the number of agency hours used per week or per month. A major problem with this method is that the actual time might quickly exceed the budgeted number of hours. This is usually a result of the agency taking too long to complete a task, changes requested by the client, or a variety of small mistakes due to poor communication among everyone involved.

The project fee is another desirable compensation method. In this arrangement, the agency outlines a proposal, which could be for creative materials, media planning, public relations activities, sales promotion programs, or digital development. Then, an estimate of the costs involved for completing the work is submitted to the client. If it is approved, the agency begins the project immediately. Payment arrangement can include a deposit, partial amounts during the project, or the full amount at the end.

Annual retainers are the preferred compensation method for B2B marketers and smaller retailer-oriented companies. The agency is guaranteed a fixed amount of money each month, regardless of the amount of work that is done. The advantage of this method is that the agency is provided with a consistent flow of income, while the client can plan a regularly monthly expense for IMC services. This method is especially fair for agencies that prepare creative advertising concepts and sales promotion programs with an inadequate amount of money for planning.

The media commission is almost extinct. While it is still used in certain situations, the process of receiving a 15% agency commission, or discount, direct from media sources is very rare. Although this method was once the industry standard, price negotiations and competition have forced percentages down and down. Now, only a few local media companies offer media commission, usually for small accounts.

The performance incentive method of compensation is more likely to be used by larger agencies that have clients with substantial budgets. This method is also being readily adapted by online companies that are paid based on their ability to improve click-through rates, page visits, and digital purchasers. The higher the numbers or percentages, the greater the amount of compensation for the agency.

It is also possible to combine several of these methods. If there is more than one agency, such as an advertising company and a public relations consultant, select the method that fits the IMC activities being performed. In all situations, the marketer should absolutely have a written contract describing the agreed-upon IMC deliverables, time schedule, and compensation method.

Employment Positions and Functions   Agencies are always organized around a centralized control manager, the account executive. This individual is responsible for daily contact and communication with their clients. The account executive works with advertising or promotion managers at corporations and small businesses to develop IMC strategies, Then, the account executive must coordinate all the activities required to implement IMC programs.

Additional team members who assist the account executive include the creative director, media manager, and promotion supervisor. The images and words for advertisements and commercials are the responsibility of the creative director. An analysis of media options and costs with purchase recommendations is the job function of a media manager. And, the promotion manager is the primary person involved with the development of incentive programs to motivate consumers to purchase more products and services.

Selection Procedures for a New Agency   When advertisers decide to find a new agency, there is a standard protocol for the selection process. It begins with the announcement of their search. Since every agency in town will want to apply, an advertiser has to do its homework. First, the decision criteria must be described. Second, a short list of agencies is prepared based on a series of visits to the agency's website. Third, a limited number of agencies are invited to make a presentation about their company, qualifications, management, and examples of successful IMC programs. Fourth, the finalists are selected and asked to make a "speculative" recommendation about their specific recommendations for future advertising programs. Fifth, a contract is awarded to the winner after negotiation of the rates and responsibilities involved with the account.

Every agency wants new clients, but they are not easy to find and are even harder to get. Since advertisers only change agencies when unhappy with their performance, there are very few opportunities. But, new product introductions, special project assignments, or entrepreneurial start-up situations are the exceptions.

Media

Want to reach people with your brand message? That's the purpose of media. They operate just like a toll road: you pay for the right to enter and use the highway. But media costs are very different. The greater the number of people who get exposed to your advertisements, the higher the prices. Costs are based on the number of viewers, listeners, or readers. So, advertisers and agencies need an estimate of the size of an audience before they even consider purchasing media. And this number can be different for every television program, channel, time period, or day of the week. Fortunately, prices for magazines and newspapers are much more predictable. Their costs are calculated from the total number of subscribers or copies of the publication distributed.

Today, traditional media (television, radio, magazines, and newspapers) are being challenged by many emerging forms of digital media. But, most of the differences are rapidly changing and merging into a complex new structure. These are really hybrid media. For example, newspaper companies are always running video commercials on their websites, and live streaming sports events are being viewed on mobile phones. What will be the new media innovation for tomorrow?

With traditional mass media, advertisers rarely negotiated directly with the stations or publishers. Media were always purchased through an agency. However, the digital world has quickly changed the business model. Corporations, small businesses, organizations, and individuals can now purchase media without using an agency. They can arrange everything online, including the method of payment. But, advertisers still need agencies. They are essential to navigate multi-platform options and to calculate the costs involved. Agencies are also more familiar with using digital media to identify, locate, and contact potential buyers with highly targeted brand messages. And, they have mastered software technology for programmatic or automated analysis and purchase of online hybrid media forms.

There is another category of advertising media, supplemental media, which is frequently used by local advertisers and in some cases, by national advertisers. Supplemental media is any form of message delivery method or opportunity that involves payment and reached a quantifiable audience. This includes many of the common but low-impact media, such as movie theatre advertising, as well as the more exotic forms of IMC, such as skywriting, doctor's office videos, and even brand images or signs posted on the sides of personal automobiles. Sometimes, the value of supplemental media is derived more from their novelty or unexpected appearance.

Suppliers

Advertisers and agencies hire many different companies to provide supplemental services. Typically, there are four major categories for these supporting companies: research firms, production companies, consultants, and technology developers. Although most relationships are based on short-term projects or assignments, IMC suppliers provide needed services that are highly specialized but essential. Let's take a closer look at each of these categories.

Research Firms While most large companies have their own marketing research departments, they are not always skilled in consumer-oriented research. Their focus is primarily on product and market research. So, when it comes to online surveys, focus groups, and personal interviews, it is much easier to hire a professional marketing research firm. The advertising agency usually makes these arrangements for clients, since this is essential for planning IMC activities. In addition, research firms help to measure the evaluate the performance of media purchases for brand advertising programs. For example, the A.C. Nielsen Company provides information about the size of television viewing audiences, while J.D. Powers offers reports about consumer satisfaction ratings of competitive brands.

Production Companies   Advertising agencies are not in the business of making films, videos, artwork, or photography. Yet, they use all of these services, and more, for making television commercials and print advertisements for their clients. How is that possible? Well, agencies are primarily concerned with the creative development of ideas and not the physical production of IMC materials. They will hire people and companies to do what they need, such as videographers and film directors, but only on a contracted project basis. The agency methodically supervises the process of producing IMC materials, since it is responsible to the client for completion. All work must be finished on time without exceeding the original budget.

Independent Consultants   There are three reasons why companies hire consultants. First, the company wants an objective, unbiased opinion of a marketing program or branding opportunity. Any consultant outside the organization does not have to deal with office politics or popularity. They only need to give good advice. Second, companies hire consultants where professional expertise is required for a very short period of time. For example, a B2B manufacturer wants to plan a three-month advertising campaign to reach new customers or expand into other countries. Third, and finally, companies hire consultants to replace individuals or even small departments during periods of severe cost reductions. It is usually less expensive to pay a consultant than a full-time employee with benefits and overheads.

Technological Support   Every agency has a website, but few can build their own without a strong and capable information technology (IT) department. While there are plenty of software programs, both free and expensive, out there to help, agencies still depend on technology to design advertisements and manage digital media platforms. Technology developers, such as coders and wireframe artists, who are proficient are quickly hired by agencies. Their skills not only keep the agency's internal systems and data storage working correctly but can also be used to provide profitable services to advertisers and other IMC agencies. And, who ever thought advertising would become more technology-oriented than any other part of marketing? Just wait. In the next few years, the influx of mobile apps, store beacons, and virtual reality advertising will be joined by programmatic media buying and steaming video analytics.

The Customer's Journey

Everyone in marketing loves to refer to the customer's journey. But, why is it so important? And, exactly what is involved in that magical mystery tour? The best definition of a customer's journey is "the cognitive and behavioral process of beginning with a perceived need or expressed want which concludes with the purchase of a product or service." What happens between the beginning thoughts and concluding events is the journey. But, it is not that simple.

Each journey has its own route and final destination. This is all part of the consumer's decision-making experience. It is not linear. It is not a series of sequential steps. It is a complex and interconnected network of actions and influences with thousands of different outcomes.

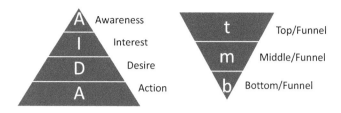

Figure 2.4 AIDA and Sales Funnel

Currently, there are three marketing communication concepts that are associated with the consumer's journey: the AIDA, sales funnel, and attribution models. The AIDA (awareness, interest, desire, action) model was always connected with legacy advertising, especially broadcast television and other forms of traditional mass media. It was also the first scientific attempt to measure the effectiveness of brand messages and marketing communication. The sales funnel (also referred to as the marketing funnel) is an extremely popular derivative of the AIDA model. The sales funnel model has been immediately adapted to all forms of digital media and online marketing. It provides a quick and easy way to demonstrate proof of performance. (See Figure 2.4.)

But, there can be thousands, if not millions, of influencing factors during a consumer's journey, including interpersonal communication, persuasive messages, and online content. Neither the AIDA model or the sales funnel takes that into consideration. Both models are designed to show results but not the activities and events that happened while getting there. That's why the attribution model was created. It can aggregate and estimate the number of influential factors influencing a customer's journey, especially with predictive analytics. This is a perfect situation for the application of artificial intelligence and predictive analytics, which can actually map and plot the number of communication "touch points" involved during an individual's journey.

AIDA Model

The introduction of the AIDA model was based on the publication of DAGMAR: Defining Advertising Goals for Measuring Advertising Results. This was the foundation of the AIDA model that was introduced way back in 1961 by the famous advertising executive, Richard H. Colley. It was also known as the "hierarchy of effects" model. The AIDA model was designed to represent the sequential steps that consumers would make before purchasing a product or service. It was a logical, practical, and easy-to-understand concept that was immediately accepted and utilized by advertising agencies and advertisers.

The AIDA model is always illustrated in the shape of a triangle. At the top level is awareness, followed by interest, desire, and action. However, some visualizations of the AIDA model invert the sequence by using a pyramid with awareness forming the base. Going from either direction, the assumption is that advertising begins to influence the consumer's decision-making process by generating awareness of a brand. Achieving a higher level of awareness provides an excellent opportunity to shift the mind and mood of shoppers and move them toward the next stage, greater interest in purchasing a particular brand, followed by a stronger desire. After a continuing barrage of advertising messages and sales promotion, the consumer is finally motivated to decide. But, the problem with any legacy media, especially with broadcast television, is that the cost of brand advertising is directly proportional to the size of the audience. However, the most desirable and responsive people cannot be identified or separated from the general audience. Thus, an advertiser might reach only 35% of a targeted audience while paying for 100%.

The value of the AIDA model was that the advertising expenditures for creating awareness, interest, and desire could be correlated with an increase in sales for a particular brand. Thus, advertising agencies had a rationale for recommending larger media budgets. And, their client was more comfortable with the large amounts of money being spent on advertising. At that time, business executives were debating whether advertising was an expense or an investment. The finance and accounting departments took the position that it was definitely an expense, while the marketing and sales department believed it was an investment. Advertising agencies prefer the calculation of a return-on-advertising-investment, ROAI, as a viable measurement of creative and media performance; however, the final decision for metrics is always made by the advertiser.

Sales Funnel

Few concepts in marketing have ever been as popular, or used as frequently today, as the ubiquitous sales funnel. Digital marketing agencies love the sales funnel and have passionately adopted it for their clients. Large companies, or small, evaluate the success of their digital advertising and promotion programs from the application of the sales funnel. Why? Because it enables them to continually monitor the results in "real time" and make required adjustments immediately. While the funnel has many advantages, it does not incorporate the large number of intervening events and activities that influence the eventual outcomes.

Today, there are literally hundreds of different funnel variations. Each uses a different shape, name, and purpose. But, the most commonly adopted visualization simply divides the funnel into three separate parts: the top, the middle, and the bottom. Agencies and advertisers affectionately refer to these as ToFu, MoFu, and BoFu. While this sounds like a foreign language, the clever abbreviation refers to the Top of the Funnel, Middle of the Funnel, and Bottom of the Funnel. The greatest amount of marketing money is spent at the Top of the Funnel, where informative content and persuasive messages are used to increase brand awareness. From there, more advertising money and new brand messages are directed toward those individuals who have entered the Middle of the Funnel. The creative and media strategies at this level are designed to heighten interest in a brand as well as to stimulate a greater conscious desire to own it. And finally, the Bottom of the Funnel uses sales promotion techniques that offer incentives to shoppers to motivate them to purchase a brand or at least take additional action to find out more about the brand.

Top of the Funnel In the digital world, the purpose of the Top of the Funnel is to drive more traffic to a brand website. The effectiveness of the marketing communication campaign is measured in the number of visitors to a website. However, there is a problem with this digital metric because of a difference between total website visits and the number of unique visitors. Website visits include returning visits from the same individual, as well as new visitors. People can come back to view a brand website multiple times, on the same day, during the week, or over an entire month. Maybe they want more information, or perhaps they are not ready to decide. But, we do know they have an interest in a product or service. What is important is that they want to continue.

Middle of the Funnel   The challenge is to turn their interest into desire. That's in the Middle of the Funnel.

Bottom of the Funnel   And, making a commitment to buy a specific brand is part of the communication that goes within the Bottom of the Funnel.

Marketing communication agencies often use the sales funnel approach to demonstrate the need to sufficiently fund a digital campaign. Let's take a look at a real-life example. Chatter Buzz Media is an extremely successful digital marketing agency in Orlando, Florida. It uses an interactive calculator, the Marketing Return on Investment Funnel, to illustrate the relationship between website visits and acquiring new customers for branded products and services. First, enter the number of visitors you want to visit your website in a month. Just type the number in the shaded box, and then push continue. The interactive calculator will instantly display your desired number of website visitors along with three "variable" factors: the contact rate, lead rate, and closing rate. The contact rate is the percentage of website visitors who have attempted to reach you by phone call, email, or filling out a form. The lead rate is the number of people who contacted you that are classified, qualified, or projected to be potential purchasers. The criteria used for determining the lead rate depends on the specific requirements of individual companies. And finally, the close rate is the percentage of sales leads that are converted into customers. This interactive calculator can be effectively used for consumer products and services and also for B2B marketing communication strategies.

Enough reading. Time to try it for yourself. Seriously, just go to this link and experiment with the results. Remember, you can change any of the four input boxes at any time. Work from the top down, and discover the website visits necessary to achieve a desired number of sales: www.chatterbuzzmedia.com/marketing-roi-calculator/

There are a few other considerations about the application of the funnel concept. First, the shape of the funnel. Is it very wide or narrow? When the funnel is wide, the marketing communication content and brand messages have been extremely effective in generating awareness, but when the funnel is narrow, the opposite is true. Second, the slope of the funnel. When the angle is very flat (or near vertical) between the level of awareness and the level of interest, or desire, then things are working well. The marketing content and brand messages have been successful in moving shoppers from simple awareness into a mindset of serious purchase consideration. But when the angle of the funnel's slope is very sharp, the opposite is true, because very few people are interested in the brand, and the conversion rate from awareness to interest or desire is extremely low. Third, the funnel's length must be considered. What is this all about? Well, once a shopper becomes a customer, then the funnel must include another level or category: retention. This involves the percentage of buyers who return for a repurchase of the brand. The importance of this concept will be explained later, since it involves the calculation of a customer's lifetime value. But for now, just imagine a longer extension of the funnel as it goes into a smaller but more valuable level: brand loyalty.

Attribution Model

Here is another upgrade in the concept of "touch points," which makes more sense in the age of algorithms and artificial intelligence. First, a trip back into the history of marketing and brand communication. The originator of the concept of IMC, Dr. Donald Schultz of Northwestern University, proposed that a consumer decision is not just the result of a linear progression from need to fulfillment; rather, it is the culmination of hundreds, perhaps thousands of individual "touch points." His theory was based on the interaction of consumers who were given multiple opportunities to see, feel, hear, or learn about a brand. While advertising and sales promotion programs were the strongest influencers, personal contact with friends, family, and associations also played an important role in a consumer's awareness, interest, desire, and potential action in purchasing the product or service.

Now, back to the future. The adoption of digital marketing analytics made it possible to create and use attribution models. Since a consumer's behavior pattern on the Internet is very visible and trackable, each exposure to a brand can be measured. This includes visits to websites, online searches, blogs, product reviews, and especially, social media. Each activity contributes to influencing the perception and attitude about a brand. But, how can this be quantified?

Attribution models create a framework for analyzing touch points. This includes legacy media, digital media, sales promotion, public relations, brand visibility, personal contact, and every other form of IMC. Values are assigned to each individual touch point and mathematically related to a formula. For example, what is the value of a television commercial compared with a social media post or a promotional email coupon offer? Or, how important is the last interaction with an online search for a brand compared with the first search for a brand? These are all part of the quantification process, which is then incorporated into a computer model that is used for predictive analytics for anticipating future consumer buying activity.

B2B marketing communication can be made more productive by using the attribution model rather than the more simplistic and less effective sales funnel. This is because the majority of B2B sales leads come from three sources: inquiries following an industry trade show, in-bound marketing responses, and online searches. Here is a quick summary. For most small businesses, maintaining a sales force is impractical, expensive, and unnecessary today. Even a major event, such as an industry trade show, is surrounded by digital communication activity before, during, and after these essential face-to-face experiences. For example, potential buyers search online to identify the companies that they want to learn more about; then, they might contact several to arrange a meeting at the trade show; and finally, there is all the activity of visiting brand websites, comparing products and services, or downloading reports from associations. In Figure 2.5,

Social Media	Online Search	Brand Website	Online Search	Retail Locations
Instagram	Email Message	Pop-up Ad	Sponsored Event	Store Visit
Twitter	Streaming Video	Radio Commercial	Influencer	Sales Person
Personal Friend	Pop-up Ad	Online Display Ad	Facebook	Coupon Offer
TikTok	Online Search	Email Message	Television Commercial	Purchase

Figure 2.5 Attribution Model

a hypothetical attribution model has been created based on a series of consumer decisions and activities that begin with exposure to a brand on social media and then progressing through multiple touch points to arrive at a final decision to actually purchase the brand.

The IMC Planning Process

In today's fast paced, ever changing digital world, do you really need to have an IMC Plan?

Of course you do. Every program and activity in marketing is so complex and interrelated that without the proper coordination, organization, and control, nothing positive will ever happen. The results are ineffective communication, wasted amounts of money, and many valuable missed opportunities. There is just too much at stake in the world today filled with intense competition, where most companies have much more to lose than to gain. It is not surprising that marketing managers believe that IMC planning is not only important but absolutely essential.

Purpose of the Plan

The IMC Plan is a blueprint or guiding direction for creating and coordinating communication between consumers and advertisers. It provides the research input needed to make strategic decisions about the creative messages and media delivery channels. The plan also includes the recommended amount of money to be spent and the method used to determine the IMC budget.

Also, the IMC Plan establishes the objectives that will be used to measure the success and impact of the communication relationship between consumers and advertisers for a specific brand.

Responsibility for Development

The individual who is ultimately responsible for the planning, development, and implementation of an IMC Plan for a brand, organization, or other entity is the company's advertising manager. While other communication functions and people are involved, the advertising manager controls the process. This is because most advertising departments at a corporation have the largest budgets (especially when traditional media is involved) and greatest number of projects that support the full spectrum of IMC activities. However, the advertising manager must always work very closely with the marketing, sales, and research departments within the company. Each department provides valuable, and essential, information for strategic IMC decision-making. Their input is the beginning of the IMC planning cycle. This information is also shared with the agency, which uses it to develop creative concepts and to analyze media options.

At the agency, the account executive is the exclusive point of contact for interacting with the client or corporation. The account executive is also responsible for coordinating all the IMC functions at the agency as well as collaborating with the advertising manager during the planning process. While the account executive makes recommendations, only the advertising manager makes decisions. Finally, after the research, strategies, and details of the IMC Plan are completed, it is presented to the marketing manager or VP of Communications. Ironically, this presentation is made by the account executive, not the advertising manager. Why? It is the responsibility of an advertising manager to first carefully review and then approve the IMC Plan. Thus, while this is all part of the development process, the Advertising Manager is also the most important evaluator of the resulting document. When that is completed, the IMC Plan is also approved by marketing and management and then finally, distributed to the entire organization. The flow of the client-agency planning is illustrated in Figure 2.6.

Figure 2.6 Client–Agency Planning Cycle

But, what about smaller companies and entrepreneurs? It might be that a single person does it all. That includes not only the marketing decisions but also advertising, sales promotion, brand visibility, digital platforms, public relations, and personal contact. This is quite a challenge for an individual with little or no experience in the area. However, most smaller enterprises cannot afford a full marketing and advertising team. The only good option is an agency or consultant.

Procedures for Approval

The amount of time allowed for a presentation usually determines the information and number of details that will be included. The actual length depends on the rate of delivery, materials and information, and responses to questions at the end of the presentation. The slide deck format includes a title slide, list of presenters, section headings, detailed contents, and ending slide.

It is essential that the words and images on each slide are minimal in number, extremely well organized, and easy to read. This means excluding complicated pictures, illustrations, and graphs. Too many visuals can confuse and distract members of an audience. The type font used must be clear, legible, and large enough to be seen by people at the back of the meeting or presentation room. Avoid an excessive number of colors or extraneous elements. Each slide begins with a bold headline word or phrase that indicates the topic, subject, or recommendation within each section of the presentation. This is supported by information, placed in a numbered or sequential design, such as "bullets," "arrows," or "stars" in a descending vertical pattern.

Never simply read the words on a presentation slide. The audience can do that alone in silence. What the visual content on the screen represents is a condensed version of what you are talking about and why it is important. This acts as a reinforcement for your intention and reason for sharing it with the audience. As a result, the presenter becomes the expert and authority who is not only delivering a persuasive package of information but also adding their own personal knowledge, personality, and passion to the content.

Structure of the IMC Plan

This textbook has been structured to help you prepare a comprehensive but practical IMC Plan. It provides essential information in each chapter and organizes the content as you begin to select your strategies, develop programs, create materials, and make decisions. After choosing the options, choices, and alternatives, include them in your IMC Plan. Then, you have a much better understanding of IMC, and more importantly, you have just created a valuable document for your own business, company brand, community project, or organization. Hope you enjoyed the process as a learning experience!

There is no single or best way to write an IMC Plan. Every approach is different, because every company is different. And, each manager has preferences based on training, experience, and skill level. Different industries have different market structures, reporting information patterns, and competitive needs. However, the IMC Plan must conform to and support the goals of a marketing

Figure 2.7 Sections of the IMC Plan

authority within a company or organization. Thus, the written format for an IMC Plan must include the most important decision-making sections for review and approval (Figure 2.7). Typically, most IMC Plans for companies, organizations, or entrepreneurs will include the following sequential information: executive summary, marketing research, segmentation strategies, communication objectives, budget allocations, creative messaging, digital and legacy media, content delivery pathways, and performance metrics.

Executive Summary

The executive summary provides top-level managers or department leaders with a brief, but accurate, perspective of the IMC Plan. It is short, precise, and meaningful. Usually limited to a single page, or less, the executive summary is a framework for the research and strategies that are being used to prepare specific IMC programs and materials. It doesn't describe everything but outlines the insights, decisions, and applications for an effective IMC program and activities.

Why is the executive summary at the beginning of the report? Basically, different departments need to know how and when the IMC Plan will impact their individual areas of responsibility. And if the recommended plan involving advertising, sales promotion, brand visibility, digital platforms, public relations, and personal contact is accepted, then this information must immediately be shared with other departments or functions. If there are questions or concerns about these activities, the Executive Summary offers a preliminary guide for what will be happening through the entire year.

Marketing Research

IMC planning always begins with research. This is a strict requirement. Since so many creative communication decisions are subjective, there is a mandatory need to support them with insights, logic, and data. The number of variables involved, combined with multiple options and choices, contributes to the complexity of IMC. While most of the IMC research reports and documents revolve around numbers, the recommendations guide decisions.

There are four parts to the research section of an IMC Plan: consumer, product, market, and communication research. Each type of research provides another perspective for effective planning and contributes to the overall quality of the strategies and programs. Consumer research uncovers the demographic, psychographic, geographic, and behavioral characteristics of both existing and potential buyers. Product research discovers the physical strengths and weakness of competitive brands with the relative importance of these aspects for motivating a purchase decision. Market research identifies the total size of an industry, plus the major competitive brands in each segment, along with estimates of their sales, unit sales, and market share.

Communication research requires a comprehensive review of both the creative messages and media expenditures of competitors. This includes an assessment of the quality, clarity, and presentation of competitive brand value propositions as well as a description of the assumed target market. The total amount of money spent on each media type is also analyzed, along with the specific programs, publications, and channels selected by competitors. The insights from these research findings are valuable input for planning a competitive brand strategy.

Segmentation Strategies

Brand communication is not designed to reach everyone. There are many differences among buyers, not only from a demographic perspective but also psychological needs and wants. So, it is necessary to identify those individuals who have the highest probability of purchasing a specific product or service. These are the most likely buyers, who will be the target of brand messages. Other factors, such as their geographic locations and product usage habits, are also important. The focus on specific segments of a larger market is the single most effective way to reach customers with the right message at the right time in the right place.

Target Audience

The target audience is the group of consumers who are most likely to purchase a product or service. This includes specific descriptions of the difference between people are interested in a brand and those who are not. There are many factors involved with a target audience, such as age, income, gender, and marital status. In Chapter 5, consumer segmentation strategies will be reviewed and explained.

Communication Objectives

The complexity of IMC requires that each of the six major strategies has its own distinct set of objectives. Why? While the overall IMC objective remains a constant, each of the strategies is measured in different ways.

Advertising objectives are based on one of the traditional models, such as the pyramid or purchase funnel, where percentages are established for each stage: for example, the percentage of the target market who are aware of the brand name or its primary user benefit. Sales promotion objectives are connected to a particular action or response with another form of measurement, such as the number of coupons redeemed, entries in a sweepstake, or walk-in visits to a retail store. Public relations objectives are associated with the value of free media coverage received, specifically, the amount of space or time multiplied by the advertising cost of a similar amount.

Other aspects of public relations can have separate objectives for the impact of internal company communications, community relations, and successful lobbying of government organizations.

Brand visibility objectives involve exposure to a product or service through methods other than traditional advertising, sales promotion, or public relations. The standards require repeated exposure to target audiences though non-paid media that have the brand name or image embedded within a program, activity, or locations.

Personal contact objectives are related to the specific function involved. A sales contact example would include the number of appointments per week or presentations made to potential customers. And for a retail sales clerk, the objective might be daily dollar revenues generated or number of items sold. Personal contact also involves any aspect of word of mouth, brand ambassador representative, or verbal dialogue with customers, such as "store greeters."

Digital objectives are the most complex of IMC activities. The measurement methods are new and relevant only to digital media or platforms. This extends to a great variety of different metrics, which are connected back to program objectives. For example, page views, unique visitors, time on page, click-through rates, or return visits are objectives for a website, while likes, posts, re-tweets, and followers are the most useful measures for social media.

Budget Allocations

The method used to calculate the IMC budget is selected and presented. This includes both the rationale and all assumptions that support the recommendation. The core element of this decision always involves the sales forecast and the method used to make this calculation. Usually, the industry "advertising-to-sales" ratio is the base number combined with a proposed increase or decrease in the percentage. However, there are many other ways to generate a budget, which result in a much more productive relationship between marketing and IMC program activities.

The allocation of IMC funds is first displayed as a percentage and then a number according to the six strategies: advertising, sales promotion, brand visibility, digital platforms, public relations, personal communications. These are the major categories. Then, the percentage allocation and numbers are further broken down into sub-categories, such as television, radio, newspapers, and magazines for advertising media or websites, social media, email marketing, and streaming video for digital media. The exact percentages are based on a combination of audience delivery size needed, target market concentration, costs involved, time frame for completion, and strategic positioning.

Creative Message Strategies

The development of creative concepts must be based on the positioning of the brand as well as its value proposition. The challenge is to maintain consistency not only for the development of brand content but also for the persuasive brand messaging that is being delivered through multiple pathways. There also has to be a balance between creativity and pragmatism. The conflict arises when creative ideas become a form of entertainment and do not include information about the brand. It is essential that the brand benefits or value proposition is embedded in the storytelling process. The needs and desires of consumers must be a priority for brand messages that are delivered through every communication pathway. As a result, the creative concepts developed by a marketing communications agency will include the applications for advertising, sales promotion, public relations, brand visibility, digital platforms, and personal contact. Achieving this integration is the ultimate measure of communication message planning.

Media Delivery Strategies

There two options for advertising: legacy media and digital media. Legacy media include television, radio, magazines, newspapers, and outdoors. Digital media are primarily social media, email marketing, brand websites, and mobile apps. The challenge is to reach the targeted consumers with the budget provided using either one, or a combination, of both media options. There is a great diversity of media vehicles within each category, but the total number of people reached by each one varies significantly, which influences the cost of the media. As a result, methodical and accurate planning is required to ensure an effective utilization of financial resources.

Performance Metrics

This section connects back to the previously established IMC objectives for each of the six pathways or categories. Performance is measured by the attainment of the separate objectives. Since there are many components for each category, there can be multiple objectives being monitored and evaluated. For example, the performance of legacy advertising can be measured with research methods based on the AIDA model, while digital advertising focuses on website visits, click-throughs, or time on page for the most relevant key performance indicators.

Marketing objectives can also be included in the measurement process. Sales volume, in either currency or product units, market share, profitability, and a return on investment (ROI) metric are the standard categories for measuring the performance of a Marketing Plan, which includes the expenditure of funds for IMC.

Summary

IMC is the process of creating and delivering a planned series of consistent, relevant, and meaningful brand messages to target audiences. This involves collecting and analyzing consumer, product, and market research and then, using the information to make decisions involving strategies, budgets, and specific programs, activities, and events. The primary goal is to combine effective creative concepts with efficient media delivery methods. Another way to describe IMC is getting the right message to the right people in the right place at the right time for the right reason with measurable results.

The IMC industry consists of four major groups: advertisers, agencies, media companies, and suppliers. Advertisers have the most control over planning, developing, and implementing IMC strategies, because they decide and approve budgets. Agencies are hired by advertisers to make creative and media recommendations. After the plans are approved, the agency, along with suppliers, produces the IMC materials and buys the media.

As an important marketing variable, IMC uses methods from six basic strategic categories: advertising, sales promotion, brand visibility, public relations, digital media, and personal contact. Advertising generates brand name awareness and preference, while sales promotion motivates people to buy products and services by offering a variety of financial and reward incentives. Brand visibility includes anything that helps people to recognize and remember the brand. Public relations is responsible for the publication of product news and information in multiple forms of media without the expenses involved in placing advertising. However, the content is controlled by publishers. Digital media include the entire spectrum of online communication, from websites and social media to streaming video and mobile apps. Personal contact describes a situation where direct, one-to-one interaction occurs, such as salespeople in a store or word-of-mouth communication among friends or associates.

The IMC planning process begins with research, followed by the development of strategies, the production of communication materials and purchasing of media, and finally, an evaluation of IMC performance using traditional marketing metrics and digital analytics. The result is a very complete IMC Plan for a company, brand, or organization.

This chapter has given you an outline for an IMC Plan. This includes a very short description of the decision-making aspects of advertising, sales promotion, brand visibility, public relations, digital media platforms, and personal contact. Each of these areas will be explored in greater detail within the coming chapters in this textbook.

Discussion Questions

1. What is the value of developing an Integrated Communication Plan?
2. Which of the IMC pathways is the most effective in reaching potential buyers?
3. How do you evaluate communication consistency? Why is it so important for brand messages?
4. Who is considered to be an advertiser? What are the qualifications? Are there any limitations?

5. Why should corporations, small businesses, and entrepreneurs hire an advertising agency?
6. How do you define the media industry? Which types of companies are associated with media?
7. Who is primarily responsible for preparing an IMC Plan? Who is required to approve it?
8. What is the difference between the AIDA model and the Sales Funnel? Which one is better?
9. Why is it essential to establish separate objectives for different components of IMC pathways?
10. What are the most important sections of any IMC Plan?

Chapter Assignments

1. Select a local advertising agency and visit its website. What services does it offer?
2. Learn more about marketing from the American Marketing Association (www.ama.org).
3. Explore the website for Advertising Age, the leading media for the industry (www.AdAge.com).
4. Find a campus or local chapter for the American Advertising Federation (www.aaf.com).
5. Discover more about advertisers from the Association of National Advertisers (www.ana.net).

Continuity Case Study

Adriana had just come back from lunch. She was surprised to find a message from Martin Lugano, Vice-President of Marketing for Athena, which is the largest fast food restaurant chain for Greek and Mediteranean food in the United States. Mr.Lugano was inviting her to attend an important meeting at 2pm. As she walked down the corridor, Adriana was thinking about her new plan to improve the productivity of the sales force. While it wasn't due until next week, there were still some issues to be resolved. No doubt Mr. Lugano had questions. When Adriana walked into the conference room, there was immediate applause. This was so unlike a typical meeting. The outburst was surprising because it wasn't her birthday, and she could think of no other reason to celebrate. Then, the big news! Mr. Lugano announced that Adriana Lopez had just been promoted to the new nationwide position of manager, Integrated Marketing Communication.

Adriana was thrilled, but puzzled. Martin referred to the importance of IMC and the challenges of being the first manager in that position. IMC? Adriana was thinking: "what does this involve?" She had previously discussed new opportunities at the company, but nothing specific had ever been proposed. Adriana was very happy as the Eastern Regional sales manager and had no plans to make any changes. Later that afternoon, Adriana began to react to the reality of the situation. Her initial task was to select a new advertising agency and begin planning for the coming year. There was no budget. However, she was expected to make a recommendation by the end of the month. The company had done very little advertising in the past and only a few promotion programs. Previously, most of this type of work had been done by the publicity department. But, nothing had been done to redesign the company's website during the past year.

Her first action was to search online for advertising agencies. Adriana was not sure what type of agency to select. The full-service agencies seemed to be the best, since no matter what was needed, they could provide the service. This could also help her learn more about the process of advertising planning and IMC. But then, digital agencies are more proficient in website design and email marketing. After spending several hours, she decided on five agencies to make a presentation, including a recommendation for budgets.

1. What type of IMC agency should Adriana hire for Athena?
2. How much should the agency be paid for its services?
3. What part of the planning process will be most difficult for Adriana?
4. Will Adriana's experience in sales be helpful in her new position?
5. What should she do to improve her knowledge of IMC?

IMC Plan Development

Step One:
>   Select your brand or product for the planning process

Step Two:
>   Prepare an outline with individual sections for the IMC Plan

Step Three:
>   Organize your team into an agency structure with specific responsibilities

Step Four:
>   Estimate the tasks, time, and challenges involved in preparing the plan

Step Five:
>   Begin preliminary research on your company, brand, or industry

Chapter 3

Marketing Research Methods

Collecting and Analyzing Input for Decision-Making

Learning Objectives

1. To understand the value and purpose of marketing research
2. To describe and apply secondary research methods
3. To describe and apply primary research methods
4. To identify consumer insights and purchasing patterns

Introduction

There are many questions you need to know about customers and potential buyers. But, the most important ones can be summarized in five short words: who, what, when, where, why?

This chapter provides you with the research methods needed to answer all these questions.

It involves learning about the entire spectrum of marketing research, including consumer, product, and industry research. The chapter also explains the differences between primary and secondary research as well as the interpretations of both quantitative and qualitative research findings. However, what is most important is how to use these different research methods to gather information and complete an analysis for Integrated Marketing Communications (IMC) planning and program development.

This corresponds to the marketing variables that will be used for the determination of target audiences, brand messages, purchase motivations, media selections, and delivery scheduling.

DOI: 10.4324/9780367443382-3

Identifying and understanding those individuals or groups most likely to need, want, or use a particular product or service is defined as determining a target audience. The primary and secondary demographic data collected and analyzed from consumer research is strategically applied for both preliminary media and creative planning. Brand messages are also composed using the same information to effectively develop relevant and meaningful content for the target audience, while industry research explains and evaluates purchase motivations. Budgets establish the financial limitations involved with media selection, and industry research influences marketing decisions for the best days, times, and locations for IMC message delivery.

Why Research Is Needed

It would nice to begin by creating commercials, but that's not how it works. Advertising is not just about having clever ideas and catchy slogans. It is about communicating with customers and potential buyers. And, we need to know all about them. A lot more. Where they live. What they do. How old they are. Why they like a product. Which brands they hate. All this important information is needed to develop creative strategies for advertising and every other form of IMC. If we did not have it, our brand messages would be meaningless and our media selection wasteful and inefficient. Research gives marketers exactly what is needed to connect brands with individuals and IMC programs with target audiences.

Here are just a few examples. An automotive company discovered that more females than males were buying a new car model, so they changed their advertising photos and increased visibility in female-oriented media. A dog food company was surprised to learn that many of its customers were older and purchased their pet as a companion, so once again, the images and advertising media were changed. And finally, a restaurant chain was surprised to learn that Hispanic customers were its most loyal customers and were geographically concentrated in California, Texas, Arizona, and Florida, and yes, surprisingly, there was even a very strong presence in Chicago.

Types of Research

The information and data from marketing research can be described as either quantitative or qualitative. This applies to all four of the categories of marketing research—consumer, industry, product, and market research. Another important aspect of marketing research is the distinction between primary and secondary research, which will be explained later in this chapter.

Quantitative Research

Quantitative research is all about collecting data that accurately reflects and describes the situation with numbers. Cold, hard facts. Rows and columns of numbers. Tables and charts. For example, quantitative research includes the number of people who are between the ages of 18 and 34 years of age who are in the United States. Or, living in the state of New York City. Or, owning a home in Los Angeles, Dallas, or Chicago. Another research report lists the number of retired people, marriage certificates, sales of computers, small dogs, or new cars purchased each year. And the possibilities continue. Quantitative research is all about numbers and what they describe.

Qualitative Research

Qualitative research focuses on gathering information about consumer attitudes, feelings, likes, emotions, beliefs, and behavior. Using a variety of methods, marketers can get feedback, comments, and opinions from both existing and potential customers. The purpose is to gain a better understand of buyer behavior, including a perspective of how, when, and why purchase decisions are made. Qualitative research is all about cognitive activity of diverse people and how these factors influence the decisions of advertisers when designing brand communication.

A simple distinction between quantitative and qualitative research is to use either descriptive numbers or subjective opinions. The first is accurate and complete. The second is estimated and only represents a sample, which may or may not be true for the entire group of people. And finally, quantitative research is relatively stable, and objective, while qualitative research is fluid, flexible, and helpful but highly subjective.

Marketing Research Categories

Figure 3.1 illustrates the four primary categories of marketing research: industry, product, communication, and consumer. Each category provides us with valuable information to make effective management decisions, especially for IMC. The information and insights derived from these different parts of marketing research are used to guide the development of brand strategies, especially creative advertising messages, media selection, promotion programs, digital interactions,

Figure 3.1 Marketing Research Categories

and other activities Data and analysis, as well as conclusions, are automatically included in a formal written document called the IMC Plan.

Any proposed or approved IMC budget must be strategically divided among each of the major categories to ensure that the brand's communication objectives are achieved. The assumption is that the total amount of money allocated represents the relative importance of a category. However, since advertising is the most expensive category, it represents a disproportionate share of the total budget for most national brands. While this is less of a problem for smaller companies or local brands, advertising frequently accounts for greater IMC expenditures than all the other categories combined.

Industry Research

Industry research includes facts about the size and structure of a market, number of competitors, leading brands, and details about recent trends or challenges that are emerging. The size of the market includes both dollar sales and unit sales, usually organized into product categories or classifications. The number of brands, and their parent companies, are identified along with a ranking of their market share. Industry research also includes information about new product developments, technological applications for productivity, and executive profiles.

Product Research

Product research looks at the physical characteristics and composition of a product or service. It is like an X-ray examination of the contents, ingredients, design, construction, and functionality. Marketing research studies for product research are designed to discover what "things" customers like, or dislike, about brands. Comparative product research actually measures the quantitative amount of approval or disapproval for specific brand characteristics.

By using a series of rankings or rating scales, market researchers can compare different brands. For example, typical questions using a five-point rating scale could be: "Which of these candy bars is the sweetest?" or "How satisfied are you with the taste of Snickers candy bar?"

Communication Research

Do you know what your competitors are doing? Which media are they using? What creative strategies appear in their brand messages? How are they using sales promotion to increase sales and profits? The answers to these questions are very important, and before you begin developing strategies for an IMC Plan, it is essential that you investigate them in greater detail. Most likely, competitors have already researched what you have done in the past and are planning to outmaneuver your brand in the marketplace. So, how are you going to approach the challenge of communication research for your IMC strategies?

Here are six categories of communication research that should be included in your IMC Plan: brand websites, social media, video content, legacy media, sales promotion, and other pathways.

First, take a close look at a competitor's brand website. It is the epicenter of their strategic focus. The website is always there on a 24/7 basis for examination and analysis. Second, examine their social media patterns, especially which social media are being used most frequently. Are they using Instagram for photos and images? Or, are they depending on a more conservative approach with Facebook? Do some social listening. Go beyond what information a brand is posting. Find out what consumers are talking about in their posts, especially if it involves a brand, product category, or life style problem. What does their social media advertising look like? Do you believe that it is effective? Third, find their YouTube channel and watch their videos, which sometimes include their television commercial and promotional programs. There are also research companies that can provide valuable information about streaming video usage. Fourth, review the media landscape for a competitor's legacy media. Do they have magazine advertisements in specialized publications? What about their television advertising? Are their brand commercials national or placed only in high-potential sales markets? What is their creative strategy? Fifth, and finally, evaluate their sales promotion events, activities, and programs. Can you estimate their effectiveness? What about other IMC pathways to customers or potential buyers?

Communication research also provides you with opportunities to evaluate the advertising and promotion expenditure level of your competitors. It estimates not only the amount of competitive spending but also the percentage of funds allocated to each media or IMC pathway. These are available through proprietary sources, and easy to purchase, but have relatively high prices for the content. But, for a large advertiser, the investment is worth the cost. As a result, companies can make better decisions about which media to use, when to use them, and what is the minimum, or optimum, amount to be more competitive in the marketplace.

Consumer Research

Consumer research is the most useful form of marketing research for IMC planning. It provides valuable data about existing customers and potential buyers as well as insights into their actions and behavior. Specific profiles about consumers can be developed from this research that are used to create brand messages, select appropriate media, and design promotional programs. Consumer research also enables company executives, small business owners, and entrepreneurs to discover new marketing opportunities with innovative strategies.

Secondary Marketing Research

Now, let's begin with a definition. Secondary research is information and data that has already been collected, analyzed, or written by an external source. It can be free or available for purchase by anyone. So, even competitive companies can obtain copies of the same research reports.

Ironically, marketing research begins with the collection of existing data and information. That's right, secondary research comes before primary research. Why? It is faster, less expensive, and easier to complete. Plus, when there is a need to find more detailed or specific information about a subject, then primary research is the only way to proceed. But, it is slower, more expensive, and difficult to complete. The compensating factor is that primary research is proprietary. You own the information. The research results and insights are exclusive, and only your company can use them for strategic IMC decision-making. This can be an extremely important competitive advantage.

Internet Search

Beginning a search on Google is a great way to start. But, the search results will not always provide the correct information or a sufficient amount. This depends on the selection of keywords. They must be precise, relevant, and phrased correctly. When a single word does not yield sufficient search results, then try a combination of words or phrases. Or, use quotation marks around the words and phrases, separated by the conjunction: and. For example, pairing the words "tea consumption" and "global brands" might produce a different grouping of search results. Another important consideration during a Google search is using industry terminology.

For example, if you wanted to find information on the breakfast cereal market in the United States, the best search term is RTE, or ready-to-eat cereal, which is a correct industry description.

The ultimate initial search strategy for information is to use databases that aggregate information. This enables you to search. For example, ABI/INFORM Global contains the full text from thousands of different journals and business trade publications. The advantage is that you can immediately find reports and studies for every industry as well as consumer studies and related marketing information. The only disadvantage is that everyone, including your competitors, can review the same documents. Another possible issue is the dates of the information. It must be recent enough to be relevant for the research investigation. ABI/INFORM Global is available online through a company called ProQuest, which has a variety of services for marketing research. While using this company can be an expensive service, the same information can also be accessed at no cost through university and college library resources. Another very powerful and valuable information source is offered through Statista, which offers insights and facts from across 170 industries and over 150 countries. Its research reports are very recent and reflect important trends needed for marketing insights and understanding.

Let's review the entire range of secondary research sources and where to find them. Figure 3.2 identifies the six major resource categories: government

Figure 3.2 Secondary Research for Information

documents, industry associations, syndicated reports, business publications, academic journals, and public library collections. Each resource provides different types of data for marketing communication decision-making, which facilitates an accurate knowledge of the consumer, market, and industry involved.

Syndicated Reports

Research companies, such as A.C. Nielsen and others, invest in funding their own projects or services. Their product is information. The data contained in the reports is extremely valuable to manufacturers of global brands and advertising agencies. So, it is much easier to buy the document and analyze the contents rather than to try to begin one's own research project. There are hundreds of professional research companies that increase their sales and profits by providing every industry with needed information on consumers, markets, and business statistics.

Industry Associations

Every industry has a professional association that requires membership to receive its services. While its most significant function is to lobby for laws and regulations that are favorable for the association's membership, these privately funded organizations also provide important primary and secondary marketing research information. The association frequently hires independent research companies, or uses its own employees, to conduct studies on topics of interest that can improve productivity and performance. The reports also investigate new products and processes as well as identifying and commenting on trends and opportunities.

Each association serves a business need and industry. And each has a website, newsletter, and information resource center that are free for members. How many associations are out there? If you want to find a specific one for any industry, even if you are not sure about the name, go to the *Encyclopedia of Associations*. At the last count, there were more than 18,000 associations in the United States. Their list includes everything from the expected to the unbelievable, such as the Dental Association of Southern California, Texas Tire Dealers Association, National Home Builders Association, and the Popcorn Growers of America.

Business Media

Every day, online industry news sources, the digital equivalent of printed magazines, report the latest happenings and activities within specific industries. These business-oriented publishing companies include sales information, new product introductions, technological developments, and a variety of feature stories. Each online source or magazine has several editions during the year that provide a summary of the leading companies, brands, and executives. As shown in Figure 3.3, there are both vertical and horizontal publications. Vertical media refers to publications that focus on a single industry or specific business activity, while horizontal describes media that contains general interest topics across multiple industries and functions.

Figure 3.3 Business Media Resources

The list of these publications is long, but it can be found in an important publication called Standard Rate and Data (SRDS). It also contains the advertising costs for each magazine as well as the circulation and other advertising-related information. Every industry in included. There are publications for the travel industry, tourism, banking, and restaurants, plus media even directed at the channels of distribution. For example, *Chain Store Age* is targeted to reach managers and executives at large national or regional companies with thousands of retail locations.

Government Documents

Your taxes paid for it. Now, it is time to get some value back. From whom? Surprisingly, the United States government is the single biggest source of secondary research information. It is offered free, or at a very nominal cost compared with private research companies. In Figure 3.4, there are just a few of the many different sources of government documents. The majority of the information that is used by advertising agencies and corporations is obtained from the Department of Census, Department of Commerce, or the Department of Agriculture. In addition, state, county, and local governments provide demographic and business information in the form of secondary research reports. Here are just a few of the U.S. Census documents that can be helpful when collecting information for an advertising or marketing research project.

If you were assigned to find the cities and states with the largest number of automobiles, where would you look? What if your job was doing marketing research for an advertising agency, and the client was a car insurance company? The *Statistical Abstracts of the United States* can provide you with the answers. It has several pages ranking cities and states according to the number of registered automobiles. For example, California, Texas, and New York are the top three geographic areas, with 17.5% of all the automobiles in the United States. Thus, your agency would recommend spending the largest percentage of the media budget in those states.

What if you needed to analyze car registrations in a different way? Then, you would use the government publication that breaks down demographic information into 7322 counties across the nation. For example, use *USA Counties* to locate the highest household income areas within 50 miles of the largest shopping area.

Another publication offered by the U.S. Department of Census involves zip codes and census tracts. Since many zip codes are large and complex, a smaller

Figure 3.4 Government Documents

division is used, called the census tract. This might be as small as several square blocks depending on the population density. For example, all the zip codes in Youngtown, Ohio are divided into 87 different census tracts for research findings.

Academic Journals

While academic journals are often theoretical and limited in their applications, these publications can still provide a broad framework and better understanding of industry problems and challenges. Professors from colleges of business and management are frequent lecturers at conferences and workshops, sharing opinions and beliefs about marketing practices. These academic papers are particularly useful when the information is relevant, recent, and comprehensive.

Consulting Companies

There are a number of large global consulting companies that publish white papers and excerpts from their reports as part of their strategy to attract new clients. These represent a significant investment in their time and money, but it is a business service that they provide. The big advantage for advertisers and marketing communication companies is that even old or partial reports are valuable for understanding the dynamics in a market segment or industry.

Library Databases

This is last stop for our fast-moving secondary research train. Libraries in large metropolitan cities, public universities, and private institutes are where an enormous amount of printed and digital information is stored. While most of the publications and reports can be accessed online, there are many very expensive reference books and proprietary documents that can be viewed through a physical visit. It might be possible to purchase or download the same information, but at a library, most published documents and records are free to read and use but not to take home.

Four of the most useful publications for advertising planning and marketing research are the *Standard Directory of Advertisers*, the *Green Book Market Research Directory*, the *Market Share Reporter*, and the *J.D. Powers Report*.

The *Standard Directory of Advertisers* and *Standard Directory of Advertising Agencies*, also known in the IMC industry as the "Redbooks" due to their color, divide companies into product categories and companies. Inside the publications are the estimated media expenditure budgets for the leading brands, including the amount of money spent on each media type, agency accounts, corporate contact information, and the names of the most important decision-makers and managers.

The *J.D. Powers Reports* are a series of brand comparison reports that cover a variety of product categories. The reports include consumer ratings for features, designs, functions, and other important product attributes. In addition, the company conducts separate research studies that measure owner satisfaction, brand loyalty, and quality ratings.

The *Market Share Reporter* is a reference publication organized according to several hundred industry classification categories. Its featured content is an estimation of the market shares by brands, which is an excellent resource for a competitive industry analysis. The numbers are most helpful in calculating advertising budgets and media strategies.

The *Green Book Market Share Directory* is a complete listing of marketing research companies. It separates the information by geographic region, company size, and area of specialization, such as field research, focus groups, personal interviews, survey research, and statistical data analysis.

Primary Research

Primary research is information, or data, that has been collected, analyzed, or written by an internal source. The process of producing this information is managed, controlled, and owned by your own company, and as a result, primary research is always considered proprietary. It is private and confidential. No one else has this information. Not your competitor. Not another organization. Only your company and its employees can utilize and apply the contents of this primary marketing research. That is the importance of this valuable research information, because it can provide a competitive advantage when planning strategic IMC programs.

But, it comes with a price and takes a lot of time. The option is to purchase, or to find online, relevant information about an industry, market segment, brand performance, consumer preferences, and other essential data. This is considered to be secondary research, or information that other individuals, companies, trade associations, educational institutions, entrepreneurs, journalists, and government organizations have already completed. Yes, there might be a price involved, but it will be much less than the cost of doing it yourself. For example, a private research company is offering a comprehensive study of the cell phone market for $1750. Expensive for a single copy, but a bargain compared with a primary study of $50,000 or more, which takes three months.

There are many techniques used to collect primary marketing research information, but the most popular ones are focus groups, personal interviews, and survey research. This trio provides a balanced perspective of consumers' attitudes, beliefs, and opinions on product categories and specific brands. Focus groups are the most likely to yield immediate insights, while personal interviews provide

Zoom Discussions	Traditional Focus Groups	Social Media Listening	Brand Website Analysis
Online Tracking	Digital Surveys	Personal Interviews	Concept Testing
Behavioral Observations	Role Playing Exercises	Immersive Experiences	Projective Techniques

Figure 3.5 Primary Research for Insights

greater depth and detail. Survey research contributes a more quantitative perspective of brands and the buyer's experiences. It is frequently used after focus groups and personal interviews as a technique to measure a larger number of consumers. Other valuable primary research methods include social listening, website analysis, store visits, role-playing, and projective techniques. The complete list of insight primary research methods is shown in Figure 3.5. The information needs of the company, or agency, as well as the amount of time and money allocated to primary insight research Insight

Zoom Online Sessions

In 2020, a new way to collect marketing research information emerged. It is fast, efficient, and produces immediate results. Of course, Zoom has been used extensively for person-to-person communication since the beginning of the decade. Zoom not only performs the same function as a traditional focus group but also allows observers to view every participant's facial reactions and expressions during the questioning period. Plus, everyone knows that a video is being made of the session, which is part of the condition for accepting participation. But, let's review what a traditional focus group is and how it functions to provide insight research results.

Traditional Focus Groups

Have you ever been to a live focus group? It is actually a lot of fun. You get to express your own opinion about products, services, organizations, and yes, every possible topic and issue.

Since the purpose of a focus group is to share individual beliefs and attitudes about brands and product usage, a well-organized set of questions must be prepared in advance. The best approach is to begin with a few general questions to begin the discussion and later, move into more specific and focused topics. For example, a focus group on breakfast cereals might start with asking "What do you like to eat for breakfast?" or "How much time do you spend eating breakfast?" but the flow of the questions must always follow a general-to-specific pattern.

Focus groups lasts for one to two hours, which gives everyone plenty of time to talk and share their thoughts. It is the responsibility of the moderator of the group to move steadily through the topics and questions without spending unnecessary time. Near the end of the focus group, the participants are asked to evaluate the image and reputation of particular brands. This can involve numerical rating scales, preference rankings, completion of a short questionnaire, or talking about what product features, benefits, or ingredients they would like to have in a new product.

The words, phrases, and expressions that are used by the participants to describe their usage of products and attitudes about brands are the most important aspect of a focus group. This information, which helps a researcher to better understand the "mind and mood" of potential buyers, can be used to prepare creative messages. Ironically, members of an advertising agency, or brand executives, are actually in the next room watching the entire focus group. They are hidden behind a two-way glass mirror, sitting in nice comfortable chairs. And, the videotape cameras with them are rolling to record the event. Too much information? No. There is more. The moderator has a tape recorder, which will be used to transcribe the sessions.

Focus groups provide a quick and easy view of consumer attitudes and behavior. When listening carefully to the participants' comments, ideas and concepts emerge for potential advertising campaigns, sales promotion programs, and even brand blogs. Other applications, which are oriented more toward product development, include taste testing as well as comparing package designs or watching television commercials.

Why do people come to focus groups? Well, the product or service category is usually one they like, and they get paid up to $50 for their time and effort. But, not everyone is invited. The brand sponsoring the research restricts the number of people based on their demographic profiles and previous brand purchases. For example, if a home furniture company wants to know what people look for when buying couches and sofas, then ONLY those individuals who said they were going to purchase new furniture in the next six months would be recruited for the focus group. Or, if a video game company was launching a new adult action series, then the attendees of a focus group would be limited to men, active players, ages 18–25. If the brand was a cookie, then married women with children under 10 years of age would be preferred target members to invite to the focus group.

Usually, there are 10 to 12 people with similar interests or backgrounds who have been invited to participate by a research company. There is often more than one focus group, held at different times and in multiple locations. National brands with large budgets always have several focus groups, but smaller companies or local enterprises might only afford one or two. While the cost can be anywhere from $500 to $2000 per session, focus groups can be arranged quickly and provide immediate feedback and information.

The important point to remember is that focus groups only provide "insights." The information obtained from a focus group is not representative of everyone, nor can it be conclusive about decisions of customers in the marketplace. However, focus groups are an exceedingly helpful research method because they help marketers to develop a much better understanding of people's feelings, beliefs, and attitudes. This includes a mixture of words, phrases, and expressions that are used to describe brands and the overall product category.

Social Media Listening

For example, social listening is more important than posting and responding to content. What are people saying about a brand or product category? Are there specific words or phrases that are frequently used to describe how, when, and why people use a product?

Social media have much more to offer advertisers than worrying about increasing the number of likes, posts, or video views. While most companies are trying hard to understand and use social media, few are listening or watching the content people are sharing. Monitoring different online websites, blogs, and mobile apps provides an excellent digital perspective of life styles, personal interests, and popular topics. And, this type of research has to go well beyond "what's trending" by going deep into the words, phrases, and images using semantic techniques. Social listening must examine the overall digital activity of a brand, along with the backend analytics available from social media platforms, before it begins launching campaigns on Hootsuite and other types of automated message delivery services.

Brand Website Analysis

Ironically, websites are an excellent source of product and market research. They are available not only for consumer viewing but also for competitive analysis. Brand websites provide a wealth of information for potential buyers with images, descriptions, and even special offers. benefits, and offer incentives to purchase. Visiting the websites of competitors should always be one of the priorities for any marketing department or IMC agency.

Digital Research Surveys

Online technology makes this one of the fastest, easiest, and least expensive methods of collecting a small, but sufficient, amount of data about customers and potential buyers. It all begins with a questionnaire, but that is more complex than you think. The problem is the amount of time that people are willing to spend completing the questionnaire. Too long, and no one fills it out. Too short, and no useful information is obtained. The questionnaire needs to be right in the middle.

So, how do you design it correctly? First, think of questions and situations that you really need to find out more about. If you can predict the answer, then don't ask it. Second, never ask "yes" or "no" questions, because it gives you very little, if any, information. The only exception is when you are intentionally separating people based on demographic characteristics or user experiences. Third, ask respondents to answer in their own words. Personal comments and suggestions are much richer in language and express the emotions and feeling involved. This does not have to be part of every question, but only when it can provide powerful insights. Fourth, use a variety of different methods for collecting responses, such as item rankings, scales, multiple choices, fill in the blank, or numerical values. Fifth, it is strategically important to save any questions about age, income, gender, or other potentially sensitive demographic information until the end of the questionnaire. Asking these questions too early can often offend people and cause them to quit immediately.

Traditionally, survey research has been conducted using paper forms, mailed to a pre-screened list of people with large sample sizes. This method took many weeks to complete, experienced low response rates, and was relatively expensive (printing, postage, and tabulating costs), but it was the best option at the time. It also required the services of a professional research company, but today, you can do it all yourself using an online platform, such as SurveyMonkey. The process is very quick, easy, and uncomplicated. No training or experience is required. And, using these online platforms is completely free. Most of the companies offering this service even provide a summary graphic with numbers for presentations.

The results of survey research provide a good estimate of the magnitude of differences or variation of preferences among consumers. It removes guessing about what people are thinking and expands the opportunities for communication. As long as there is a sufficient number of respondents, the research findings are valid. Thus, a marketing manager or business owner can make a more informed decision about people's attitudes, beliefs, and opinions. Utilizing online tools such as Mentimeter is an excellent way to obtain data. The results displayed are not only the visual representation of the word entered by the respondent but also the size of the word. The larger the size, the greater the number of times that a single word, or phrase, was entered into the system. You can easily sign up for a free account, which is provided at www.mentimeter.com.

Personal Interviews

Talking directly to a customer or prospective buyer is the single most effective way to get a realistic perspective of any marketing environment. The problem is the cost and time involved. It can be very expensive to find and recruit people for an interview and even more expensive to hire a professional research interviewer. The process of asking people questions can be a challenge, especially when you do not want to influence their answers. The interviewer has to do more listening than talking and always be alert for opportunities to learn more. Spontaneity must be encouraged, as well as honesty and openness. Perhaps, what is not said is the most important part of the interview. A respondent's non-verbal messages often clearly indicate a preference, dislike, or confusion. For example, a frown or smile when a question is asked, raised eyebrows when reading a statement, or a puzzled facial expression when discussing a brand. That is why corporations hire experienced research companies, who are trained in the nuances and subtleties to conduct personal interviews. But, it is still a good idea to try a few interviews on your own to feel the pulse of the marketplace and better understand how customers think and react.

How many personal interviews are needed? That is a very subjective decision. The answer is a combination of funds available, time frame for completion, and purpose of the research project. Typically, companies like to have 10 to 12 completed interviews in multiple cities or locations. While the results are not statistically projectable, overall patterns emerge that are extremely relevant. The findings can also be used for designing a questionnaire for survey research or planning advertising messages, promotional programs, or other IMC activities.

Behavioral Observations

There is no better way to understand consumers than to physically observe them shopping, discussing, or using a product or service. This often involves unobtrusive observations, which ensure that no one knows that you are watching. While this can also be completed by using video surveillance, the feeling of being there contributes to a realistic experience. This gives the observer a real opportunity to watch how they pick up a product from a store shelf, listen to them talking to their friends or asking a question of a store employee, or just to watch the expression on their face. It is all part of the buying experience and final part of the customer's journey.

Role-Playing Exercises

In the movie *What Women Want*, Mel Gibson's character is an experienced, talented, but over-confident creative director who wants to become the vice-president of an advertising agency. Unexpectedly, an attractive, savvy, and aggressive new leader has just been hired.

In her first meeting, the agency executive, played by Cheryl Ladd, passes out colorful boxes containing female-oriented products from all the agency clients. She insists that every member of the creative team goes home and experiences using each brand. If you saw the movie, then you know the challenges Mel Gibson had with face cream, leg razors, and pantyhose.

But without trying them, how else would a male begin to understand the brand benefits?

Personal product usage is just one method. Role-playing also involves simulations, such as comparing different products or even making purchase decisions, but taken from the actual perspectives of other people. This is a great way to get a better feeling for a brand, its competitors, and the challenges of marketing in retail environments. Role-playing quickly demonstrates a consumer's need, a product's solution, and an IMC opportunity to connect.

Projective Techniques

This collection of qualitative methods comes direct from the methods used by psychologists, sociologists, and anthropologists. They are called projective techniques because they depend on the mental ability of people to complete missing information, structure ambiguous situations, or project their own opinions, emotions, attitudes, or feelings. This information can provide valuable insights for planning the most relevant words, phrases, images, and content for brand advertising messages. That is why projective techniques are so popular with marketing communication agencies and research companies. However, since advertising agencies are most interested in understanding the mind and mood of customers and potential buyers, these techniques are used only with those individuals who fit into the desired demographic, psychographic, geographic, or behavioral segmentation profile.

In Figure 3.6, the seven most frequently used projective techniques are displayed: word association, sentence completion, photo caption, forced comparison,

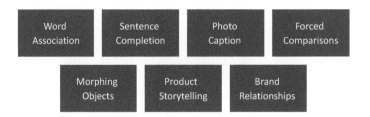

Figure 3.6 Projective Techniques

morphing objects, product storytelling, and brand withdrawal. Here is a brief description and example for each of the techniques. The results can provide information to guide the development of persuasive brand messages for advertising as well as informational content for social media posting or targeted email marketing campaigns.

In word association exercises, an individual is presented with, either orally or written on paper, a series of stimulus words and asked to immediately provide only a single response word. The instructions should always emphasize that each answer must be the first thing that comes into their mind. There is no right or wrong, or good or bad answer. It is a simple, easy-to-administer, and valuable method to gain deep insights about how people think. The technique utilizes the Theory of Cognitive Structuralism, explained in Chapter 6, which describes the conscious and subconscious association between stimulus and response words with neural brain networks.

In a sentence completion exercise, people are asked to fill in a single word that is missing from a sentence. For example, I like Cadbury chocolate bars because it always makes me feel_____. The responses from this projective technique can also indicate the mental associations that consumers have with a brand and its relationship to their shopping and life style behavior.

In a photo caption exercise, people must provide a short title or headline for a picture or image. For example, if three attractive men, or women, are shown standing next to a black Land Rover parked in front of a pub, a possible caption might be? This is another quick and easy way to discover the attitudes and opinions about brands. Go ahead, it's your turn to provide a caption!

In a forced comparison exercise, individuals are asked to imagine relationships between two dissimilar objects, people, or places. For example, a beach in Florida and a new winter coat, or a hungry dog and a private jet plane. While it might sound ridiculous, the forced comparison does provide insights after repetition of multiple comparisons. Eventually, brand names in different products are introduced, such as Walt Disney and Outback Steak House, during the process of searching for the perception of images, reputations, and the attractiveness of the brands.

When people are asked to morph objects, they must be creative. Morphing requires changing as many characteristics as possible for a specific product or service. The purpose is to explore the possibilities of unusual, but acceptable, variations that might be used for new product concepts. For example, if people were asked to change the color, shape, texture, aroma, and taste of a breakfast cereal, then responses could include a new ready-to-eat cereal that is a blue triangle with a smooth surface, smells like vanilla, and tastes like walnuts. Interesting results!

In a product storytelling exercise, the customer is asked to imagine a situation involving a familiar company and then describe a sequence of events. For example, what would you expect to happen if you were going to open an account at Barclays Bank? Or, how are you treated as a customer every time you go inside the local branch of Barclays Bank? The way that the person answers provides a clear perspective of their expectations, uncertainty, or previous experiences.

In brand withdrawal, the purpose is to evoke the emotions involved with an imaginary situation where an individual must describe how they feel if they cannot purchase or use a favorite brand. The first possibility is based on the brand being discontinued, while a second is focused on temporary unavailability of the brand. Other options include modifying the characteristics of the product or service and then asking the person how this could change their attitude to that brand.

Summary

The purpose of marketing research is to minimize the risks associated with decision-making by providing detailed information about industries, products, communication, and consumers. There are two types of research: quantitative, which revolves around statistics and numbers, and qualitative, which focuses on information and insights.

The marketing research process begins with secondary research, which includes industry, product, communication, and consumer. This is immediately followed by primary research methods, which are initiatives taken by agencies and advertisers to investigate competitive brands and consumer behavior. After that information is reviewed and analyzed, the need for primary research includes focus groups, personal interviews, survey research, store visits, website analysis, social listening, role-playing, simulations, and projective techniques.

Next, product usage insights and perceived brand advantages are discovered, evaluated, and prioritized. And finally, the combined results of secondary and primary research are incorporated into IMC Plans.

Discussion Questions

1. Why is it important to complete secondary research before beginning primary research?
2. What is the difference between quantitative and qualitative types of research?
3. How can each of the four categories of marketing research provide valuable information for planning IMC activities?
4. What kind of consumer-oriented research can be obtained from the U.S. Census Bureau?
5. What is syndicated research? What are its advantages and disadvantages?
6. Are trade associations and business publications good sources of information?

7. Can online surveys be an effective method for gathering primary research data?
8. What are projective techniques? How can they provide input for brand communication?
9. Are focus groups on Zoom or a similar service better than using a physical room? Why?
10. How can social media listening provide important information about competitive brands?

Assignments

1. Explore a data base

   Log in to your university or college library. Try a simple search for a product, service, industry, or topic using ABI/INFORM Global. If you are not sure how to access this data base, request an appointment with a research librarian.
2. Design your own online survey

   Go to SurveyMonkey.com and set-up your own survey. It is free to use but limited to only 10 questions. So, be sure that each question focuses on the information you need.
3. Discover the U.S. Census Bureau

   Go to www.census.gov and learn what type of information is available. Look up the population of your favorite state or city. Find out how to use data visualization graphs.
4. Analyze competitive brand websites

   Select a product or service category. Identify three or more competitors. Visit each of these websites and analyze their brand content, visual appeal, and ease of navigation.
5. Complete your own focus group

   Now, it's time for you to control the Zoom meeting. Just prepare your list of questions, send invitations to the participants, and begin the discussion. Remember, it's quick and easy to establish your own free account, but the scheduled time is limited to 40 minutes.

Continuity Case Study

Since the digital marketing agency did not have a research director, Adriana had to find an outside supplier. Fortunately, the monthly meeting of the American Marketing Association featured a panel on using insight research for advertising. Adriana attended, and was introduced to a company that specialized in primary research. She invited them to make a presentation to both her and the agency as a collaborative project for insights before developing the IMC Plan.

She was intrigued by the number of choices that the research company offered. While some took several months, others could be completed in only a few weeks. After listening to everything, she decided on a series of in-depth personal interviews. However, it would take more than 10 weeks to finish and would cost a lot of money. The research company originally proposed a series of focus groups across the country, but Adriana did not believe that the information would be helpful.

Later that day, she called Martin to ask his advice. He abruptly responded that the company had plenty of information about its customers already, and that any more research was just a waste of time and money. It was a difficult situation for Adriana, since she had already agreed to work with the research company. What should she do? After thinking about it, she called Tony at the agency. He proposed that Adriana purchase a syndication study about consumer attitudes and beliefs about fast foods, eating habits, and brand preferences. Adriana had to make a decision.

1. What type of marketing research is most important for Athena?
2. Do you think Martin is correct about having enough research?
3. Are focus groups the best choice for insight research?
4. How will secondary research help Adriana to develop an IMC Plan?
5. What should Adriana do to better understand Athena's customers?

IMC Plan Development

Step One:
> Select the types of secondary research resources that you are going to begin investigating.

Step Two:
> Immediately launch an online search using key words and phrases to identify specific reports, documents, and publications.

Step Three:
> Analyze the information that has been collected and determine what questions need to be explored in greater detail. Continue searching for additional data from multiple resources.

Step Four:
> Select the primary research resources that can provide you with additional insights, perspectives, and understanding of the marketing environment.

Step Five:
> Prepare a summary of the information and insights from the marketing research that has been completed for the industry, product, communication, and consumer.

Chapter 4

IMC Objectives and Budgets

Funding Methods and Allocating Financial Resources

Learning Objectives

1. Recognize the funding sources for IMC
2. Understand the various methods to determine IMC budgets
3. Write specific objectives for each separate IMC pathway
4. Design a strategy to allocate IMC funds by category and purpose
5. Reflect on the different ways to anticipate a change in budgets

---

Introduction

Spending money in business is easy. Anyone can do it. But without a goal or purpose, the results can be disappointing or ineffective. That is why marketing managers always insist on a plan to structure their programs and activities throughout the year. And, brand communication is an important part of their annual plan. Depending on the product category, advertising and sales promotion will account for a sizable amount of the marketing budget. But, how much should be allocated for Integrated Marketing Communication (IMC)? That is the question that will be discussed in this chapter, along with the methods for estimating expenditures and the allocation of financial resources. We begin with the funding sequence itself, which eventually ends up with an amount of money allocated to IMC. Then, once that number is established, IMC objectives can be written and the funds allocated to each category with strategic decisions.

DOI: 10.4324/9780367443382-4

Funding Sequence for IMC

The effectiveness of IMC programs and activities depends on three important financial factors: the amount of money available to spend, the most productive allocations of funds, and the flexibility to modify previously approved IMC plans, strategic decisions, and budgets. Who determines the exact amount of money for IMC, and how is it connected to the Marketing Plan? And, what method is used to develop an appropriate budget? There are three possibilities. In the first approach, the marketing management is in complete control of the process and determines the amount of money that can be spent on IMC. In the second approach, the IMC department estimates the costs required to achieve the sales objectives established by the marketing department. And in the third approach, a collaborative arrangement is made between both departments for a budget.

Here is a big paradox. Where does the process begin? Marketing managers demand accurate cost information, along with specific advertising, promotion, public relations, and digital media recommendations, to finalize their IMC budgets. But, advertising managers need an initial estimate to develop a "proposed" IMC program. As soon as the amount of money changes, so will the recommendations. Ultimately, marketing managers make the final decision about how much money will be spent, but individual IMC managers, such as the person responsible for advertising, promotion, public relations, or digital media, will be making hundreds of detailed choices as to precisely where, when, and how these funds will be used. To summarize, the funding process begins with the marketing department asking the advertising department for a plan. The final result is the number that the marketing department approves, but the input from the advertising department is essential to arrive at a realistic and satisfactory budget. It all depends on the communication objectives that are proposed and the cost for implementation.

Estimating Costs

This is the reverse of a situation when marketing management, or the company owner, decides how much money will be approved for IMC. It begins with the complicated process of estimating the expenditures that are needed to achieve the proposed IMC objectives. This involves the combined cost of programs, events, and planned activities for advertising, sales promotion, public relations, brand visibility, digital platforms, and personal contact. In most situations, advertising is the largest component of the estimated costs, followed by sales promotion and brand visibility. Eventually, this number is calculated and shared with the marketing department or company owner. Then, the final budget is determined based on what is affordable, acceptable, or necessary to effectively compete in the marketplace.

Marketing Approvals

In most business circles, objectives are considered as achievable goals or actions. But, they are much more than that simple definition. Objectives need to have a specific number as part of the objective, otherwise it would be impossible to measure and determine whether the actions taken were successful. Along with that initial number, a time frame has to be identified. Does the goal have to be reached in one week, one month, or one year? It certainly would make a big difference. And then, there is the budget involved as a resource for building and implementing a plan. Other factors to be considered are any restrictions that might be placed on the programs and activities that are used to achieve the goal, and finally, a clear and meaningful description of the results category or the actual measurement criteria that are being used to evaluate performance.

The flow of funds now moves from the marketing areas into IMC planning and a new round of decision-making. The first major division of the IMC budget is the allocation of money by IMC component or category. This decision involves the percentage of funds for advertising, sales promotion, brand visibility, public relations, and digital media. The percentages remain the same even if the overall IMC budget is changed at a later date. This is done to retain the importance of each component based on the financial resources used for program implementation. In Figure 4.1, the direct flow of budgets from marketing to IMC is graphically shown, which is the IMC Funding Sequence, as well as the next two steps in the sequence, the advertising budget and the media allocation budget.

Since the total amount of advertising funds is from a percentage of the IMC budget, the next decision is which media categories will be used strategically. Then, the estimated amount of money needed or recommended will be determined or once again, allocated by a percentage. Later, the dollars will be split up and assigned to individual media selections based on analysis and strategies. Typically, these include individual magazines, television programs, radio stations, newspapers, and other media choices. The procedure and methodology used to make these decisions will be explained and discussed in other chapters.

In Figure 4.2 , the factors that influence Integrated Marketing Communication budgets are displayed. These include: the specific IMC category, stage of the product life cycle, target audiences, and media costs. The factors are complex because each one has an impact on the decision, and when used in combinations, there are a variety of results. Ultimately, the decision of the marketing manager, or the owner of a retail business, will be based on the amount of financial resources that can be allocated to the brand communication activities.

Figure 4.1 IMC Funding Sequence

Figure 4.2 Factors Influencing IMC Budgets

Budget Calculation Methods

Eventually, a decision must be made on how much money will be needed or allocated for an effective and highly competitive IMC Plan. In Figure 4.3, the twelve most frequently used methods to calculate or determine an IMC budget are summarized.

These methods include historic patterns, annual increase, industry ratios, percentage of sales, price per unit, market share, share of voice, IMC objectives, media models, competitive plus, break-even point, and new brand entry. Each of the methods has its own strengths and weaknesses. And, several of the methods are more appropriate for smaller businesses and entrepreneurs, while others can only be used by larger corporations and complex organizations.

Historic Patterns

This is the quickest, easiest, and simplest method. Just look up what was spent last year. Then, add a percentage increase, or decrease, and your work is done. But, how effective is this method? Is the IMC budget number the right amount to spend? Or, is the budget too low? Will increases in the cost of advertising put a strain on the budget? What if several new brochures have to be produced, or major changes have to be made to the company website? Any change means that more money will be needed. Unfortunately, the historic method is used most often, because most of the people involved do not know any other way. Even in larger companies, there might not be enough time to analyze past results, or there may be uncertainty about the effectiveness of past efforts.

The historic pattern is an excellent reference point. It does provide an initial level of IMC expenditures and offers an opportunity to review the adequacy of this amount. Perhaps, more funding is needed? Or, not. At least everyone knows the starting point for now.

In situations with no historic pattern, the maximum affordability method can be used. This method is very common with new business ventures, small

Historic Pattern	Annual Increase	Industry Ratios	Percent of Sales
Price Per Unit	Market Share	Competitive Plus	IMC Objectives
Share of Voice	Media Model	Break-Even Point	New Brand Entry

Figure 4.3 Budget Calculation Methods

businesses, or entrepreneurs. It is not dependent on sales, profit, market share, or any other factors. The money for an IMC budget is based on either what is available today or what is estimated for tomorrow. This involves predicting the future of sales for a product or service that has not even been launched. While this might make sense from the perspective of daily cash flow, it is not a viable long-term strategy.

Annual Increases

This method is pretty plain and simple. Just take last year's budget and increase, or decrease, the amount. It could be a percentage formula or just a number based on the estimated needs of the company. For example, here is how the historic pattern method is calculated. Assume that last year's IMC budget was $40,000, and 10% is added for increased expense and inflation; then, the new budget would be $44,000. Logical and easy, but if the top manager decides to cut the budget by 30%, or more, the IMC budget is reduced to $28,000. Not too difficult a strategy.

Industry Ratios

Products and services within the same industry or business category have a similar pattern of advertising expenditures and promotional budgets. This is a result of being competitive with other brands. One of the best ways to find out how much to be spending on IMC is the relationship of advertising to sales for individual product categories. This is expressed as a ratio, such as 7:1 or 3:1. The higher the ratio, the greater the amount of advertising dollars compared with total category sales. For example, the fast food industry has a ratio of 9:1. Based on the average of each of the major competitors, approximately $9 million in advertising is spent for every $81 million in sales.

Another way of looking at the advertising-to-sales ratio is the relative importance of advertising within the overall marketing environment. The ratios illustrate combined "averages" for a particular industry or product category. This is not a question of good or bad, or too high or too low, but the most acceptable standard for competing products. For example, the cosmetics industry has an exceptionally high advertising-to-sales ratio with heavy television advertising and expensive national magazine advertising. At the other end of the spectrum, most industrial products, such as construction equipment or office desks, have a very low ratio. An extensive list of advertising-to-sales ratios for both consumer and business-to-business (B2B) product categories and major industries can be found on the website for this textbook.

Should a brand spend above the industry ratio to generate greater visibility? Or, should it spend less to keep its selling price lower? That is a strategic marketing decision. Aggressive companies will spend above the average to increase market share, but how much above can only be estimated. There are no certainties with budget decision, only quality assumptions.

Percentage of Sales

This method of budgeting is directly connected to a company's internal numbers and financial marketing requirements. It is calculated using brand strategies and targeted level of gross sales and net profits. The percentage of sales is a very quick and easy procedure, especially if there are multiple brands involved. Just take the percentage and do the math. It is not a good move to select a percentage on an arbitrary basis, because there is no relationship to the market. Even if the industry ratios are used as a guide, and a calculated percentage is derived, there is no direct connection to the communication needs of the brand. What are the size and structure of the target audience? Where are they located? How effective are traditional, or digital, media in reaching them? The percentage of sales is a fast, easy, but highly ineffective budget strategy.

Fixed Amount per Unit

This budget method is very quick and easy. Just multiply the estimated number of units that are expected to be sold by an amount per unit. For example, a total of 135,000 lamps by $20 per unit yields a budget of $270,000. While the amount per unit is also an arbitrary decision, a number of factors need to be considered, such as previous history, competitive activity, affordability, and value of the product or service. Typically, the higher the retail selling price, the greater the fixed cost per unit. For example, automotive manufacturers use this method to generate advertising budgets for their dealers. If the decision is made to set aside $500 per vehicle for advertising, then a market with estimated sales of 3000 cars per year would have a $1.5 million budget. This method has a major flaw because aggregate funds based on the performance of a "sales forecast" can be frequently misleading or incorrect. Just like today's weather report!

The fixed amount per unit is usually calculated once a year to establish an annual IMC budget, but it is also frequently used to determine a mini-budget for short-term sales promotion programs. Why? In the annual budget calculation, the units probably have not yet come out of the factory or been completely assembled. So, when the demand for a brand declines, the units originally scheduled for production will immediately decrease, and consequently, the amount of money for advertising will also decrease. For sales promotion programs, the units have already been created and distributed, but the managers or company owners have an urgent need to quickly reduce inventory for financial reasons. And, as you will discover later in the textbook, there are many incentives and special price offers that can stimulate consumer purchases and increase profitability. Many companies prefer the fixed amount per unit method over the percentage of sales. The fixed amount means fewer calculations and less complexity. This is especially relevant for high-priced items, including luxury goods, or brands with an assortment of different sizes, price points, and options and a variety of models.

Market Share Strategies

A brand's strength against competitive products can be described in many ways, but one of the best is its share of market. This number can also be used to plan existing and future advertising budgets. Let's assume that a brand records a 23.7% share of dollar sales in a market segment. If this budget planning method is used, then the same brand could be expected to also account for about the same percentage of advertising expenditures. Rarely does this happen. The market share for dollar sales compared with advertising depends on many other variables. IMC budget strategies could include spending more than a brand's market share, or even less. As a result, this method does not work very well.

Share of Voice

This parallels the concept of market share, but in this instance, the share of voice is calculated based on the money that a single brand spends on advertising, or IMC, divided by the total amount of money spent by the entire category. This indicates the relative position of each brand compared with the competition. For example, if a brand has an 18.9% share of voice, that represents nearly one out of every five dollars spent on advertising within that product category. Or, that same brand might be listed as spending the smallest amount of money compared with two other brands that have at least a 30% share of voice. It is a relative measurement of the strength, or weakness, of a brand calculated on the money that it spends on advertising compared with its competitors.

IMC Objectives

There are many different media planning models used for developing IMC budgets. The majority of them involve a variation of the classical approach, also known as DAGMAR. This was the abbreviation for Defining Advertising Goals for Measuring Advertising Results. At the heart of this model was a series of stages, including awareness, attitude, purchase interest, and action. Other media planning models include the "purchase funnel," "pyramid," and "customer's journey," which follow a similar method of descending numbers. While the labels and stages might be different, the basic method of moving toward the top, or bottom, level is consistent.

The process begins by identifying the target market and estimating the total number of people who can be included in this description. Then, specific communication goals, or levels, are established for each stage of the model. These are always expressed as percentages of the total number of people in the target market. For example, if the awareness goal was 70%, then the total number of individuals who could remember the brand name after being exposed to the advertising campaign would be 70%. Here is how it works. If the total target market is estimated to be 20 million people with an awareness goal of 70%, then a successful IMC program would "potentially" make 14 million people aware of the brand name.

The debate among IMC managers is the amount of money and media strategies that are required to achieve success at each stage. For example, if the awareness of a brand is low, then most likely, the amount of money for advertising will have to be dramatically increased. But, what about the impact of a creative message? Or, a more efficient selection of media? The creative department will argue that low awareness can be eliminated with a persuasive brand message, and the media department will emphasize the need for more expenditures or a new combination of delivery methods. While more money does help to increase awareness, it is not a guarantee.

Share of Media Expenditures

This calculation is the percentage of total advertising expenditures within an industry or market segment that can be attributed to your brand. Essentially, share of voice represents your brand communication strength relative to competitors. For example, if the share of voice is 46%, then are dominating the market, but if you only have 8% share of voice, then you have little, if any influence over the total amount of money being spent on advertising.

Media Models

Programmatic media buying, powered by predictive algorithms, is a powerful and dynamic new way to simultaneously analyze, select, purchase, and place advertising. Although it was designed primarily for traditional television, it can be effectively used for digital video delivery platforms. This automatic system is based on complex mathematical algorithms that include media prices, availabilities, and audience sizes. These sophisticated computer software programs run 24 hours a day following the decision rules established by an advertising agency or advertiser. These models are used by larger corporations with gigantic budgets as well as agencies that service their companies. In the future, sophisticated and inexpensive versions will become available to anyone else who has the knowledge and experience to apply them correctly to local businesses.

Competitive Plus

This budget method approaches the market with a more aggressive strategy. It is designed to spend more than any other brand, or at least, an amount greater than the nearest competitor. For example, if the strongest competitor is spending 21.4%, then the budget strategy would be to spend anywhere from 25.0% to 35% or more to dominate the market with advertising messages. This has to be considered a short-term strategy because of the amount of money involved. It is used to stimulate a spike in sales, which also leads to an increase in market share. The strategy also involves forcing a competitor to respond by matching the level of advertising, which can lower the profitability of the other brand. As you might assume, a competitive plus strategy should only be used by a very financially strong company with a high-quality brand.

Break-Even Points

Marketing managers in manufacturing and packaged goods industries use a break-even analysis to arrive at the number of units of a product that must be sold to make certain that the total revenues match the total costs. When that occurs, anything sold beyond that point indicates revenue in a break-even analysis graph. Where advertising comes into this equation is in the role of an important cost variable, which can be modified to increase or decrease on a per unit basis. This means that each product sold contains an amount allocated to advertising or IMC. In reality, the consumers are paying for advertising that will be used to motivate them to buy the product!

New Brand Entries

How do you plan a budget or IMC program before a new brand is introduced into the marketplace? The challenge is very different for a new brand compared with an existing brand that is already using a proven method for its budget generation. This requires going through the list and selecting the best alternative. The process should begin by examining the IMC objectives based on several hypothetical budget levels and then refer to a few marketing-oriented approaches, such as industry ratios for a base combined with an application of the results of a break-even method. Many corporations go beyond this approach to include a payback model to estimate the unit sales required to recover the total amount of funds invested in advertising.

Predictive Algorithms

The use of artificial intelligence is a powerful method to anticipate consumer behavior. It utilizes information from previous activities, such as online search for products and services, and then calculates the probability of a repetitive pattern. This includes the frequency of action, time of behavior, or any other characteristic of consumer behavior. For example, have you ever noticed how you get a series of advertising posts or text notices on a website that appear almost immediately after you complete an online search for a particular brand? That is just one example of artificial intelligence being used to predict consumer behavior by using complex algorithms.

Writing IMC Objectives

In most business circles, objectives are considered to be achievable goals or actions. But, they are much more than that simple definition. Objectives need to have a specific number as part of the objective; otherwise, it would be impossible to measure and determine whether the actions taken were successful. Along with that initial number, a time frame has to be identified. Does the goal have to be reached in one week, one month, or one year? It certainly would make a big difference. And then, there is the budget involved as a resource for building and implementing a plan. Other factors to be considered are any restrictions that might be placed on the programs and activities that are used to achieve the goal. And finally, a clear and meaningful description of what is expected as measurable results.

Requirements for Objectives

The five requirements for writing an effective IMC objective are shown in Figure 4.4. These requirements include the measurement criteria, a specific number associated with the criteria, a pre-determined time frame, marketing restrictions, and the most important, an approved or estimated funding budget. The criteria for measuring an objective change with each of the basic IMC strategies. For example, the objective for advertising is measures of brand name awareness and purchase interest, while the sales promotion objective has several parts, such as the number of coupons redeemed, sweepstake entry forms submitted online, or even retail store traffic. The important fact to remember is that every IMC strategy has a different set of objectives. There is no single IMC objective for a brand, but different ones for advertising, sales promotion, brand publicity, public relations, digital media, and personal contact.

There are several variations of the criteria required for writing IMC objectives. Many companies adopted the SMART approach, which is easy to remember and effective in its intent. The five letters of this acronym refer to the following criteria: smart, specific, measurable, achievable, relevant, and timely. While this can be a very effective approach, it must be applied separately to each of the six IMC pathways because there are different criteria for measurement and communication effectiveness.

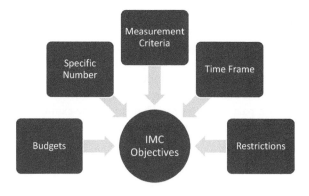

Figure 4.4 Writing IMC Objectives

Budget Allocation Strategies

The development of an IMC budget never ends. Even after the numbers are finalized, changes occur. These changes can be in the money allocated to each IMC category, geographic areas, timing, or other areas. While most of the time, the shifts are internal, there are other situations where the total amount of money is suddenly and unexpectedly reduced. In rare situations, extra funding is provided for expanded IMC activities, especially when new ideas or programs are submitted during the middle of the year. And if approved, and not funded with additional money, the original budget has to be used to implement IMC activities that were never anticipated.

Any proposed or approved IMC budget must be strategically divided among each of the major categories to ensure that the brand's communication objectives are achieved. These categories are listed in Figure 4.5 and include IMC pathways, time periods, targeted audiences, and geographic potential. The assumption is that the total amount of money allocated represents the relative importance of a category. However, since advertising is the most expensive category, it represents a disproportionate share of the total budget for most national brands. While this is less of a problem for smaller companies or local brands, advertising frequently accounts for greater expenditures than all the other categories combined.

Allocation by IMC Category

There are many different approaches to this process of dividing funds by IMC category. Here are three factors to consider. First, the total number of people who need to be reached for the brand to be successful from a marketing perspective. Second, the importance of generating sales on a regular basis or during short time frames. And third, the desire to maintain or increase a relationship with existing customers. The first approach emphasizes a traditional advertising strategy, while the second points to a greater number of sales promotion programs. The

Figure 4.5 IMC Allocation Strategies

third approach is a mixture of public relations and digital media, especially social media interactions.

Compared with the other IMC categories, public relations are not very expensive, especially when most of the work and activities are completed internally. Since larger companies have more complex needs and a greater variety of public relations audiences, a professional public relations firm is usually hired. The amount of money allocated for digital media is often misleading. Low in cost. High in value. Not a lot of funds are needed for major impact, especially compared with the prices for advertising in any media. The importance of digital activities, such as websites, social media, and mobile apps, is much greater than their expenses or percentage of an IMC budget.

After the initial allocation for advertising is finalized, a series of budget decisions must be made for the five sub-categories of media: television, radio, newspapers, magazines, and outdoor media. The costs involved with each of these media will be reviewed. Until then, the most important concept to understand is that the number of people reached by traditional media advertising is proportional to the price of the medium. This means that there is a direct or linear relationship between people and media cost. For example, a magazine with 200,000 readers has an advertising cost of $500, while one with a circulation of 600,000 would cost $1500.

So, how do you decide how much to spend in each medium? First, take a close look at the product or service being advertised. Does it benefit from a visual demonstration, detailed explanation, or experiential enjoyment of the brand? Do you need more time or space to communicate the story of the brand promise or user benefit? How important is the visual appearance of the product or service? Second, what is the typical cost of this media for either local or national advertising? Third, how many weeks or months will be involved? Fourth, what is the strength of your competitors, and what amount of advertising are they using now? Fifth, how popular is your brand? Does the brand need more recognition and awareness, or do you have to concentrate on forming a new and more targeted image?

Allocations by Product Life Cycle

IMC budgets for a brand or company can dramatically change over time. This is based on their position in the six stages product life cycle: introduction, growth, maturity, decline, extension, and elimination. This progression can occur at different speeds. Each stage also requires a different funding level based on the IMC programs and activities that have been planned.

The introduction stage is the most difficult budget category to estimate. How much is really needed to launch a new product? Too little, and the product fails. Too much, well, that does not happen very often, especially when media prices are so high. The challenge is to generate enough sales, or reorders from retailers, or trial usage from customers, that the initial financial forecast is reasonably achieved. Caution is helpful, but being bold and daring is better.

The growth stage is the most expensive part of a brand's life cycle because sales are soaring and expansion is everywhere. Since the popularity of the brand has been established, it is the best time to capture sales away from competitive products as well as discover new users for the category. Depending on the method of budgeting selected, there is plenty of money for national advertising and related IMC programs.

At the maturity stage, the market and the brand have slowed down. Sales are still high but not increasing at the same rate per month. There are fewer competitors, since the weaker ones were eliminated during the growth phase. It becomes harder to find new buyers, and the customer acquisition cost begins to climb. The amount of advertising should be slowly, but carefully, decreased and shifted to promotional programs.

When entering the decline stage, advertising funds should be reduced to an absolute minimum level. Promotion programs, if any, would be used to get a few extra sales from extremely loyal buyers or those individuals who are willing to purchase products when prices are substantially reduced. Most likely, the decreasing amount of communication between the brand and remaining customers would be handled through websites, blogs, emails, or text notifications.

The extension stage is optional as a marketing communication strategy. If management decides to make one last and final marketing push to revitalize and refresh the brand, then a quick increase in advertising funding will be arranged. It is a short burst of activity, perhaps only a few months in length. Sometimes, a successful response can lead to continuing the IMC programs, but usually, this is only a temporary action to delay the eventual termination of the brand.

During the elimination stage, just watch and wait. Public relations might be the only important aspect of the brand's disappearing IMC activities. Digital activities will remain due to their low cost of operation and ability to deliver communication efficiently to the shrinking target market.

Allocation by Time Periods

IMC funds can be organized according to four different periods of time: annual, quarterly, monthly, and weekly. And for smaller companies, and sales-driven retail organizations, the budget period might be as short as weeks. The majority of large national companies use quarterly periods for planning promotional programs, but the annual IMC budget remains constant.

Quarterly budgets are planned well in advance and built around specific themes or activities. Often, the promotions are linked to the seasons, such as the Winter Sales Event, Spring Festival of Savings, Summer Fun Discounts, or Fall Spectacular Sale. Or, they could be connected with popular sporting events, like the Super Bowl, NCAA Basketball Tournament, Olympics, or World Cup Soccer Championships. And finally, quarterly promotions can be organized around a brand, or a product line, incorporating a life style situation, activity, or experience into the creative message. Each promotion is supported by a smaller, but essential, advertising budget to announce the promotion program to targeted customers or potential buyers. These quarterly promotions also provide an opportunity to create excitement and enthusiasm in a sales force as well as to encourage retailers to accept larger shipments of products to earn incentives. In addition, seasonal sales variations, such as holidays, consumer usage patterns, or industry trends, can be easily incorporated into the IMC planning process by allocating a different amount of money for each month. This provides a way to plan advertising based on when it is needed most or where it will yield the best results. Monthly budgets can also be used as a method of budget control by limiting the total amount of IMC expense within each month.

Allocation by Geographic Potential

The total sales potential for any branded product or service will vary based on the profile of the target audience and the composition of a geographic region. The higher the concentration of a preferred audience profile, the greater the sales potential. For example, the State of Florida has the highest concentration of older or retired people compared with most other states, while at the same time, Florida is among the top states for citizens with Hispanic ethnic background, along with Texas, California, and New York. This is all part of developing an effective media strategy.

Demographic factors are used to allocate funds for IMC programs, especially for advertising, which is very much connected to the prices for legacy media. If the sales potential for a geographic region is very high, then a larger amount of money will be allocated for advertising because a greater return on investment is expected.

Flexible Budget Adjustments

So, smart marketing managers always reserve extra money in a special IMC budget category called "contingency funds." These are financial resources that have not yet been committed to any IMC category, activity, or program. There are different views on how much money to place in a brand's IMC contingency account, but conservatively, 10% of the total is a safe number. While it is not required, incorporating a contingency fund into an annual IMC plan can eliminate many problems during the year. And, provide money for special new opportunities.

What does a flexible budget adjustment cover? As shown in Figure 4.6, budget adjustments can include unpredictable situations and unavoidable circumstances, such as competitive activity, new brand introductions, media cost increases, unexpected opportunities, and fiscal year-end budget reductions.

Figure 4.6 Flexible Budget Adjustments

Competitive Activity

They act. You respond. If a competitive brand, store, or sales organization begins a new creative campaign that is unexpected, disruptive, and might immediately impact sales and profits, then you must respond quickly and correctly. This probably means a change in your media selection, message delivery pattern, or a requirement for more money. The options are to divert a portion of funds already committed, or more strategically, use some of the money that has been allocated to your IMC contingency account. While you are not sure what is coming next, being prepared is a good way to avoid unwanted IMC expenses.

New Brand Introductions

The most challenging part of IMC budget planning is determining exactly how much money to commit to launch a new brand. If the budget is too low, the brand might not get enough exposure or recognition and hence, fail. It the IMC budget is too high, the brand's expenditures could make it unprofitable, also causing it to fail. What is the correct amount? It is a combination of a "threshold" level of sales needed to achieve the break-even point for profitability along with the difficulty of penetrating a market segment that is already highly competitive and exhibits a high level of brand loyalty.

Media Cost Increases

Price hikes happen! It can occur at any time, but being prepared helps. Even after you have negotiated for the lowest rates with one medium, or signed a contract, another media company announces a price increase, effective immediately. Or, you get a favorable quote for printing a new brochure, but the following month, prices go up by 10%. It is inevitably going to happen several times this year, so you always need to be prepared. A good time to go back to the contingency fund for a few extra dollars.

Unexpected Opportunities

IMC programs are planned well in advance, but there is always something new coming over the horizon. These are events or media buys that have not been announced until after the IMC budget has been approved. Unless funds are waiting in a contingency fund, there has to be a change or reduction in the original plan to accommodate the addition of a new element. Typically, these are opportunities in traditional media, which have a high price tag.

Fiscal Year-End Reductions

The quickest way to increase profits is to immediately decrease expenses.

Financial managers recognize that one of the fastest and easiest ways to increase profits before ending a fiscal year is to reduce expenditure. The elimination of IMC expenses goes directly to the bottom line, a plus for financial statements but disaster for an IMC plan. Advertising and media activities are natural targets for these short-term cuts compared with personnel and materials. But, there is a caution. Many commitments involve discounts based on the amount purchase or the frequency of placement. So, cutting these expenses can be unwanted and highly disruptive to future plans and programs with suppliers.

Summary

IMC budgets are derived from marketing funds. Eight methods can be used to calculate the amount of money needed to implement an annual IMC Plan. These budgeting methods include historic patterns, maximum affordability, industry ratios, percentage of sales, fixed amount per unit, competitive market shares, media planning models, and finally, predictive algorithms. The allocation of funds begins with a distribution among IMC categories. The amount of IMC money allocated to advertising, promotion, public relations, and digital activities is based on the resources, situations, and marketing needs of individuals, brands, causes, companies, and organizations. Estimated expenditures are based on the exact stage in a product's life cycle, affordability of media, or management strategy. Additional considerations are the IMC objectives as well as the size, cost, and complexity programs, including strategies for geographic segmentation, monthly scheduling, cash flow, and competitive brand activities.

After making the budget allocations, traditional advertising is further divided according to the media category, frequency of brand message delivery, and amount of funds needed to effectively implement a planned media purchase. Digital media follow another pattern, which depends on the online platform, communication strategies, and size of the target audience to be reached.

Discussion Questions

1. What is the importance and value of having IMC objectives?
2. Which criteria for writing an IMC objective are the most difficult to estimate?
3. Can the same IMC objective be used for each of the IMC pathways?
4. When is a break-even analysis used for developing an IMC budget?
5. What are the advantages and disadvantages of using an advertising-to-sales ratio?
6. Is the market share method of generating an IMC budget a proactive strategy?
7. What information is used to plan allocation by different time periods?
8. Can geographic allocations increase the effectiveness of advertising budgets?
9. How does competitive brand activity influence budget planning and resource allocations?
10. What percentage of an IMC budget should be allocated to a contingency fund?

Chapter Assignments

1. Discover brand expenditures
   Let Google do its magic. Maybe you'll be lucky. Try searching industry category or brand name.
2. Prepare a sales forecast
   It's easier than you think. Take the total number of potential buyers and project a market share.
3. Use the AIDA model
   Complete a hypothetical situation using percentages for each of the four stages in the model.
   Explain how this could be achieved and justify why you selected those specific numbers.
4. Calculate a sales funnel
   Provide an example for a health club marketing agency using a ToFu, MiFu, and BoFu approach.
5. Write an IMC objective
   Not just one objective, but six objectives. And, each pathway has separate performance criteria.

Continuity Case Study

The Vice-President of Marketing had just reviewed the initial budget proposal submitted by Adriana but was not pleased. He felt it was much too low and did not include enough money for quarterly promotions. When asked why there was no television or radio advertising in the plan, Adriana responded that digital media were less expensive and more focused. That answer was not enough to satisfy Martin. He asked her to go back to the agency and revise the entire plan.

At the next meeting, Adriana asked Tony Perez, the account executive at the agency, to help with the solution. After explaining the "marketing funnel" and its relationship to IMC, he recommended another budget. Tony used the AIDA model, which was compatible with the company's objectives. The problem was that Martin expected advertising to immediately increase sales. In his view, that was the only reasonable objective for marketing. While Adriana really liked Tony's approach, she remembered Martin's objections but was not sure how to solve the problem. Adriana had found information about restaurant advertising expenditures. Perhaps using the industry advertising-to-sales ratios would convince Martin.

1. What budget generation method should Adriana use?
2. Why did Tony recommend using communication objectives?
3. Is Martin correct about the importance of sales objectives?
4. Should Adriana consider increasing the budget and include television?
5. How would you allocate the funds among the six IMC categories?

IMC Plan Development

Step One:

> Write your IMC objectives for the pathways selected.

Step Two:

> Determine the best method for generating an IMC budget.

Step Three:

> Estimate the total amount of money needed to achieve the IMC objectives.

Step Four:

> Complete your allocations by pathway, time period, and geographic area.

Step Five:

> Develop a strategy and recommended budget for changes and modifications.

Chapter 5

Segmentation Strategies

Prioritizing Target Groups for Effective Brand Communication

Learning Objectives

1. To understand the purpose and value of segmentation
2. To describe and select different segmentation categories
3. To prioritize primary and secondary target audiences
4. To build and apply consumer demographic profiles
5. To utilize geographic, psychographic, and behavior segmentation

---

Introduction

The cost of advertising is based on the number of people who are watching, listening, reading, or exposed to brand messages within a medium. The more people involved, the higher the cost of an advertisement. But, not everyone is a potential buyer. And, even fewer people are interested. So, advertisers need to identify only those people who are most likely to buy their brand within a particular product or service category. As a result, brand messages are directed toward only the most responsive people, which reduces the size of the audience along with advertising costs. How do advertisers do this? With segmentation, the general audience is divided into smaller and more specific groupings. This also enables advertisers to deliver a more relevant and highly targeted brand message to individuals who can benefit most from buying a specific product or service.

This chapter describes four primary Integrated Marketing Communications (IMC) consumer segmentation categories. These categories include demographic,

DOI: 10.4324/9780367443382-5

psychographic, geographic, and purchase/usage segmentation. Within each category, there are even more ways to identify and separate consumers based on their differences, not their similarities. The purpose is to provide information to advertisers and agencies for creative planning and the selection of the most appropriate and efficient media for delivering brand messages within multiple pathways of IMC.

Importance of Segmentation

Marketing segmentation is absolutely essential because it provides a better perspective of the type of people who are most likely to be interested in purchasing specific products or services. However, there are six external factors that influence the segmentation process. These factors include: the size of the population, along with advertising media prices, relevance of creative content, financial affordability of products and services, positioning of competitive brand, and the total advertising expenditures in the market. Let's explore several of these factors that influence segmentation and IMC planning and implementation.

Size of the Population

The larger the marketing area, the greater the number of potential buyers. The marketing area can be defined in many ways, such as a country, region, state, city, or local community. This data about the targeted geographic area will be used to analyze the sales and profit potential for a company that is going to be using Integrated Marketing Communications to promote its brand.

Advertising Media Prices

There is one advertising rule that is always the same: the price of any media, digital or legacy, is directly proportional to the number of people who will be reached by the advertising message.

The prices for all traditional forms of media, such as television, radio, magazines, newspapers, and even digital media, are based on the total number of people reached by those media. This means that advertising prices are proportional to the size of the audience. The relationship between media prices and number of people is a linear or straight line relationship. This means it has a 1:1 ratio. If the number of people exposed to an advertisement is doubled, then the media cost is doubled. Or, if the media cost is reduced by 50%, then the audience size is also decreased by 50%. For example, if a television commercial on a television station is seen by 500,000 people at a price of $5,000, then a commercial on another television station that reaches only 250,000 people would cost about $2,500.

Segmentation is a way of estimating and controlling the size and composition of a media audience. By limiting the number of people, advertising costs are reduced, but those individuals being selected must have "high potential" user characteristics and buyer profiles. This information should have already been identified through both quantitative and qualitative marketing research studies and reports.

Relevance of Creative Content

Is a marketing strategy designed to appeal to 25-year-old women the same as for 60-year-olds? Definitely not. Sure, there might be some similarities, but the life styles and psychological motivations are different, along with associated brand benefits. For example, sports shoes for running, kick-boxing, or yoga are more interesting to younger buyers, who are looking for performance and style, while older buyers would be more concerned about comfort and safety.

People like to identify with others who look, act, or behave as they do. That is why the graphic images, photos, and activities in advertising must be selected carefully. And the words, too, make a big difference. Slang terms, jargon, and contemporary styles of speaking and communicating need to reflect the tastes and life styles of those who are being exposed to advertising messages. Thus, it is essential for advertisers to use the most relevant combination of images and words for those individuals who are most likely to purchase their brand.

Financial Affordability of Products and Services

This is a financial paradox. Anyone can afford most products and services, but for many people, it is a severe financial sacrifice. Purchasing power is determined by individual or household income. And even with credit cards, payment plans, and loans, there is a limit to how much can be spent. So, when the price of a brand exceeds its ability, that consumer becomes an unlikely shopper or buyer. Advertisers must estimate these financial barriers and determine the "threshold" income levels required for the brand's preferred audience profile. Although people might express a strong interest or admiration for a brand, if they cannot easily afford the product or service, they should not be included in a targeted group.

Positioning of Competitive Brands

The user benefits, product features, and perceived images of a brand represent yet another business reality. Incorporating these segmentation aspects into a perceptual map with competitive products indicates exactly where each brand fits in the consumer's mind. Product positioning is a direct application of research findings and provides an initial framework for planning IMC segmentation strategies.

Maximizing Return on Investment (ROI)

Which comes first, the sales objective or the marketing budget? The chicken wins in this case. The number of units sold, dollar volume, and market share are the driving forces that dictate the financial investment that a company or organization is willing to make in its marketing budget. A sizable budget allows heavier advertising schedules, frequent promotions, and plenty of digital media activity. But, an under-funded budget leads to limited IMC programs that cannot adequately support aggressive sales objectives or corporate demands for profit. Success with segmentation strategies is also connected to the number of people in each of the profile characteristics. For example, if a company was evaluating the age ranges of 18 to 45, 18 to 34, and 34 to 45, then a major consideration would be the total number of people in each category. And if other criteria were included, such as selecting females only, the size of the audience would be cut nearly in half.

Consumer Segmentation Categories

What is a segmentation category? It is defined as the identification, selection, and aggregation of individual consumers based on their differences in physical characteristics, location of residence, method of thinking and behavior, and usage of products in a specific market segment. As shown in Figure 5.1, there are four major segmentation categories that can be used to identify and separate consumers based on their individual differences: demographic, geographic, psychographic, and behavior. The process of consumer segmentation is an essential prerequisite for selecting specific target audiences to be used for the creation and delivery of brand messages. The combination of segmentation categories and individual elements provides the foundation for the initial development of the IMC Plan.

Let's take a closer look at the multiple layers within the segmentation structure, including sub-divisions. Later, we will learn more about their role in planning IMC programs and activities.

Demographic Segmentation

The purpose of demographic market segmentation is to identify and describe the differences between people using their physical, social, and cultural characteristics. The 10 most frequently used sub-categories of demographic segmentation include age, gender, income, marital status, family composition, ethnicity, race, religion, sexual identity, type of residence, and physical attributes. The most essential demographic segmentation characteristics are age, gender, and income.

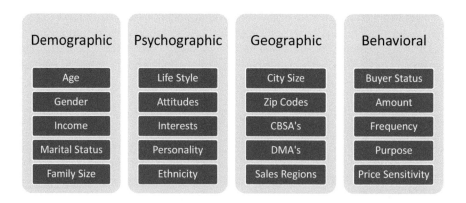

Figure 5.1 Consumer Segmentation Categories

Why these three? First, age is an extremely good predictor of life style activities, personal beliefs, and social behavior. No other variable tells us so much or so quickly. It is almost always included on survey research questionnaires and is the most frequently used classification category for secondary research reports. Second, gender immediately adds another powerful dimension to demographic segmentation. As with age, the life style activities, personal beliefs, and social behavior of women, compared with men, has been found to dramatically influence their purchase patterns for products and services. And third, the income factor is a consistent predictor of an individual's, or family's, ability and willingness to spend money on brand name products, especially as the price level increases. The ability to purchase is more important than the desire, especially with higher-price premium items.

Age But, how does age get involved in planning IMC programs? It is all about dividing age into a number of different categories. There are several ways, but the whole idea is to make the divisions as small as possible, but realistic, for intelligent consumer analysis. If the age groupings are too broad, then no discernible patterns will emerge. For example, separating female buyers into only three age categories is one possibility. The first group might be women between the ages of 18 and 34, while the second group is from 35 to 49, and the final group aged 50 years or more. This is very helpful, because the desired brands and purchasing behavior should be significantly different. The assumption is that women aged 18 to 34 will act differently than those in the other age groups.

This type of information is extremely useful for creating advertising messages but less helpful for media planning. Here is the problem. While the three categories separate the women, there is no indication about the relative distribution of individuals within each age category. For example, what if more than 70% of the women in the 18 to 34 category were over 30 years of age? Are they more similar to the next group, or not? That is why age groups are divided into even smaller categories for media planning. In the previous example, the preferred analysis would include five divisions: 18 to 29, 30 to 39, 40 to 49, 50 to 60, and 60 plus. Consider the importance of these numbers when comparing a brand profile with a media profile. The better the match, the more efficient the media purchase. And the more effective the creative message, the more favorable the results for a brand.

Gender This segmentation category is pretty equally split into two nearly equal halves. However, when paired with age and income, the profiles of males and females will be remarkably different. Women, as well as men, tend to spend their money in a variety of ways that support the need for this type of segmentation. The creative messages and media selected should always appeal to one group more than another. While there are situations where both are similar, whenever possible, it's better to have separate IMC programs directed toward each target audience.

Income The purpose of segmenting by income is primary connected to the affordability factor of a product or service. It does not need to have rigid criteria. But, the amount of disposable or available income will influence a brand's sales forecast. There are two types of income to be considered: individual and household. This distinction becomes important when either a husband and wife are working, or other members of the family are contributing their share of living expenses. It is also possible to target either the man or the woman, or another relative who is in the same residence, as a separate consumer. Then, the personal income is directly connected with the individual who is actually earning the money. When is income used for segmentation strategies? Here are a few examples. Buying a new automobile for family transportation would require marketers to examine their household income, while purchasing a movie theatre ticket probably would not be very important.

Marital Status   Of course, the implications of this category are obvious. Single versus married. But, also, divorced and widowed. As the population ages and cultural beliefs change, the number of people in each of these four sub-groups increases and decreases. Also, the life style of first time married people, compared with those who have been married multiple times, is unquestionably different. The ages of those involved, their children, and other factors make this segmentation category increasingly complex, but still important.

Family Size   A young married woman with three children under the age of 5 has problems that are no longer experienced by another married female with children already over the age of 14. This means that family composition is a mixture of the number of children, their ages, and their gender. As you can imagine, a completely different set of consumer needs and wants exists, depending on which sub-groups are targeted for marketing brands. Are there too many divisions for this category? Probably, but the answer is a function of the brand's positioning and user benefits.

Ethnic Heritage   This segmentation category is a reflection of cultural heritage and ancestral background. Whether first-, second-, or third-generation descendants, there are ethnic predispositions that can influence a consumer's decision-making process. They can be real or imagined, perceived or imitated, but there is always a certain amount of stereotyping about attitudes and behavior. Is ethnic association necessary? Not unless the brand is clearly positioned to appeal to a particular cultural group. For example, the Hispanic population in the United States is extremely large and growing, but marketing to this important segment requires deep cultural and linguistic understanding. Spanish is their common language, but the similarity ends quickly when the country of origin is considered or the ages of the people involved.

Race   No doubt, this segmentation category can be viewed as controversial, but it is only a method to connect brands and people based on what is important to them. The most important goal for any IMC program or activity is to deliver the right message to the right audience at the right time and in the right place. So, if Asians, African-Americans, or any other group want to see people who look or talk just like them in advertising media, then that's perfect. It is all part of IMC planning.

Religion   In the United States, a person's religion is a pretty minor consideration compared with previous years and circumstances. While segmentation strategies are possible for groups who strongly identify themselves as Christian, Jewish,

Muslim, Mormon, or even agnostic, the homogeneity of the American culture makes this unnecessary. There are plenty of exceptions, such as Kosher foods or religious abstinence from coffee, alcohol, or cigarettes, but these will be discussed in the chapter on culture.

Sexual Identification   LGBT is a sizable and valuable market. As legal barriers and personal prejudices are reduced, marketing and advertising campaigns targeting these consumers will dramatically increase. Although LGBT communication and promotional programs have existed for many years, the messages have not always been included in mass media. There are plenty of specialized options to reach this rapidly expanding and lucrative market with a choice of very efficient and effective media options.

Choice of Residence   House or apartment? Where you live makes a difference to advertisers and agencies. The size, location, and age of your residence are all factors important to brands that specialize in housing products and services. This includes interior items, such as appliances, lighting, flooring, and furniture, as well as the exterior. And, the details of your housing location are also connected to the purchase of automobiles, parking, gasoline, public transit, and insurance. While sub-categories are instrumental in planning, the most important question remains: house or apartment?

Physical Attributes   How do you segment a market based on a person's physical attributes? Take any one, and consider what it means. For example, height, weight, eye color, fist size, body type, skin texture, hair length, or dress size. The clothing industry has plenty of opportunities to specialize in products based on variations in physical attributes. Here is a simple demonstration. Three women could all wear a size 8, but for jeans, it would be difficult if one was 5′2″, another 5′7″, and the last 5′10″. The demographic segmentation category is usually reserved for brands that have a product feature, benefit, or ingredient that depends on physical attributes. It is not a common marketing strategy, but there are a few aspects that subtly flow into the photos and graphic images contained in advertising, promotion, and digital media.

Health Status   While this might be dependent on the age of a person, there are definite ways to assess, evaluate, and even predict their health status. This can be attributed to life style habits, such as drinking coffee, heavy consumption of alcohol, recreational drugs, and smoking. It can also be related to the amount of daily exercise, the type of activities, and choice of foods. For example, the trend toward healthy eating can impact not only on the physical attributes of a person but also on their attitude and approach to life. Ultimately, preventive health is a growing concern, but it requires establishing a relationship with doctors prior to experiencing any problems. Health status can be described in many ways, including categories from poor to below average to above average to excellent.

Geographic Segmentation

There are five categories for geographic segmentation: traditional locations, zip codes, Core Based Statistical Areas (CBSAs), Designated Market Areas (DMAs), and corporate sales regions. Most of the traditional categories are created by different levels of government, such as states, counties, cities, and villages. A similar pattern exists in other nations around the world, but the names and methods are based on cultural perspectives. Large corporations, advertisers, and even media organizations have been responsible for the addition of several new categories of geographic segmentation, specifically DMAs and sales regions.

Traditional Definitions   The list for traditional locations is based on government definitions, including states, counties, cities, and local communities. This can be aggregated into regions, such as the Northwest, Western, Southeastern, Midwest, Mountain, New England, or any other groupings with a specific description. Other variations can include time zones or clusters with a large metropolitan area, such as districts, neighborhoods, suburbs, or satellite cities.

When marketing outside the United States, the focus shifts toward individual countries or large geographic political organizations, such as the European Union, and broad regions, such as Asia/Pacific or the Middle East. These areas have similar divisions and sub-categories but use different names and operate under separate laws and relationships.

Zip Codes   This has been a favorite form of geographic segmentation since it was introduced way back in 1963. Do you know what ZIP means? Originally, it was a shortened version of Zone Improvement Plan, which consisted of more than 42,000 codes. Now, that is a winning answer for a trivia game! The primary beneficiaries from the zip code structure were companies that designed and printed promotional pieces. In 1983, the addition of an extra four digits was introduced. Since then, the federal government has compiled and published census information based on zip code. These reports and documents contain enormous amounts of information about people living within each zip code, including selective demographic data.

Core Based Statistical Areas (CBSAs)   The U.S. Office of Management and Budget created a series of population clusters that are used for collecting and reporting demographic information. There are three variations based on the density of the population and the proximity of neighboring locations. A total of 955 CBSAs are part of this structure, which is composed of 374 centralized urban areas and 581 micro areas with smaller cities, towns, and villages. These population clusters provide a simple, comprehensive, and unified method for organizing geographic segmentation.

Designated Market Areas (DMAs)   The global research company A.C. Nielsen introduced the concept of DMAs as a media planning tool for television. Those famous program "ratings," which entertainment reporters frequently talk about, are based on the total number of people in a geographic area. The areas are defined by the counties that are receiving a television signal from a local station. For example, the Orlando DMA includes the people living in nine different counties. Every county in the United States is assigned to one of 210 DMAs. This is arranged by the Nielsen company according to a station's signal strength and other factors, such as viewer preferences and historic patterns.

The strategic value of a DMA as a segmentation strategy is that demographic information has already been aggregated by county. Why is this so important? First, the total number of people reached by television coverage in that DMA is confirmed. Second, the cumulative delivery of advertising messages from other media can be added to the television coverage. How this works is explained in a later chapter. And third, the 210 DMAs can be ranked according to multiple demographic characteristics, such as age, gender, or ethnicity. For example, DMAs in California, Arizona, and Texas have larger Hispanic populations, while Florida has the highest percentage of retired adults who are 65 years of age.

Media companies use DMA to demonstrate their effectiveness in reaching target audiences. The only problem is that each television or radio station has different strengths and weaknesses. And so, the data presented to advertisers and their agencies is often biased or modified to emphasize favorable coverage of specific age ranges and other information about income levels and purchasing power.

Company Sales Regions Geographic segmentation can even include companies establishing their own boundaries. For example, the entire country can be divided into areas based on individual sales regions, districts, or territories. Of course, this only applies when companies use a geographic structure based on marketing and not traditional maps. The advantage is a more accurate and precise measure of performance, but the disadvantage is that these structures are incompatible with competitive analysis.

Psychographic Segmentation

While demographics describes the physical and personal characteristics of individuals, psychographics explores the mental or cognitive aspects. This method of segmenting consumers is a collection of several sociological, psychological, and anthropological attributes: personality, life style, values, attitudes, behavior, and culture. Each attribute provides another perspective on the potential target audience and customers. The entire purpose of psychographic segmentation is to help advertisers better understand how the customers think about their lives and what they really believe about themselves. It is not what an advertiser wants but what a customer needs.

Personality Using personality as a method of psychographic segmentation is a surprisingly effective way to humanize numbers and descriptions. The essence of an individual's personality can actually be compressed into a single word or phrase. Just think of your best friend and then, describe either him or her using only one adjective. It's that simple. For example, your response words might be: impulsive, cautious, extravagant, thoughtful, happy, caring, curious, organized, or serious. When you complete a psychographic profile or pattern for a target audience, several descriptive words must be included. Why? Because each word projects an image of a different person and their pattern of behavior. And when a brand is trying to communicate, this information is essential.

Think of it this way. Each descriptive word projects or suggest the types of products or services that a person might like to purchase. For example, how well does each of these brands match the psychographic segmentation profile for you or your friends? Rolex? Apple? Toyota Camry? L'Oréal shampoo? Or, Nintendo? If they do not, then what type of behavioral or personality characteristics could you be associating with these brands?

Life Style   The ways people work, spend their time, and interact with others are the best ways to describe a life style. How many different activities do you think this includes? The list is long: from sports to hobbies, and from traditional routines to adventures. And, even within a life style, such as sporting activities, there are variations and multiple levels. For example, there are professional sports, college sports, high school sports, amateur sports, and casual sports. And are they passionate or passive about sports? Which ones, too? How often, where, and with whom? And finally, are they enjoying this life style by reading, watching, or participating in sports?

Values   People normally have four sources of values: personal, family, institutional, and cultural. They might be identical or in conflict, depending on the circumstances. These can include issues or positions on politics, religion, or social, economic, or ethical issues. While values can be a method of segmentation, this is extremely hard to quantify for individuals but easier for larger groups or clusters of people. There are other ways to use this for creative and media planning, covered in later chapters.

Attitudes   We all have attitudes. Most likely, hundreds of attitudes are in our mind are many more arrive when a circumstance or individual triggers them. Why is this important for Integrated Marketing Communication? First, identifying the types of attitudes provides an advertiser with a better understanding of a consumer's motivations and interest. For example, do they like fast cars or love racing? Or, are they more concerned about safety and always obey speed limits? Second, understanding attitudes enables advertisers to be more connected to the inner thoughts and feelings of individuals. For example, are they worried about getting older and not being married? Or, are they eager to go out to and have fun with their friends until late in the evening? Third, leveraging and demonstrating support for attitudes can provide advertisers with a strong message that resonates with consumers and connects the brand with a cause or purpose. For example, the "me too" movement is part of a cultural attitude that has recently shaped brand communication.

Activities   Just consider all the possibilities. Sports. Music. Painting. Photography. Gardening. Motorcycle racing. Movies. Social media. And, the list continues. But, there are two basic levels of involvement with any activity. Watching is one, and participating is the other. For example, you can enjoy watching soccer on television every weekend, or you could be going to actual matches. Plus, if you really enjoy the sport, then you will be kicking a ball around with a few friends or organizing an informal game. The bottom line is that any activity that you spend time on, other than working or interacting with your family, is considered to be an activity of your own choice.

Behavioral Segmentation

Behavioral segmentation organizes consumers into four groups: buyer status, purchase rates, benefit motivation, and product application. What are their motivations for selecting a particular brand? And, why will they change, or keep the same buying behavior? How will they use each brand? The motivations for any purchase can also be an effective form of segmentation. For example, people might buy a new car for its styling, economy, speed, performance, safety, or reputation. And, the usage patterns of the product have a similar purpose for segmentation. Consider these sub-categories: frequency of usage, amount of usage, and occasion of usage.

Each reveals individual likes and differences for the same brand, which can be applied to marketing and IMC strategies. What needs to be done is to connect specific numbers to usage behavior, especially for light, medium, and heavy usage patterns. For example, someone using mouthwash once at day only in the morning is a light user, after every meal is a moderate user, and before any form of social interaction could be a heavy user.

Buyer Status   As shown in Figure 5.2, buyer segmentation status includes: first time buyers, brand switchers, and brand loyal. It is important to distinguish among these categories because each of them will have a different demographic, psychographic, geographic, and behavior profile. This again is essential to know and understand before beginning any creative development, media planning, or other aspects of Integrated Marketing Communication. Let's take a close look at each one.

First Time Buyers   Why is this group so important to advertisers? Well, if the customer's initial experience is favorable, then many more opportunities are created for repeat purchases. And, a continued pattern of buying again and again evolves into brand loyalty. The financial implications are sizable. It is not a single sale, but hundreds of purchases, which results in thousands of brand revenue dollars over the years. First time buyers also require more information about a brand. They spend more time searching online or talking to friends. This

Figure 5.2 Buyer Status Segmentation

is particularly important if the buyer is unfamiliar with the product category. Even after repeated explorations, the motivating IMC message that moves them into action might be a television advertisement, a sales promotion offer, or just an attractive point-of-sale display.

Brand Switchers   Advertisers and agencies describe customers who purchase brands that are different from their previous selection as brand switchers. Why does this happen? There are three logical reasons. The first is dissatisfaction. The brand did not meet up to their expectations or did not perform as promised by a sales person. The second, and most frequent, reason for switching brands is price sensitivity. This could be the result of a price increase, comparison with similar brands, or more likely, a short-term sales promotion incentive. However, will the customer quickly return to their original brand when the promotion is over? Or, do they choose brands based on the lowest price, best deals, or greatest value at that time? The third, and final, reason for brand switching is experimentation. Once in a while, people just like to make a change, try something different, or discover a new experience from the process. It is all part of the challenge of strategic marketing.

Brand Loyal   Perhaps, buyers in this category are completely comfortable with their brand or just continue to buy it again and again as a regular habit. Either way, their buying patterns remain stable and fixed. Brand loyal buyers have a very strong resistance to promotions and special price offers. They also are cautious of substitutes and ultimately, will refuse to buy any other brand if their favorite is not available. The financial impact of brand value, as a continuing income source, has already been explained. That is why companies are placing a greater emphasis on customer service, which occurs after the sale. And, that relationship can be dramatically improved using social media, special promotions, and other forms of IMC.

Purchase Rate   Another type of behavioral segmentation is purchase rate segmentation, or how people are using a product or service including the amount, frequency, purpose, and price sensitivity. The single most important pattern is the purchase rate of a product. Since this is directly related to the rate of product usage and sales volume, marketing management is always extremely interested in this information. Typically, consumers are divided into three separate categories, as illustrated in light users, medium users, and heavy users. But, these categories need to be quantified. If not, then they are just abstract and vague words without definition. So, estimated numbers must be assigned to each of the three categories. In the example, light users are assumed to purchase the brand on a monthly basis, while medium users follow a weekly pattern, and finally, heavy users purchase the brand daily. Can you guess which product category this describes?

Remember, each brand and product category will have a different pattern. What is essential is to complete either an estimated or a calculated number for light, medium, and heavy users. Then, the demographic profiles are compared for each category. Nearly every time, there is a difference in the age, gender, or income of a heavy user. And, why are they so important for marketing management? Just do the math. As a result, advertisers and agencies are always striving

Figure 5.3 Purchase Rate Segmentation

to attract and retain the brand loyalty of heavy users within a specific product or service category.

Developing Audience Profiles

What are the most effective ways to use segmentation strategies? Brand strategies that utilize a combination of all four of the major categories with specific descriptive requirements can benefit from the application of a Segmentation Spectrum. This concept is illustrated in Figure 5.4, which has very precise demographic, psychographic, geographic, and purchase/use characteristics for a brand. The result is the optimum profile for a potential buyer or a description of an existing customer. What is important is how this information will be used for the development of creative ideas for brand messages, the selection of media for delivery, and the implementation of other types of IMC activities, events, and programs.

Each brand must have a very specific combination that identifies a group or sub-group that will be the primary target audience. The more detailed the better, and being narrow is preferred. While others might wonder why so many are being excluded, the reason goes back to the cost of media. Why pay to reach people who have a low probability of purchasing your product or services? And finally, the most important reason is really to better understand the mind and mood of consumers. This will become more apparent in the chapters on creative development and media selection, where being specific improves the quality and effectiveness of brand messages.

Knowing who is buying a particular brand, and why, is only the beginning of effective IMC planning. The first phase is a review of the target audience profile for current purchases of a brand. Advertisers need to evaluate a brand's success and competitive performance in the marketplace. IMC agencies are required to substantiate their continuing effectiveness in delivering brand messages and achieving measurable results. For example, sales promotion companies will monitor the response rates of consumers coming from different demographic, geographic, and psychographic segments. Profiles of competitive brands must also be considered. Where are the best opportunities? Can market share be increased? Which is the fasting growing segment? Answering these questions is the next phase of planning

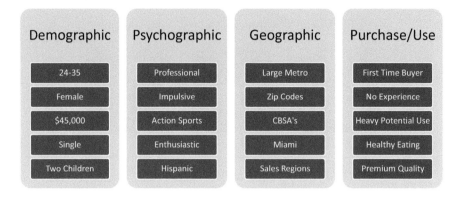

Figure 5.4 Targeting Audience by Segments

target audience profiles. And finally, media companies go through the same process of creating their own current customer profiles, comparing them to their competition, and developing a strategic focus for the future.

Existing Customers

This is a brand's reality. The segmentation profile of current customers indicates who is buying the product or service, why they are buying it, and how they use it. This segmentation profile provides an excellent perspective for planning brand advertising, sales promotion, brand visibility, public relations, and digital media strategies. However, there can be substantial differences among customers who are purchasing product variations of the same brand name. For example, honey or fruit-flavored Cheerios are more popular with children, while adults prefer the traditional taste. Or, fewer women drink regular cola brands compared with men, and they are much more likely to select a diet version, especially cola drinkers who are single women under the age of 25. The difference among existing customers can actually provide important insights for IMC planning and implementation.

Competitive Brands

What are your competitors doing? And, what are their segmentation profiles? This information isn't a trade secret, because a well-planning marketing research project can quickly develop a suitable competitive profile. As might be expected, every company is doing the same thing by trying to learn more about shoppers, buyers, and loyal customers. The information is a perfect input for IMC planning. What happens next is like a chess game with moves and countermoves. And, there are few winners, since the process is constantly producing new strategies. The only losers are companies that do not try to adjust to competitive market activity.

After a brand examines segmentation profiles of its own customers and analyzes the strengths and weakness of competitive brands in each segmentation category, a new strategic focus should emerge. This is based not on what the profile is but rather, on what it should become in the future. A decision to pursue different types of buyers, such as younger or older, male or female, married or single, can be made. Or, advertisers or IMC agencies might begin to place a greater emphasis on alternative segments. The results are a different allocation pattern of budgets for media, expenditure amounts, and most important, the timing or scheduling of advertising campaigns.

Media Composition

The segmentation profile of media audiences is just as important as a company's brand. Exactly what type of people are watching a television program, reading a magazine, subscribing to a newspaper, listening to a radio show, or visiting websites? As part of the triangle of advertising, media companies cannot effectively sell or promote their products or services to agencies without a brand profile. Media companies follow the same methodology as advertisers. They examine themselves, as well as competitors. In this case, the strengths of their own brand are emphasized, and the weaknesses of other media companies are pointed out. As a result, advertisers and agencies must be vigilant about the truth of media statements, because each company is manipulating the audience information.

Prioritizing Target Audiences

The most successful IMC programs are based on using two separate, but related, target audiences: primary and secondary. This distinction enables advertisers and IMC planners to appeal to both groups while prioritizing their approach and favoring the most important audience. The amount of money that will be allocated and the sequence of IMC spending are also important strategic decisions involving primary and secondary target audiences.

Primary Target Audience

A primary target audience is defined as "the segmentation profile of people with the highest probability of purchasing a brand within a product category." And, the secondary target audience is "the segmentation profile with a moderate, or lower probability of purchase." The best approach is to make the target audience as narrow as possible. This means selecting the most specific and detailed sub-categories within demographic, psychographic, geographic, and behavioral segmentation categories. It is essential to use marketing research to focus the selection strategy on a limited, but viable sub-segment. These decisions must be based on the likelihood or probability that the sub-group will have a strong interest, desire, and high probability of purchase a product or service. Even if a brand can be used by most people, appealing to everyone results is unproductive and expensive. For example, an incorrect choice for a target audience would be: adults, 18-65. This audience selection includes too many people which makes media buying more difficult, as well as expensive. Remember, media prices are proportional to the size of an audience. If you double the size of an audience, then the cost of media

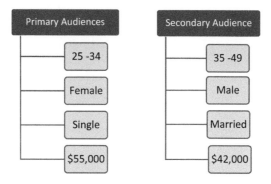

Figure 5.5 Primary and Secondary Audiences

is also doubled. In addition, creative brand messages that are effective with adults who are 25 years of age might be very different from those who are 45 years or older. So, a much better target audience selection, as shown in Figure 5.5, might be females 25 to 34 years of age as the primary target audience men women 35 to 49 years of age.

Secondary Target Profile

So, which is more important, primary or secondary? The best approach is to go after the primary audience before the secondary. Both are important, but a strong prioritization is necessary. It is not that one will be excluded from the other. The primary audience should always be pursued first, especially when IMC funds are limited or there is intense competition among brands within a product category.

The preferred strategy is to apply a pre-determined amount of financial resources that is allocated using unequal amounts for primary and secondary audiences: for example, 60% for the primary audience and 40% for the secondary audience. Use the media expenditures to reach the primary target audience first; then, go back and begin to spend money on the secondary target audience. Both are important, but the primary audience represents the highest probability of an actual purchase.

Focused Target Segment

Eventually, a segmentation spectrum should be developed for creative development as well as media buying. As shown in Figure 5.6, there are very specific sub-sections and criteria included for the demographic, psychographic, geographic, and behavioral segmentation profiles. Here is another example involving both primary and secondary target audiences developed for the same brand using all four major segmentation categories. The primary audience consists of men, aged 34–49, married but with no children at home, residing in smaller cities or suburban areas, who are also condominium owners, enjoy going to artistic events, are very religious, are active in community events, travel frequently for business, and like to cook. The secondary audience for the same brand might be women,

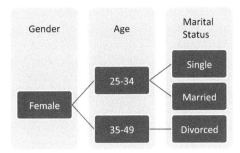

Figure 5.6 Segmentation Spectrum

aged 24–34, single, living in large metropolitan areas, apartment renters, active in sports and physical fitness, users of public transportation, heavy consumers of fast food, who love and really enjoy science. They are different, but both can be loyal brand customers.

Summary

Identifying brand purchasers and potential buyers is essential for IMC planning. Creative and media decisions cannot be made without accurate descriptions of intended audiences for brand messages. This process is called segmentation. There are four kinds of consumer segmentation: demographic, psychographic, geographic, and behavioral segmentation. Demographic segmentation includes variables such as age, gender, income, marital status, family composition, occupation, education, ethnic association, and other characteristics that separate people based on their differences. This is necessary to use the right language and images for creating brand messages and for selecting the right digital media, traditional publications, and broadcast programs for delivering brand messages. Psychographic segmentation involves the cognitive aspects of their behavior, such as personality and life style. The focus is on attitudes, interests, opinions, and communication styles. Geographic segmentation is based on where people live. This includes government and industry classification categories as well as advertising-defined boundaries, such as DMAs. Behavioral segmentation identifies first time buyers, brand switchers, and loyal customers, while usage segmentation relates to the motivating reason for buying a product or service as well as the physical amount, occasion, time of consumption, actual need, and frequency of purchase.

Discussion Questions

1. Why is segmentation important for planning marketing communication?
2. How is the cost of advertising media related to the number of people reached?
3. Which demographic variables are the most essential for media planning?
4. How can psychographics be used for the development of creative ideas?

5. What are the most effective applications of product use segmentation?
6. How can geographic segmentation be used for brand advertising?
7. Does a brand need to analyze the demographics of its competitors?
8. What is the purpose of a secondary target audience? Why is it needed?
9. Why is sales promotion so effective with first time buyers?
10. Can the demographic composition of a market influence communication strategies?
11. How are target audience profiles used for planning digital marketing?

Chapter Assignments

1. Profile a national brand
    Select a national brand for any product category. Try to describe its most likely customer profile.
2. Take a psychographic survey
    Want to find out which VALS type you are? Take the Value and Life Style Survey for results (www.strategicbusinessinsights.com/vals/presurvey.shtml).
3. Evaluate television markets
    Look at Nielsen's list of metropolitan markets. Select three and compare (www.nielsen.com).
3. Segment by product usage rates
    Demonstrate your understanding of this concept by creating an example involving toothpaste.
4. Calculate the value of new customer
    It's not just one sale, but every time that person continues to buy your brand far into the future.
5. Create your own cluster group
    Identify different customer groups within the same demographic profile and give them a name.

Continuity Case Study

Adriana wasn't satisfied with the agency's target audience profile. Surprisingly, their recommendation was to deliver brand messages to men and women over the age of 18. Perhaps the agency was concerned about Martin's statement that Athena needed to reach everyone who loves good food and a fine restaurant. That wasn't the end of the problem. Adriana knew from her sales experience that prioritizing markets was a secret to marketing success. But when she asked the agency's account executive to review the company's individual market sales analysis, Tony only complained about how it would add more work plus slow everything down. She still insisted that he come up with a reasonable solution.

At the same time, Felicia, the creative director at the agency, wanted to begin designing advertisement, but Adriana told her to wait. There were too many undefined issues involving demographic and psychographic segmentation. No one had clearly defined either the primary or the secondary audience. Julie, the media director, was asking for this information to begin the planning analysis, but neither Tony nor Adriana responded. So, nothing more was done.

1. Did the agency provide a sufficient target audience profile?
2. How could the demographic segmentation be improved?
3. Why is geographic segmentation important for advertising planning?
4. Should the agency use more psychographic segmentation?
5. Why should Adriana insist on very specific target audiences?

IMC Plan Development

Step One:

Identify a primary target audience using each segmentation category: demographic, psychographic, geographic, and product usage. Be specific and narrow with your descriptions.

Step Two:

Identify secondary target audience using all of the four segmentation categories.

Step Three:

Estimate the total number of people in both primary and secondary target audiences.

Step Four:

Compare your target audience profiles with possible profiles for competitive brands.

Step Five:

Recommend a list of prioritized geographic market areas based on sales potential.

Chapter 6

Creativity Strategies and Advertising

The Storytelling Process, People, and Procedures

Learning Objectives

1. Understand the process and theories of creativity
2. Recognize and develop the characteristics of creative thinking
3. Develop the contents and information in a brand brief
4. Compare and evaluate the applications of storytelling frameworks
5. Utilize the methods and formats for presenting creative concepts

Introduction

Creativity is a complex topic. It is so easy to recognize the results but difficult to explain how it happened. This is because creativity has multiple dimensions. There are at least five ways to describe the phenomenon of creative thinking. First, creativity is a cognitive process. It is an unconscious, but systematic, method for solving problems, developing new ideas, proposing original theories, and inventing unique products. Second, creativity is a subjective experience. What you think is a good idea may not be acceptable to others. Most evaluations of any creative idea or product are based on personal opinions and preferences: for example, modern art exhibits, literature, clothing styles, car models, and movies. Third, creativity is a behavioral characteristic. This reflects how you interact with people, places, and things. The world around you is a great source of stimulation and inspiration. The more you explore, the greater the probability of discovering creative ideas. Fourth,

DOI: 10.4324/9780367443382-6

creativity is a transformative event. It can change anything and everything. But, does it add value or just result in an impossible and impractical situation? The perception of a creative idea must include a meaningful contribution or benefit. And fifth, creativity is an entertaining activity. It makes us laugh, smile, cry, feel happy, or even get angry. That's the purpose of an imaginative thought that surprises, delights, and keeps our attention.

What Is Creativity?

Definition of Creativity

Creativity is a cognitive phenomenon that can be defined in many ways. Perhaps, the most practical definition is that creativity is the "process of combining existing ideas, concepts, facts, and physical objects in new ways that are unique, surprising, entertaining, and valuable." This implies that creativity is a learned, manageable, and structured behavioral pattern. And, it is. Surprised? Well, after you finish reading this chapter, you will not only understand the process of creativity but also be able to activate your own imagination, ideation, and inventiveness. Are you ready to begin the journey? Then, let's go!

Cognitive Structuralism

Your brain is designed like a computer. Or, is it that a computer is like our brain? In a machine with artificial intelligence, there are millions of connecting wires, microcircuits, and electrical pathways. Not too surprisingly, our brain has an even greater capacity for connectivity, with billions and billions of cells woven and intertwined together in microscopic networks with endless possibilities. No, this is not a biology lesson but the foundation of the theory of cognitive structuralism. In a single word, this structuralism approach is the way different types of knowledge, information, and experiences are organized. Each point of connection, called a node, leads to another cluster of connections and pathways, which are linked together in intricate formations. Figure 6.1 provides you with a visualization of a

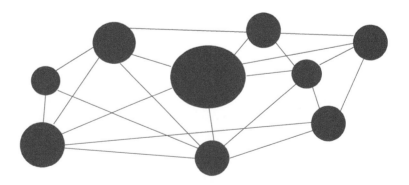

Figure 6.1 Cognitive Structuralism

simple node. Need an example? Sure. Imagine all the words that you can associate with the word "dog." There are the different breeds of dogs, activities involving dogs, foods that dogs eat, places that dogs live, and many experiences you personally remember about dogs. Just take any word and then, make a list of all the other ideas or words that you can associate with that concept. Put several thousands of these together in your brain, and the result is cognitive structuralism.

Physiology of Your Brain

The physiological structure of your brain is quite remarkable. In the cerebral cortex, there is a simple division of your brain into two equal parts, the left hemisphere and the right hemisphere. Since this is not a biology course, there will be no further medical terminology or Latin names. Most of us have a basic understanding of the functions of each hemisphere. The left hemisphere is involved with developing, expanding, and controlling our language skills and capacity to think rationally.

This includes both oral and written communication as well as our ability to use numbers, understand mathematics, and engage in decision-making. The right hemisphere is the primary source of our emotions, visual processing, and creative thinking abilities. This includes the entire category of non-verbal communication, such as facial expressions, and non-linear thinking.

Left-brain people are more logical, verbal, objective, linear, and planned. Right-brain people are more emotional, visual, subjective, circular, and spontaneous. Which side do you utilize the most? Take a look, then decide, based on the comparison of left-brain activities compared with right-brain activity shown in Figure 6.2. Everyone uses both sides of their brain, but there are distinct differences in the amount of time spent using each side. Each of us has an awareness of our preferences and abilities based on which hemisphere of our brain is performing best for us. That's why some people work in accounting and finance, while others are more comfortable in graphic design, architecture, or advertising.

Left-Brain	Right-Brain
Logical	Emotional
Verbal	Visual
Objective	Subjective
Fixed	Flexible
Linear	Circular
Planned	Spontaneous

Figure 6.2 Brain Physiology and Function

These differences are important, because they enable everyone to achieve success in areas that are best suited to their cognitive abilities.

Consider these two different ways of thinking when you are developing brand messages. If the product or service requires a consumer to understand or utilize information in their decision-making, then a left-brain approach is preferred. Jumping to the other side of the brain, a right-brain approach is the best way to appeal to those customers who are visually oriented or moved by messages that involve evoking emotions. This can make a big difference in the successful delivery of brand communication and the motivation of individuals to make product purchases.

Cognitive Spheres

People live in their own worlds. Their reality is the only one that exists. And, they don't believe in any others. Yet, their lives intersect with many other individuals. Family and friends. Neighbors. Co-workers. And, even complete strangers. Still, each person lives in a separate world. Undetectable. Impenetrable. Hidden deep inside. Filled with a flow of emotions and facts.

Let's try a new approach. It is completely egocentric. Not ours, but theirs. The idea is based on viewing everything from the inside-out. Becoming "one" with the person on the inside. Knowing what they know. Thinking like they think. Acting like they might act. Being inside their world.

While this is never really possible, we can attempt to replicate it or at least, better understand it. To do that, a different conceptual approach is required. Something beyond personas, target audiences, and demographic profiles should be conceived with a high degree of dependence and integration with artificial intelligence software.

Consider this possibility: cognitive spheres. It's a hybrid of ancient Zen thinking and modern behavioral psychology. So, what is the definition? A cognitive sphere is a replication of the internal processing of visual, verbal, and sensory data for a continuous interaction involving input, storage, organization, access, and output. There was a famous Beatles song written way back in 1967, called "The Walrus." It still has relevance today. While it was great music, the lyrics were even better. It encapsulates what cognitive spheres are all about: "I am he, as you are he, as you are me, and we are all together." Crazy? No. Just a different way to be more creative.

Measuring Creativity

Is it impossible to measure an individual's creative thinking ability? No, but the challenge is difficult. While there are many popular quizzes and attempts, there has been only one scientific study of this phenomenon. It was developed by the famous psychologist Paul Torrance, who designed a comprehensive series of tests for assessing creative potential. Those being evaluated are given abstract images to interpret or challenged by utilizing a simple object to perform as many different functions as possible. The scores are then coded and tabulated along with a comparison of norms involving the fluency and flexibility of an individual. Fluency refers to the number of creative ideas generated in a fixed amount of time, and flexibility refers to the variety of different uses derived from a single object. The

Torrance Test of Creativity Thinking still remains as the gold standard for assessing creativity, innovation, and imagination.

Personality Characteristics

How you interact with people, places, and things in your daily life provides fuel for creativity.

Your responses, or behavior, are called personality traits, and they connect you with your environment. Psychologists have identified hundreds of different traits, but only a few are relevant to creative thinking. In this textbook, we will be taking a quick look at only those traits most frequently associated with creativity. Do you have to have all of them? Absolutely not.

But, try to incorporate more of these personality traits in you daily behavior. The result will be a dramatic increase in your ability to think creatively, solve problems, and always come up with innovative ideas. It won't happen overnight, but with a little practice and patience, you'll arrive!

How many of these personality traits do you exhibit on a regular basis? There is a list of 30 different personality characteristics in Figure 6.3, along with a few short descriptive words or phrases that reflect that particular trait. The greater the number of traits that you exhibit, the more likely you are to be creative. But, that does not mean you need to be proficient with all of them. Even five good ones will make you stand out from everyone else. So, to be more creative, it is simple as practicing the ones that you enjoy the most and becoming better at the others. Make a list of the ones you want to improve or experience. And, have fun and enjoy the experience!

Curiosity.
Wants to find out more. Discovers how things work. Needs to know why. Always searching.

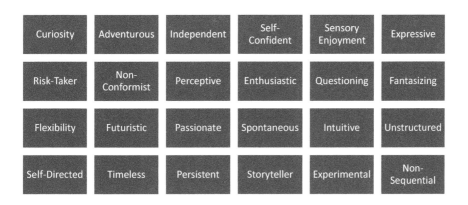

Figure 6.3 Creative Personality Characteristics

Adventurous.

Enjoys the unknown. Comfortable with uncertainty. Desires exploration. Makes bold decisions.

Independent.

Not committed to tradition. Investigates alternatives. Works toward solutions. Compromises.

Humorous.

Attitude of happiness. Loves to laugh. Capable of immediate comedy. Alters perception of life.

Self-confident.

Projects image of success. No doubts about personal abilities. Completely in control. Destiny.

Sensory enjoyment.

Visually oriented. Detects sounds. Discriminates tastes. Describes smells. Desires touching.

Expressive.

Highly interactive. Animated hand gestures. Maximized eye contact. Multiple facial responses.

Risk taking.

Not afraid of failure. Assumes success. Extremely confident. Ignores consequences. Fearless.

Non-conformist.

Independent thinker. Not afraid of criticism. Proud of actions. Likes to be different. Eccentric.

Perceptive.

Detects differences. Observes behavior. Sensitive to situation. Recognizes details. Always alert.

Enthusiastic.

High energy. Positive mental attitude. Quickly motivates others. Belief in activities. Passionate.

Questioning.

How? Why? When? Childlike approach. Enjoys answers. Digs deeper. Always wondering.

Fantasizing.

Frequent day-dreamer. Wild imagination. Likes role-playing. Doodler. Excellent storyteller.

Flexibility

Easily adapts to change. Eager to try new things. Comfortable with learning. Quick to respond.

Futuristic.

Attracted to technology. Thinks about tomorrow. Innovative behavior. Visionary perspective.

Passionate.

Believes in mission. Fueled by emotions. Patient. Persistent. Determined. Driven to succeed.

Spontaneous.

Immediate response. Reacts to stimulus. Sometimes impulsive. Prefers to agree. No limitations.

Intuitive.

Beyond logic. Inner guidance. Unconscious motivations. Feelings and not facts. Instinctive.

Unstructured.

Without barriers. No restrictions. Free thinking. Wandering search. Shapeless structures. Open.

Self-directed.

Never needs instructions. Determines own priorities. Dislikes authority. Acts independently.

Timeless.

Unaware of the clock. Always absorbed in the activity. Takes a long time. Completely focused.

Persistent.

Never stops trying. Always optimistic. Driven to succeed. Believes there is always a solution.

Storyteller.

Enjoys talking about experiences. Easily interacts with people. Captures attention quickly.

Experimental.

Continually trying new things. Craves the unusual. Wants to see what works. No expectations.

Non-sequential.

Never starts at the beginning. Frequently changes lists. Jumps topics. Focuses on the present.

Developing Creative Ideas

There is the classical model of creativity developed by James Webb. This four-phased approach, shown in Figure 6.4, begins with preparation, incubation, illumination, and evaluation. While there have been many models, extensions, and new descriptive terms, the basic concept has remained the same for many years. Let's apply it to Integrated Marketing Communication (IMC). First, the preparation stage equates to marketing research. What do we know about potential buyers and existing customers? What do they believe about our brand? What is really important to them? Second, the incubation states. This is the easiest part of the process. Do nothing! That's right, after you have reviewed all the research and insights, just go and do something else. Leave everything else to your subconscious

Figure 6.4 Steps for Development of Creative Ideas

mind. Never force creativity. The harder you try, the less you will get done. It just needs time! Third, illumination, or the moment you recognize the creative idea. Haven't you experienced getting a great idea after talking a walk, making dinner, or just before texting a few friends? It's often referred to as the "ah-ha" experience or visually illustrated with a glowing lightbulb. The fourth stage, which is evaluation, completes the creative thinking process with a left-brain examination of the concept or idea. Is it feasible? Will it work? What are the potential problems? If all the questions can be answered with satisfaction, then the creative idea is ready to move forward toward the implementation of the original creative idea.

Brainstorming

Can you improve your ability to be more creative? Absolutely. Take a close look at the amount of time you spend exercising to improve your physical strength and endurance. A lot of people join health clubs, go to yoga classes, use machines at home, ride bicycles, or just take long walks around the neighborhood. And, what about expanding your intellectual abilities? Hopefully, attending classes, reading your textbooks, writing term papers, and taking examinations (well, maybe not, no, not really) will help you improve your mental abilities. But how much time do you devote each day to improving your creative thinking abilities and imagination? Why not?

There are a number of techniques that can be used by individuals and groups to encourage and stimulate creative thinking. Advertising agencies use these methods, along with a series of outside programs, to maximum the creative potential of their employees. In addition, there are numerous books and magazines devoted to the topic of creativity, including the Institute of Creative Thinking, located at the University of New York in Buffalo, which teaches techniques such as brainstorming. Alex Osborn, an advertising legend is credited with the development of this technique for his agency.

The purpose of brainstorming is to come up with as many different ideas, concepts, thoughts, and solutions to a creative problem as possible within a very limited amount of time. In brainstorming, the total number of ideas is always more important than the quality of the ideas. The purpose is to build a long list of possible answers but without making any comments or criticisms about the ideas. The theory behind brainstorming is that each idea will lead in a different direction, and by constantly exploring different ways to get there, a greater number of solutions and alternatives will emerge.

A brainstorming session should be limited to a small group, usually about 5 to 10 people. If the size of the group is too large, it is difficult for everyone to participate and confusing when people begin to talk at the same time. The principle behind brainstorming is that the number of creative ideas is more important than the quality. Ideas that initially make no sense can often lead to other ideas that are original and innovative. The objective is to encourage people to think in different ways without fear of criticism or judgment.

Here are the rules for a brainstorming session. First, participants must spontaneously react to every idea, regardless of its quality or value. Second, members of the group cannot criticize, discuss, or reject any idea that has been presented. This is especially important because one of the barriers to creative thinking is fear of rejection. Third, everyone in the group must come up with ideas as fast as possible. The shorter the time lags between responses, the greater the number of ideas that can be generated. The fourth and final rule for a brainstorming session is that every response must be written down for review and evaluation at a later time or date.

Morphing and Visualizing

While there are many other methods for coming up with creative ideas, a few proven ones stand out, like morphing and visualizing. The ability to morph, or radically change and modify, objects in your mind is a very powerful tool. It is like having your own creative factory, where you can change the color, shape, texture, aroma, or packaging of a product—in an instant! Just imagine it, and the product idea is finished. What is most important is not the result but practicing the technique, especially when morphing is done just for fun. Try it! The more times you try this technique, the easier it gets. Then, when you have an assignment, your brain is ready to respond.

So, what is visualization? When you use this technique, you are not changing anything; you are creating everything from the beginning. Perhaps, another way to describe this creative idea development process is that it becomes unlimited fantasy. For example, just close your eyes for a minute and be silent. Imagine a small lake that is filled with chocolate and not water. Then, a helicopter begins flying overhead and begins dropping giant scoops of vanilla ice cream everywhere while playing Korean hip-hop music. And finally, you see yourself there, standing next to a big red Harley-Davidson motorcycle, wearing a yellow raincoat and eating a Mexican burrito. Perhaps, it is a good time to stop this crazy visualization? Next time, you begin a silent visualization with your own imagination. No storyline is required. Just let the ideas flow!

Creative Planning at Agencies

Since the majority of companies and small businesses use advertising or marketing communication agencies for the development of brand messages and media placement, it is important to learn more about the internal structure of agencies and the people who work there. The primary focus in this chapter is creativity and creative teams, but other individuals are involved in the process. This includes the account executive, who is the exclusive point of contact with the client, the media team, and at some agencies, the account planner, who has the responsibility of sharing research and information with everyone involved with the advertising and IMC programs.

Take a look at Figure 6.5, which visually indicates the flow of materials and processes involved at an advertising or marketing communications agency. It begins with a brand brief, which is a short one-page summary that contains the most essential information about the product and people who typically purchase the brand. Along with the brand brief, the buyer persona is presented to illustrate what type of people are interested in a product or service, along with a narrative with images about who they are, what they do, and how they think. Then, the creative team begins to generate ideas and concepts for brand communication,

Figure 6.5 Creative Planning at Agencies

eventually leading to a storytelling framework, creative approach, and a presentation of the proposed advertising and digital content, which ultimately, is approved with changes and modifications.

Creative Teams

Digital marketing agencies, as well as traditional advertising agencies, need a combination of media strategists and creative talent. People with experience in analyzing consumers, sales opportunities, and the business needs of the agency's client become the strategists. Others with exceptional creative abilities become generators of digital content and advertising. And, in the middle of all these right-brain and left-brain thinkers are account executives. They are the ones responsible for guiding the planning, implementation, and management of brand messages.

The creative team at an agency is composed of four individuals: a creative director, a content writer, a visual or graphic artist, and a digital specialist. This is the core group, which can include more than one person in each category, except the creative director. The number of people in the group will depend on the needs of the client, time required, and IMC budget.

The creative director is the leader of the group and makes the final decision on the concepts or materials for brand messaging and content development. The content writer, who is also called the copywriter, focuses on the communication process between the brand and the consumer. This includes the words used in television and radio commercials, as well as video content for online purposes, plus printed materials, such magazine and newspaper advertisements, brochures, and direct mail pieces. The visual artist, who is also called the art director, designs, selects, and recommends the images that will be used in digital media, traditional advertising, promotional material, and all other forms of IMC. And finally, the digital specialist is the lead expert for everything online, from search engine optimization to the performance analysis of website and social media activity.

At some agencies, there are account planners, who are involved in both consumer research and strategic IMC development. Their job is to understand the overall psychology and behavior of consumers, especially those who are purchasing brands made by the agency's clients. Typically, the account planner prepares a creative brief, presents it to the creative team, and works with the account executive to prepare the creative and media materials that support the brand. Not all advertising or digital marketing agencies use account planners; usually, it is a position available when there are large advertising budgets, multiple accounts, and different brand assignments.

Brand Briefs

Creative people at an advertising agency are more interested in ideas than research reports. Numbers don't excite them, but visual and verbal concepts do. So, how do you get the most talented creative minds to connect marketing strategies with advertising and IMC programs?

Most agencies use a brand brief. What is it, and why is it so important? The purpose of a brand brief is to concisely and accurately select the most relevant and helpful information from a marketing plan. This includes a summary of consumer, product, and market research for the client's brand as well as competitive products or services. If written well, the brand brief provides enough information for the creative team to begin generating ideas using a solid strategic communication perspective.

At advertising agencies, the brand brief is prepared by an account executive. It is their responsibility to review the marketing research, search for key insights, and make recommendations for IMC strategies. In large agencies, there is often a position called the account planner, who is assigned a portion of these activities, since an account executive's main role is to manage the interaction with a client. The account planner has a hybrid responsibility that combines the duties of a research manager with the primary functions of a communications strategist. Account planners are the "go to" people when creatives need to know more about consumer psychology and the reputation of a brand. The account planner must think, act, and feel as if they are potential buyers or users of a brand. At the same time, account planners often come up with their own creative ideas from insights and personal observations, which are shared with the agency's team.

In Figure 6.6, the most essential parts of a brand brief are reviewed. The account executive must answer five basic questions: who, what, where, when, and why? Simple, but essential information for the creative team. Each of these questions corresponds to a marketing communication planning activity. The "Who" is the target audience. The "What" is a brand message. The "Where" is the geographic areas for advertising, as well as the media selected. This will ultimately include the specific magazines, newspapers, or radio and television stations that are purchased and in addition, any other activity that is recommended as part of an IMC plan. The "When" is the time frame for scheduling the advertising. For example, the daily, weekly or monthly appearance of advertising or promotional programs. This is exceptionally critical with social media, where messages can be posted at any minute of the day. The "Why" includes the perceived purchase motivations for both potential buyers and existing loyal customers.

Another way of summarizing the brand brief is the formal categories of buyer profiles, which include the specific demographic, psychographic, geographic, and behavioral segmentation descriptions of existing or potential customers. The brand brief also includes information about the brand, such as the brand positioning, competitive product analysis, and basic value proposition that will be offered

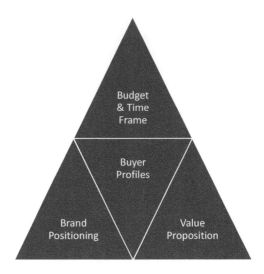

Figure 6.6 Components of Brand Briefs

in the marketplace. Finally, the budget that has been allocated to the advertising and other IMC pathways is an important element of the brief, accompanied by a launch date and time frame for completion, which shapes the structure of a creative proposal.

The format and style of a brand brief change from agency to agency. This is because each IMC company approaches the development of creative concepts in its own unique or slightly different way. As a result, there is no best way to write a brand brief, and there is no single way to present this information to a creative team. However, the most essential components of a marketing plan must be compressed into a single document. It also has to center around one, or more, consumer insights about a brand, competitors, product usage, or other important aspects of the marketing environment. All this in a single page, perhaps with a short PowerPoint, and an inspiring approach when presenting the brand brief to a creative team. Writing this document is difficult for anyone involved and even more of a challenge when it is given to a creative team.

Buyer Personas

The presentation of demographic and geographic profiles can be boring and uninteresting to the right-brain minds of a creative people at an agency. They need something more exciting to capture their attention and to provide a better understanding of consumers. That's why most agencies also include a buyer persona in the brand brief, as well as many other documents and presentations. Essentially, a buyer persona is a narrative about a person who is the most likely buyer of a brand. This includes a taste of their life, including their job title, personal interests, participation in sports, favorite television programs and movies, and choice of clothing styles. The composition of a persona includes many specific

Figure 6.7 Development of Buyer Personas

demographic, personality characteristics, and behavioral variable about the target audience. In Figure 6.7, the sample persona for a potential buyer of cosmetic products includes their occupation, social media preferences, and favorite activities, as well as demographic and geographic information. What other products or services might be desired by the person described by the sample persona?

This narrative is always accompanied by a photo or drawing of the hypothetical individual. But you can get a pretty good idea of who that person is and what they are all about by discussing the information in a buyer persona. It is not a strategy of numbers and facts but an exposition of a person along with everything in their life.

Storytelling Frameworks

The definition of a creative strategy is "the conceptual framework for a series of brand messages delivered with continuity through multiple media channels, IMC pathways, and other exposure opportunities." A strategy is not an individual idea, or a completed advertisement, but a method of implementing storytelling with a persuasive message. The creative strategy is a combination of different elements, including the style of communication, method of expression, and flexible interpretation of a creative concept. It is not a single message or series of commercials but a continuous expression of a brand positioning with highly effective verbal and visual content.

Each advertisement on television, social media post on Facebook, coupon offer on Twitter, video on Instagram, podcast invitation in an email, and free music download offer from a website is an important part of an IMC Plan. And, it is essential that the brand messages are consistent across all media and every interaction with customers and potential buyers. The creative strategy is the foundation for delivering brand content and value propositions, which can transform ideas into effective and productive communication.

Creativity itself is a subjective experience. And, what appeals to you might not appeal to others. The problem is: how can you decide which one is the best? It isn't easy. To begin, ask three questions before selecting a creative strategy. First, which creative strategy is most compatible with the persona for existing customers? Second, which creative strategies is most likely to attract the attention and interest of potential buyers? Third, which creative strategies are being used by your competitors? The answers to these questions will provide a good indication of the optimum strategies for brand content in social media and brand messages in advertising media.

Remember the functions of the left brain and right brain? They most certainly apply here as part of the selection process. One way to organize them is into two separate groups. One to appeal to the left-brain functions of people, such as the strategies of demonstration; comparisons of problem/solutions, before/after; testimonials; scientific proof; information; and new report formats. And another set for the right-brain thinking people: humor, storytelling, imagery, mystery, fantasy, animation, fear avoidance, and surprise. This is not an easy choice. There is no single solution. It's an IMC decision made from subjective opinions rather than logical, analytical judgements. At the end of the day, there is never only one way to know which creative strategy was the best. The best solution is to measure the results using the AIDA (awareness, interest, desire, action) model. Until then, a combination of consumer insights, brand knowledge, competitive intelligence, marketing research, professional agency experience, and personal instincts are the main guiding forces for selecting the optimum creative strategy for a brand.

In this textbook, there are 30 different creative frameworks that can be used for ideas and brand messages. Most of them you already know or probably have experienced. Sometimes, frameworks are combined to produce a completely new hybrid message or brand story. For example, a famous celebrity can demonstrate a brand benefit using a humorous approach. Or, an animated spokesperson helps a customer solve a financial problem using the comparison of the before and after situation. There are a lot of options. And, it is difficult to really know which one

Figure 6.8 Storytelling Frameworks

is best. You should not just select the one you like or enjoy. The choice has to be made based on the accumulated knowledge and understanding of the potential buyer or customers. That is why it is important to hire a professional digital marketing communication agency with advertising skills, technical expertise, and creative judgement for IMC messaging.

Now, it is time to review the description of the 30 creative frameworks for creative brand message communication. They are shown in Figure 6.8 and reviewed in detail in the following sub-sections in alphabetical order. Which one is the best for your brand? And, how will you decide?

Animation

From Disney cartoons to Pixar movies, we have grown up with animated characters. They have made us laugh, smile, and even cry. Animated cartoons have always been part of our cultural, social, and entertainment environment. The list is long and begins with the iconic ones: Mickey Mouse, Donald Duck, Bugs Bunny, Roadrunner, Yogi Bear, and Daffy Duck. Later came another wave of more modern and controversial characters and programs: The Simpsons, South Park, and SpongeBob Square Pants. Whether you watched them or not, their visibility and reputation were everywhere. So, who were your favorite cartoon characters? Go ahead, think about it.

But, there is another category of animated characters. These are the ones involved in the sales promotion of products and services. Going back over the years, can you name a few? How about the Jolly Green Giant for vegetables, Mr. Clean for household products, and Tony the Tiger for Kellogg's Corn Flakes? Or, remember Cap'n Crunch, Charlie the Tuna, and the Pillsbury Doughboy? Over the past several decades, these anthropomorphized figures have appeared in television and radio advertising as well as being viewed in magazines, newspapers, comic books, and many other forms of printed media. And, their visibility extended to images on posters, outdoor signs, and life-size reproduction in grocery stores and supermarket aisles.

The oldest cartoon personality, Mr. Peanut, tragically died at the age of 104 years. In a famous television commercial appearing before the Super Bowl football game in 2020, it appeared that Mr. Peanut was killed in an automotive accident. And, the shocking news of his death was confirmed in his own Twitter account. Yes, confirmed. But, there is no need to cry or send flowers. In a second humorous commercial, an animated funeral was attended by many famous cartoon celebrities, including Mr. Clean and the Kool-Aid Man. The happy ending featured the birth announcement of "baby nut," who can still be found today using the hashtag #BabyNut.

There is always an opportunity for a new animated character to promote a brand. It can become a recognizable spokesperson in media advertising, social media, and many promotional activities. Physical appearances at retail stores, public events, schools, restaurants, and other locations can be a boost for publicity, brand awareness, and customer engagement. Ronald McDonald did this successfully for more than 60 years with appearances around the globe. It just demonstrates the power of brand personification. Do you have some ideas for cartoon characters for a brand?

Announcer

This is a very old-school method, but it has relevant applications. Using announcers to promote a brand can be a vibrant part of a retro strategy, filled with nostalgia or even a satirical approach. The most important aspect is finding the right voice to match the visual appeal of the announcer. Should it be male or female? Young or old? About what age? And, are there any particular regional accents that would be more appropriate? It's all about the consumer's perception of the speaker and relevance to the product category. Strategically, the choice must be based on a brand's persona as well as the intended target audience. For example, if a brand's persona included a description of a rugged-looking young man hiking with friends in the woods, the choice would be different than in the case of teenage girls comparing their most recent Instagram posts.

Aspirational

Everyone wants to look or feel better. The promise of both benefits is frequently contained in advertising. Madonna's desire to be a "Material Girl" sure has relevance in this context. Or, the motivation of getting a new job, meeting someone special, or making a big pile of money are other personal goals that can capture the attention of potential buyers. The importance of understanding and applying this basic psychology to brand messages can yield incredibly productive results. "Be all that you can be!" was the recruiting slogan for the U.S. Army for more than 20 years. It was extremely effective in attracting young people to consider a military career.

Before/After

It's dull. It's ordinary. But, it works. Who is going to pay attention? Anyone with a problem that needs to be solved will immediately pay attention. These are things can that happen at any time, such as a coffee stain on shirt or sore muscles from exercising too much. Or, young mothers with children who don't like to eat their breakfast food. And men who cannot decide between an electric razor and a traditional shaving blade. Simple things, but highly relevant. How many before and after commercials can you remember? Which ones were the most effective?

This is a time-tested creative strategy that always delivers results. It follows a predictable and proven sequence: show a real-life problem, explain the solution, and visually compare the difference. Every time that a brand "promise" is included, the amount of interest and consumer involvement increases. The only thing that remains is for the consumer to purchase the brand. Proctor & Gamble, along with many other package goods companies, have been incredibly successful with this creative strategy. While they seldom win many advertising awards, their financial statements clearly have consistently reported increased sales and profits.

Blended

A blended strategy is kind of a "mash-up." Just take a little bit of this, some more of that, and combine them in an original way that communicates a brand story.

Blended is a mixture of sights, sound, and images that delivers a message in its own unique way. It doesn't have to conform to any pre-established idea of a strategic category or creative approach. This is a situation where it is good to break the rules and come up with a most unusual and unexpected idea. Don't worry about how things come together with this advertising. Just get in there and give it a go!

Celebrities

Who is your favorite celebrity? Are they associated with any product or service? And if you had to hire them to represent another brand, which one would it be? How much should they be paid?

Advertisers are spending millions of dollars, pounds, or Euros to have them appear in television commercials. And even more for endorsements, public appearances, or live performances. Is it worth the money? Advertisers think so. And, the results are usually worth the investment.

There are several reasons for this. First, celebrities come with their own audiences. They already have millions of followers on Facebook, Instagram, or Twitter. Few media vehicles can offer the same exposure. For example, the famous football player Ronaldo has an estimated 92 million followers on Facebook. That's extremely impressive, especially since it's more than Eminem, Rihanna, and Vin Diesel. But today, the top spot goes to Shakira, who enjoys a worldwide audience of slightly over 100 million followers. Who know what new celebrities will join the ranks of the top 10 during the decade of the 2020s?

Social media have transformed celebrities into an important part of our daily lives. Talking about them makes people feel good. What are they wearing? Where are they going? What did they do? Who are they dating? Or, if they are in sports, then how well are they playing? There is always a flow of celebrity gossip on Facebook, Instagram, and Twitter. So, the brand does not always have to be involved, only the celebrity. The association or connection comes later with advertising and sales promotion activities. The greater the visibility of a celebrity, the more value for the brand.

Second, celebrities can leverage brand marketing. This is a perfect example of how IMC can be combined with advertising and sales promotion. There are numerous opportunities to have a celebrity do much more than appear in a series of television commercials. For example, their image can be featured on point-of-sales displays in retail stores, a sweepstakes program can be created with a trip to Hollywood, or a private dinner gathering or entertainment can be arranged with business-to-business (B2B) customers at a large trade show or industry exhibit.

However, each extra activity comes with a fee, unless previously agreed upon in a contract.

Third, celebrities create excitement in the marketplace. Is this enough to increase sales? As you have already learned, there are many complexities involved with the customer's journey. But in a global marketing environment, celebrities can be very influential in generating awareness for a brand. A sports figure, pop culture, or entertainment celebrity gets immediate attention. This can be very beneficial for a brand, as long as the life style of the celebrity is compatible with the brand. What celebrities do in their private lives can be a major problem for advertisers. The tabloids are always searching for shocking news, and the paparazzi are everywhere, complete with their cameras. Controversial words or actions quickly become headlines for video reports on the evening news. It's enough to receive negative publicity, but the severity of the situation can result in a canceled contract. That means no endorsement, no appearance, and no millions of dollars for representing the brand. Bad news. Really bad news!

Comparison

Brand comparisons intentionally match one product against others, usually the leading brands. There several ways to do this. The comparisons can be done by using on-camera talent, or an announcer who explains the differences, or by displaying graphics, illustrations, or simulations that provide evidence of brand superiority. A frequent technique is featuring the "exclusive" ingredients or benefits of the advertised brand. These can be real physical differences, like the powerful pain-relieving xylocaine-5, but often are expressed in a more relevant and understandable form, such as the magic scrubbing bubbles of a household cleaner.

Is it a mistake to compare brands? No. When brands are unknown, it is an excellent idea. Comparing immediately boosts awareness and image of a less familiar brand. That brand is quickly perceived to be equal to the competition, perhaps even better. And, it helps consumers understand the details of the brand proposition. The entire purpose of a brand comparison is to encourage people to know it, buy it, and like it.

The only danger with this strategy is when a leading brand emotionally rejects or rushes to disprove another brand's advertising content. It is only falling into a trap by including the new brand's name again and again in more advertisements. Its communication response is actually helping the new brand get established. One word that should never be used in advertising is "the best." This immediately invites a requirement for proof from consumers, competitors, and even governments in the United States or the European Union. There is some room for bragging, puffery, or boasting, but too much exaggeration of the truth turns off customers and incurs the anger of competitors. Depending on a brand's questionable claims or false promises, companies have several options for taking legal action. Superlatives, like the greatest, fastest, or easiest, must be used with caution. To be safe, a brand should emphasize comparative, not superlative statements in its marketing communication materials.

Most companies hire independent test laboratories for comparing brands. The results are thought to be more believable and acceptable to consumers. And they are, but the sponsor already knows what to expect based on their own product research. Still, proof of product claims is essential, and comparative information must always be substantiated. If it is not, the risks are bigger, with distorted customer expectations and disappointment with less than desired results.

Demonstration

Which brand is better? There is only one way to find out. Prove it. Show the advantages. Explain the benefits. Compare the differences. Anytime a brand has superior characteristics or performance, it is a perfect candidate for a product demonstration strategy. Product demonstrations are logical appeals to the left side of an attentive brain to listen, learn, and believe. This is especially true for food products with discernible differences in taste, color, texture, or appearance or brands that have advantages in their operation, application, or assembly.

While product demonstrations are highly effective in retail store environments, they are expensive, time-consuming, and complex to arrange. But, that is why visual demonstrations are perfect for television advertising and streaming video. The communication challenge is to compress the action and information into a short, but impactful, 30-second commercial. The results are often simple but memorable occurrences, like spilling coffee on a shirt to demonstrate a laundry detergent or playing with a basketball while ordering a pizza with a mobile app.

The problem of using a product demonstration strategy is producing a boring or uninteresting advertisement. Obvious, consumers not the brand are not going to pay any attention, but those who do can easily become unmotivated or negative. Why watch a poorly presented or uninteresting demonstration? The brand benefits must be easy to understand, or the advertisement is a complete waste of money for the advertiser.

There is one final point about product demonstrations. They are very important for leveraging other activities with IMC. For example, a sales promotion that offers gifts or coupons to anyone watching a short brand demonstration. Or, entering their name in a sweepstake for participating. Other applications include direct mail pieces or digital demonstrations with interactive features for visitors to a brand website. As you know, the silent purpose is to get information about everyone who is watching or participating in the product demonstration. The data is valuable for learning more about the people who have purchased a brand, as well as those who didn't. If a company has their email address, or phone number, then a digital marketing offer can be delivered directly to them. It is just another way to maintain contact with potential buyers.

Dramatization

Everyone loves a dramatic movie or television show. There might be plenty of overacting and exaggeration, along with improbable situations. But, will the same approach work in a short-form video advertisement or television commercial? It can. And, dramatization does generate attention, even when you are not interested in the product category. The right mix of reality and exaggeration has to be woven into the dialogue, with a believable character with a legitimate problem. Fortunately, the solution can always be found with the appearance of the brand. It becomes a hero in the dramatized situation and subtly promises the same for a shopper.

Emotional

Stir up the feelings, arouse the passions, and ignite the heart! This right-brain strategy is always right on target. An endless number of commercials and advertisements have proved how effective this approach is for a variety of products. The secret is discovering the emotional "trigger" for the person, situation, or brand. But, emotional strategies still need to be developed around the value proposition of a brand. Here is where marketing research can provide the insights needed to tap into the creative strategy. Involving and motivating potential buyers depends on the approach and presentation of the content. Just push the right button, and bingo!

Traditional Japanese commercials are the most proficient and skilled in using emotional creative strategy. Typically, the best commercials devote the entire content of their television advertising content to telling a story, a very emotional story. The advertising agency that produced the commercial wants to get your feelings involved as you continue to watch. Then, in the last five seconds, the name of the brand is revealed in a very subtle way. This might be the silent display of a logo within the last frame, accompanied by a short phrase that reflects the philosophy of the company. This is shocking by American standards, where hard selling and persuasion are always king. But, in Japan, emotional strategies are enormously successful. For example, here is an emotional strategy commercial that won an advertising award. Imagine a young boy and his grandfather walking down a dusty path. They stop to talk to people, look at some animals, and finally get a drink of water at an ancient well. Can you guess the product in that television commercial? It was never shown. It was never mentioned. But at the end of the advertisement, the famous logo was displayed. The advertiser was the Japan Railroad system.

Entertainment

This is pure storytelling. It can be filled with great characters or funny situations. Or, it can direct your attention to an important social issue. At the end of the day, the purpose of an entertainment strategy is to make you enjoy experiencing brand messages. It can be when you are watching a television commercial, listening to a podcast, or downloading free music from a sponsor's website. Entertainment is a fusion of the brand value proposition and effective storytelling.

The danger is that an excessive emphasis on entertainment can dilute the brand message. The result would be for an advertiser to be spending a lot of money to make people happy but with no financial return to the company. Another caution is the tendency of many young and talented creative people at the agency to favor this form of strategy. Their preference is based on their own personal behavior without realizing how it impacts upon a marketing plan for a brand.

Episodes

People love to binge-watch old television programs. This addiction comes to life on Netflix. Watch episode one, then two, three, and four ... continuing late into the night. The origin of this concept goes back to the days of "silent movies." The powerful movie studios loved to create episodes where there was an improbable or dramatic ending. The hero was usually trapped in a car on the railroad tracks with a train coming right at him. Or, a beautiful damsel was trying to escape from a burning building. The purpose was to lure you back to the movie theatre next week to find out what happened. Can this approach work today? Why not?

Fantasy

Let your imagination run wild here. No rules. No reality. All illusions and fiction. Whatever you can dream up works here. It's like Cirque Soleil, where most things are just hard to believe. Or, the Blue Man Group, where experiencing the unexpected is why you came in the first place! But, a fantasy strategy is very similar to an entertainment strategy when imagination gets in the way of a brand message. Still, this strategy is always a consideration for luxury products and services as well as brands that want to project an unconventional and sensationalistic image with fantasy.

Fear

Make no mistake about this strategy. Fear motivates. It's part of our inherent DNA to take immediate action to survive. But, there is no big bear chasing us down the street or tsunami in our backyard. Yet, there are strategies that invoke fear about problems, situations, or conditions. And if not fear, the feeling of strong concern, worry, or discomfort is always there. At this psychological level, a good creative strategy will stir up those emotions, then connect them to a fear reduction option.

A simple example is toothpaste. The fear of having tooth decay, or worse, can be minimized by brushing daily. So, purchasing a tube of toothpaste is a small price to pay for avoiding a trip to the dentist. And, toothpaste advertising likes to remind us of other calamities, such as plaque, tartar, bleeding gums, and a few hard-to-pronounce diseases. Fear works. It is not a gentle approach, but the message can resonate deeply with those individuals who want to avoid things.

The use of a fear, as an advertising strategy, can be applied to nearly every product category. Just think about all the possibilities. Do you feel safe on the road with worn tires? And what about your family? What about a home security system for your house? Or, the importance of virus protection on your computer, or an Otter brand outer covering for your Apple phone? The consequences and costs of not having this type of security can stir up a level of fear in anyone.

Historical

How many commercials have you seen that involve people from past times and places? This is a frequently used strategy that is actually not very creative. Too many advertisements are built around historical figures, cultural heroes, or political icons. Let's discover new things with Christopher Columbus, Galileo, or Albert Einstein. Or, engage the audience with images of gladiators, cowboys, pirates, sailors, sword fighters, or the ubiquitous cavepeople. Really?

The problem is that good storytelling, while funny, dramatic, or inspirational, can interfere with the brand message. The historical approach has to be focused and methodically communicating the benefits of a product or service or its competitive advantage. Anything less is a waste of time and money. But, many historically based advertisements are legendary. It still takes a lot of skill to select the right characters and deliver the right message to effectively resonate with people.

Humor

Why does humor work so well? Well, everyone enjoys laughing, but what makes something funny? No one really knows. Sure, psychologists might have theories, but there is no magic formula for laughter. But, there is a big problem with humor. What is funny to one person may not be considered humorous by another. Plus, there is always the danger of accidentally being offensive to other groups by using certain words, images, or content. It is a very delicate balance between making people laugh and keeping people happy. Apparently, humor is a subjective experience, which is unpredictable, uncontrollable, and most certainly, unexpected.

So, why is humor used in advertising? First, humor gets your attention. It can surprise us in the first few seconds, or at the end. Humor can be woven through the entire advertisement or selectively inserted at important points. Second, humor keeps a person engaged. It can take an ordinary situation and make it entertaining, or create a fantasy situation with absurd characters and events. Third, humor is memorable. It is easier to retain in your memory, because you want to remember it. Fourth, humor is sharable. When a post, photo, or video is funny, we all like to share it. This can be done through social media, forwarding email, or just when talking to friends, family, or work associates. It is a process of both sending and receiving. Humor travels fast, and great humor can immediately go viral. Fifth, humor provides enjoyment. If you liked it, you want to see or read it again. And again. And again. Sometimes, even anticipating when the commercial could appear, or just being pleasantly surprised when it does. This repetition is very important. If the brand message has been correctly embedded in the advertisement, then the most important parts have been effectively communicated to the audience. Many advertisers believe that this moment of "feeling good" can be transferred to the brand's image. What do you think?

The biggest challenge in using humor as a creative strategy is to not let it distract from, or dilute, the brand message. This becomes more apparent during advertising pre-testing research. People frequently describe the entire story going on in a television advertisement, including many details, but then, when asked for the name of the brand, they cannot remember it. The advertiser is paying a lot of money to promote a product or service, not just entertain an audience. Laughter is a very powerful audience-engaging creative strategy, but it must still deliver measurable results.

Inspirational

When people accomplish difficult tasks, overcome challenges, or finally reach impossible goals through struggle, hard work, or perseverance, the result is inspirational to everyone. Leverage the feeling with adverting and brand messages. Publicly acknowledging these individuals is just another way to gain the respect, trust, and loyalty of customers as well as potential buyers. Those who inspire us need to be honored, and it is our duty to make certain that the news travels far and wide, especially in social media. Is this being too manipulative? Not really. This strategy is not going to work for every brand and company. But for those who match up well with the purpose and intent of this strategy, the world is ready to listen and learn.

Life style

Deep dive into the demos. Zero-in on specific categories. Read and study the personas. Take every piece of information from marketing research and use it to construct a life style advertising campaign. The formula is to reflect the activities and interests of very specific demographic, psychographic, and geographic groups. Be very specific. For example, people who are between the ages of 21 and 25 can be very different from those who are 25 to 29. Not convinced? Just look around, ask your friends, or observe people at work. The music. The movies. The games.

Study the components of their life, especially psychographics. Think like they think. Act like they would act. The life style commercial you create is the environment where your brand belongs. The strategy must resonate with their mind and mood, and overall, the brand must be perceived as an important part of their personal identity or life style. Black. White. Young. Old. Rich. Poor. LGBT or straight. And, the list goes on. Make your brand a part of their world.

Mystery

Who is that person? And, what are they doing? If there are any questions, people are motivated to keep watching and find out. Creating a mystery storytelling experience is a challenge for a 30-second television commercial. But, it can be done. And, the results can be very impressive. There are many ways to begin the mystery, such as an opening scene that is unexpected, startling, or even shocking. The plot can revolve around an individual, a location, or a situation. There can be heroes and villains, favorites and fools, champions and losers, or just regular people whom viewers can identify with, just for the moment. Just keep the secret until the end. It always works better that way. But, be sure to involve the brand. This creative strategy is about the unraveling of the story, not the name of the product. That part should never be a mystery!

Negative

There are a few situations where negative advertising strategies really work well. They are particularly effective for political advertising. Negative content creates doubt. It does not have to be true, or not true, just controversial. Negative content raises suspicions. The more times negative advertising is repeated and viewed, the greater its impact. Negative content dilutes trust. And, that is the core of its powerful influence, which is destructive and difficult to erase among voters.

Brand advertising is always held accountable for its claims and statements. It must always follow guidelines and rules that have been established by the Federal Communications Commission (FTC). This is all part of the truth-in-advertising laws, which include financial penalties and court actions to prevent and stop false advertising. In the most severe cases, companies are legally forced to pay for corrective media adverting that acknowledges any errors or misleading information. Ironically, fact-checking is required for brands but not for political campaigns.

So, what is a negative creative advertising strategy for a brand? It could be describing the many undesirable characteristics of a competitive product. It could point out a competitor's weaknesses, deficiencies, or unfavorable social media reviews. All this can create doubt, raise suspicion, and dilute trust. As you might conclude, even if the information is true, there is a delicate balance between disparagement and aggressive marketing communication.

Problem/Solution

This is a classic creative advertising strategy. It is a legendary approach used by packaged goods companies that is consistently dull but highly believable. Nothing fancy or exotic. Just introduce the problem at the beginning of the commercial and logically explain how your particular brand is the solution. It can revolve around several people discussing what has happened in a situation. Another approach is a friend or family member who is offering a solution. Or, it can be the intervention of an announcer, animated character, or fantasized individual who has the answer.

Real people

Advertising content is always full of pretty faces and beautiful people. Not anymore. Reality has finally joined the party, and visual images of what shoppers, buyers, and customers look like have changed. People relate to those individuals who look, think, and behave like them. Nothing more, and certainly, nothing less. Reality sells more than fantasy images or illusions.

Romantic

The romantic strategy has been a favorite to appeal to women, but times have changed here, too. There still are plenty of situations to use romance as a lure, but it is going to be limited by the age of the people being exposed to the advertising and their status in a family, or as a single, or couple, or any number of other possibilities. Romance is being re-defined, as well as beauty.

Sexual energy

This has been a controversial topic for many years, and only recently have advertisers and agencies got the right message. The "Me Too" movement made certain of that, as well they should. The explosive combination of sexuality and advertising has always been controversial. It is much better to use a soft sensuality that is not blatant. Or, create an advertising message that is filled with romantic imagery and subtle possibilities. The "sex-sells" needs to be immediately removed from consideration from professional marketing communication agencies and advertisers.

Shock value

Stop reading this, now! That short sentence got your attention, didn't it? Shock value is whatever you think will disrupt and disturb people from what they are doing. This is not recommended for established brands that have an image to protect and a loyal buying group to cultivate. If you're new, different, and need to cut through the clutter, this strategy is for you. A shock value strategy is frequently used by entrepreneurs who need to attract investment capital, or a brand that does not have enough money to compete with much larger competitors. Just be concise and relevant.

Slice-of-life

The most popular creative strategy on the entire list is also the most boring. Oh, yes, and most effective, too. Everyday events in your life are the primary focus with this creative strategy. This includes washing the dishes, doing your laundry, taking out the garbage, cleaning the house or apartment, and making breakfast, lunch, dinner, and all those tasty snacks without a time limit. It is very similar to the problem-solution approach, where people are having problems and brands are providing solutions. But, the difference is that a slice-of-life strategy might concentrate more on depicting the brand in regular and normal usage without any difficulty. Or, at least a little.

The slice-of-life strategy was adopted as a proven winner by companies like Proctor and Gamble, Unilever, and many other package goods manufacturers. While they didn't win creative awards for their brands, the sales and profits continually soared higher and higher.

Teaser

This creative strategy just gives you a little piece of the puzzle. Typically, it does not use the product or brand in the initial campaign. The messages are mysterious and cryptic. Why? Because the advertiser wants to arouse your curiosity! The entire idea is to get you to be thinking about what is coming soon. For example, a new way to fly into Chicago, or the ultimate online battle game, will be revealed in five days. The teaser is most often used for launching movies, promoting television shows, and most famously, for introducing new brands. What could be more appealing than wanting something that you know nothing about?

After the initial series of teaser ads, the brand messages quickly change. The tone is different, as well as the content. At this point, media strategies come into the planning. How many advertising messages are needed to sustain the brand, and which media are best to reach potential buyers? The entire spectrum of IMC options is available for market entry.

Technical

A technical approach is the perfect left-brain strategy. Just fill the entire advertisement with an abundance of data, facts, figures, chart, graphs, and information. The more the better. Make it compelling to read and logical to come to a single conclusion. With digital content, use links to even more resources, reports, and professional opinions. Even if your numbers and charts are not understood, an impression has been made that your brand has been scientifically proven.

Technical creative strategies are often essential for B2B marketing. As you might expect, the products and services are very different than in consumer categories. And, decisions are made by business managers, who are utilizing a cost-benefit analysis with competitive comparisons. These advertisements are filled with speci-fications about the brand plus information about meeting industry standards. It's difficult to be creative with these restraints, but marketing communication agen-cies have many innovative ways to present and persuade new buyers.

Testimonial

There are three categories for a testimonial strategy: real people, paid spokespeo-ple, and celebrities. Trust and believability are the highest when viewers, listen-ers, or readers recognize, and relate to, what are perceived as real people in an advertisement. They can associate with the same identity. This includes looking the same, acting the same, and responding in the same way. Paid spokespeople are professional, essentially highly skilled actors and actresses, who can deliver a written script with an extraordinary level of persuasion and enthusiasm. Even when everyone knows that they are paid to pitch a product, the results are the same. Spokespeople are worth the price when sales and profits increase. And finally, using celebrities for testimonials is an awareness-generating strategy, but risky at the same time. You know the dangers. Be cautious.

User-Generated

It's real. It's natural. It's fun. But, it can be so unpredictable. There are advertisers who like to use video content that comes from social media. Whenever the user-generated content is shared, the greater the number of viewers. This is almost like free advertising. But, there is the danger that these clever and original videos will not always present the brand image is a desirable way.

Every year, there are a few companies that promote a user-generated contest. Submit a video and win cash, prizes, and a backstage concert pass. For example, Frito-Lay sponsored a "Crash the Super Bowl" video contest, which attracted 36,000 entries. No wonder. One year, the cash prize was $1,000,000. The win-ning video was also shown during the famous American football game. This user-generated promotion for Doritos continued for more than 10 years and became part of the tradition of Super Bowl Sunday. That's a lot of crisps and Doritos for everyone to enjoy.

Format for Creative Proposal

The idea is in your mind. Now, how do you get it out? Let's briefly review each of the four basic methods for sharing, discussing, or presenting a creative concept. The formats for presenting a creative proposal are shown in Figure 6.9. These include copy and layout, storyboards, audio scripts, and wireframes. Each has a purpose used by marketing communication agencies for delivery through both legacy advertising and digital media.

Basic drawings are used for designing brand messages that will appear in a printed form, such as magazines, newspapers, brochures, and promotional materi-als. But, this method can also be applied to the development of digital content, such

Layouts	Storyboards	Scripts
Magazines & Newspapers	Television Ads	Radio Ads
Posters, Signs, Printed Material	Short Form Videos	Podcasts
Websites	Social Media	Streaming Audio

Figure 6.9 Formats for Creative Proposals

as websites or blogs. It puts the ideas in a visual format that can be easily changed or modified. Storyboards are for preparing television commercials, social media videos, or short-form films. They are even used for organizing the content for movies, live performances, and streaming programs. Audio scripts are used for making radio commercials, podcasts, and other sound-only forms of communication. And finally, wireframes are the preferred method for providing technical specifications for digital page outlines for websites and other online display media forms.

Copy and Layout

A simple drawing, sketch, or illustration is the best method for sharing and discussing creative concepts. At an advertising agency, members of the creative team quickly understand. Few explanations are needed. Their individual imagination fills in the details and explores the possibilities. Just a few stimulating words and images can immediately ignite a creative mind. It's always been that way. You would be surprised how many famous advertising campaigns began from a rough drawing on a napkin, a paper plate, or even an unused envelope.

Now, a description of the standard presentation format, copy, and layout. If you're wondering about the title, it evolved from the early days of newspaper advertising. Copy refers to the words, and layout refers to the placement of images. Headlines are short phrases located at the top of a page, and the copy, also known as body copy, is placed below. There are variations and rules. But, rules should always be broken. And, variations make everything more interesting. Today, we refer to everything as content. Words and images have transitioned to websites, social media, and mobile apps. But, the basic structure of a layout remains the same: Positioning + Content.

Storyboards

A storyboard is a simple, easy, and efficient way for organizing, visualizing, and presenting a sequential event or activity. Walt Disney Studios began using this technique in the 1930s. That's more than 90 years of planning and producing cartoons, movies, video games, and television programs. The purpose of a storyboard is to illustrate what will happen, how it will happen, when it will happen, and who will be involved. Basically, it illustrates a complete story.

Storyboards are traditionally printed on white paper with a series of rectangular boxes called frames. Inside each frame are drawings, sketches, images, photographs, or illustrations. They can be in a pen and ink format (black and white) or multiple colors. Along with each frame is a smaller box that is used for including the exact words that will be used during that part of the commercial. Information about music, special effects, or even camera instructions can also be placed in the box. This provides a complete description of the flow and audio content of the video commercial.

There can be 6, 8, or even 12 frames in a storyboard. The number of frames depends on the complexity of the creative material or the type of media involved. For example, a television commercial can be illustrated in 10 frames or fewer, while a full-length movie might need several hundred frames. Ask your instructor for a sample storyboard or find a blank template online.

Paper storyboards are still used today, because they are inexpensive, informal, and an excellent way to present a visual narrative. But, the shift today has been to digital replication, animation, and other forms of visual narratives. This involves everything from "drag and drop" templates to sample videos made on a smartphone. First, storyboard templates. There are software packages that enable anyone to effortlessly create a professional-looking storyboard using "drag and drop" technology. What makes this possible is the abundance of royalty-free images and videos. In addition, some packages provide you with the ability to insert music tracks, sound effects, and animated titles. The best example of this technology can be found at www.animoto.com.

Here's a secret. If you don't want to spend the money on these software packages, then use your PowerPoint for the same purpose. Just go online, download the most relevant images, and include them in your slides. Finally, to make your presentation go more smoothly, use the built-in timer to automatically advance each frame of your PowerPoint storyboard. It's fast, efficient, practical, and easy to make any required creative adjustments.

And now, let's discuss cellphone videos. People do this every day and post them on Instagram, Facebook, or even TikTok. But, the purpose of an advertising video is different. You are not trying to entertain everyone but rather, to demonstrate an important aspect of the creative concept or strategy. So, the storyboard format is replaced with a video sequence that has a beginning, middle, and ending. These videos are not finished products but another method to visualize a storyline that involves people, places, situations, problems, and experiences, and most importantly, to incorporate the value proposition and user benefits of a particular brand.

Audio Scripts

If you're presenting ideas for a radio commercial, digital podcast, or any other form of audio communication, then you need a script. Sounds simple, but there is a hidden challenge. Writing is not the same as speaking, and listening is not the same as talking. Prove it to yourself. Just look at voice-to-text translation of a message on your cellphone. Did it make sense? Or better yet, record a message using text-to-voice technology. Then, analyze what happened. You will discover that whenever we are speaking to others, the phrases become shorter, sentences are incomplete, or there are frequent pauses. Sometimes, we even use words or phrases that are simply awkward.

No matter how fast or slowly you speak, the average number of words will be about 120. Use this as your base number of words. If you have too many words in a script, then the announcer or actors will have to speak faster. This is a big risk for listener comprehension. But, there is a way. Just keep the words simple and sentences short. Don't try to say everything. It is more effective to focus on the communication of a single, well-defined idea. Let that be your best guide.

The basic format for an audio script is a single-page document. It is divided into two sides. The left side identifies the people who will be speaking, while the right side contains the content. Be sure to capitalize the left side of the page. This is a visual aid to quickly identify who is speaking during the recording session. The words for a script are located on the right side of the paper in lower case letters. Quotations are used. And, double space everything to make it easier to read.

Here is a short example for a 30-second radio commercial:

JOHN: "Did you see the soccer game last night?"
MARK: "No, I missed it. But, I saw the replay of the winning goal."
JOHN: "It was fantastic! I was really surprised."
MARK: "So was the losing team."

Sound effects, music, and even silence can also be part of a radio commercial. Since people have to use their imagination to listen to a radio commercial, it is important to help them by inserting relevant sounds, noises, and audio back-grounds. This can include anything from a thunderstorm to the crowd cheering at that soccer game. Use the abbreviation "SFX" and put it on the left side of the page with the description of the sounds on the right side. For music, first select the genre that is most appropriate for the creative idea as well as appealing to the target audience. Next, capitalize MUSIC and place it on the left side with the description of the genre. And finally, indicate the volume level, speed, and other aspects involving the musicians or performers.

That's it. Now, you have a script. The next step is recording the commercial. That's when you need an advertising agency or production company to complete the process. Every aspect of the commercial must be executed correctly. It takes longer than you think and can become very complicated. The biggest challenge is to remain within the required media time limits of either 60 (:60) or 30 (:30) seconds. The average person talks at the rate of 115 to 135 words per minute. That means about two words per second. Not much time to deliver a brand message, but you always can. And finally, before the entire recording session is finished, everything has to be approved by the advertising agency, the production company, and the client.

Wireframes

Since this textbook is not going to describe the details of developing a brand website, the most important thing to remember is that a basic visual layout of a home page that includes images, copy, embedded videos, and navigational links is sufficient for advertising management. The codes that must the written and their precise positioning can be completed by technology experts. The only caveat is that the process often takes much longer than expected and involves a level of complexity reserved for trained personnel. Be careful of making too many unnecessary changes, because the price will only go up and further delay the completion.

Evaluating Creative Presentations

Agency Perspective

The agency created it. They proposed it. But, they want the advertiser to accept it. The advertiser has already provided the agency with information about the company, brand, marketing strategies, IMC budgets, competitors, and buyer profiles. And, the agency has done its best to come up with the best creative concepts, media implementation plan, and promotional programs.

Now, the moment of truth has come. The account executive, along with several other agency team members, will make a presentation and request an approval. If the advertiser agrees with their recommendations, then the agency can begin immediately to implement the IMC Plan. If the plan is not approved, then changes must be made according to the advertiser's instructions and requirements. Obviously, more time and money will be needed. But, who pays for these modifications?

Agencies' expenses are determined by multiple compensation systems, but the majority are based on a fixed price per hour worked. The number of people involved, complexity of the task, and hours associated with preparing and implementing marketing communications will determine the total fee paid to the agency. In many situations, agencies charge a different hourly rate for working on a creative assignment compared with a media assignment, or variable rates based on experience level or position at the agency. For example, account executive versus assistant account executive, or junior versus senior art director. And finally, agency rates will definitely vary if their people are working on an advertising campaign, a social media program, a promotional activity, or a public relations event.

Since agencies have contracts with advertisers, the compensation methods and procedures are well defined. But, there are situations where the advertiser disagrees with the creative content presented by the agency. The question of who is to blame often shifts from an advertiser's reluctance to accept the proposal toward the agency's interpretation of a communication plan. The solution is to maintain a continual collaborative relationship between agency and advertiser.

Advertiser's Reaction

The advertising manager is responsible for making the final decision involving the agency recommendations. However, there are other individuals who participate in the approval process. At larger companies, the marketing manager, sales manager, or Vice-President of Marketing will provide input and comments about the agency's work. There also could be separate departments for advertising, promotion, and public relations with their own managers. The process is much easier in smaller companies, where the final decision-maker is always the owner.

There are a few other voices from the marketing department that might also express their views about an agency's recommendations. In some industries, a very selective group of important dealers or distributors are invited to review the proposal. This is done internally and informally without the agency. The reactions and opinions are only advisory. Another vocal group is the company's sales organization. These are the people who have daily contact with customers. The assumption is that salespeople have an excellent relationship with people who buy their products and services. That is correct, but since they are not advertising experts, any responses should be used as input and not a mandate for changing individual aspects of the plan or IMC strategies.

Opinions are not facts. That's why marketing communication experts frequently use multiple forms of testing. This doesn't eliminate the risk of making incorrect, or ineffective, decisions; it only provides advertisers with information to make better judgments and improvements. This type of research includes copy pre-testing, focus groups, and most frequently, online comparison of two different versions (changes in copy or images) of digital advertising concepts.

The advertiser, not the agency, makes the final decision. While the agency has the creative and media expertise, the advertiser has the money. While a favorable performance is expected from advertising, sales promotion, and public relationship activities, marketing success is never guaranteed. The results depend on decisions made by advertisers, agencies, and suppliers.

The purpose of IMC is to deliver a single unified message about the brand. There can be no deviations or exceptions. The advertising, digital content, sales promotion, and public relations must be synchronized, coordinated, and controlled. It is the agency's responsibility to manage these functions but the client's obligation to monitor the entire process. If this partnership is successful, the communication will be clear, consistent, and effective.

Summary

Creativity is not a mysterious phenomenon but a cognitive process and ability that everyone possesses. While there are individuals who are more proficient than others, the opportunity to improve and practice is always available. Understanding the difference between the right-brain and left-brain functions, combined with a knowledge of the behavioral characteristics that enhance creativity, is the foundation for cognitive growth, imagination, and innovative thinking.

Advertising and marketing communication agencies follow a set of procedures for developing brand messages, which include the preparation of a brand brief, buyer persona, and insights from marketing research reports. This leads to the generation of creative ideas that are expressed using different creative strategies and storytelling frameworks. Finally, the creative concepts using storyboards, scripts, layouts, and wireframes are presented to an advertiser for approval before proceeding to their implementation. This results in the brand messages for pathway distribution.

Discussion Questions

1. Why is creativity so important for advertising and marketing communication?
2. Evaluate your own creativity. Rate yourself on a scale of 1 to 10.
3. Which of the personality traits do you believe are the most essential for being more creative?
4. What information is typically included in a brand brief? Who needs to use this document?
5. Is humor always an effective creative approach? What are its advantages and disadvantages?
6. Which types of products are best for demonstrations or competitive comparisons?
7. Who is better for promoting a new brand of shampoo: a sports figure or a movie star?
8. How effective is the problem/solution approach for getting a potential buyer's attention?
9. What kind of information is contained in a storyboard for a video or television commercial?
10. Who has the final authority to approve creative concepts and implement IMC programs?

Chapter Assignments

1. Develop a brand persona
   Try to understand the psychology of a brand purchaser by describing their life style and attitudes.
2. Design a magazine advertisement
   Can't draw? No problem. Use PowerPoint to insert uploaded images and insert headline and copy.
3. Create a brand website
   No coding required. Use PowerPoint again. Layout graphics to appear on a computer or phone.
4. Record a radio commercial
   Radio is a great local medium. Learn how to use it by writing a script. Then, read and record it.
5. Make a video commercial
   Complete a simple storyboard based on the slice-of-life strategy for a product found in the kitchen.

Continuity Case Study

Everyone at the company agreed with the brand brief but not with the agency's creative ideas. They presented a very funny video commercial that involved an exaggerated "Greek wedding" but did not use the Athena name until the last few seconds. Tony–was excited about using the video as part of a social media campaign and thought that it might become a viral sensation. He explained that this was a very cost-efficient media strategy, because Athena would avoid the high prices for traditional television advertising. But, Adriana was not convinced, and neither was Martin. They both felt it was too risky, because even if people laughed and enjoyed the commercial, it did not do anything to help brand name awareness. As a result, the storyboard was rejected, and the agency had to come up with a new approach. This also included using television and not social media.

Later that week, Adriana called Jeanette, who was a communications consultant. She suggested that the agency create a few theme lines that were memorable and could easily be adapted across different media. Adriana requested the agency to come up with several concepts, and within a few days, the agency came up with two excellent theme lines: "Athena—Not Just a Meal, but a Greek Experience!" and "When You Dine In with Us, You Go Out On a Holiday." Adriana liked them both but could not decide which one was the most appropriate and effective for Athena.

1. In your opinion, what is the best creative strategy for the Athena brand?
2. Why was Adriana so reluctant to approve a social video commercial?
3. Which theme line will be most appealing to the target audience? Why?
4. Did the agency make a mistake by not presenting more creative concepts?
5. How can these themes be used in other IMC activities, such as promotions?

IMC Plan Development

Step One:
   Develop a consumer persona that reflects your primary target audience and their life style.
Step Two:
   Write a brand brief with the value proposition of your brand and relevant marketing information.
Step Three:
   Select a storytelling framework that complements your creative strategies and brand positioning.
Step Four:
   Prepare a creative concept presentation that includes multiple pathways and digital platforms.
Step Five:
   Implement your brand message with a layout for a magazine ad and a storyboard for television.

Chapter 7

Digital Media Strategies

Owned and Shared Pathways for Delivering Brand Content

Learning Objectives

1. Understand the differences and characteristics of paid, owned, and shared media
2. Recognize the multiple relationships between online search and increased website traffic
3. Know how to place advertisements on social media and other online media platforms
4. Establish a business profile on LinkedIn for networking, promotions, and job searches
5. Utilize streaming video for brand messages that generate awareness, interest, and action

Introduction

There is a complex relationship between digital media and legacy media. That is why this chapter focuses only on digital media marketing, while the following chapter concentrates on legacy media. The purpose here is to review the categories of digital media and introduce the process of advertising on specific platforms, such as social media. This will be presented in the context of Integrated Marketing Communication (IMC) and its utilization for creating and delivering brand messages. Since there are more specialized courses and programs involving website design, search engine optimization, email marketing, and social media,

DOI: 10.4324/9780367443382-7

this textbook will only provide a framework for coordinating a combination of digital and legacy media programs.

Digital Media Pathways

Digital media are a complex collection of many different technologies. While they are independent, there is also a very powerful interactive relationship among each and every one of them. So, what is included in the list of digital media categories? In Figure 7.1, there are 12 digital media categories that will be discussed in greater detail: mobile apps, brand websites, search engine optimization, social media, business networking, electronic print, email marketing, streaming video, entertainment gaming, consumer-generated content, influencer marketing, and retargeting platforms. It is important to remember that digital media are a major component of the attribution model, which theoretically identifies and tracks the movement of existing customers and potential buyers as they progress through their journey of discovery.

Each category of digital media has its own unique properties and functions, but all are seamlessly connected through the Internet. Since digital content is compatible with nearly every viewing device, from desktops and laptops to tablets and portable displays, IMC planning has a multitude of options to reach customers and potential buyers. And now, mobile apps make it even easier to view, access, and share information, photos, and videos between individuals, friends, associates, or nearly anyone else with an online capability. But, the real advantage of digital media is the opportunity for response and interaction, something that was impossible with traditional media.

The most important aspect to remember is that every brand message must be consistent, not just for advertising and promotion, but for every form of traditional, as well as digital, media. This is the eternal mantra of IMC, which includes every aspect of traditional advertising, digital media, and personal contact from creative messages to delivery.

Figure 7.1 Digital Media Pathways

Paid, Owned, and Shared Media

There are other ways to categorize media based on their functional purpose. For example, digital marketing agencies in the United States frequently refer to the concept of paid, owned, and shared media. While there is very little consistency with industry definitions, this classification method is used as part of their planning process. The simplicity is helpful to clients but can lead to confusion and misunderstanding of the various options and their impact on communication.

Paid media include any persuasive message or purposeful statement, such as advertising, that involves the payment of money to a third party for the right to display, incorporate, or distribute content online. This includes both digital and legacy media. The amount paid to a media company for the right to deliver a brand message, visual image, text copy, or video could be fixed or negotiable. Let's look at legacy media. Typically, magazine and newspaper advertising has a fixed price list, which is also called a rate card. These two media delivery options offer discounts for the volume of advertising during a specific time period or an annual contract. There is also a cost menu for extra requests, such as preferred position in the publication or special features. However, television and radio are negotiable, because there is a very limited supply, and the demand always determines the price. The most popular shows have the highest prices because the audiences are larger or they deliver a target audience that is desired by advertisers for their brand category profile. Outdoor advertising has a fixed price structure with discounts based on the number of locations, geographic coverage, and contract terms for an extended period of time.

Digital media are more complex because they involve the process of establishing daily budgets for advertising. This money is spent for advertising on social media. While the policies and procedures for each social media platform are different, the basic requirements for implementing advertising campaigns are very similar. Although this process will be explained later in the chapter, the amount of social media advertising is always related to the number of people who can be reached but filtered by specific demographic or behavioral characteristics.

Owned media are defined as any form of proprietary content that is original, exclusive, and completely controlled by the company or organization that has published this material online.

Websites are the primary form of owned media. Short-form videos that are designed and displayed for entertainment purposes are also considered as owned media. Digital publications created by an advertiser or company can also be identified as a form of owned media.

Shared media comprise any method of online communication based on open access and unrestricted posting of text messages, images, or videos through a digital distribution platform. The problem with this categorization is the potential overlap across different forms of media. It can be very confusing, with various sub-sections, such as websites and YouTube channels, as owned media. While the use of paid, owned, and shared media remains a convenient phrase to use in marketing discussions, it is a simplistic and generalized way to separate brand message delivery options. There are too many details and complexities involved, especially with digital media.

Consumer-Generated Content

Until the Digital Age, the possibility that individuals with little, if any, experience with advertising, marketing, or communication would be flooding the media channels with products of their own creation was simply unimaginable. But, the Internet provided the method, motive, and technology to accomplish that impossible dream. As smartphones replaced traditional cameras, the ability to generate video expanded exponentially, and then beyond. There was apparently no limit to the amount of self-made content propelled relentlessly into the online world. Why was it so effective? Did it really have that amount of attention-grabbing power and influence? The answer is definitely yes, because everyone likes to experience another person's story, from the plain to the exotic and from the happy to the sad. It's a reflection of their own life.

Where does all this new content go? Why does it continue to grow? Basically, it is the never-ending fuel for social media, with posts, tweets, and sharing anything and everything. It does not matter which platform is being used; the audiences find their way to whatever is trending. And when you inject the phenomenon of famous celebrity or global personality, the numbers soar. That's why it is so attractive for marketing communication. The ability to generate a sizable audience that is equal to, or greater than, that of a television program is an amazingly effective way for companies to connect with existing customers and potential buyers.

There are two strategies for brands to leverage consumer-generated content. The first strategy is actively participating in the process by posting text, images, and videos. But, is this perceived to be authentic communication or excessive and intrusive commercialization? The second way is to provide a brand message within the framework of social media through the process of paid advertising. If this is subtle and blends into the communication environment, then it can be highly effective. At this point, the only thing that matters is not the quality of the consumer-generated content but the size of the audience. The larger the numbers, the greater the value.

Understanding the Media Spectrum

What are the connections among the multiple forms of digital and legacy media? How do they contribute individually, and collectively, to building a brand image in the mind of a potential customer? Why is omnichannel marketing so complex and involved? How much money is needed to build an effective social media campaign? Which measurements should be used to evaluate digital media marketing? Why is this related to the attribution model as well as the sales funnel and the AIDA (awareness, interest, desire, action) model? Should an advertiser develop an IMC plan based only on digital media? There are just some of the topics and issues that will be included in this chapter. Let's begin by examining the entire media spectrum from several different perspectives involving the advertiser, agency, and ultimately, the consumer.

Web-Centric Marketing

The word "media" is always associated with digital marketing. But, that is only half of the media equation. There is a category of advertising that has budgets much larger than those of digital media. This is legacy, or traditional, advertising, which includes television, radio, magazines, newspapers, and outdoor. Before

Figure 7.2 Web-Centric Marketing

digital, this was the only form of advertising media. Legacy advertising still exists, but it is being transformed into hybrid media. For example, if you go to the website of your local television station, there will be banner ads on the page along with pop-ups and display advertising along the side. There might also be paid content along with video commercials for branded products and services. This is a new revenue source for television stations, which maintain broadcasting signals through transmission towers or cable systems.

Today, there are three parts to the media spectrum for IMC: legacy, traditional, and hybrid. In this chapter, digital media will be discussed and explored, including hybrid media. Since there are numerous courses and webinars on digital marketing, this textbook will only focus on the most essential elements and provide an overview of the options and strategies. In the next chapter, legacy media will be described, along with the terminology required to analyze, purchase, and measure advertising in those media forms.

It is more extensive because very few textbooks cover this information in detail. However, knowledge of legacy media, especially for television and radio advertising in local markets, is needed for small business, non-profit organizations, and entrepreneurs. As you will learn, both digital and legacy media require a substantial amount of basic mathematical calculation.

So, what is web-centric marketing? The conceptualization in Figure 7.2 indicates that the most powerful and important digital media activities are focused on driving visitor traffic to a brand website. This includes all activities involving social media, mobile apps, online search, and supplemental programs, such as affiliate marketing. The result is reflected in the sales funnel, which as you have learned, is also called the marketing funnel. Digital marketing strategies always emphasize increasing the number of people entering the top of the funnel with other programs and activities, such as sales promotion offers and financial incentives, designed to move them down into the middle and eventually, the bottom of the funnel. It is all about websites.

Omnichannel Media

Here is another word that is frequently used but confusing. Originally, a channel referred to the signal frequency of a television, with numbers going up from 2 to 13, called VHF or Very High Frequency, to channels with numbers from 14 to

51, called UHF or Ultra High Frequency. While this lasted for many years, the growth and expansion of cable television changed all that. With cable, the number of channels has grown to hundreds and even thousands. And finally, the introduction of digital technology enabled the possibility of an unlimited number of viewing options. So, it was possible to have millions of potential channels based on upload content.

YouTube still maintains the word "channel," reflecting the reality of digital media. But, many marketing communication companies use the word "channel" to refer to social media platforms, email marketing, and even blogs as online channels. It appears that absolutely every possible pathway to reach a customer or potential buyer involves some form of communication or channel. In Chapter 1, the concept of pathways was applied to the connections between media and consumers, which is actually a reflection of the common reference to a channel. Thus, the inclusion of an omnichannel approach is identical to every type of marketing communication.

Television Delivery Systems

There are other transformations in the linguistics of media, such as television. Once considered the ultimate method of mass marketing, capable of reaching millions of people with a single message that was distributed simultaneously, the meaning of the word "television" became blurred with the appearance of new distribution methods. For example, there are four different physical ways to transmit a video program to a viewer. The first is broadcast television, which is the traditional way of using a high-energy signal from a tall tower or building that can be received by any type of home television equipment. The second is a more recent method, cable television, which is based on direct fiber optic wires connecting through a router in homes, apartment buildings, or other structures. The third is satellite distribution, which is based on signals that travel up to orbiting satellites, continuously uplinking and downlinking content. And, the fourth and most recent delivery system, digital media, operates through the Internet in an interconnected global network using browsers and software protocols.

What about the grey distinction between video and live? We can enjoy streaming video on the Internet or communicate with people live in real time through social platforms. Plus, there are new forms of television, called connected television, interactive television, and over the top television. These are basically other ways to describe delivery of content through high-speed Internet connections rather than cable or satellite. This process avoids the complex price bundling strategies that have been used by local service providers, prompting the popular description of "cable cutting" as a method of selecting another delivery system. Direct digital transmission enables anyone to get content, such as Netflix, HBO, or Amazon Prime, directly from their computer or smartphone.

Mobile Apps

In 2020, an estimated 1,800,000 mobile apps were available for download from the Apple App store. That includes many different possibilities, including plenty of exciting options for entertainment, communication, information, education, and hundreds of thousands of brands apps. These apps are an essential link between consumers and companies. They provide the connection pathway from buyers to brands, and as discussed in Chapter 1, they also represent a new frontier of electronic commerce using seamless voice selection, payment, and delivery for nearly every product or service imaginable. As the current trend continues to shift the amount of online search activity from desktops and laptops to mobile devices, mobile apps will only become stronger and more powerful in both the frequency of usage and volume of operation.

The value of a mobile app is the instant connection to a brand website. It is also an essential accessway to social media, which in turn, can drive more traffic toward a brand website. The combination provides a flow of targeted and interested audiences into the top of the sales or purchase funnel. From there, sales promotion techniques can be used as financial motivation forces to stimulate a call to action and evoke an immediate response. Hopefully, this will result in a purchase, or if not, it will be a contributing factor in the attribution model that was explained in Chapter 2 of this textbook. As you remember, there are always multiple influencers and factors that impact a purchase decision, and it is nearly impossible to identify all of them.

Advertising Costs in Digital Media

Before we begin to go deeper and explore the various forms of digital media, it is important to introduce three essential concepts: the audience/pricing model, cost-per-thousand (CPM), and advertising impression. The audience/pricing model is used for media planning for both legacy and digital media. The model provides an estimation of the amount of advertising that can be purchased with a specific budget by comparing the size of the audience with the cost required to purchase a fixed amount. CPM is a concept that is based on media buying efficiency. This uses a mathematical calculation to determine what price must be paid to obtain units, comprised of 1000 individuals, within a pre-determined target audience. Advertising impression is defined as a measurement of the total weight of a media campaign. This enables advertisers to aggregate the exposure value of every type of digital and legacy media.

Audience/Price Relationship Model

The price of media is directly proportional to the number of people reached by that media type. This is true for both legacy and digital media. This is called the cost of advertising model. However, the relationship can be described in many ways. It is defined as a linear relationship with a one-to-one ratio, which means that when one variable increases, the other increases at an equal or similar rate. It is also referred to as a direct or proportionate relationship. Since media prices and audience sizes are always proportionate, any increase or decrease in one of the variables will automatically change the other variable. Here is an example of how a cost of advertising model works, as shown in Figure 7.3. Notice that when the size of the audience doubles on the horizontal axis, the price of the advertising doubles on the vertical axis. Or if the audience size is decreased by one-third on

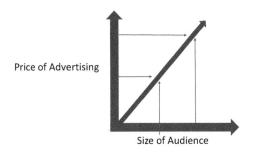

Price of Advertising

Size of Audience

Figure 7.3 Audience/Price Relationship Model

---

the horizontal axis, the price of the advertising is also reduced by one-third on the vertical axis. Why is this model needed? It is used to quickly estimate costs and determine what is needed to achieve specific audience size objectives. Thus, everyone can determine exactly how much advertising can be purchased with a fixed or limited budget.

Does the legacy media category make any difference? No. The price/audience relationship is the same for every form and sub-category of television, radio, magazine, newspaper, and outdoor media. Digital media follow the same pattern. The prices for advertising on social media go up as the audience size increases. It does not matter if the messages are delivered through Facebook, Instagram, or YouTube. Prices and the size of the audience are always directly related, which means that the cost of advertising can be determined in advance based on the number of people that an advertiser wants to reach. Remember the importance of prioritizing demographic profiles for a product or service and distinguishing between primary and secondary target audiences? This is where you apply these important concepts. Later in this textbook, you will learn how to evaluate media based on the percentage of a target audience within the total number of people who are viewing, listening to, or reading a specific legacy media publication or program.

Cost-Per-Thousand

The concept of CPM provides advertisers and agencies with a method to determine the relative efficiency of individual media. It is used to evaluate choices between and among individual media delivery options. While the CPM calculation is primarily used in legacy media, the same concept is used to purchase advertising in every form of digital media.

OK, so why isn't it called CPT? That would make sense, but unless you majored in Latin in high school or regularly watch *Who Wants to Be a Millionaire* on television, the fact that the Roman numeral for 1000 is "M" could easily elude you. But now, this is the most important part of speaking the language of media. Whenever you are buying advertising on television or social media, you will need to know how to calculate or use the formula shown in Figure 7.4.

The formula for calculating cost-per-thousand is quite simple: CPM = cost ÷ delivery.

Figure 7.4 Calculating Cost-Per-Thousand

This is the basic unit of comparison for every form of advertising media. The cost is defined as the price of the media, or what is paid to have the right to display a brand message. The delivery is defined as the number of people who are exposed to the advertising messages. But, the word "exposed" does not guarantee any change in awareness, interest, or attitude. It is only an opportunity to read, see, or listen to a brand message. Nothing more, but a measurable number. Here is another way to understand this concept. The basic component of the CPM calculation is a theoretical package of 1000 people. Therefore, the first thing to do is always divide the number of people who are exposed to an advertisement by 1000. The result is one "package" or the "M" component of CPM. The bottom line is that a CPM is used to compare the relative efficiency of individual media options to reach a desired target audience through a specific media vehicle.

Here is how you use the CPM concept in media planning. If all the packages of people are identical, then you begin to purchase them at the lowest price per package. This is the most efficient way to save money on the same commodity. For example, if you were buying cans of Red Bull at a local grocery store, and you needed to buy 150 cans for a party but were running out of money, where would you go first? Store #1 is selling Red Bull for $1.79, store #2 is offering the same product for $1.99, and Store #3 has it for $1.59. Obviously, you start buying cans at Store #3, the least expensive purchase price per unit, until there is no more Red Bull left to buy. Perhaps, you were able to buy 100 cans, but now you have to go to Store #1, the next lowest price. If you could only get another 35 cans, then you would have to end up at Store #2, which has the highest price per can. Eventually, the required 150 cans of Red Bull are purchased but with several different prices. The product is the same, but the cost to purchase varied.

Here is a more complex example that involves legacy media. If a magazine charges $1500 for a full page of advertising, and the total number of people who receive the magazine is 150,000 (or 150 units of 1000), then the CPM is $10.00 ($1500 ÷ 150 units). The cost has been divided by the delivery, which in this case is the audience. A quick and easy way to verify the accuracy of a CPM calculation is to take the original CPM number and then multiply it by the number of "packages" of 1000 people. This will immediately confirm that the advertising cost is correct. In the previous magazine calculation, a $10 CPM times 150 packages of 1000 people is $1500 ($10 × 150 = $1500). As a general rule, the CPM for mass media vehicles will range from $10 to $25 per thousand for television or radio, while for more selective media for highly specialized target audiences, such as doctors or company CEOs, the CPM might be $65 to $85.

Finally, legacy media use CPMs to compare the relative buying efficiency to reach a pre-determined target audience. It is a balance of the size of the audience versus the actual price charged for an advertising unit. Low costs might reflect smaller audiences, but most likely, there will be higher CPMs. The objective is to match the demographic profile of a specific media type with the demographic profile of a brand. Thus, success is measured by building large audiences, which satisfies this matching requirement, but achieving the maximum audience size with a low CPM.

Impressions

The media definition of an impression is the "opportunity for a reader, viewer, or listener to be exposed to an advertising message." This is the same for legacy media as well as digital. But, there is an important distinction for every form of media communication. An opportunity for exposure does not mean that the person paid attention to the message or engaged with the content. It simply indicates the "opportunity." Is this bad? No, the purpose is to provide a standardized and universal way to estimate the amount of advertising that is received based on the money that will be or has been spent. This allows comparisons within similar media categories as well as the aggregation of brand messages across the entire media spectrum.

Impressions are both a planning tool and a measurement. As a planning method, impressions can be directed at a targeted audience, which can be indicated as a media objective. As a digital or legacy measurement, impressions indicate the amount of advertising weight, or volume, that has been actually delivered. While there are many variations and exceptions, impressions still remain one of the most important concepts in media planning.

There is a simple formula for calculating gross impressions. Figure 7.5 shows the method to multiply the number of advertisements by the size of the audience that is exposed each time the advertisement appears. This is the same for both legacy and digital media. For example, if a magazine has 500,000 subscriptions or readers, then that is the size of the audience. And if 5 ads appear in the publication, then using the formula for gross impressions yields 2,500,000.

A similar example for digital media could involve website visits per day or the number of display advertisements appearing on Instagram for a specific brand. Using the formula, the number of gross impressions would be the audience size, which is the total number of website views per day, but the calculation for Instagram might involve 3 separate advertisements during the day with an

Figure 7.5 Formula for Gross Impressions

average of 2,000,000 people who viewed the brand message, which is 6,000,000 impressions.

What gets complicated and confusing is that each individual viewing of a magazine or social media advertisement represents an impression. But, the same person could account for 3, 5, or even 10 viewings of the same advertisement during the day. They are all counted as impressions because they are an opportunity for exposure to a brand message. That is why the word "gross" is used to identify them. There is duplication with multiple exposures. Fortunately, there are other methods to calculate a net unduplicated audience, such as unique visitors, using website metrics.

Brand Websites

How many different websites do you visit in a week? Or, a month or a year? Some are dramatic and keep your attention, while others engage and encourage you to explore other pages. What makes a website attractive? And, why are brand websites such an effective strategy for IMC? These are difficult questions to answer because the evaluation of websites is a subjective experience influenced by many personal characteristics.

This section will briefly review several of the most important dimensions of brand websites, as shown in Figure 7.6, which is a checklist for the requirements involving visual page design, navigation strategies or functionality, relevant content, and digital analytics. Along with these important dimensions, there are also search optimization, remarketing potential, and real-time measurements. It is essential to remember that websites must be developed based on marketing objectives and strategies as well as communication objectives and strategies. Although both marketing and communication plans are coordinated and aligned to achieve the same ultimate goals, each has a different focus and emphasis. Marketing is customer-oriented, but focuses on sales, profits, and market share, while communication emphasizes involvement, engagement, and interaction between brands and customers, prospects, or potential buyers.

Landing Page

Visitors to a website often arrive at a landing page before being connected to the homepage of a brand website. After concluding an online search, you might click on a link that takes you there. Ironically, there is only one page on this website, called

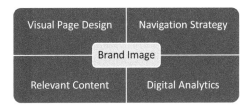

Figure 7.6 Website Development Checklist

a landing page. The entire purpose is to encourage visitors to take immediate action to purchase a product or service. It is not the homepage of the actual brand website. It is only a call-to-action page location. But, how did you get there? Most likely, you were directed there through advertisements placed in any one of the social media platforms, including Facebook, Instagram, or Twitter. Or, you might have clicked on a link embedded in an email message. And, there are many Google and Bing ads everywhere that subtly guide you to a landing page. Remember, this page has only one purpose, and that is to sell. As a result, everything involving the visual design will be more concise and simplistic with fewer graphics, words, and possible action. It's all taking the bait, as a fish does in the water.

Remember the marketing funnel and the three levels: top of funnel, middle of funnel, and bottom of the funnel? The landing page represents the top of the funnel, the conceptual location where people interested in a brand arrive to find out more. But, the landing page is designed to focus on persuasion. So, there won't be a lot of options for the visitor. What does appear is a very positive story about the benefits of the brand and reasons for buying the product or service, including social proof, such as testimonials from satisfied customers, video clips, or detailed case studies.

As for navigation, there is a link to the actual brand website, but the atmosphere of the landing page encourages visitors to remain there or continue into a link that requires a purchase action.

Home Page

What are your favorite brand websites? And, what makes them special? There are plenty of differences among brand websites. Here are three common characteristics that are frequently associated with a superior website: simplicity of design, clarity of message, and ease of navigation. The best advice is never to put too much information on the home page. That is because a first-time visitor will not spend a lot of time there if the website appears too cluttered or disorganized. It must be visually attractive and have relevant content, or the visitor will be quickly shifting to another online location. This aspect becomes more important when you consider that a customer or individual doing a search will be comparing different brands.

Simplicity of design also means a very limited or moderate number of images, words, and information. This is a minimalist approach, which is intended to engage a visitor without confusion or excessive content. While there is always room for more elements, it is often unnecessary and counterproductive to fill up the entire page. White space, the small sections of the website without images or words, makes a viewer's eyes quickly move around the entire page, scanning and noticing different elements. This motion allows a viewer to pay more attention to both visual and verbal messages. Images must be correctly proportioned and harmonious with other elements on the page. There is no set rule for this, only experience and personal judgment. Everything on the homepage should be not too large, and not too small, but just right. Clarity of content includes the length of sentences, choice of words, and brevity of expression. Paragraphs should be short and kept to only a few sentences, at most. The style of writing should be concise and very similar to the communication of magazine advertisements both visually and verbally.

Visual Design

In business or life, you only get one chance to make a good first impression. For example, when a new person is introduced to you at a social gathering, entertainment event, or business function, you make an immediate decision about how the person looks, talks, acts, and behaves. This most likely occurs in the first 10 seconds, or less, and continues for the duration of the introduction. Just think about how quickly you formed a first impression about that individual. The same is true for a brand website, but it probably took even less time. If you didn't like it, you closed the page and moved to another website. Just a click of the mouse and the website is gone!

The initial impact of a visual design is highly relevant for building a brand website. What factors influence its appearance? There are many different design elements, including colors, type styles, images, physical sizes, balance, and the overall proportions in a digital format. When website designers are thinking about all these elements, it does not involve their personal tastes or attitudes but rather, the mind and mood of the consumer or client. Their challenge is to design a website that appeals to the target audience or specific persona associated with a particular brand. As you will recall from earlier chapters, the demographic, geographic, psychographic, and product usage characteristics must guide all forms of communication in marketing and digital media. As a result, the colors, type styles, images, physical sizes, balance, and overall proportion of brand website must reflect the persona of the target audience to maximize the visual impact.

Interior Pages

How many pages are needed on a brand website? Well, there is no exact answer. It all depends on the product or service, as well as the marketing strategy. There are many variables involved, including the number of variations of the brand, such as differences in package size, colors, features, and other characteristics. Many websites resemble catalogs or showrooms with absolutely everything available to view in a single place. This is necessary if a market basket page is being used for purchasing check-out. But, other websites will display the variety of products being offered and then direct visitors to retail locations. In these situations, prices are never shown, because the website is owned by the manufacturer, who wants to stimulate awareness of their brand. There is another way to answer the question of how many pages are needed. Cost. Each page adds more expense to the website development as well as the amount of time required. So, the economics of the project and budget can shape its design even more than a marketing need.

Navigation

Easy of navigation is finding what you need and getting to where you want to go—fast, and without complications. This depends on several important factors: the menu tabs, the linked pages, and the ability to go back and forth without losing the connection to the brand website. Menu tabs must always be easy to read, understandable, and helpful. Since they are the quickest route to get to other pages, menu tabs have to be well organized, well labeled, and accurate. The linked pages should have the information promised as well as more options for expanded content. And finally, the "back" button has to be large, visible, and located in a user-friendly place, based on where the button is needed and not where a web designer always wants to put it.

Navigation is all about making it as effortless as possible. When using a website takes too long, visitors will spontaneously decide to stop and immediately leave the site. The amount of time might be only seconds, so brands must be sure that the functionality operates at a high speed.

Dashboard Metrics

This is the epicenter of digital marketing. It is the hub, the source, and the best location for brand information. Even though social media platforms, such as Facebook pages, are being used more frequently to communicate with customers, a brand website is the place where people can learn the most about a company, its philosophy, and its brands. It does not change often but truly projects the image and personality of its creators. So as digital media evolve and expand, the brand website will also change and adapt to new communication environments. There are many different digital media analytics and metrics available on most digital media platforms, but the ones that most people used to evaluate the flow of traffic and engagement activity are listed in Figure 7.7. These include unique visitors, page views, time on page, and the click-through rate. The complexity of website analytics and online measurement will be left to more specialized textbooks and instructions involving digital media marketing. However, a basic understanding and recognition of the four metrics involved is an excellent foundation for future planning.

Retargeting

Remember the purchase funnel? The intended purpose of driving traffic to a brand website is to get as many people as possible in the top of the funnel. However, the percentage of people who immediately purchase a product or service will be very, very small. While some of them will spend time exploring different pages on the

Figure 7.7 Brand Website Basic Performance Metrics

website, or even select a few items to put in a digital market basket, the vast majority will leave the website and probably never return. But, there is a way to lure them back. It's called retargeting, or remarketing. And, this is a highly effective strategy for increasing the conversion rate of shoppers, turning them into buyers and eventually, into brand-loyal customers.

Remarketing is just like going fishing. Even if you never had this outdoor experience, a fishing analogy is perfect to explain remarketing. Imagine that you are in a small boat alone on a lake. You select a lure, which you believe will attract a fish, and place it onto your fishing pole. Then, you carefully select a desirable location on the lake and slowly lower the pole down into the water. Then, you wait. And wait. Perhaps, nothing happens. Suddenly, a fish grabs the bait on the pole, and you think you have caught a fish. No. It got away. No fish. No luck. Maybe you want to try again. Why not? Maybe you will select a different lure or change locations on the lake. But, you are determined to try again. Success! This time, the fish was caught. And, you got what you wanted. You can continue this process or stop anytime that you want. So, the adventure is over.

Some people use the term "retargeting," but this is not the same as remarketing. Retargeting is changing where the message is directed or who is the intended recipient. While this appears to be similar to remarketing, the two concepts are very different. Remarketing is going back to try to capture the same people, while retargeting is changing the demographic, geographic, or specific psychographic characteristics of a previously identified and targeted audience. So, be sure you know when to use each one in your communication planning and strategic development.

So, what happens when a shopper goes to a brand website but then leaves? If a retargeting advertisement has been purchased, then a brand message or promotional image will immediately appear on that individual's computer or mobile device as soon as they begin another search. The paid advertisement might feature the exact product or service from their initial search, or it could include a similar item with different features or characteristics. For example, what if you were searching for a new pair of pants, shirt, or shoes? Most likely, a retargeting advertisement about what you just looked at will quickly appear during your next search. The colors, styles, and prices might change. Or, a promotional code for a discount might also be included to motivate you to return to the original website and make a purchase. No surprise. This happens every day.

As search activity continues to rise, more people are using their mobile phones to look for products and services than their desktops or laptops. So, retargeting represents an excellent marketing communication opportunity. Let's briefly explore one company, Waze, a navigation software app that is owned by Google. By incorporating global positioning satellite technology, or GPS, Waze incorporates maps into its platform. It provides help with driving directions, store locations, and information about places provided through a community of users. Waze offers three advertising formats to reach consumers: pin ads, search ads, and takeover ads. Here is how messages are delivered. Pin ads function just like a store sign by attracting attention when a customer is getting near or passing by a physical location. In this case, the sign is a circle that pops up on a mobile phone screen. Search ads are small boxes that list essential business information, such as the name, address, and phone number of the company. Takeover ads are like a small billboard but only appear on the screen when a vehicle comes to a complete stop. Clever use of technology. While giving the appearance of being safety-oriented, these ads might be very disruptive to a consumer, especially when in the middle of heavy city traffic.

Social Media Platforms

We know them. We use them. But, how well do we really understand them? Figure 7.8 lists 12 of the most popular and frequently used social media platforms: Facebook, Instagram, Twitter, YouTube, Snapchat, Pinterest, Periscope, LinkedIn, WhatsApp, WeChat, MeetUp, and TikTok. Each platform has its advantages and disadvantages. Figure 7.9 compares six of them based on the size of the audience, demographic composition, functionality or purpose, type of engagement allowed, and several other factors. However, the best way to understand the communication differences is to take the perspective of an advertiser and not a consumer.

There are plenty of differences in the type of content that is displayed and the methods for sharing information. While it is very easy for us to quickly insert our photos, post our comments, and launch our video messages, companies and retail businesses have a different purpose. They want to sell and promote their brands

Facebook	Instagram	Twitter	YouTube
Snapchat	Pinterest	Periscope	Linkedin
WhatsApp	WeChat	MeetUp	TikTok

Figure 7.8 Social Media Platforms

Multi-Format Platforms		Video-Oriented Platforms	
Facebook	**Instagram**	**YouTube**	**TikTok**
Largest Global Social Media	Younger and More Engaged Users	Long Form Videos	Short Form Videos
Multifaceted Options, Sharing Videos & images	Emphasis on Images and Sharing Experiences	Entertainment and Information	Trendy and Fun, Music-Oriented
Collected Content, Prolonged Engagements	Original Content, Spontaneous Responses	Second Largest Search Engine	Personalized Feed, Local Content
Advertising Can Be Duplicated on Instagram	Owned by Facebook	Owned by Microsoft	ByteDance (Chinese)

Figure 7.9 Comparisons of Social Media

as well as offer very specific products and services. And when they do, it can be perceived as artificial and manipulative. Overcoming that obstacle has been quite a challenge during the past years. Fortunately, as advertising became part of the social media platform, things changed, and a larger amount of a company's budget was directed to advertising messages but placed within the context of a social media environment.

Advertising on Social Media

While most of us are using social media every day, few of us know much about the requirements for social media advertising. So, we are moving away from the activity of posting photos, texts, and videos on our favorite social media and moving into another realm of communication. This journey begins with the process of having a business page, or opening a business account, with one of the 10 major social media platforms. It does not require very much information. Basically, most business pages can immediately be connected to your personal account. As a result, you are able to monitor activity of your business pages and then switch back to your personal account. However, large corporations or advertising agencies have dedicated accounts exclusively for business with links to their website as well as functionality with mobile apps.

Each social media platform encourages small companies, especially entrepreneurs, to actively become involved with their advertising process. Their goal is to make it as effortless as possible, so that you continue to spend money, particularly if you are receiving financial benefits, such as an increase in sales and profits. However, the initial development requires more time to completely understand the options, pricing, and creative mechanisms for a social media advertising campaign. While there is a steep learning curve, everything becomes more familiar very fast after all those decisions are made, leading to better results and continuous improvement.

There are five major categories for planning social media advertising, as shown in Figure 7.10: the development of budgets, audiences, messages, scheduling, and measurements.

The most difficult decision involved with social media advertising is the selection of the best platform for a brand, company, or organization to use to achieve its objective. Most likely, this will involve more than one type of social media. This is a strategic decision based on the target audience, product category, and competitive marketing environment. No matter which social media platform is finally used for advertising, there are five important decisions to make during the process of planning social media advertising: daily budgets, audience selection, time scheduling, creative messages, and performance measurement. Let's explore each of these categories in greater detail along with several questions that must be considered for brand advertising.

Budgets

How much money should you spend on social media advertising? The answer depends on the amount of money that has been allocated to digital media, as

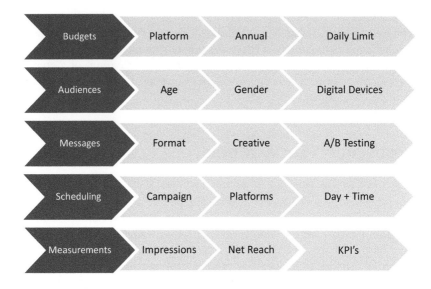

Budgets	Platform	Annual	Daily Limit
Audiences	Age	Gender	Digital Devices
Messages	Format	Creative	A/B Testing
Scheduling	Campaign	Platforms	Day + Time
Measurements	Impressions	Net Reach	KPI's

Figure 7.10 Social Media Strategic Planning

well as the total budget for Integrated Marketing Communication. Social media advertising is less expensive than traditional legacy advertising, but as the number of people targeted and included increases, so does the media expense. This relationship has already been explained in the audience/price model. Global corporations spend hundreds of millions of dollars per year on legacy advertising, but the percentage allocated to social media is much smaller. These companies have the ability to reach very large national audiences. Mid-sized or smaller companies might depend more on social media because legacy media are too expensive. Still, their combined expenditure levels are significant and represent a sizable portion of the entire output of social media advertising. However, smaller companies, along with local retail stores, depend heavily upon social media to attract new buyers and maintain relationships with existing customers.

Here is the big challenge. Social media requires a daily commitment. Every day is a new opportunity. Every day is a new situation. Every day requires a new budget. Because, every day provides different results from an advertising campaign. That is why social media management must examine the results of an advertising campaign regularly and make immediate adjustments. Typically, a social media advertising campaign begins with a fixed amount of money that is allocated per day. Yes, per day! While the budget can be established for a week or even a month, the daily budget is the best way to go. The reasons for this are complex and involved but can be explained by three variables: competitive changes in daily prices due to competitive bidding, increases from the social media platform for the CPM to reach a specific audience, or fluctuations in planning amounts for daily budgets that are planned and scheduled in advance.

Advertisers are told by digital marketing agencies, as well as social media companies, that advertising is an investment. And, it is, but advertising is also considered an expense, especially by accountants. In the first situation, a financial return on investment is very easy to provide. You spend a fixed amount of money, and you receive a larger amount back as sales or profits. The magical part of the equation is that the return on investment in social media is immediate. For example, if $100 is allocated for social media on Wednesday, then by Thursday, a return on investment calculation can be made from a performance report that included 40 new customers who spent an average of $17.38 based on the social media advertising that was used for that day.

Since this advertising money is considered an investment, the greater the return, the more likely it is that additional money will be allocated until a point of diminishing returns. However, the total annual budget for social media must always be considered to avoid spending it too fast.

Audience Selection

The audience targeting strategies are based on demographic, geographic, psychographic, and product usage or behavioral characteristics. This is the same for digital media as well as legacy media. But, the difference is that digital media focus on a limited number of categories, such as age, gender, and personal interests. The exception is the astonishing technological ability of digital media to target and select audiences by the type of communication technology that consumers are using to access social media, such as Apple iPhones or iPads. The selection process is easy. For example, identify the exact age, or age range, that is your target market; then, the filter being used by that social media platform will indicate the current CPM to reach that group. Then, divide the advertising budget that you are using by the CPM to calculate how many packages of 1000 women can be reached. For example, if your budget is $700 and the CPM to reach women aged 24–39 is $7.00, then the number of packages of 1000 women in this age category is equal to 100. As a result, your advertising message can be sent to 100,000 women ($700/$7 = 100 × 1000 = 100,000). This is the way you connect your advertising budget and the target audience selection filter. Change the demographic age filter on any social media, and the CPM will be different. Change the amount of money, and the total number of people you will reach will be different. Changing both the age filter and the budget gives another result.

Buying advertising for social media is essentially the same for every platform. While there are minor differences among Instagram, Facebook, YouTube, and TikTok, the basic rules of media analysis, planning, and purchasing remain the same. It is a combination of having a desired CPM along with a daily spending limit. The difference in using social media advertising compared with legacy advertising is that the CPM determines the number of people who can be reached within the limits of a fixed budget expenditure, as shown in Figure 7.11. However, in legacy advertising media, the CPM is a result of calculating the audience delivered by the price paid or cost of the specific advertisement being scheduled. Finally, the measurements are very different between legacy and digital. Legacy advertising depends on the measurement of changes in awareness, interest, desire, and action through marketing research completed through surveys and interviews,

Figure 7.11 Buying Advertising in Social Media

while digital advertising effectively and immediately measures results through real-time metrics, especially website visits, click-throughs, and other combinations of social media analytics and digital monitoring.

Time Scheduling

Social media are the ultimate real-time form of advertising. It can be launched during any hour of the day. Social media advertising can appear continuously or intermittently. It can run continuously, or an advertising message can be sent out at 11 am to promote a luncheon special or at 11 pm to promote a flash sale tomorrow. The advertiser has the absolute power to decide exactly when, where, and how its brand message or persuasive communication will appear. Strategically, there are preferred times of day for social media advertising based on the platform and the brand being advertised. These are important factors to take into consideration for planning because of the number of people who are using social media and the reasons for their engagement.

Scheduling patterns can be done manually through the social media platform or connected to a separate social media management platform, such as Hootsuite, which has the capability to schedule creative brand message advertising from multiple social media accounts simultaneously. For example, Hootsuite can initiate the exact day and time to launch social media advertising from Twitter, Facebook, and Instagram. The creative content and delivery might be different, with rotating photos on Facebook, 10-second videos on Instagram, and a sequence of separate tweets on Twitter with hashtags. Finally, links to a brand website can be included in the advertising to drive traffic using the purchase funnel model or to improve the level of interest in a brand using the AIDA model. As you would expect, different scheduling patterns will yield different results in responses. This is where the number of variables involved becomes very complicated and complex. A good social media planner knows the best patterns and combinations to use, but it is also important to consider the amount of money that is being spent. The daily or weekly budgets are the tools that should be used for scheduling, along with any special sales promotion programs, such coupon codes or offers, that have a definite time limit.

Messages

Each social media platform has different requirements for the size and format of a brand message. This includes a variety of text, image, and video advertising with varying lengths.

And, there are numerous combinations, such as a carousel format, which automatically rotates a series of images, a storytelling format that is longer with a sequential progression, or a promotional format that is built around coupons, special offers, and discount codes. The most powerful connecting message is a video of any length, but too long can be a problem. Since the number of words involved and themes are limited, the emphasis should be placed on the most concise and relevant brand messages that will attract and motivate the target audience to respond. This goes back to the creative storytelling framework in an earlier chapter, which can be consistently used for both legacy and digital media advertising. The creative message is always the same but expressed in different ways through social media.

One important feature contained in every social media platform is the ability to do A/B testing. This is when you compare the performance of two separate advertisements. The first is identified as A, while the second is B. What is the difference? It could be a single word, a phrase, or an image. Or, there could be two entirely different creative concepts. This can include changing the physical image of an individual who is shown in a photo or the type of motivational appeal. For example, an digital advertisement for a cough medicine could feature a young female doctor in a white coat in the A-version, while the B-version could feature an older male doctor. Or, the same cough medicine could include a mother with young children, or the same mother alone coughing.

In A/B testing, the advertisement that gets the greatest or largest response will be selected and repeated again and again. There are always new ways to communicate the same brand message.

Measurements

This is the dashboard or the reporting center for digital metrics and analytics. While there are variations in the visual appearance and functionality, most social media platforms focus on the real-time display of activity, especially the number of impressions, age demographics, and response rates. There are plenty of charts, graphs, and columns of numbers involved with the movement of people coming into, leaving, and engaging with the social media platform. The data that is included on the dashboard of a social media platform is unique to that platform.

The challenge is not the collection or reporting of data but the interpretation of the metrics. What does it mean, and how can the results be improved? Is enough money being spent each day? Has the best target audience been selected? Is the number of advertisements per week sufficient? Are the brand messages resonating with potential buyers? Have enough people responded to a call to action? Should the advertising formats be changed? If so, how often should they be refreshed? What is the best scheduling plan? Is this the correct social media platform?

The answer to these questions indicates the incredible number of variables involved in the decision-making process within social media advertising. The

List Building	Content Creation	Performance Metrics
Existing Customers	Subject Headline	Open Rate
Opted-In Prospects	Visuals & Text	Bounce Rate
Purchased Data	Call-to-Action	Conversion Rate

Figure 7.12 Constant Contact Email Marketing

most difficult to effectively manage and control is the costs of advertising. Since each day could involve a different amount of money, either by intentional choice or through a bidding system, it is easy to spend more than originally expected. That is the reason for having daily spending limits. The amount can be changed to maximize the return on investment and efficiency in reaching a target audience.

The best way to learn more about the performance metrics for each social media platform is to examine each platform. Many of them include video tutorials for learning how to read and interpret the results. The complexity increases with skill and knowledge of each system, but even a first-time user can understand the visual data displays that indicate increases and decreases in the number of impressions, or the percentage of demographics reached, shown in a pie chart or bar graph. This is used to compare what was actually delivered by the social media with the desired target audience for the branded product or service.

One of the best way to plan, monitor, control, and measure social media advertising, as well as email marketing, blog posts, and other forms of consumer communication, is Hootsuite. As shown in Figure 7.12, Hootsuite provides the technology required to manage the delivery of brand messages, including content and timing. For example, a specific advertisement can be scheduled days in advance, or even hours, based on the strategy selected. These messages can be repeated on a regular basis or limited to only a single promotional event. Hootsuite provides maximum flexibility for complex digital communication by providing options and combinations. This platform is the single best way to organize, manage, and measure digital media performance.

Email Marketing

The attractiveness of email marketing has steadily decreased over the years due to a combination of factors, including excessively aggressive and frequent sending of email messages, as well as spam and untargeted distribution with massive bulk mailing. Perhaps the greatest contributing factor to this reduction in the utilization of email is technology. Mobile apps have basically taken over the marketplace with direct connection to websites and purchasing options. And when the full

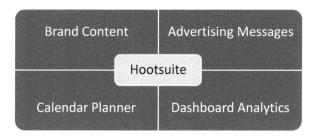

Brand Content	Advertising Messages
Hootsuite	
Calendar Planner	Dashboard Analytics

Figure 7.13 Hootsuite Scheduling Platform

potential of voice marketing is realized, Siri and Alexa will be driving continuous traffic to brand websites along with seamless voice commerce with search, selection, purchase, payment, and delivery. But, email marketing still has a very important place in the spectrum of IMC, especially for small businesses and local retail establishments.

However, there are plenty of third-party email marketing companies thriving in the United States and around the world. The largest and most popular are Constant Contact, Mail Chimp, and Vertical Response. While the majority of their business in oriented toward consumers, they are also utilized for business-to-business marketing. The advantage of using a third-party supplier is the complex technology required for information storage, security, and access. It is their responsibility to maintain all records and data about individuals who have interacted, or even not interacted, with their clients. This includes the basic information, such as the person's email address, phone number, or interest in a product category. Most of this data comes from customers who are in the process of purchasing a brand or have opted in to newsletters, special offers, or other forms of communication. Third-party email marketing companies can also help with testing, list segmentation, targeting, and performance evaluations.

There are three important components for implementing an email marketing program: list building, content creation, and performance metrics. This is summarized in Figure 7.13 using an application for Constant Contact. While there are many details involved with email marketing, the targeting of existing customers and potential buyers remains unchanged. This includes the use of personas, number of people involved in the mailing, budget limitations, competitive considerations and timing strategies.

List Building

Without a viable list of email addresses, there can be no communication. While it is still a one-way message with the hopeful possibility of a response, the quality and quantity of email addresses are essential for effective marketing. The quality is related to the potential interest of the consumer in the brand message. The greater the interest, the more likely a positive response. However, the quantity is a different situation. If there is a high-quality list, then the more names the better.

The only limitation is the cost to implement the mailing. Selection and wording of the most appropriate appeals is another factor that will influence the ability to evoke a favorable response.

Typically, companies build their own lists from existing customers. This input comes during the purchasing process or in any situation where an individual can opt in to receive information. Advertisers also have the option to contact a list broker who can offer categorized lists of names and email addresses from other third-party sources. Some of these lists are obtained from public information, while others are derived from private companies that are willing to share or sell names from their data base. In either case, there are plenty of sources to discover email addresses that can be used to target new customers based on demographic profiles or previous purchases.

Subject Headlines

What attracts your attention when you receive your long list of emails in the morning? Most likely the majority of the email messages are unsolicited advertising, sales promotion, or prospecting messages, but there are also brands that you have previously purchased, stores you have frequently visited, and activities that you have previously enjoyed. Here is the best way to answer the initial question of the attractiveness factor of an email. First, does it match their previous buying behavior in a product category? Second, is the topic interesting or creating a feeling of curiosity? Third, how likely is the demographic and psychographic profile of the reader a good reflection of the typical profile of an existing customer? Fourth, is the subject headline fresh, original, or attention-getting? Fifth, does the message content resonate with the recipient of the email and motivate them to take immediate action?

Testing a headline is the best way to know its potential effectiveness. This involves using a smaller group of customers, dividing them into two groups, and then sending out two separate messages with different subject headlines. Which ones get opened? And, which ones get a pass? This is not a one-time event but a continuous process, especially when many companies send out several messages a week. Is that too many emails? Most likely, but even if the average is once a week, there are still many different opportunities for creating new subject headlines.

Open-Rate Analysis

What percentage of the emails that are sent are eventually opened and read? The answer to that question depends on the industry, product category, specific brand, and headline. Most large companies believe that an average of 20% is a good number, while others are content with substantially lower numbers. It is logical to want a very high open rate, but what if most of the people who opened the email, just looked for an instant, then closed or deleted the email? Or, think about how many of us have automatically deleted an email without opening the message because of the subject headline. So, analyzing the open rate is a measurement that must be evaluated in the context of the purpose of the email, the contents, and the type of people who have received that specific email. Quality is better than quantity. Why? Because quality leads to the next important metric for email marketing, which is the conversion rate from a click-through to an actual purchase, transaction, or request for information.

Conversion Rate

The conversion rate is the number of people who have opened an email and then, visited a website and purchased a product. Typically, a good conversion rate for a retail store is 3% to 5%. Again, the low number appears to be inadequate, but it is not. If the email marketing campaign is well planned and successfully managed, the income derived from the consumers who have made a purchase should be much greater than the cost involved. Plus, the acquisition of a new customer translates into many future sales, which can be quantified by calculating their lifetime value. This can include the average order of an existing customer, and email marketers need to maintain a strong and beneficial relationship with them for the purposes of financial sustainability.

Other factors to be considered in email marketing involve the churn rate, or the number and percentage of people who have decided to unsubscribe from the list. The cause can be anywhere from a poor evaluation or previous unsatisfactory experience with the brand or irrelevant content. No matter what the cause, it is not a good sign when the churn rate, or number of individuals who are canceling or unsubscribing, is greater than the number of new opt-in customers.

One of the best way to plan, monitor, control, and measure social media advertising, as well as email marketing, blog posts, and other forms of consumer communication, is Hootsuite. As shown in Figure 7.13, Hootsuite provides the technology required to manage the delivery of brand messages, including content and timing. For example, a specific advertisement can be scheduled days in advance, or even hours, based on the strategy selected. These messages can be repeated on a regular basis or limited to only a single promotional event. Hootsuite provides maximum flexibility for complex digital communication by providing options and combinations. This platform is the single best way to organize, manage, and measure digital media performance.

Streaming Video

While you think it's fun to talk with your friends using Facetime, or any other form of digital streaming, this technology in part represents a new form of entertainment and eventually, advertising. CBS, NBC, ABC, and FOX networks have been quietly allowing their traditional television programs to be viewed online through their corporate websites. But now, there is a race to offer free apps for direct online viewing. CBS was one of the first, offering live news and video reports, along with ESPN, which featured sports programming. But, their real competitors were not the other television networks but social media platforms. For example, in 2016, Twitter was the first social media platform to live stream a complete NFL football game. Not a video tape. Not a highlight clip. Not even a special YouTube program or channel. Twitter was the first company to have a live, real-time sports event way back in 2016. While it was not promoted, the game was seen by more than 7 million people. This was not as many as a regularly scheduled NFL Sunday football game, but pretty close. Very, very impressive!

Is there a difference between video and live streaming? Yes, absolutely. Video streaming is limited to what has been recorded or previously saved in a digital format. Live streaming refers to any real-time transmission of content without interruption or delay. This includes large audience viewing situations, such as sports events, artistic performances, and world-wide activities, as well as business or government speeches or conferences. Live streaming is an important part of social media. However, there is the potential to expanded its current popularity with live WhatsUp and Facebook communication and create entirely new media channels.-Imagine this. As the most popular singers, movie stars, or sports celebrities continue to use and expand their live streaming content, audiences will grow. And grow. And eventually, reach the same levels as recorded video television programs. But, there is no television network involved. And, no local TV station. And, no advertising messages. That is because live content is delivered online and can appear on a mobile device, tablet, watch, phone, laptop, desktop computer, or even a large monitor screen. Who controls the content? The sender. Who controls the time, length, and moment of distribution? The sender. There is no longer any need for intermediaries.

The three basic revenue models for streaming video are displayed in Figure 7.14. Historically, advertising paid for the creation and development of content for television viewing. But, times have changed, and today, the pay-per-view and the subscription method are quickly becoming the dominant forms of revenue generation. Netflix proved just how effective this can be for viewership and profitability. It assumed that people wanted a greater variety of news, sports, and entertainment programming without the intrusion and interruption of television commercials. It was more than correct! And now, the major television networks in the United States are attempting to adjust their business models. For example, NBC has just launched the Peacock Network. If you are wondering about that unusual name,

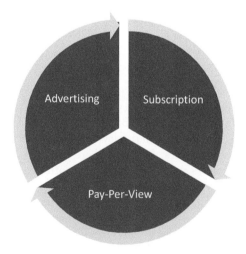

Figure 7.14 Streaming Video Revenue Models

it comes from the animal that was used as their official logo when people could watch television in color and not just in black and white.

To be sure, CBS and ABC are planning similar models, along with the competitive threat of thousands of Starlink satellites, launched by Elon Musk's SpaceX, circling the globe and offering low-cost viewing, new programming, and even private Internet systems in the future.

The bottom line is that people, celebrities, organizations, or brands can build very large viewing audiences. Just as in social media, where the number of "followers" translates into popularity, live streaming has the potential to challenge network and local television. But, live streaming has a characteristic that existing forms of social media do NOT have. That is, the ability to deliver content simultaneously. Just as with television, live streaming content ensures that every viewer receives the same sounds and images at the same time as it is distributed around the world.

That use of a social media platform for live sports clearly demonstrated that people are ready, willing, and eager to use their mobile devices for sports viewing and entertainment. What could be next? Movies, concerts, or video game competitions? Why is this important? Advertisers need to reach large numbers of potential buyers, but within pre-determined segmentation categories. And digital technology, especially mobile apps, social media, and streaming video, is combining to provide an effective delivery method for all forms of IMC.

Here is one final thought on the topic of digital media. Amazon has the capability for selling video advertising space on its website but has decided not to proceed. It makes sense to permit brands to place advertisements in this environment to promote their products and services, but there is the downside of becoming cluttered and full of excessive communication. Most likely, there will be experimentation in the near future with shopping websites that accept external advertising. Facebook might also be a candidate for leveraging its enormous audience size for video advertising, especially if there is a strategy change at YouTube or another competitor modifies its social media delivery platform to combine business pages with video advertising.

Summary

This chapter explored different types of digital media: brand websites, social media, email marketing, digital print, and streaming video. Websites still remain the anchor for brands that are actively marketing their products or services. Every business has a functional website, and most individuals can easily create one with online templates. Effective websites require simplicity of design, clarity of message, and ease of navigation. Social media are the most active and popular form of digital communication, but recently, the focus has been on inserting a greater number of advertising messages into their platforms. Email marketing is also changing, with a more sophisticated approach to targeting and data base marketing. Digital print remains underutilized but still provides high-level graphic delivery for online magazines, publications, catalogs, and brochures. Streaming video, the most exciting part of today's digital media environment, has already disrupted the television industry and movie distribution companies.

Discussion Questions

1. What are the advantages of having a mobile app for a branded product or service?
2. Which is the most important aspect of a successful website: design, content, or navigation?
3. Compare the advantages and disadvantages of Facebook, Instagram, and Twitter.
4. How do you determine which social media platform should be used for brand advertising?
5. Why is LinkedIn such an important method for business networking?
6. Is email marketing more effective than social media marketing? Explain and provide a rationale.
7. What is the purpose of having a YouTube channel for a product or service?
8. How would you use electronic print for a public relations strategy for an organization?
9. What is the role of consumer-generated content in a marketing communication plan?
10. What is the value of retargeting? Is it worth the expense, and what are the results?

Chapter Assignments

1. Go to Facebook and learn how to set up a business account page (www.Facebook.com)
2. Select any website design template and search for available URLs (www.Wix.com)
3. Discover what is required for a business networking profile (www.LinkedIn.com)
4. Learn more about the costs and requirements for video advertising (www.Adroll.com)
5. Explore Hootsuite, the social media scheduling platform (www.Hootsuite.com)

Continuity Case Study

Most of the managers at the company were surprised by Adriana's decision to hire a digital marketing agency. There was the expectation of having brand-oriented television and radio commercials to attract new customers. Most of them wondered how things like social media could help sales. Perhaps a lot of emails with bold images would be able to get more business for the company?

During the first week, the agency outlined the potential program that could be used for IMC. Obviously, they focused on digital technology. Adriana wanted to begin with social media. She was excited that millions of people could view her brand messages every day on Facebook, Twitter, and Instagram. But, Adriana did not know about business pages for social media. When the agency began talking about CPMs and audience sizes, she became confused. Weren't the posts free? And why did they have to pay for ads? How much money would be needed to manage a successful social media program for the company?

Adriana also thought that the agency's monthly charges for maintaining their social media accounts were too high. So, she hired an assistant to handle the posts and monitor the content internally. However, a compromise was reached with the agency to prepare the creative content but not to schedule any posts. Adriana thought that this was something she could do herself.

During the second week, the agency discussed email marketing, followed by inbound marketing. This included specific proposals for using Constant Contact and Hubspot. Adriana liked the idea of emails because the costs were reasonable and creative materials could be made very quickly. There wasn't much discussion of the website or its role in the IMC program. The agency said it needed more input before the design process could begin. Adriana didn't agree. She wanted to have the website completed in two weeks before the next marketing meeting.

1. What does Adriana need to know about the digital media environment?
2. What is the value of advertising on social media? And, which one is best?
3. Will her assistant be able to effectively schedule and monitor social media?
4. Do you think email marketing is a good option for the company?
5. Is Adriana being unreasonable about the time needed to design a website?

IMC Plan Development

Step One:
>   Develop a layout for your brand website, including multiple pages and navigation instructions.

Step Two:
>   Select the social media platforms that will be used along with a specific advertising strategy.

Step Three:
>   Determine how you will use email marketing in your IMC plan, especially for sales promotion.

Step Four:
>   Create a YouTube channel based on the demographic segmentation for your target audience.

Step Five:
>   Establish the performance metrics that will be used to evaluate the success of your digital media.

Chapter 8

Legacy Media Strategies

Paid Pathways for National and Local Advertising Campaigns

Learning Objectives

1. Understand and explain the meaning of legacy media terminology
2. Calculate and apply essential media formulas for legacy advertising
3. Analyze media costs and compare with target audience delivery potential
4. Prioritize and recommend alternative media choices with rationale
5. Develop skills to evaluate and purchase legacy media for local advertising

Introduction

Prepare to learn a new language. Get familiar with abbreviations for media concepts. Expect to learn several simple, but important, formulas. And finally, prepare to make a few calculations. This is all part of understanding and applying the principles of media planning, buying, and analysis. Before finishing this chapter, you will be comfortable using words, phrases, and concepts that are unique to the world of traditional, as well as digital media, advertising. While many of the terms sound familiar, the definitions are different from what you might expect. This is what makes media planning so difficult. The utilization of media is easier than you think, but without understanding the terminology, nothing will make any sense. Got it?

In this chapter, you will experience a deluge of numbers and calculations. The purpose is not to overwhelm your brain or make the chapter extremely boring to read. What is important is that you appreciate and understand the complexity of making advertising media decisions. While we all admire and applaud great creative concepts, the delivery of brand messages through media channels. So whether

DOI: 10.4324/9780367443382-8

you are managing or buying digital, marketing, legacy media, or any other form of marketing communication, there are nine essential concepts that will guide your decisions: cost-per-thousand, impressions, unduplicated reach, average frequency, coverage, duplication, rating, gross rating point, and target rating point. Once you learn and understand what they mean, then you will be better prepared to make excellent media choices.

Legacy Media Categories

There are five basic categories for legacy media, as shown Figure 8.1. These include all forms of television, radio, magazine, newspaper, and outdoor. The term "broadcast media" refers only to the television or radio. This is because they were originally designed to send signal waves from large transmitting towers. Perhaps, you have seen these large structures, which are usually located just outside large cities. Later forms of legacy television included cable and satellite, which deliver signals through fiber optic cables or orbiting satellites. Television programming can originate from either a national or regional network or a local station. Streaming video is delivered through the Internet, even though it might contain the same content as live or recorded television stations.

Radio is also a broadcast medium because it also involves using large towers to deliver signals, but these are more limited in their geographic range and pattern of delivery. Later technological developments enabled radio to be transmitted through cable systems and satellite downlinks and also through the Internet as an online digital medium. And, as with television media, radio programming can originate from a national or regional network or a local broadcasting facility.

The term "print media" primarily refers to magazines and newspapers, but it could also include virtually anything that uses a printing process for reproduction, such as direct mail pieces, single sheet promotion flyers, or catalogs. Magazines are usually national publications, but most have regional editions for advertising. Or in other cases, a regionally based magazine gains popularity in a specific geographic area. The content of a magazine can be categorized according

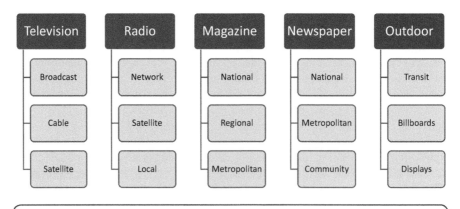

Figure 8.1 Legacy Media Categories

to a variety of special interests, such as life style, occupation, or topic. This will be explained in greater detail later in this chapter. Newspapers follow a similar pattern but have dramatically declined in popularity and circulation due to the emergence of online digital media platforms.

Outdoor advertising includes a combination of sub-categories, specifically transit, billboards, and displays. This medium is frequently used in larger metropolitan areas and includes multiple points of contact or media exposure at locations such as train stations, airports, and bus stops. It can also include moving vehicles that have advertising messages placed either outside or inside, such as taxis, trains, and buses. Billboards are the large structures along highways or city streets. And finally, permanent displays that appear anywhere are also considered to be outdoor advertising.

Media Terminology

The language of legacy media begins here with the introduction of eight basic concepts, listed in Figure 8.2. Each of these terms will be explained in this section, but here is a quick overview of where they apply. The concepts of reach, frequency, impressions, and cost-per-thousand (CPM) are used with every form of legacy media; however, the terms that include rating points, gross rating points (GRPs), and target rating points (TRPs) are associated only with television or radio. The description of each terminology contains several examples with plenty of numbers. It is a good idea to read those sections several times to gain a better understanding of exactly how calculations are used to make the best media decisions with cost efficiency and maximum delivery of audience size.

Reach

Reach is defined as the total number of *different* people who were given the opportunity to be exposed to an advertising message in a medium. This definition contains several words that need clarification. The number of "different" people is the core concept. In the dynamics of media, there are only two possible outcomes: an individual has been exposed (or not exposed) to an advertising message. It is like the binary system, which consists of only two numbers, 0 and 1.

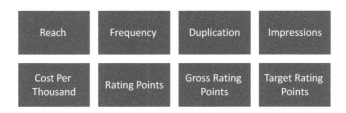

Figure 8.2 Media Terminology

A more common analogy is a light switch in your home, which is either turned "on" or "off." Thus, a member of the target audience will be reached, or not reached, by a brand advertising message delivery through a medium.

There are three distinct characteristics of the concept of reach that are involved in the process of media planning and strategic advertising. First, reach is expressed as a percentage. However, the media planner must know the size of the target audience to be able to calculate the "reach." This means that the demographic profile has to be quantified and expressed as a discrete number. The result is the base number for calculating reach. Here is a simple example. If the target market is women between the ages of 25 and 34 living in the United States, then the resulting "base number" is 38.9 million. How did we get this? Just use some simple research and an easy calculation. Here it is: the population of the United States, which was 304 million in 2008, was multiplied by the percentage of women who were in that specific age category of 25 to 34, or 12.8%. (This statistical data was obtained online from the Census Department of the United States.) Here is another way to look at reach. If the "reach" of a medium used in an advertising campaign was 21.7%, then 8,441,300 women aged 25 to 34 were exposed to the advertising message (38.9 million × 21.7%).

Second, reach does not include the total number of commercials. This is irrelevant because the number of times that a person views, reads, or listens to an advertisement is NOT included in the calculation of reach. As soon as a person is exposed to at least one advertisement for a particular brand, they are automatically counted as reached and added to this media planning number. Remember, each member of the target audience can only be counted once when calculating the "reach" for a brand campaign, no matter how many times they have actually been exposed to an advertisement. Just remember, an individual can only be counted once. They were either reached or not reached. There is no other way to explain the definition of reach.

Third, reach is a cumulative process. The percentage of "reach" will increase over time, but the standard length of measurement is four weeks. This means that the "reach" number indicates the percentage of the target audience that has been exposed to a specific brand's advertising message during a four-week period. However, the maximum reach that can be attained is 100%.

Fourth, reach does not equal awareness. It only indicates that people have had the opportunity to be exposed to an advertisement. Just because they had the opportunity to watch a TV commercial, read a magazine advertisement, or listen to a radio promotional message means nothing. If the creative didn't get their attention, there is no impact. And if the people were multi-tasking or doing something distraction, it was another wasted opportunity for the advertiser. There are plenty of research techniques and methods that can be used to test the creative effectiveness of brand message, but for now, the important thing to remember is that reaching a potential buyer and increasing the level of awareness are two separate, and often unrelated, psychological events.

The concept of cumulative reach can be quickly demonstrated. It involves calculating the reach among a hypothetical audience of 10 individuals. A weekly program will be used as the medium selected for viewing a television commercial for a particular brand that is a sponsor of the program. At the end of the first week, only Ron, Kent, and Arnold had watched the program, which means that they were the only people in the target audience exposed to the advertising message. Thus, the reach can be calculated as 30% (3 people reached ÷ 10 people in the target audience). During the second week, three people viewed the program and commercial, but only two of them had previously been exposed to the advertisement.

So, what is the reach at the end of the second week? The correct answer is 40% (4 people reached ÷ 10 potential viewers). Why? Julia was the only person who was exposed to the advertisement for the first time. Ron and Arnold had already been reached, so they cannot be counted again. What about the end of the third week? The reach has not increased, even though four people watched the advertisement. The reach remains at 40% because everyone who watched that week has already seen the commercial at least once. However, at the end of the fourth week, the reach has jumped to 70% because three new people (Alex, Rafael, and Adriana) have been added to the calculation of reach. The same concept of reach can be applied to audiences of 1 or 10 million people. As a result, the reach of any medium can be estimated for media planning purposes and the development of effective communication strategies.

Frequency

Although you can only be "reached" once, there is no limit to the number of times that you can see, hear, or read an advertisement. For example, two people might have seen a particular television commercial during the week, but the first individual saw it only twice, while the second person was exposed to the advertisement a total of eight times. Each individual had technically been reached, but one of the viewers had seen the commercial more often and as a result, would be more likely to recall it or be influenced by the message.

What is the right level of frequency will depend on how many times you have to see, hear, or read an advertisement before you remember its contents. If the creative approach is good, the frequency number should be very low, but if the advertising is mediocre or poor, then a greater number of exposures will be necessary to get the attention of the target audience. The average number of times that an individual must be exposed to an advertising message to achieve a minimum level of awareness is known as effective frequency.

Ever wonder why you see the same commercial so many times? Is more really a better strategy? Many years ago, the Naples Study concluded that effective frequency could be attained with a surprisingly low average frequency of three. Is this enough? The issue of effective frequency has been debated since the Naples Study, but the most influential variable in the equation, the "ability of a single message to penetrate the mind of the consumer," is different for every brand and advertisement campaign. Thus, it is possible for some advertisements to achieve an effective frequency with just 1 exposure because of a superior creative approach, while other advertisements might require 5, or even 10, exposures to achieve the same result.

However, there is an inverse relationship between reach and frequency. This means that as the frequency of the advertising messages increases, the reach will automatically decrease in the same proportion. And when the reach goes up, the frequency will correspondingly drop. Thus, it is impossible to increase both reach and

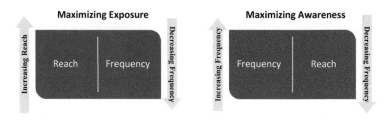

Figure 8.3 Inverse Relationship of Reach and Frequency

frequency at the same time. As shown in Figure 8.3, the inverse relationship is used for different purposes. If a company is launching a new brand, then the best strategy is to maximize exposure by reaching as many people as possible. However, if a company has a brand that is experiencing a lot of competition, then the media strategy shifts toward maximizing awareness through high frequency, or extensive repetition of the same advertising message among a smaller, more targeted group of consumers.

Duplication

Often, the same people read different magazines and watch different television programs. While we know that everyone has a different media consumption pattern. Some read magazines, others watch television, and even more are streaming movies. That means that the same person might be exposed to advertising and brand message from multiple sources during the same day. That is where duplication exists. But in the world of media calculations, impressions are the number of people exposed to each advertising opportunity according to circulation or audience size. However, impressions cannot be equated to the number of people. That is because impressions continue to count and include the same people. For example, if magazine A has 100,000 readers and magazine B has 250,000, then the total number of impressions for one advertisement in each magazine, combined, is 350,000 people.

But if there are two advertisements in each issue of the magazine, then the impressions go up very fast to 700,000. These are not 700,000 people but 350,000 people. And getting deeper into media planning, the actual number of people who read both magazines has an overlap, or duplication, factor. This has to be subtracted from the combined circulations. In this instance, 700,000 minus an "assumed" duplication factor of 50,000 would leave a net audience of 650,000 people. If you remember the concept of reach, an individual can be counted only once, so the number of times a potential buyer is exposed to an advertisement does not increase reach but only the average frequency. In this case, the impressions still remain the same at 700,000.

Impressions

Late one evening, while you are watching a television program, a funny commercial comes on to promote a product. At that very moment, you have been given the opportunity to be exposed to an advertiser's message. It does not matter if you watched the commercial, or left the room, began talking to a friend, or continued to search for things on the Internet. The opportunity to be exposed to the advertisement just happened. What you just experienced was an advertising impression, the real-time opportunity for a single individual to be exposed to a persuasive message or advertisement. So, what if 1 million people also saw the same program and had the opportunity to view that same commercial? The correct answer is 1,000,000 impressions.

The formula for calculating impressions is very simple. As shown in Figure 8.4, impressions are the number of advertisements multiplied by the audience size associated with that particular medium. Impressions are considered an opportunity for exposure, but this does not mean that anyone will remember the advertisement or will be influenced by its message. Impressions are an opportunity for exposure to an audience. Nothing more. The calculation for impressions is the same for television, radio, newspapers, and magazines. And surprisingly, digital media also use the concept of expressions for indicating the amount of brand messages that are delivered.

For media planning purposes, impressions can be added together. If you saw the same commercial five times while you had the television turned on, then five advertising impressions occurred. If those same 1 million people also saw the television advertisement 5 times, then 5,000,000 impressions happened. Since impressions are the same in any medium, they can be added together to form a concept called "gross impressions." The formula for calculating impressions is simple. The exposure per advertisement is multiplied by the number of ads that appeared. Exposures are the number of copies of a magazine or newspaper, while exposures for television are the number of people watching a particular program, and for radio, the number of people listening.

Here is an example of how to calculate the total number of gross impressions. If 500,000 people receive a copy of *Sports Illustrated* magazine, and the Schick

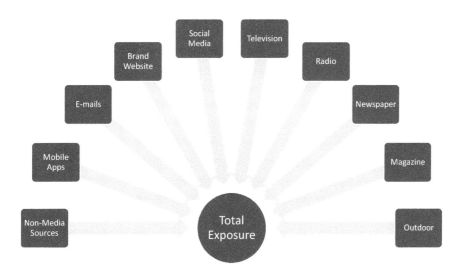

Figure 8.4 Aggregating Media Impressions

razor advertisement appears twice during the month, then the gross impressions will be 7,000,000 (3,500,000 opportunities for exposure multiplied by 2 advertisements). Then, Schick runs a television commercial on the CBS evening news. The commercial appears a total of three times during the same two-week period. Since this program attracts an average of 5,000,000 viewers per night, the gross impressions for the evening are more than 15,000,000 (5,000,000 people and 3 advertisements). Since the number of impressions from different media can be added together, the number of gross impressions is 22,000,000 for the 2 weeks of Schick advertising.

Did this advertising campaign include 22,000,000 people? Absolutely not! The maximum number has to be fewer than 8,500,000 people (by adding 3,500,000 readers to 5,000,000 viewers). However, many of the individuals who subscribe to *Sports Illustrated* magazine also watch the CBS evening news. This is duplication. So, the statistical challenge for the media department of an advertising agency is to find the "true number" of the exclusive or unduplicated audience. That's where the concepts of reach and frequency are applied again with other media research.

Advertising impressions indicate the amount of advertising "weight" that can be achieved with a budget and a specific media plan. Conceptually, impressions are the same as GRPs. For example, GRPs can be converted into impressions by dividing the number of GRPs by 100 (the maximum amount of reach that can be attained, or 100%) to get another number that shows how many times, theoretically, the entire population has been reached. For example, if there were 850 GRPs, then the entire population was reached 8.5 times. Assuming the population used in this calculation was 2,000,000 people, then the total number of gross impressions would be 2 million multiplied by 8.5, or 17,000,000. Specific reach and frequency numbers are used to establish objectives for a media plan, such as "achieving an 85% reach of the target market with an average frequency of 7.5 times."

Rating Points

What is your favorite television program? How many other people are watching this show? As we learned before, the total number of viewers directly influences the cost of advertising in a proportionate relationship. Media planners use the concept of a rating point to estimate the size of a television audience for individual programs. It is a useful tool for quick and easy comparisons among different shows, time periods, and networks.

A rating point is the number of people actually watching a television program compared with the total number of people available for viewing. Since this concept is expressed as a percentage, 1 rating point is equal to 1% of the base number. Thus, 12 national rating points mean that 12% of the entire population of the United States was exposed to an advertising medium.

However, there are two other types of rating points that are even more important to media planning: household rating points and TRPs. A household rating point is the estimated number of households exposed to an advertising medium, expressed as a percentage of the total number of households that exist within a specific geographic area. Using the same concept, a TRP is the estimated number of people in a particular demographic group exposed to an advertising medium expressed as a percentage of the total people that can be classified as members of that demographic group. For example, an estimate of 15 target rating points for men who are between the ages of 35 and 49 indicates that 15% of the people in this category were exposed to the advertising medium.

Rating points are also used to compare the performance potential of television programs. The higher the number of individual rating points, the greater the number of people watching the show; the larger the amount of household rating points, the more households are exposed to the medium; and the greater the number of TRPs, the stronger the ability of the medium to reach the target market. However, in media planning, the rating only indicates the size of the audience involved. If the efficiency of a specific medium is being analyzed, then the CPM calculations can be used, or the cost per point (CPP) method, which is the number of rating points divided by the cost of the television commercial. For example, a television program having 20 individual rating points (reaching 20% of the population) and costing $100,000 for one commercial would yield a CPP of $5,000 ($100,000 ÷ 20 points).

Gross Rating Points

There is another important characteristic of media rating points. They are additive from medium to medium, and from exposure to exposure. As a result, the rating for one media program can be combined with the ratings for other media programs. For example, if the household rating for television program "A" is 8, program "B" is 9, and program "C" is 14, the resulting number of household rating points is (8 + 9 + 14 = 31). However, it is important to understand that while rating points are primarily used in media planning for television, the concept can be equally applied to other media, such as radio, newspapers, magazines, or outdoor advertising.

The process of adding together the total number of people, households, or members of a target group that have been exposed to a medium, expressed in the form of a rating, provides an indication of the total amount of advertising that is being delivered into the marketplace. The addition of rating points from different television programs yields a number referred to as the gross rating points, or GRPs. It indicates the total number of people who have been "potentially" exposed to television advertising.

Calculating GRPs is the most important formula for planning television advertising. This calculation method is shown in Figure 8.5. Reach is multiplied by Frequency to get Gross Ratings Points: GRPs = R × F. Using the other variation

Figure 8.5 Calculating GRPs

of this media formula, determining the reach of an advertising program that uses 400 GRPs per month with an estimated average frequency of 5 would indicate that 80% of the target market had been reached by the advertising (R = GRPs ÷ F = 400 ÷ 5 = 80%). Any time that a media planner knows the number of GRPs involved and one of the elements in the formula, then the other can be found easily by solving the equation for the missing variable. For example, if an advertising campaign is being planned for 400 GRPs per month with a media objective that requires an 80% reach factor, the required frequency is 5.0 (F = GRPs ÷ R = 400 ÷ 80 = 5).

What can you buy in a discount store with $100? There are lots of options and choices. How and what you buy is determined by your needs. And what you end up with is a result of how well you shopped. The same is true for media planning and buying. If an advertising agency just allocated money to each media category and vehicle, it would not indicate the value or the importance of the decision. Agencies and media buying services use planning tools, like GRPs, to allocate advertising weight rather than dollars.

GRPs are used to estimate the amount and intensity of an advertising program. The higher the number of GRPs, the greater the combined impact of reach and frequency. For example, if 600 GRPs are spent during a 4-week period, then the advertising campaign has, according to media theory, generated a frequency of 6 if the maximum reach of 100% is used to complete the calculation (600 GRPs ÷ 100% reach = 6 frequency). Although the maximum reach is a theoretical number, it can still be used to establish the limits of an advertisement's exposure potential.

In this example, a total of 600 GRPs can also be achieved with a frequency of 15 and a reach of 40% (15 × 40 = 600). While the number of GRPs has remained the same, the relationship between reach and frequency has changed. Another option for a media plan with 600 GRPs will result in a reach of 80% with an average frequency of 7.5 (600 = 80 × 7.5) Thus, the first plan focuses on a target audience that is smaller in size, with many of the "same" people receiving the advertising message again and again with continuous repetition. The second plan would emphasize reach, rather than frequency, by delivering advertising messages to as many "different" people as possible within the target audience.

Target Rating Points

In the previous section of this chapter, an individual rating point was defined as the "number of people (or households) exposed to an advertising message, expressed as a percentage of the total number within that particular geographic area." So, what makes a TRP different? It is more focused and direct. A regular rating point just counts individuals, while a TRP is based on the demographic composition of a group of consumers. For example, a TRP could be men aged 18–29 years or women aged 34–49 years. In this example, the total number of people in each of the two categories would be estimated, and then the percentage of that number that was achieved by a television program would be considered to be a TRP, such as 18.2. This means that 18.2% of the targeted audience was reached by using a particular television program.

TRPs will have a higher CPM, but they are delivering a more concentrated amount of the target audience. They also provide the effectiveness of going after only the desired audience demographics rather than everyone. Thus, TRPs can help to decide the best selection from alternatives based on their ability to reach the target market at minimal cost. Since the price or cost of advertising is proportional to the number of people reached, a media planner will try to keep the absolute cost down by purchasing the programs that deliver the highest concentration of the target audience. If a media planner is not using TRPs, then the client is paying for a lot of people who have a much lower probability of purchasing the brand.

Characteristics of Legacy Media

Television, radio, newspapers, and magazines have their individual strengths and weaknesses. In Figure 8.6, these characteristics are compared. Television is a medium that delivers high levels of reach, while radio is utilized when high levels of frequency are required. Television is the most expensive medium for both national and local markets. Radio is the opposite. It can be a very inexpensive and affordable medium for small-budget advertisers. Magazines are considered to be a national rather than a local medium, although there are excellent magazine publications in each metropolitan market. However, the percentage of reach for magazines is lower than for most television media, and the average frequency is limited due to the reduced number of opportunities for advertising. Specifically, most magazines are published monthly, except for the limited number that publish weekly. Magazines can be extremely efficient at reaching audiences based on life style interests and specific demographic categories. Newspapers are high-reach media within a metropolitan area but not very efficient for reaching a target audience. In previous decades, the majority of the population received or purchased a daily newspaper and depended upon it for multiple purposes, such as movie times, stock reports, and personal ads.

New product introductions require media strategies that provide extensive reach. The purpose is to expose as many people as possible in the target audience to a new brand. However, there is no way of really knowing how shoppers will respond to the advertising, regardless of the media or creative message. Thus, the traditional approach is to maximize reach at the expense of frequency.

Figure 8.6 Characteristics of Legacy Media

For example, a reach objective of 70% might be selected along with an average frequency of 3.5. This is not surprising, since reach and frequency are inversely related, as you have previously learned. The communication challenge is to achieve that high level of reach within a fixed time period and limited budget. The results are reported using the AIDA (awareness, interest, desire, action) model, such as changes in the levels of awareness derived from year-long surveys and marketing research tracking studies.

Established brands, especially those in highly competitive product categories, often depend on high-frequency strategies. This is because the brand awareness levels are already sufficient and the communication challenge is shifted more toward interest, purchase intention, and action. In these situations, radio is an excellent medium, since it can be flexible by delivering brand messages during different times of the day or within relevant programs. The driving force behind this media strategy is to turn shoppers into buyers with constant reminders, repetition, and messages.

Determining Media Objectives

Ironically, legacy media objectives do not include any references to sales, profits, or market share. These objectives are related to the planning concepts and terminology that were explained earlier in this chapter. Media objectives provide the direction that a company or marketing communication agency requires to properly analyze, select, negotiate, and purchase legacy media. Typically, broadcast media, which include television and radio, are flexible during price negotiations because of their business model. This is because their audience levels are never consistent. The number of individuals watching television or listening to radio changes every minute. Since the audience numbers are always fluctuating up and down, the prices also follow the same pattern. Print media, which include magazines and newspapers, are rigid, with a fixed price and few opportunities for price concessions or reductions. The number of subscribers for magazines is very consistent with slow growth or decline over time. There is only a slight variation due to magazine and newspaper sales from retail store purchases and other locations.

In Figure 8.7, the most common criteria used to determine legacy media objectives are reach, frequency, impressions, time frame, and budget limits. The reach objective is expressed as a percentage, the frequency objective is expressed as a smaller number, the impressions objective is expressed as a very large number,

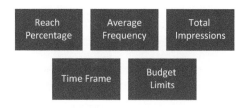

Figure 8.7 Determining Media Objectives

the time frame objective can be expressed as days, weeks, months, or even a year, and the budget limit objective is expressed in the authorized amount of money for legacy media. The performance of these objectives contributes to the overall levels of awareness, brand interest, and purchase consideration and ultimately, results in successful marketing.

Media objectives need to be specific. For example, a media objective could be expressed as achieving 75% reach of a target audience with an average frequency of 4.5 during a 6-month period with a budget not to exceed $5,000,000. Media objectives also need to be relevant to the marketing plan. For example, another media objective might be expressed as achieving 45% reach of women aged 24–39 with an average frequency of 7.2 during a 4-week period with a minimum of 7 million impressions using a budget of $1,500,000. These two examples indicate the complexity of media planning and the requirement of being as specific as possible.

The challenge is to select the optimum combination of each of these five elements. While there are no incorrect decisions, there are good, better, and best choices. There are often trade-offs among the criteria, such as balancing the relationship between reach and frequency, and achieving high levels of awareness in a very short time period without overspending a budget.

This depends on the skill of a media planner and media buyer at a marketing communication agency or company. It is essential that this individual has an extensive amount of training and professional skills in the process of analyzing media and spending a client's money in the most efficient and productive way possible. The real problem for an advertising or marketing communication manager at a company is knowing the proficiency level of a media planner or buyer. For example, how can you evaluate the ability of a person to speak French, German, or Spanish if you do not speak that language yourself? So, knowledge of the language of media becomes an extremely important aspect for selecting a marketing communication agency.

Purchasing Legacy Advertising

It's very easy just to spend money buying advertising media but very difficult to know what you're getting for your dollars. After learning the media concepts and terminologies, the actual process of selecting the types of media and specific magazines, television programs, and radio stations begins. It involves a lot of details, calculations, and record keeping. While the contents of this section have more detail that you need, it is a demonstration of the complexity of the process and an exploration of legacy media that can still be effectively used for local advertising purposes. If you are in the position to spend money on these categories of media, then the best approach is to contact the local representative for the major stations or publications for prices and information.

Magazines

In the United States, there are more than 23,000 different magazine titles published each year. With all these choices, how does an advertiser decide which one is best? The process will be reviewed in this section using an eight-step procedure to analyze, select, and purchase specific magazines. First, identify the most appropriate magazine categories. Second, evaluate the editorial content for compatibility with the brand. Third, analyze the circulation of the magazine. Fourth, select the size and type of advertising pages. Fifth, review the prices listed in the rate card. Sixth, compute and compare CPMs. Seven, prepare a sample schedule. Eight, check the dates for publication and distribution. Nine, recalculate prices to include multiple discounts. And finally, ten, prepare a summary spreadsheet of the costs, circulation, impressions, CPMs, pages, and any other information involving target audiences.

There are two major categories of magazines: consumer and business. Each category has publications that appeal to different target audiences for many different reasons. For consumer magazines, the editorial content should be matched to the life style, interests, and activities of the readers. That is why people buy the publications. For business magazines, the content must provide valuable information about a particular industry or retail operation.

The single best source for media costs and circulation numbers is the Standard Rate and Data Service (SRDS). This source of media information is sold to advertising agencies, corporations, and research organizations as a printed book, DVD, and online website access. For both consumer and business publications, SRDS organizes the magazines alphabetically according to categories, or classes based on editorial content. For example, there are at least 87 different class categories for consumer magazines, and within each of these categories, each of the available publications is listed alphabetically. If the media planner is not familiar with a specific, then it is important to review the editorial description. Within each category, there are plenty of choices, such as 14 different magazines for automotive.

If the media strategy calls for a geographic emphasis, publications that are targeted toward a region, such as *Southern Living* or *Sunset Magazine*, are more appropriate choices. In some cases, there are magazines that focus on a particular city or state, such as the *Michigan Fisherman*, *Texas Rancher*, or *Chicago Magazine*. There are also many magazine choices involving every possible demographic group and personal interest: *The American Association of Retired People (AARP)*, *Golf for Women*, *Pottery Collector*, *Trucks in Action*, *Bass Fisherman*, *Cooking*, or the *American Cheerleader magazine*.

Editorial Content Within any category, there are a great variety of magazines, from cooking to snowboarding and from gardening to football. Since a media planner will not be familiar with every publication, the editorial description provides an immediate glimpse or insight about the magazine. Compare the content, intent, and focus for these two magazines. How are they similar to each other? What makes them different? What does a media planner need to get a better understanding of the publication? For example, *Sports Illustrated* covers "the world of sports through in-depth articles, photography, and stories." Compare this description with *Sporting News*, which concentrates on baseball, pro and college football, pro and college basketball, hockey, and NASCAR and claims to be "the definitive source for the sports fan that always craves insider information about athletes, teams and the games they play."

Another important thing to watch is the number of pages within a magazine. If there are too many advertisements within a particular issue, it reduces its desirability from the perspective of the reader. This, in turn, can eventually lead to a decline in the popularity of the publication and lower circulation. Too many ads also represent "clutter" to an advertiser, which is basically an environment with extra competition for attention. A media planner uses the editorial-to-advertising ratio, the number of pages of editorial divided by the number of pages of advertising, to analyze the balance of a publication.

Circulation Media coverage is an important factor in the media selection process. For magazines, coverage is estimated by using the circulation of the publication. The total circulation of a magazine is composed of three parts: subscriptions, single copy sales, and finally, complimentary copies. Annual or semi-annual subscriptions are the best indication that consumers are interested in receiving a particular magazine. They have paid money in advance for the publication and if satisfied, will continue to renew their commitment. Subscriptions are a stable indication of a magazine's popularity. However, there are many other magazines that depend on impulse buying at newsstands, grocery stores, drug stores, and other mass merchandising outlets. These single copy sales will increase or decrease each week based on the cover stories or topics of interest. The third part of the circulation number is complimentary subscription and also non-paid distribution. Complimentary or free copies of a magazine are given to people who work at advertising agencies and corporations to encourage them to better understand the contents of the publication. Non-paid copies are issues also given away at shows and special events or used as part of a promotion. Complimentary and non-paid distribution numbers typically are very small and not included in a media analysis. To ensure that publishers are reporting the correct circulation numbers, an independent organization, the Audit Bureau of Circulation (ABC), verifies the accuracy through industry reports. The numbers in SRDS are based on the ABC reports. In the online version of SRDS, you can click the ABC Audit Report to see a more detailed summary of the circulation by week or by month, and even the total number of copies sold within each state.

Another factor to consider in selecting a magazine is the geographic coverage of the circulation. If the advertising plan has a special geographic concentration, then these numbers must be examined in greater detail. The ABC provides comprehensive information about the number of copies of each magazine distributed in each state.

Sometimes, publishers emphasize the total number of people who read a magazine. While only one name is on the subscription list, there are always other people who will read all, or a portion, of each issue. This is called the "pass-along" readership or what media planners refer to as readers per copy. Have you ever "borrowed" your sister's (or brother's) magazines? Most people do. For example, if a subscription to *People* magazine is sent to a family in Los Angeles, five individuals might read it, including the wife, three daughters, and the husband. The same copy of this magazine might also be given to a neighbor, friend, or relative, or taken to a place of employment. All these instances qualify as pass-along readership, because they expand the total number of people who were given the opportunity to read the magazine and potentially, be exposed to the advertisements inside. The concept is used to promote the value of advertising in a particular magazine. By comparing the number of readers per copy, the popularity of the magazine is demonstrated. For example, magazine A has 5.3 readers per copy compared with magazine B with 3.7 and magazine C with only 2.9 readers per copy. Since pass-along readership is very difficult to accurately quantify compared with circulation numbers, it should be viewed as helpful but peripheral information for media planning. Pass-along readership numbers are an important component of media planning, but the numbers are NOT as accurate as subscriptions or the rate base.

Size of Advertisements   There are three factors that determine the cost of advertising in a magazine: the size of the page, the color involved, and the physical placement of the advertisement within the magazine.

While magazine advertisements are usually sold as a full page, it is also possible to purchase a portion of a page, also known as a "fractional page." This can include a variety of sizes and layouts, but the most popular are the half-page horizontal, half-page vertical, quarter-page, and one-third-page vertical. However, the cost of a fractional newspaper advertisement is not always in proportion to its size, dimensions, or creative layout. For example, the cost for one full page of advertising in *Sports Illustrated* using black and white is $176,700. That's a lot of money for a single advertisement, but then, the publication reaches 3,150,000! So, you would expect that a half-page advertisement in Sports Illustrated is $88,350 or 50% of the full-page cost. Wrong! A half-page black and white advertisement in a horizontal format is actually $121,000. This pricing policy discourages advertisers from dominating the page. When do these fractional pages work? If an editorial story is continued over several pages, then the readers will follow the story and eventually encounter the fractional page advertisement.

Second, the use of color in an advertisement increases the cost of a page. The lowest price for a full-page advertisement in *Sports Illustrated* is the black and white rate. In this case, black ink is the initial color. Additional printed colors can be added for a cost per color used, such as adding $750 to the black and white rate, or listed separately. Four-color advertising, or full color, is considered to be the maximum needed for high quality.

Third, the physical location of the advertisement within a magazine determines its price. However, there are only a few choices for advertisers. The "cover" positions carry a very high premium cost. Why? Although the circulation of a magazine remains the same, readers are much more likely to notice and read advertisements on the inside front page, which is often called the 2nd cover. The inside back page is referred to as the 3rd cover, while the back cover is the 4th cover. Advertising rates for these positions are always the most expensive. For *Sports Illustrated*, the cost of the back cover is $378,235 compared with $290,950 for a four-color page inside the publication. Neither the advertiser nor the agency has any control over the page location for a specific advertisement. The publisher always determines where each advertisement will be placed, but whenever possible, competitive brands are separated. The publisher tries to produce a magazine that aesthetically mixes stories with advertisements and make it appealing to the readers.

Comparison of CPMs   The easiest way to initially compare similar magazines is to first find the advertising prices for each publication. This information is contained in a document called, the "rate card." This is basically a non-negotiable menu for advertising prices. The numbers will be combined with the circulation to calculate the CPMs, but it is still important to know the basic cost of each full page. Rate cards are provided by media sales people, and the same information is posted on the magazine's website.

Media buyers calculate the CPM by dividing the cost of advertising in a medium by the number of people delivered. In calculating the CPM for magazines, the page cost is divided by the circulation. If enough information is provided, an advertising agency or media buying service can calculate the CPM based on the target audience. This is a targeted CPM calculation, and it is a much better measurement of the delivery potential of a magazine. Because this CPM is based on a specific demographic group, such as men aged 18–49, the cost-per-thousand measurement is more meaningful. For example, let's assume that the rate base circulation of a magazine is 1,000,000, but only 40% is the desired audience of men age 18–49. This means that the number of readers who have the preferred demographics is only 400,000. If a single 4-color page costs $20,000, then the rate base CPM is $20, but the targeted CPM is $50. In this case, a higher CPM is acceptable because it reaches a selective audience.

Let's compare *Sports Illustrated* with the *Sporting News* using a CPM analysis. To keep this example simple, let's limit our analysis to a single four-color page with no discounts. *Sports Illustrated* has a paid circulation of 3,245,284 (rate base of 3,150,000) with a 4-color page cost of $290,950. The *Sporting News* has a paid circulation of 713,158 (rate base of 713,000) and charges $51,735 for a single page of color advertising. The CPM for the Sporting News is $72.54, while for *Sports Illustrated*, it is $92.36. The *Sporting News* is definitely the more cost-efficient, because it delivers these media packages of 1000 people with the lower cost. However, *Sports Illustrated* provides greater coverage of the market because the total circulation is more than four times larger than *Sporting News*. Which one should be selected? If the media strategy is "reach-oriented," then it is important to get the advertising message out to as many people as possible. In that case, *Sports Illustrated* is the better magazine. If the media strategy is "frequency-oriented", then the *Sporting News* offers a different advantage. It does not reach as many people, but it does provide a greater number of opportunities for exposure of a targeted group to the advertising message.

The optimum choice is to use both magazines but with more emphasis on *Sports Illustrated*. Why? By including the *Sporting News* in the media schedule, the total reach of the media plan is increased (because new people are added who don't read *Sports Illustrated*). Another option for a frequency-oriented media plan is to reduce the size of the advertisement in *Sports Illustrated* to save enough money to purchase a greater number of total advertisements (but remember, smaller sizes actually cost more in the long run). Again, these media decisions may not be welcome by the creative department, the account executive, or even the client who is paying for the advertising. So, many times, the final media schedule is a compromise based on the most efficient numbers and the expressed needs of an advertiser.

So, what happens when 10 or 20 magazines are being compared? The same procedure is used, and the magazines are ranked in order with the lowest CPM at the top of the list. This indicates the most "cost-efficient" magazines based on the target audience selection criteria. As a point of reference, the magazines are also ranked by circulation with the highest numbers first. This indicates the potential coverage of the publication. As previously indicated, a mixture of efficiencies and coverage is needed to produce a media plan that maximizes advertising expenditures. Time to put it all together. Not to buy, but only to see how it looks. This means summarizing expenditures that are included in the proposed media plan according to the magazines on the list and their scheduled appearance during the year. It is the second part of this sentence that is very important. This information needs to be checked against other IMC activities to make certain that is it coordinated and supports the advertising and media objectives.

There are three primary types of media discounts: frequency, trans-media, and corporate. First, let's take a closer look at the application of a frequency or volume discount. It is pretty simple—the more you buy, the less you pay. For example, as the number of total pages of advertising in a particular magazine increases, the cost for an individual page decreases. The symbol used to indicate the number of times required is: "ti" or "×." For example, 6× represents six pages, while 12× indicates 12 pages of advertising. Using these symbols, a media planner can calculate the frequency discounts. Here is an example for the *Sporting News*. The listed price for a single full-page advertisement is $41,829. However, if 12 pages are purchased, then the price per page drops to $35,463, and with 24 pages, the price per page falls to $29,280.

Second, the trans-media discount is given to advertisers who purchase more than one magazine "title" owned by the same company. This discount is given as a percentage of the cost for pages in each magazine based on the total amount spent with the parent company. For example, Time Life owns more than 162 different magazines, including *People*, *Newsweek*, and *Sports Illustrated*. If an advertiser buys all three of these magazines, then Time Life gives the advertiser an extra 15% discount. In addition, several of the largest media companies own properties in television, newspapers, radio, and magazines. Thus, discounts can be received in more than one medium at the same time. For example, a contact with Clear Channel Communications could include a newspaper, a radio station, and an outdoor advertising display.

Third, the corporate discount is based on the accumulation of advertising money spent by different divisions or parts of the same company. This means that the advertising funds for individual brands can be combined with other brands owned by the same company. For example, if the company had 4 brands, and each purchased 3 pages in the same magazine, every brand would qualify to receive the 12-time rate (4 brands × 3 pages of brand advertising =12 pages with the same publication). Just imagine how much this financially benefits multi-brand, global companies like Proctor & Gamble.

Most national and regional magazines require that the advertising materials needed for reproduction, even in a digital form, must be at the publication at least 60 and in some cases, 90 days before printing. This is called the "materials closing" date. It is necessary so that the advertising can be combined with editorials and other parts of the magazine. The other type of deadline is the "space closing" date, or the last day that a publication will accept a commitment for an advertiser. The media buyer needs this information so that the correct paperwork can be completed and the advertising materials delivered on time. If not, and the advertisement does not appear in the scheduled issue, then someone at the agency will be in big trouble.

Once the recommended magazines are assembled, and the costs are summarized, then this portion of the media plan is submitted for internal review.

However, this is only one medium. If television, radio, or any other medium is used, then the entire process is repeated in the same way. Finally, the media director will review the entire media plan. Once it is approved, the account executive will review the document and then make arrangements to present the media plan to the client, that is, the advertiser.

Newspapers

Most likely, you have already placed a classified advertisement in a local or community newspaper. Maybe you wanted to sell something. Or, perhaps, you were looking for a new job, or a used car. At several different times in your life, you will look at the classified section of a newspaper. While the physical size of these advertisements is small, the amount of money spent in this section of a newspaper is quite large. According to information from the Newspaper Advertising Association, about one-third of the newspaper advertising expenditures in the United States were classified advertising. Local retail advertising represented about half of the total with national advertising accounted for less than 20%.

Size of Advertisements   Since newspapers first appeared in the United States, their physical layout has been based on a series of vertical columns that measured anywhere from 1 inch to 1½ inches wide. However, the number of columns and the exact width of each column changed from newspaper to newspaper. National advertisers encouraged the industry to adopt a uniform sizing system, the Standard Advertising Unit (SAU), which at least minimized the problem. However, during the past several years, many newspapers have actually reduced the overall size and width to conserve paper and reduce costs. Essentially, the entire newspaper page is divided into a number of squares or rectangles, each representing the physical size of the advertisement. Numbers are assigned and then used to identify the advertisement and find the cost. Since the prices will vary by newspaper based on circulation, each newspaper has to be checked independently.

Categories of Newspapers   The majority of newspapers in the United States are local, but the metropolitan markets dominate the advertising with their coverage and expenditures from brand advertisers. National newspapers have a large circulation but still cannot compete in numbers with television advertising. This is also a medium with rapidly declining popularity and circulation due to digital media. In addition, the profile for the average newspaper reader is older and not always as desirable as alternatives.

In the United States, there are only two major national newspapers. The first, *USA Today*, is a consumer-oriented newspaper that reaches more than 2.2 million people per day. Started in 1962, this publication was designed to combine the flexibility and responsiveness of a daily newspaper with the national coverage of a magazine. Here is why the concept of *USA Today* was very attractive to an agency. The advertising agency only had to contact 1 company, not 20 or 30 different newspapers, to arrange national advertising. While it has been financially successful, *USA Today* must compete with an increasing number of smaller, geographically targeted newspapers that now have the same expertise and technology to customize their publication to local market interests. The circulation of 2.2 million is still a fraction of the total number of people who claim to read some type of newspaper on a daily basis.

The second major national newspaper in the United States, the *Wall Street Journal*, is a business-oriented publication. The daily circulation, estimated at 2,400,000 copies, provides an extremely cost-efficient way to reach a high-income, well-educated audience. The *Wall Street Journal* also covers a variety of topics that take it well beyond finance and investment articles. Surprisingly, the *Wall Street Journal* is not the largest business newspaper in the world. The *Japan Economic Journal*, published and distributed in Japan, is the largest single business newspaper in the world, with a daily circulation of more than 3 million copies per day.

There are 1456 daily newspapers in the United States. As you would expect, the cities with the largest populations also have the newspapers with the greatest circulation. For example, the daily circulation of the top three metropolitan newspapers includes the *New York Times* with 1.1 million, the *Los Angeles Times* with 740,000, and the *Washington Post* with 755,000.

Suburban publications are also an important part of newspaper media advertising. Although they are located in cities and towns surrounding a metropolitan area, these newspapers do an excellent job of combining news from local areas. In many ways, these newspapers compete with the leading publication in the metropolitan area. Their advantage for a local advertiser is coverage in a geographic area close to their location without having to pay a lot for the entire circulation of the larger, metropolitan newspaper.

Everyone has one. No matter where you live, there is a community newspaper that exclusively covers the events in your city, town, or village. It could be across a rural area, a particular neighborhood, or a geographic area around a metropolitan market. The content of a community newspaper is always more relevant to readers. In this type of newspaper, you can read about people you actually know, find out about local activities, and become more informed about issues that are important to everyone in the area.

The rates are low, the circulation is low, but reader interest is high. Is it worth the price? If you are a local advertiser, the answer is most likely "yes," but other types of media will reach most of these people.

Newspaper Formats Newspaper advertising comes in three formats: display, classified, and pre-printed inserts. In traditional newspapers, display advertising is very similar in appearance to magazine advertising, while classified advertising is basically a single column of words and does not include any pictures or illustrations. Pre-printed inserts are advertising materials produced by companies not associated with the newspaper but can be included with the distribution of newspaper editions. Let's take a closer look at all three to learn more about how a national advertiser, local advertiser, or individual can use each one.

The majority of advertising in a newspaper that involves pictures, graphics, illustrations, headlines, and body copy is called display advertising. This type of advertising appears throughout the entire newspaper with the exception of special sections, such as the obituaries, legal notices, and the editorial pages. Display advertising comes in a variety of shapes and sizes, including different horizontal and vertical formats. The exact size selected is a combination of the funds available and the creative requirements.

Classified advertising in a newspaper is all about buying and selling. Any product or service can be placed in the classified advertising section. Some people use it to find a new job, while others search for the right used car. It is a giant marketplace organized in alphabetical order by category. Classified advertising in a newspaper offers individuals, companies, and organizations the opportunity to list, describe, and offer an incredible variety of items. Organized alphabetically, the classified section of the newspaper uses a pricing structure based on the total number of individual lines placed in the newspaper. The width of each line corresponds to the width of a column in the classified section of the newspaper. The price is also a function of the time or times that it will appear in the newspaper, the specific editions, and any special features, such as bold face type, colors, or other elements.

Newspapers offer other ways of effectively delivering creative messages beyond traditional display advertising, such as a pre-printed insert. This involves the placement of advertising materials, such as a catalog, brochure, single page flyer, or a loose collection of pages, inside the main fold of a newspaper. Since these items have already been prepared and printed in advance by an advertiser, the newspaper is responsible for mechanically putting these materials inside the publication. The purpose of a brand-oriented, pre-printed insert is to get the reader to remove the advertising materials from the newspaper and save them for future usage. Since most of the newspaper will be discarded the next day, or put in a pile in the corner of the kitchen, it is important to motivate readers who are potential customers to respond immediately. If these people are in the final phase of their purchase decision cycle, then a pre-printed insert is an excellent way to promote brands and retail selling locations.

The most common pre-printed inserts are coupon pages, which are called freestanding inserts (FSI) in the newspaper industry. Just take a look at most Sunday newspapers to discover the amount of sales promotion activity delivered through this medium. How many coupons do you think are in that edition? 50? 100? Perhaps, even more? It is not too surprising to learn that more than 80% of all the coupons in the United States are distributed through newspapers. The cost for placing pre-printed inserts into a specific edition of a newspaper will vary by the publication. However, the basic cost to advertise is computed by the total number of copies inserted as well as the type of material involved.

Newspaper Rates   Newspapers have a pricing structure that is very complex. First, newspaper advertising, especially display advertising, comes in a variety of different sizes. The Newspaper Advertising Association reports that there are 57 different sizes. In the following paragraphs, you will discover the many choices that an advertiser has to evaluate when buying newspapers.

The total amount of money spent with a newspaper during a 12-month period ultimately determines the cost. A newspaper's pricing policy begins with the "open rate," a fixed cost for a minimum amount of advertising space. This minimum is based on the size of one column inch, an area that is measured by the width of the column and one vertical inch. However, when a contract is signed, the advertiser makes a commitment to purchase a minimum amount of advertising during the year. The greater the volume of advertising planned, the lower the contract rate.

However, if the advertiser does not meet the volume requirements in the contract, then the "short rate" is applied. Basically, the contract rate is then recalculated to make up the difference between the anticipated and the actual amount of advertising. If the advertiser actually spends more money than agreed to in the contract, then the cost is revised upward based on the "earned rate," which is the amount of money spent above the annual contract rate. For example, the open rate for the *Chicago Tribune* is $52.17 per column inch. If the size of the ad were equal to 10 column inches, then it would cost $521.70 for a single insertion. If the advertiser contracted for 200 column inches per year, then the contract rate might drop to $49.87 for each column inch. If the same advertisement were run again, the cost would be $498.70.

Newspapers have a two-tiered pricing structure. The first rate, the local rate, is offered to companies, organizations, and individuals that have a physical presence in the marketplace. Typically, this includes local retail stores, small businesses, and professional services. The national rate is quoted only to large corporations that market their products or services across the country. The local rate is always less than the national rate. This is because most of the sales revenues for a newspaper come from local retailers and small businesses. These are the regular customers of a newspaper, and many of them advertise on a daily basis. On the other hand, large corporations do not use newspaper advertising as often and do not spend as much money as local advertisers. In addition, if a national advertiser wants to cover a metropolitan market using newspapers, the options are limited. However, national advertisers can take advantage of local rates through the use of co-operative advertising programs. Since an individual dealer, distributor, or franchisee is usually reimbursed for 50% of the cost of an advertisement in any medium, there is a strong financial incentive for retail locations to advertise. In these situations, newspaper advertising is a preferred medium due to its ability to display prices, maps, store hours, specific items, and other information. In addition, newspapers provide the opportunity to quickly change prices in a competitive marketing environment.

Newspapers also offer a variety of discounts involving advertising in a combination of morning and evening editions, or weekday plus weekend editions. For example, if an advertisement appears in the morning edition, it can be included in the evening edition for only half the original price. As expected, the Sunday edition of a newspaper has the largest circulation and attracts the greatest number of advertisers. To encourage more use of the weekday editions, many newspapers offer a combination purchase of the Sunday paper with either the morning or evening editions during the week. How do advertisers select which edition to use? The type of product or service being advertised will generally determine this selection. A grocery store, mass merchandiser, or drugs store might favor the Thursday food section, while an electronics store prefers the Friday entertainment section. Automotive dealers want to dominate Sunday with pages and pages.

Would you believe that in some newspapers, restaurants pay less for their advertising than car dealers? Why? There are plenty of car dealer ads. Most likely, every dealership in town has an annual contract and is getting a big volume discount. However, some product categories, such as restaurants or clothing stores, might be reluctant to advertise. So, to stimulate businesses that do not advertise on a regular schedule, newspapers will have a price list based on the category of business. For example, while some categories pay a premium price, others are offered a deep discount.

What about a retailer that has only one store location? It doesn't make sense to advertise in a newspaper that covers a large physical area. However, large metropolitan newspapers provide an opportunity for excellent geographic segmentation. The circulation can be divided into separate areas or parts of the city. These are called city zones. Most newspapers have between 6 and 8 different city zones, but there can be as many as 12 or more. The basic advantage for a retailer is that copies of the newspaper are delivered in a well-defined geographic area. Thus, the people who live the closest to the store are reached first, and others who can easily travel to that location are also included. The advertiser does not have to pay to reach individuals who would have to travel a great distance to get to the retail locations.

The city zone pricing strategy also enables metropolitan newspapers to more effectively compete with small, local newspapers. For example, the *Palm Beach Post* newspaper has an 8-zoned edition with a total daily newspaper circulation of 833,000 copies, but the northern zone edition is only 117,000. Why pay extra money to reach people who most likely can never travel very far to go to a location when there is a much closer alternative?

Newspapers are organized into regularly appearing sections. Inside most newspapers, there are the sports section, business section, food section, entertainment section, travel section, real estate section, automotive section, and main editorial section. This is good for life style and psychographic segmentation. While the total circulation of a newspaper covers a broad population, individual sections concentrate on attracting different readers. It is logical that an advertiser requests a specific section of a newspaper. However, a newspaper does not automatically guarantee this. The location of an advertisement within a newspaper, or placement, is a complicated process controlled by the publisher. A daily newspaper has the challenge of designing, printing, and distributing its product within 24 hours or less. As a result, newspapers need a high degree of control over what goes where.

There are four basic types of placements or positions in a newspaper: run-of-press (ROP), preferred, full, and next to reading matter. In an ROP, the newspaper decides everything, including the section and the exact position on the page for an advertisement. In this case, the advertiser has no control over where an advertisement will appear in a newspaper. However, the newspaper compensates for this situation by offering a lower cost. ROP is the least expensive way to use display newspaper advertising. For a few dollars more, an advertiser can request a specific section or preferred position. This ensures that an advertisement will be in a particular section on a specific date. For example, if a company's target audience is men, the sports section would be requested, or the entertainment section for younger target audience, or the travel section for a target market with higher income. The other placement option is next to reading material, which ensures that an advertisement is located close to written content rather than advertising on the same page. The final placement category is a full position, which involves specifying a precise location, such as the top right corner or in the center of the page. If an advertiser wants to ensure a full position, then the cost will be at least 25% higher than the normal rates.

Television

When you go into an automotive dealership to buy a car, the price listed is never the price you pay. But, how do you know that you got the best deal? Hopefully, you did some research to find out about the differences among the models and the options you want. And, a smart buyer also checks out what competitive dealers are offering (if you can get out of the showroom) before you begin to negotiate. Purchasing television commercials is similar. A media buyer has to have a clear idea of the type of program and audience profile that is best for a brand. This includes comparing alternatives and being ready to negotiate for the lowest price. In this section, we will review how to purchase television based on costs, CPMs, and program ratings.

The total number of advertising opportunities, including the length of each television commercial and the time (or program) when it will appear during a broadcast day, is called the station's inventory. Network and local television stations can offer advertisers anywhere from 150 to 250 commercial minutes per day, and cable systems can offer even more. Commercial advertising minutes are broken up into units of 30, 20, or 10 seconds. The most frequent length of a television commercial in the United States is 30 seconds. This offers plenty of time to get the attention of a viewer and communicate the brand message. However, there are also examples of using 60, 90, or 120 seconds for the introduction of new brands. They cost more, but then, these longer commercials get attention, since there are fewer of them. Surprisingly, nearly all the television commercials during the 1950s and 1960s were actually 60 seconds in length. Yes, a full minute was the way it used to be.

Today, the entire pricing system for television advertising is built around selling a 30-second commercial. Stations usually charge premium prices for shorter versions to maximize their profits and discourage the rate of media bombardment. For example, imagine the psychological impact of viewing six 10-second television advertisements in a row, rather than watching just one 30-second commercial. However, all the expanded new digital platforms are designed to deliver shorter and shorter forms of video communication. So, within a few years, a 5- or 10-second video commercial might replace the 30-second commercial as the most popular form, especially as digital media distribution through social media and streaming services expands.

Each television station, or network, has an assortment of individual programs and shows that contain a pre-determined number of minutes of commercial advertising time. These are called in-program advertising positions. In addition, there is a limited amount of advertising time that can be sold immediately preceding and following each regularly scheduled program. These are referred to in the industry as adjacencies. In terms of cost, adjacencies are generally much cheaper than in-program advertising.

Availabilities   The inventory of a television network, cable system, or individual station that has not yet been purchased is referred to as the availabilities (usually abbreviated as the avails). This changes every day as advertisers, agencies, and buying services make their media decisions. That is why a decision has to be made relatively fast before a specific program or advertising opportunity becomes "unavailable." Once a commercial position is sold, it cannot be offered to anyone else, even if they offer to pay more money.

Knowing this policy, the television stations intentionally price the most popular programs higher than their true market value. Why? If a media buyer waits too long to make a commitment, another advertiser or agency will quickly buy the availability.

Local television stations have a more complex situation with advertising availabilities. Not the entire inventory is under their control. National sales representatives will sell a percentage of the time during network or syndicated programs. Sales people do this from the network, or even the national sales manager for a local station. Fortunately, most of this is done months in advance. The local stations, which are affiliated with a network, are always guaranteed a certain number of commercial minutes within each program that can be sold to advertisers in their marketing area.

Syndicated and bartered television programs have a very different set of circumstances. In most of these cases, the local station controls most of the available airtime for broadcasting commercial minutes. This can range from having nearly all the commercial minutes available (when the station agrees to put a specialized show on its broadcast schedule) to an equal sharing of commercial minutes with the producers of the program. In this case, since the syndicated show already has incorporated a brand's commercials within the program, but the local station has the opportunity to go into their market and find advertisers or agencies who would benefit from have their commercials placed within the program.

The Pricing Grid   Unsold inventory is bad. This means that the television station will not receive any income for these commercial minutes. What happened? Perhaps, the programs had low ratings or did not offer a good demographic profile. Or, the cost for this commercial time was too high, and advertisers found better bargains elsewhere. So, it is time for the station to lower its prices.

The situation is similar to what happens in the airline industry. A company might offer a special sale price for "unsold" tickets a few days before the scheduled departure. The rationale is that the plane is going to leave anyway, so why go with empty seats? It doesn't take a financial wizard to figure out that some money is better than no money.

The sales manager for a television station is responsible for maximizing profits from the commercial availabilities. This requires an analysis of the market and an estimate of the demand for particular properties. However, since the laws of supply and demand are involved, the pricing of individual properties begins with the most desirable showing being assigned the highest prices, and as an incentive to buy, the least desirable showings have the lowest prices. What is hot for media buyers? Certain demographics and low CPMs are always the driving forces behind the selection of availabilities, but the program content and its compatibility with the psychographic profile of the target audience is also a major consideration in a media decision.

The amount of time between the official day when the availability is first offered for sale and the actual broadcast date is critical. As the time between these two dates decreases, the requested price for the availability also decreases. As a result, a pricing grid (unknown to the advertiser or media buying organization) is calculated and used by the sales manager of the station. If program or commercial position remains unsold, then the sales manager authorizes another reduction in the acceptable price that will be offered by the station. Sometimes, media buyers wait until the last minute to take advantage of the situation. However, as with any television availability, the buyer who makes a commitment owns the television time position. Those who hesitate or take too long to make decisions will usually end up with nothing.

One of the biggest problems that a media buyer experiences is a television station that promotes its audience strengths while ignoring its weaknesses. It always happens that each station becomes the leader in one of the categories for comparison. For example, a television station wanted to demonstrate their superiority in attracting the largest possible audience, regardless of age, so they displayed the total number of viewers aged two or older. Somewhat misleading, but a true number.

The numbers game is actually quite serious. The television stations understand that media buyers are looking for the right profile to match the target audience established for particular brands. So, whether the target is men aged 18–29 or women aged 18–49, the station will find a time period, program, or special event that indicates its ability to deliver the desired audience. The media planner or analyst should have already gathered this information for the media buyer, so that when it comes to negotiating, everyone knows the facts and isn't fooled by the fiction.

The Cost-per-thousand (CPM) is the foundation of media decision-making in television. The goal of a media buyer is to select those programs that deliver the greatest number of people in the target audience but at the lowest CPM rate possible. Again, the CPM can be based on the general population, household, or a specific demographic group. It is calculated by dividing the cost of one advertisement unit, regardless of its length, by the rating points for a particular program or time period. For example, if a program has a rating of 20 and the cost for one 30-second commercial is $300,000, the CPM will be $15,000. Now, let's take a simple look at how the CPM is used to make effective media purchases.

If we compare six different television programs and their CPM: Program A is $17.21, Program B is $15.89, Program C is $16.30, Program D is $15.77, Program E is $17.21, and Program F is $19.46. Since program D has the lowest CPM it would be selected first, followed by program B, which has an almost equally low CPM. Would a media buyer purchase television time on all six of the programs? No, probably not. This is part of the complexity of implementing a media buy. Depending on the budget, the timing, and the specific media objectives, the media buyer might also purchase programs C and A. Why? Their CPM is definitely better than E and F, and adding different television shows to the schedule can theoretically extend the reach of the entire media plan.

Although a CPM calculation can be used here as a measurement of media buying efficiency, it is not as helpful as rating points. This is because in print media, such as magazines and newspapers, the number of people reached and the frequency of their exposure to advertisements are more precisely measured. Television ratings are estimates, derived from a statistical sampling of a larger population. However, as digital platforms become more influential in the delivery of video content and advertising messages, there will be a more precise identification of who is watching and how they are responding.

Radio

In national advertising campaigns, radio is used as a support medium. It quickly provides high levels of frequency against a target market without spending a lot of money. The cost of producing radio materials is very inexpensive compared with television, and with today's digital technology, radio commercials can be recorded in just a few hours. Since most radio is a locally based medium, it gives national advertisers the opportunity to concentrate on rapidly growing or high-potential markets. The relative low cost and affordability of buying radio time also makes it an excellent medium for dealers, distributors, and franchisees to make a connection between retail selling locations and nationally advertised brands.

Station Formats   The type of information, entertainment, or program content that dominates a radio station is known as a format. A station needs to select a particular format not only to attract listeners but also to differentiate itself from competitors. In small markets, where there are only a few radio stations, the station format will reflect the life style or culture of the environment, such as a farming area, university town, or ethnic community. In mid-sized or larger markets, there is a greater variety of formats to appeal to different musical tastes and listening interests. In metropolitan areas, where 20 or 30 radio stations are competing for advertising business, there is something for everyone.

Dayparts   The total number of people listening to a radio station depends on the time of day. This is reflected in the way radio commercials are sold. Each 24-hour broadcast day is divided into 5 categories, or dayparts, based on the major listening periods during the week: morning drive time, afternoon time, evening drive time, late evening time, and overnight time. There is also another category, that includes the weekend period. The number of people who listen on Saturday and Sunday depends on the type of programming or format of the station.

The most popular dayparts for radio are morning and evening drive time. These vary by station but usually include morning drive from 6 am until 9 am, mid-day from 9 am until 3 pm, evening drive from 3 pm until 7 pm, late evening from 7 pm until midnight, and overnight from midnight until 6 am. The actual time sections often depend on the population size of the market.

Each daypart segment also offers an opportunity to reach different types of consumers based on their occupation. Drive time reaches people who work in offices or are in one of the service industries. The afternoon daypart primarily reaches mothers at home, salespeople who are traveling, and perhaps, a greater number of retired people. The late evening daypart could be most anyone who would rather listen to the radio than read or watch television And finally, the last daypart, overnight. While you might think there are not too many people in this daypart, there are plenty of truck drivers, security guards, and factory workers driving home from the second shift.

Average Quarter Hour (AQH)   How many times do you change a radio station when you are driving? That is one of the problems when trying to estimate the size of a radio audience. People tune in and tune out based on the song, the topic, or (woefully for advertisers) when a commercial is being played. The actual number of people listening is continually changing by the minute. So, the audience levels for any given station, if put on a graph, would take on the characteristics of a wild roller coaster. The average quarter hour is a media measurement number that includes an estimate of the individual people who listened to a specific station at least once during a 5-minute period, within each 15 segments of a daypart, divided by the total number of people who tuned in at any time during the daypart. This number is expressed as a percentage of the population of the broadcast area and represents the "average" number of listeners that a radio station would have during a particular daypart. While the concept of an average quarter hour "listenership" was created to compensate for station changing, it still remains a rough estimate of what people are actually doing.

Cumes   This sounds like a strange word, but the "cume" (short for cumulative) is the total number of different people, or the unduplicated audience of a radio station over a specific daypart. Again, anyone who listened to a particular radio station for at least five minutes during a quarter hour is included, but this time, there is a separation based on the number of times that a person tuned in. As a result, the cume of a radio station is very similar to the general media concept of reach, but in this case, it is measured within a very short time period. As we learned in the previous chapter, the reach of an advertising campaign is usually calculated using a four-week period.

Why do media planners use cume numbers? Overall, they indicate how well the station is doing in building a total audience throughout the broad-cast day. However, the use of these numbers gets complicated when a cume is used for each daypart, including cume ratings, which are expressed as a percentage of the unduplicated audience of a particular radio station divided by the total population that lives in the broadcast area. When you need to get involved with these types of numbers, it is best to call your radio sales representative.

The standard length of a radio commercial is 60 seconds. The other two options are 30 seconds and 10 seconds. The reason why the standard length is preferred by advertisers is that the radio stations have priced them to be the best value for the money. Here's why. The price of a 30-second commercial is always about 75%–80% of the cost of a 60-second commercial. The price of a 10-second advertisement is almost 50% of the cost of a full 60-second radio commercial. In addition, a radio station believes that two or three longer commercials are more acceptable to its listeners than four, six, or eight shorter commercials. Imagine the tune-out rate if 15 advertisements, lasting 10 seconds each, were played in the middle of the news or between songs. That's why the 60-second commercial rules!

Just as in television, broadcast time is highly negotiable. Each radio station has advertising prices, organized and arranged by dayparts. This information is printed on its rate card or posted on its website. But then, the media buyer has to use audience delivery numbers, CPM calculations, and geographic coverage patterns to maneuver for a lower price. The sales representative for a local station, or the radio network, tries to maximize the selling price for the number of advertising units involved. Their selling strategy will be to emphasize the number of commercials that can be purchased with a given amount of money rather than the delivery of specific demographic groups.

Total Audience Plans (TAP)   Sometimes, you have to take the good with the bad. In radio, this is more likely to happen than in television. Since every media buyer wants to get the largest audience for the lowest possible cost, the radio industry has figured out a good way to do this. It is called the TAP. This is essentially a "package" of advertising that skillfully mixes the most desirable audience dayparts, drive time, with moderate and lower audience numbers, such as those experienced during late evenings and weekends.

There are three important advantages that a TAP purchase gives to an advertiser. First, the advertiser is guaranteed a certain number of radio commercials during drive time, the highest-rated daypart or time period. While these advertisements can be obtained without buying them through a TAP plan, the purchase price per unit is always more expensive with a premium cost. Either way, drive time can quickly generate a high level of awareness for the brand if the creative is strong enough to get the attention of listeners. Second, TAP plans maximize the potential reach delivered by an individual radio station. Advertising during other dayparts will increase the size of an audience, especially the number of unduplicated listeners.

Third, the average cost per commercial is reduced with a TAP purchase, since the most expensive dayparts are combined with a percentage of less expensive dayparts throughout the day or over the weekend.

Although radio is considered a traditional broadcast medium, things are rapidly changing. Digital technology has already begun to restructure the industry by expanding its delivery capabilities. First, the introduction of satellite radio makes it possible for a single station to be heard around the world. We will get to an explanation of how it does that in the next section. Second, radio signals can easily be sent over fiber optic connections shared by cable television companies. There are a lot of people who are already tuning in to their favorite music channel. Third, the Internet lets anyone listen to music, discussions, sport events, or other content by going to the website controlled by a radio station. So, you may never again need to have a radio to receive "audio only" information and entertainment.

Drive too far from your hometown, and eventually, the signal fades. Maybe your favorite station can last up to 75 or 100 miles, but eventually, it all becomes the sound of static. Now, with satellite radio, you can listen to your favorite radio station, even if you are eating dinner in Boston or going to a club in Los Angeles. Why? Because your Sirius or XM radio receives its signal from a high-tech satellite orbiting the earth more than 23,000 miles away. It's the same with satellite radio; you may never have to change the channel again, no matter how far away you are from home. Now, that's great reception! How does this type of radio differ from regular AM or FM broadcasting? With traditional stations, the distance and range of a radio signal are limited by a combination of factors, including the location of the transmission tower, the height of the broadcasting antenna, the amount of power allocated to deliver the signal, and the presence of large physical objects or structures, such as mountains, geographic elevations, or tall buildings. In addition, the federal government regulates the distance, direction, and broadcast patterns of individual stations. This is done to prevent overlapping signals and eliminate any unnecessary electronic interference among geographic areas.

What the emerging new form of satellite radio creates is the simultaneous access to a "national radio" medium. This means that the same content (music, sports, talk, or other formats) is delivered across the country at the same time from a single location. Since satellite radio does not depend on traditional transmission towers, there is no physical limitation on the ability to receive a digital signal. Get to the right website, and you can listen to a radio station over the Internet. For those who enjoy multi-tasking, it is a great way to play the music you like while doing something else on your screen. Click on the correct icon, and the audio begins. Although the sound is only as good as the speakers attached to the computer, the signal will be continuous until you close that particular window. Should an advertiser have to pay extra for those who are listening over the Internet? That is a question that is still being debated.

The perspective of the radio station is that it is delivering a greater number of listeners and as a result, can charge a higher price per commercial. A national advertiser can recognize the value of connecting to a larger audience and might consider that it is reasonable to pay more when you get more. In addition, the big opportunity is to get the person who is "listening" to the radio on the Internet to respond at some time during the broadcast and actually visit the website for the brand being advertised. This is another excellent example of the synergy that digital technology opens up for the advertising media industry. On the other side of the argument are local advertisers who do not want to pay to reach people who might be hundreds, or even thousands, of miles from their store locations. It is an easy fix for the stations. Two pricing schedules: national and local advertising—just like the newspaper model. This enables local advertisers still to reach customers at an affordable price.

Outdoor/Transit Advertising

It sounds like a strange name for an advertising medium, and it is. But, how else can you describe the hundreds of different ways you can get a message in front of customers and potential buyers without using traditional methods? Ironically, the first forms of media were outdoor signs and posters that began appearing several thousand years ago. These crude advertisements were basically designed to provide directions to a business establishment or indicate its exact location. Today, we have not only paper and plastic versions but digital applications as well. So, how do define this collection of advertising vehicles that existed long before mass media? Out-of-home advertising is a marketing communication opportunity that delivers advertising messages to individuals, and large groups of people, when they are physically in, or moving through, an assortment of public places, private locations, or retail store environments.

Although this includes hundreds of different applications, there are five major categories for out-of-home advertising: outdoor, transit, venues, displays, and posters. The essential feature shared by out-of-home advertising is a dramatic graphic and very few words. For example, how much can you read when driving an automobile at 60 mph? Or, will you really notice the theme line for a brand posted on the side of a city bus? Consequently, out-of-home advertising becomes more of a "mental reminder" or "visual identification" rather than a persuasive message. But this medium still has a vital and important role in multi-media advertising campaigns.

Outdoor Bulletins   The most common standard outdoor advertising structure is called a bulletin. According to the Outdoor Advertising Association of America, it measures 14 feet high by 48 feet long or wide. This is typically the type of billboard or outdoor advertising that you encounter while driving down the expressway. The advertising message on a bulletin can be painted or made from large pieces of paper that have been printed, organized, and prepared for posting. Bulletins are purchased for periods of 3, 6, or 12 months, but in the case of painted bulletins, 1- or 2-year contracts are required.

Thirty-sheet poster panels (given that name because it takes 30 separate pieces of paper to cover the physical viewing area) are also a popular form of outdoor advertising. Compared with bulletins, 30-sheet posters are smaller in size with a height of 12 feet and a width of 25 feet. Produced at special printing plants, the advertisement is actually glued onto the outdoor display structure.

However, the effects of weather and time will require a reposting of the original paper or the production of new creative materials. Another favorite outdoor advertising method that is frequently used inside congested metropolitan areas is the junior panel, or eight-sheet posters. Since these panels are much smaller (6 feet high by 12 feet wide), they can easily be placed near store locations, in parking lots, or attached to the sides of buildings.

Showings   What is the cost for an advertiser to purchase space using a standard outdoor advertising structure? It depends on the market, the amount of time, and the geographic coverage required. The industry uses the concept of a showing, which is a theoretical number representing 1% of a market's total population. Outdoor advertising space is sold in block units of 25, 50, 75, or 100 showings. For example, a 50 showing indicates that at least half of the population has been exposed to an advertising message. The number of outdoor bulletins, or posters, needed to achieve a 50 showing varies. Since an outdoor advertising company has hundreds, perhaps thousands, of different locations throughout the city, it is important to identify the ones that generate the highest levels of exposure to the targeted population.

Other forms of outdoor advertising include painted surfaces, mobile signs, or video projection. Advertisers can contact the owner of a building and negotiate a price to have an advertisement painted on one of the sides of the structure. It provides a unique way to frequently communicate an important selling point for a brand. For example, an old warehouse that is still visible from the expressway is a perfect candidate for this type of innovative outdoor advertising. Or, they can install a large sign on a flat-bed truck and begin driving it around the city, as many outdoor companies offer in metropolitan markets. In this case, the outdoor advertising message comes directly to the target audience. This technique is frequently used at trade shows to get attention and generate awareness in the physical area immediately surrounding the convention or exhibition facility.

And finally, there are the extra-large digital displays, which are also a form of venue advertising that is used in sports stadiums and entertainment locations. It offers advertisers the opportunity to prominently display their names, logos, and promotional theme lines. In addition, high-resolution digital imaging projects video commercials onto the screen. How can you not watch one?

Transit Advertising   Any form of advertising that includes images or messages that are placed on, in, or around a mode of transportation is classified as transit advertising. This can include a variety of different types of applications with trains, planes, buses, taxis, trucks, or any other method of physical mobility. The audience for transit advertising involves three separate groups: passengers, pedestrians, and observers. The first group, commuters or travelers, have the opportunity to experience advertising messages while being in a transportation vehicle or while they are waiting for one to arrive. For example, small display signs may be placed inside the entry doors to a train or larger posters attached to the side of a bus stop. The second group, pedestrians, includes those individuals who are passing close enough to read or view advertising messages. The third, and final, group, observers, includes anyone who is in a stationary location, or at a distance from the advertising, but can still be exposed to its message through a transit medium.

Transit advertising is made from printed materials, primarily paper and cardboard with an increasing amount of plastic. As expected, new types of digital displays are also becoming incorporated into transit advertising. There are examples of some of the most frequently used forms of advertising: a taxicab topper, a bus shelter panel, an inside vehicle poster, and a fully painted bus graphic. Transit advertising can be placed on the side, back, or top of a vehicle.

How do transit companies charge for their advertising? It once again involves the utilization of advertising impressions. Fortunately, the number of people using different modes of transportation is fairly well documented by reports generated by local, county, state, and of course, the federal government. Computer trains and metropolitan subways, along with city buses, have published numbers about their daily usage. Traffic on the roads can be measured by electronically counting cars and trucks; city planners have a good estimate of the numbers of individuals moving around.

Just as with outdoor advertising, there is a high duplication factor. Many of the same people are counted again and again. So, the maximum "reach" that is possible with transit advertising is achieved very quickly, and from there, the "frequency" of exposures among the target audience continues to build on a daily basis. The estimated number of impressions with transit advertising is always high, but this is not an indication of the actual number of people who have been exposed to an advertising message.

Portable, or movable media, is another category of out-of-home advertising. This includes advertising incorporated into display, kiosks, or self-contained small structures that have interactive DVDs, computers, or access to the Internet. Other options with an advertising display are areas specifically designed for demonstrating the product, distributing catalogs, or having a spokesperson discussing the benefits of the brand in an entertaining way. Where do you usually find these displays? The majority of these displays are in trade shows or exhibitions for marketing business-to-business products. However, there are plenty of displays at shopping malls, store locations, and when permitted, even right in the middle of a public place or sidewalk.

Print them and paste them. Put them on any surface from a door to a wall, or in a construction site, hallway, or storage bin. They are inexpensive, easy to reproduce, and often saved by college students. The same goes for stickers and adhesives. Both are definitely guerrilla advertising that can be most effective for small, local companies, or even national companies that want to get edgy. Consider this medium as an unrestricted form of exposure. But now, enter the digital poster. This is a serious new medium. The size can vary from a 12-inch square flat screen to a 3-foot by 5-foot panel. So, it is just small enough to put anywhere, but technologically savvy.

Preparing Media Spreadsheets

Get ready for your first advertising spreadsheet (Figure 8.8). While most people put the information into an Excel document, the media data can be displayed in many other ways, including complex software displays and real-time dashboard reporting services. But, let's keep it simple for now. To begin, what is the purpose of an advertising spreadsheet? It is a method of displaying and presenting the advertising media plan, which has been developed by an agency or consultants. The advertiser, who is a client of the agency, can view the summary of media activity before approving the final document. Once the plan is approved, then the advertising agency or media buying service actually purchases the media and also schedules the creative materials that have prepared. The media spreadsheet enables the client to communicate this information to other divisions and parts of the corporation. This is especially important for the sales department, which needs to know when the advertising is starting and what products will be featured. As you can imagine, a sales promotion program must be coordinated with everyone involved, from manufacturing and shipping facilities, to the wholesaler delivery, to stores and retail outlets.

The media spreadsheet contains three separate summaries organized by months, media, and money. These are the 3Ms of media reporting. The first summary is the total number of dollars, or other currency, that have been planned or are being spent on advertising. The second is the accumulated number of impressions or the number of unduplicated people exposed to the advertising. The third is the identification and counting of advertising materials, such as the number of television and radio

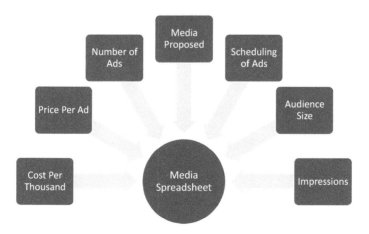

Figure 8.8 Preparing Media Spreadsheets

commercials or magazine and newspaper advertisements. There are complications and complexities in reporting this section of the spreadsheet. Each of the five legacy media categories has different reporting units or methods of delivering advertising. For example, the broadcast media have 5 different lengths for advertising commercials: 60-second, 30-second, 15-second, 10-second, and 5-second commercials. Magazines can be full pages, half-pages, fractional pages, or special combinations such as spreads or gatefolds. Newspapers are usually purchased according to the SAU, which has pre-determined size dimensions. Outdoor advertising is reported accounting to the number of billboards or showings, or another method of indicating the potential number of exposures based on the movement of people or traffic.

Media spreadsheets vary in the information contained, the method of displaying the advertising expenditure, and the audience delivery. Figure 8.8 highlights the most common types of information arranged in a media spreadsheet. The list includes total impression, audience size, media selected, scheduling of advertisements, number of units, price per advertisement, and CPM. The numbers for all these reporting categories are displayed on a calendar layout by month. Thus, the combined activity for the entire advertising program can be summarized by month and by media: for example, the amount of money spent on television commercial during February or the number of magazine pages scheduled during October; or, the total number of impressions occurring during January and the advertising expenditures during July and August. And finally, the supporting portions of a spreadsheet can also provide the identification title of a television or radio commercial as well as the headline of each magazine advertisement that has been prepared by the creative department of an agency.

Summary

Advertisers usually hire advertising or marketing communication agencies to research, plan, and implement media purchases. The media department at an agency must collect advertising costs, estimate audience sizes, and analyze demographic profiles for the most relevant media categories. The ability to perform this IMC function depends on a complete understanding of the terminology and vocabulary of traditional and digital media. The five most important media concepts are reach, frequency, impressions, CPM, ratings, and GRPs. Recommendations for purchasing media are based on a set of specific and measurable objectives. Specific publications, programs, and media vehicles are selected based on a combination of cost efficiencies, coverage of the target audience, and the quality content environment for a brand. The methods for analyzing and purchasing each legacy media category are different for television, radio, newspapers, magazines, and outdoor advertising.

Discussion Questions

1. What is the difference between reach and frequency? Are they important for media planning?
2. Define an impression. What is the purpose of using impressions for legacy and digital media?

3. How do you calculate the cost-per-thousand? Why is it so essential for media buying?
4. Is a CPM analysis more relevant for magazines, newspapers, radio, or television advertising?
5. What are SAUs? How can you use them for planning local advertising campaigns and programs?
6. How do GRPs help advertising planners? What is a Target Rating Point?
7. Is it better for brand advertisers to use a TAP, or drive time, rate from a local radio station?
8. When should outdoor and transit advertising be used to promote a product or service?
9. Why do advertisers and agencies need a media spreadsheet? What data should be included?
10. What is the effectiveness of legacy media advertising compared with digital media advertising?

Chapter Assignments

1. Select a magazine about an activity you enjoy and find the advertising rates from its website.
2. Find the website for a newspaper in a large metropolitan area. Explore its advertising options.
3. Search online to discover the number of radio stations in your market. Compare their websites.
4. Choose five network television programs that could match the profile of a targeted audience.
5. Investigate the companies that sell outdoor and transit advertising in your marketing area.

Continuity Case Study

Adriana learned about rating points during a seminar sponsored by the American Advertising Federation. She invited a representative from the Nielsen company, whom she had met at the seminar, to give a presentation at Athena. But during the meeting, there was a dispute over the quality and desirability of different programs. The Nielsen representative made clear that viewing numbers and audience profiles are the most important aspects. Personal tastes, prejudices, preferences, or opinions about social issues are not relevant for media planning.

At the end of the meeting, Adriana got approval from Martin to hire a media buying service. This was necessary, since the digital marketing agency did not have the experience needed to handle this assignment. Their leader, Fritz Schulz, was a leading expert in negotiating prices and had extensive experience in the television and cable industry. But before Adriana approved a television budget, she had to evaluate the effectiveness of each of the traditional media categories. Which medium was best to promote a coupon? Or the family travel sweepstakes?

There were also the marketing problems, such as declining lunchtime sales, along with the lack of familiarity with Greek foods and side dishes.

1. Which traditional medium is best for Athena's advertising campaign?
2. Is television advertising worth the cost to get maximum exposure?
3. Can radio advertising stimulate greater lunchtime and dinner sales?
4. Should local newspapers, or digital media, be used for coupon promotions?
5. What types of national magazines are most relevant for Athena?

IMC Plan Development

Step One:
>Review budget allocations for legacy media and make changes required by IMC strategies.

Step Two:
>Decide which type of legacy media is best for your brand based on the primary target audience.

Step Three:
>Write your media objectives using specific performance numbers for each legacy medium involved.

Step Four:
>Determine the individual units of media used for delivering creative content with estimated costs.

Step Five:
>Prepare a spreadsheet that summarizes media expenditures, audience delivery, and impressions.

Chapter 9

Sales Promotion Strategies

Motivating Shoppers to React and Respond to Special Offers

Learning Objectives

1. Describe and understand the purpose and value of sales promotion
2. Develop the skills to write a specific sales promotion objective
3. Recognize the relationships between promotions and Integrated Marketing Communications (IMC)
4. Know how to select the most appropriate promotion for a brand

Introduction

In this chapter, we will review the functions of sales promotion activities, events, and programs and their relationship with IMC. Sales promotion strategies are frequently combined with advertising messages to motivate shoppers, potential buyers, and customers to purchase a product or service. A variety of incentives are offered to stimulate action and accelerate the decision-making process for those searching online or comparing brands.

Sales promotion activities, events, and programs can originate from manufacturers, wholesalers, or retailers. Promotions designed to reach consumers can include financial incentives, value offerings, psychological rewards, or targeted interactions. The effectiveness of a sales promotion strategy is based on measurements that are relevant to the strategy selected.

Consumer promotions and business-to-business (B2B) promotions use similar strategies, but B2B concentrates on negotiated prices and concessions. Both consumer and B2B marketing involves accelerating the movement of product inventory through channels of distribution.

DOI: 10.4324/9780367443382-9

What Is Sales Promotion?

Definition of a Promotion

In classical marketing terms, promotion is one of the original four Ps. But, it frequently caused confusion because advertising was included in this definition. To complicate the situation even more, the common term in the marketing industry is sales promotion. Is the only purpose of a promotion to stimulate sales? What about the other benefits from promotional activities? And, how does sales promotion relate to everything else from IMC?

The American Marketing Association defines promotion as "media and non-media marketing pressure applied for a predetermined, limited period of time in order to stimulate trial, increase consumer demand, or improve product availability." Why? Because the concept of IMC includes a multitude of strategies and tactics. Achieving increased sales and profits is only part of the process. Other important aspects are obtaining data about shoppers, purchasers, and loyal customers as well as reinforcing the image of a brand. The limited time period is a motivational factor. But, the purpose of a promotion is to accelerate the decision-making process for branded products or services. It should always include a strong call to action. At the same time, the value proposition of a brand, including its competitive advantages or user benefits, must also be reinforced.

Promotions are used for both consumer and B2B markets. While many of the techniques and strategies are identical, consumer promotions are more dependent on advertising and social media for their success. B2B promotions require personal contact or frequent communication.

Consumer promotions involve much larger audiences, multiple market segments, and a wide range of buyer needs. They are targeted according to the most likely buyers based on demographic, psychographic, and geographic profiles. B2B promotions are significantly smaller but have a more clearly defined target market. That is because audiences for B2B customers are limited to wholesalers, brokers, distributors, dealers, agents, and retailers.

Media Advertising Support

Sales promotion events, activities, and programs cannot be successful without a sufficient amount of media support. This includes a strategic combination of advertising, social media, publicity, and personal contact. Promotions cannot exist without an effective method of communication with the individuals who will be interested in the benefits or value of an offer.

Advertising is the most efficient way to reach a very large number of shoppers and potential buyers, but this communication is also the most expensive. Social media cost much less than traditional television advertising but do not always get the same level of response. Sales promotion also involves the people working at a retail store or business. For example, they can answer questions about the promotion and explain specific details. Their personal contact and interaction contribute to the success of a promotion by building customer relationships.

Push and Pull Strategies

The classical approach to marketing focuses on a combination of "push" and "pull" strategies. These are two different approaches for moving products through a distribution system. Here is a quick explanation of the process. As soon as a national manufacturer sells its products to a wholesaler, the company receives payment, and the items are shipped. Then, a smaller quantity of the same products are sold, once again, but this time to a retail store. The wholesaler receives payment for those products, and the items are delivered to retailers. And finally, the retail store sells the same products to a customer at a store, or even online. At the end of the day, the same product has been sold three times: manufacturer to wholesaler, then wholesale to retailer, and finally, retailer to individual shoppers.

In a push strategy, a manufacturer arranges to place an extra amount of product into the channel of distribution. The quantity is much more than any wholesaler normally wants or maintains on a regular basis. So, why would a wholesaler agree to purchase a larger quantity? This is because financial incentives are offered by the manufacturer to lower the average cost per item. This can mean greater profits when these products are sold to retailers. But then, retail stores will have the same problem with more products than they need. As a result, retailers lower prices, and shoppers get a bargain. The overstocked inventory is quickly reduced because it has been pushed through the channel of distribution by using a combination of financial and psychological incentives.

Pull strategies are designed to create an increase in the retail demand for a specific product or service. Shoppers are made aware of a brand through advertising, social media, and other forms of marketing communication. As a result, more people become interested in the brand and order it online or go into stores and purchase the product. The entire process is accelerated by a substantial amount of money spent by national manufacturers on advertising. As individual store sales increase, retailers must replenish inventory by purchasing additional quantities of the brand from wholesalers. And yes, you guessed it, these wholesalers will be ordering more from the manufacturers. This is a seamless and effective way to "pull" products through a consumer distribution channel using a combination of IMC methods.

Promotional Objectives

At large corporations, the marketing manager or advertising manager is responsible for planning sales promotion activities, events, and programs. In most cases, there is a specific sales promotion manager with the responsibility for developing programs. Frequently, other managers will also be involved, such as a sales manager or a brand manager, but they are more the recipients of the decisions. In smaller companies, the owner or general manager must take on these important responsibilities, while in entrepreneurial ventures, everything depends on that person alone.

The development of a sales promotion objective requires six essential components: the target audience, time frame, promotion strategy, program budget, legal restrictions, and performance measurement. Each of these variables influences the development of a promotion, but a priority must be placed on the desired marketing outcome, especially sales, profits, or market share.

Target Audience

Promotions do not always have the same target audience as traditional advertising, social media, or other forms of IMC. This is because the purpose of a sales promotion activity, event, or program is to generate immediate sales. To differentiate the buyers, it is important to separate them into three different categories or promotional groups: existing customers, previous purchasers, and first time buyers. Existing customers continue to buy the same brand. They are less motivated by price and more attracted to psychological motivations, such as loyalty programs. Previous purchases are price shoppers and search for bargains, especially coupons and special offers. First time buyers are cautious and want more information about a product or service. This group is more influenced by product demonstrations, sampling, and free trial periods for experiencing the brand.

Sales promotions programs also need a very clear and specific description of their demographic and psychographic profiles for planning advertising support. Behavioral segmentation and brand usage patterns are the next level to be considered when identifying the best possible target audience for a promotion. And finally, geographic considerations based on the specific determined strategies of the brand, or company, will again influence the selection of advertising media as well as communication on social media and other digital platforms.

Time Frames

Promotions can be too short, too long, or too frequent. When a promotion is too short, there is not enough time for the advertising, social media, and digital marketing program to have any impact upon the targeted audience. And as a result, few people will respond. Sales will be very disappointing, and the promotion will be a failure. When a promotion is too long, there is no sense of urgency. This means that only a limited number of people will be motivated to respond. Once again, sales will fall below the anticipated number, and this promotion will also be a failure.

When a promotion is too frequent, and is constantly being used as a marketing strategy, it does not have any importance. When a brand is always having a promotion, or discount sale day, the offer is usually ignored. Still, a limited number of people will respond because they need to purchase a product in that category, and they want the lowest price.

How do you find the time frame that is just right for your brand? Here is a good way to begin. Construct a matrix that compares purchase rate frequency and the value of a product or service. Put the purchase rate in the left column of the matrix. Be sure to define the average number of times for each purchase rate category. For example, occasional might be once a month, while regular is once a week, and frequent is several times per week. Then, put three columns across the matrix for value. Label them according to high, medium, and low value based on price points.

Expenses and Budgets

Promotions cost more than you think. That's because there is more to planning, organizing, and implementing a promotion than you would expect. First, the lost profit, or revenue, connected with the promotional offer must be calculated. Second, the cost of the marketing communication budget to support the promotion must be estimated. Third, the expenses involved in the management of the promotion event, activity, or program must be accurately identified.

The lost profit or revenue for a promotion is calculated based on the manufacturer's wholesale price. This is not the retail price but the amount of money a company receives when a product or service is sold to the first link in a channel of distribution. Marketing communication budgets are estimated on the basis of the type of media strategy selected, duration of the promotion, and intensity level of brand messages. For national brands, this could include advertising costs for television, as well as social media, along with other supporting materials. Launching a promotion program goes beyond Facebook posts and Instagram videos. It can be a series of new brand messages that are included in an ongoing campaign with Google Ads. This means either using existing funds or allocating an additional amount of money for the promotion. The expenses involved in a promotion will be related to the activities and personnel required beyond internal staff and employees: for example, hiring a software company to design a coupon redemption program or a management firm that specializes in arranging a brand-oriented sweepstakes promotion.

Ethical and Legal Issues

Promotions will always involve attorneys and legal consultants. Their expertise is needed to review the wording, mechanics of the program, liabilities issues, discrimination rights, consumer protection laws, and finally, contractual arrangements with suppliers. This also involves the full disclosure of the promotional offer in the advertising. As a result, the "fine print" is always part of the commercial or advertisement as well as any printed literature or online digital statements.

The most difficult challenge in the United States is state and local regulations. Since there are few national laws, states can make their own requirements. That means that it is necessary to check the advertising regulations and promotion laws for each of the 50 states. For example, the word "free" cannot be used in many states unless the items can be obtained without making a purchase. In other locations, "free" cannot be used in any form of advertising. So, it is essential to know the laws, especially what can and cannot be done with brand-oriented promotions.

Performance Measurements

Evaluating the effectiveness of promotional activities, events, and programs is very similar to advertising, but with one important difference. The criteria used to measure the performance of a promotion change with the individual strategy selected. As you will read later in this chapter, there are specific measurement criteria associated with each promotion category. These can be incorporated into the promotional objectives and used for evaluating the effectiveness of the promotion during the pre-determined time frame. It is important to remember that increases in sales, profits, or market share that occur during a promotional period might be attributed to many other factors, especially competitive activity. So, the performance measurement of a promotional activity, event, or program is a combination of metrics. Let's save that discussion for later.

Sales Promotion Strategies

Now that you know the requirements for planning a promotion strategy, let's take a closer look at each of the major categories along with the most frequently used methods. There is no single best way to motive a customer to purchase a product or service. Each strategy has a different appeal and attractiveness for shoppers, buyers, and loyal customers. And, the amount of the purchase incentive is an important variable. Because the competitive marketing environment is always changing, any adjustments or additions must be flexible and responsive.

Incentive Categories

There are several ways to organize these sales promotion strategies. In Figure 9.1, the potential strategies are categorized into four major groups: cost reduction strategies, value invitation strategies, psychological reward strategies, and targeted interactions strategies. Each strategy provides a different incentive, motivation, or reason to purchase a product or service. That is why knowledge of consumers and their buying behavior is essential. Now, you will realize the value of both primary and secondary research, since it guides decision-making.

The complete listing of the 15 most frequently used sales promotion strategies is contained in Figure 9.2. Since the final selection of a strategy depends on the current positioning of a brand and its value proposition, as well as the stage in the product life cycle, every brand decision will be different. It is the responsibility of the advertising or sales promotion to make that selection and allocate the required financial amount to design and deliver an offer to the targeted audience.

Figure 9.1 Sales Promotion Strategies

Figure 9.2 Implementation Tactics for Sales Promotion

Price Reduction Strategies

Coupons, buy-one/get-one, cash back, purchase volume, minimum quantity, special models, and featured items.

Retail Deal Offers

Extra product, free trial, amenities, free gifts, self-liquidations, and on-pack items.

Psychological Rewards

Loyalty programs, exclusive experiences, membership clubs, reward points, special recognition, event privileges, and VIP treatment.

Targeted Interactions

Brand sampling product demonstrations, sweepstakes, contents, digital problem solving, online game access, and virtual events.

Price Reduction Strategies

Although financial incentives are classified as sales promotions, they also can be described as "invisible" pricing strategies. By reducing the final purchase price of a product or service, these incentives make a brand more attractive and affordable for consumers. When shoppers are more aware of these financial incentives, the probability of a purchase increases. Lower prices always motivate people, especially when they are searching online. It is a proven strategy that attracts new customers and immediately takes sales away from competitive brands.

The most frequently used financial incentives for consumer promotions are paper coupons, digital coupons, BOGO (buy-one, get-one), cash back, rebates, minimum quantity, special models, and sale-only items. B2B promotions also involve financial incentives, but how and when they are offered are different than the reduction in the cost for a consumer product or service. The relationship between a manufacturer and a wholesaler, or any channel member and a retailer, determines the final amount paid. The majority of discounting is based on the types and value of the products and services purchased, but there are many other forms of concession. In Chapter 12, the last chapter of this textbook, there is a more detailed description of business-to-business sales promotion and communication strategies.

Paper Coupons Paper coupons are still descending upon us. They come from many directions. Some are familiar, while others are not. They are a reminder of another period of history: a time when people cut them out of newspapers, magazines, brochures, postal mail, and anything else that was made of paper. Even today, people continue to bring hundreds of millions of paper coupons into stores, restaurants, and retail businesses. But, the times are now changing. Paper coupons are still here, but with digital technology, what's next? So, it's good-bye scissors! And, hello mobile apps!

Free-Standing Inserts (FSIs) Historically, the largest distribution method for paper coupons in the United States is the free-standing insert (FSI). It is also called the Sunday Supplement because it was always placed in the center of the newspaper. The FSI is basically a collection of special sale announcements, featured brand promotions, and a treasure chest of paper coupons. It is either a single sheet of glossy paper, a multi-fold tabloid brochure, or a large broadsheet that opens up like a small magazine. While you probably don't get a Sunday paper, talk to someone who does.

More than 84% of all the paper coupons in the United States are still distributed through the Sunday edition of metropolitan and medium-size city newspapers. While the popularity of FSIs has diminished, billions of paper coupons per year are still being distributed. Why are they so appealing? It is because being in an FSI is much cheaper than placing a display advertisement inside a section of the newspaper. Besides, the life of a newspaper is only a few days, and coupons from an FSI might be kept for weeks or even months. The only cost is the printing of the insert and the insertion expense charged by each newspaper. While this can be expensive, there are plans and lower prices based on targeting city zones or zip codes.

The demise of newspapers has drastically lowered their circulation. Fewer readers means a reduction in the attractiveness of this medium for advertising. As a result, newspapers have begun to lose advertising revenues from local movie theatres, real estate listing, and the very profitable personal ads. Netflix, Zillow, and Craig's List are just some of their digital replacements.

Post Office Mail There is a large tsunami of paper coupons that frequently fills your mailbox. It arrives daily at your home, apartment, or any location connected to your name and street address. And all too often, these paper coupons and promotional offers are delivered to "occupant" or "current resident." That really makes you feel special, doesn't it? So, why is postal mail still being used?

Postal mail is very effective at reaching people in a pre-determined geographic area. Local businesses can use zip codes to connect with potential buyers who are living close to their establishments. It is affordable, since the cost is low. And, coupons delivered by postal mail are effective, since many people keep them until they want to use them. It could be a coupon for a hamburger at lunch the next day, a new pair of shoes next week, or new tires for next month.

Single Sheet Flyers   They are everywhere. Where you live. Where you work. Where you exercise. Where you drink coffee. And occasionally, they find their way to your car window. Perhaps that is why they are called flyers, especially when the wind blows. This promotional technique is a very inexpensive way to promote a local business, organization, event, or any other activity. These coupon flyers can be printed professionally, reproduced at an office, or just printed at home from your computer.

The only real cost is the number of coupons redeemed, not distributed, which is a big advantage.

Digital Coupons   Remember, coupons used to be made out of paper. Well, they still are, but disappearing fast. That's good for multiple reasons. Just think of the ecological implications. Paper is made from trees, and green forests are necessary for replenishing oxygen It's better for the planet. And, it's better for us. But, there are many more reasons why digital coupons are better than paper coupons, especially for IMC programs and activities.

Advantages of Digital Coupons   Digital coupons offer five distinct advantages for companies and marketing communication. First, digital coupons prevent fraud. They cannot be photocopied, duplicated, or modified in any way. Since a digital coupon can only be used once, millions of dollars are saved from false coupon redemptions. Second, digital coupons are easier to redeem. This is a benefit to shoppers. No more searching for those clippings from newspapers, flyers, and store brochures. No more difficulties presenting them to the check-out clerk. No more missing the expiration date without a notification. Third is the cost of processing and redeeming digital coupons. The old way was awkward, old-fashioned, and time-consuming. Here is what would happen. The paper coupons were collected each day from retail stores, packaged into bags, and sent to a special redemption house that sorted coupons, and finally, payments to the retailers were arranged. Today, one click does it all, instantly! Fourth, digital coupons are flexible. They can be created in minutes and distributed at the push of a button. As a result, their delivery can be targeted on the basis of geography, store locations, or previous shopping behavior. Fifth, digital coupons are trackable. Since they are connected to individual telephone numbers, retailers and global companies have the opportunity to personalize messages and promotion offers and most importantly, collect data about the shoppers' purchases and brand preferences.

Digital coupons also provide a model for measuring consumer responsiveness to a specific offer along with a method for tracking their effectiveness. In Figure 9.3, the cycle of digital coupons and their ability to generate incremental sales is shown. This is structured around a simple four-part process of create,

Figure 9.3 Incremental Sales from Coupons

distribute, redeem, and repurchase. Specific measurable objectives can be determined for each part and then measured in real time during the promotional time period.

Digital Coupon Distribution   Let's take a quick look at digital coupons from the consumer's perspective. Mobile search is the most frequently used method for discovering, evaluating, and purchasing products and services. Branded or generic. Expensive or low priced. Popular or unknown. Easy to find or hard to get. Everything is out there in the online world. So, how do most people get their digital coupons? There are four sources: mobile apps, brand websites, coupon aggregators, and coupon generators.

First, mobile apps are the most popular way to get coupons. Nearly every major brand has a proprietary mobile app that can be downloaded, for free, from either the Apple App Store or Google Play. Since most online search is done on phones, these mobile apps enable users to connect and interact with a brand or organization. Along with the ability to purchase products and services, mobile apps are perfect for discovering deals and obtaining coupons.

Second, brand websites. Shoppers can easily obtain and download digital coupons directly from a brand website. But many companies, or brands, use a different approach. A "coupon code" is provided for use during the online check-out or redemption with purchase at a retail store. This code can be very simple and relevant, such as June Savings, or a more complex series of letters and numbers, such as XMB47512. Other companies give shoppers the choice to download a "coupon image" and then print a paper coupon at home or in an office. This coupon can then be used for instant redemption at a retail store with a traditional bar code or the square QR image.

Ironically, there is also an option to download an image of a coupon, print a copy, and then use it like a paper coupon. This seems counterproductive, and it is for many large companies.

Third, coupon aggregators. These companies are "discount intermediaries" that search, find, and display coupons from thousands of different companies, including hotels, resorts, airlines, and entertainment events. They do not create coupons. They do not redeem coupons. Their entire business model is based on the click-through traffic generated through their website. The problem with many of these websites is that they do not always remove coupons that have already passed their expiration dates. This is both an annoyance and an inconvenience for shoppers.

Fourth, coupon generators. This is a new hybrid type of company. It combines coupon savings with deal discovery using a number of new techniques. We all know, and most of us have used, PayPal. This online financial giant is now in the business of "deal discoveries" with its acquisition of the Honey Science Corporation in 2019. PayPal has a network of 24 million merchant partners, and its website extension technology works with more than 30,000 merchant websites. This massive retail connectivity enables Honey to provide multiple functionality, including product discovery, price tracking offers, promotional codes, and loyalty rewards.

Here are three of these programs available through the Honey website: DropList, Amazon Badge, and Honey Gold. DropList automatically searches and alerts users to lower prices with continuing updates. Amazon Badge searches through the pages of the largest online retailer in the United States for specific brands and items. Then, customers are notified of the lowest price from those intermediaries who ship and deliver the items. Honey Gold is a user reward program that shares a portion of the earnings that the company receives when a customer shops at any one of more than 4500 independent brand websites. At the end of 2020, Honey had an estimated 27 million active users. How sweet it is to grow so quickly! www.joinhoney.com

Buy-One, Get-One (BOGO)   Buy-one, get-one always has a money saving appeal for shoppers. In reality, BOGO is a 50% discount from the regular purchase price. This retail strategy is highly effective because most customers know, or at least believe, that a significant amount of money has been saved with each purchase. As a result, people will spend more money during a shopping visit. So, any lost profit from offering a BOGO will be made up by people spending more money.

   BOGO strategies can also keep competitors away from your customers. Since a shopper now owns two packages of your brand and not one, it will be extremely difficult for a competitor to get a sale until the customer's next purchase cycle. While this is only a temporary advantage, the brand purchased with a BOGO strategy has an excellent opportunity to increase customer satisfaction and owner loyalty. Since a BOGO promotion moves products off shelves faster, this boosts retail sales and provides a faster and more predictable cash flow for stores. This is especially important for grocery and drug store chains that purchase a large volume from wholesalers, providing a boost in sales. Plus, the entire process accelerates the reordering process.

Cash Back   Getting any amount of money back, after purchasing a product or service, is always a satisfying experience. But, this is just another form of an "invisible" pricing strategy. It is a very effective sales promotional method because the offer is perceived to reduce the final cost of buying an item. This is very attractive and appealing to potential purchases. However, the manufacturer or retailer who is offering a cash back has planned to automatically include the amount of the cash back in the sales promotion price that is being given to the customer. While the selling price appears to be lower, it is actually an inflated price that has been discounted only for the promotion.

Rebates   When people are searching for the lowest possible price, rebates always get their attention. Since they are already interested in the product, the financial incentive involved in receiving some money back, or having it applied to the final purchase price, is a strong incentive for consumers. Rebates also provide people with an opportunity to save money by comparing brands. For example, let's assume that an online shopper is comparing two large screen televisions. The first has a published retail price of $450 but offers a $100 rebate. But, the second television has a discounted price of $375. If both are perceived to have the same quality, then the first offer with the $100 rebate will be more attractive. Since the final purchase price is only $350, the decision is easy to make. This is the power of a rebate as a financial incentive and motivating factor.

Value Invitations

Deal Discovery   Deal discovery is the process of using mobile apps to search, compare, and identify the lowest prices for a particular brand, product category, or service function. It can indicate the location where the item can be purchased or display a price comparison chart on the website of the deal discovery search app being used.

Extra Content   Has the size of a chocolate bar shrunk since you were a child? Or, what about last week when you noticed that your favorite box of crackers had become smaller? No, it is not your imagination. Making a product smaller in size can keep the retail selling price down. This is much better than raising the price and losing customers because they think it costs too much. The secret for the brand manufacturer is to make the physical reduction large enough to achieve meaningful cost savings but not too visible or recognizable by consumers.

As an experiment, here are a few possibilities to consider. Compare the number of ounces between two cans of soda, breakfast cereal, or laundry detergent. Would you know if there was 10% less of each? That 8-ounce can might be the same size but contain only 7.2 ounces inside. And that soap package has 1 inch less of product inside. Those poor Americans have to deal with metric conversions, too. Imagine a regular-sized bottle of purified water that has all three of these measurements on the label: 16.9 fluid ounces (1.07 pints) 500 ml.

On-Pack Bonus   Attaching a small box or a useful item to the original package is called a bonus pack. It can be a sample of another related product, an extension of the brand, or an item that relates to the utilization of the brand: for example, a free toothbrush attached to a tube of Crest toothpaste or a foil squeeze sample of hair conditioner for L'Oréal shampoo. Marketing creativity is unlimited for non-related bonus pack items, such as free DVDs, discount tickets, or sunglasses. The only restrictions are the challenges of attaching or inserting the item to the package. The perceived appeal of the item should determine its selection, especially to the correct market segments and potential buyers.

Free Trial Usage   The offer is so appealing. But, read the fine print on the promotion offer. Or, just continue with the registration process. Eventually, there is a request for your credit or debit card number. That is because the terms of your promotional agreement include a monthly charge after the initial 30 days. Sure, the service can be canceled at any time. Netflix is a great example. Most companies are honorable and respond promptly to your request, while others take longer than expected. They are hoping you will reconsider. Look at it this way. What is the company giving up? Actually, nothing. Offering a free trial is a strategy that is literally a form of publicity because it makes consumers more aware of a brand, and actually boosts the brand's image. And, if a customer does decide to accept the free trial offer, the company has the opportunity to continue the relationship. While there are no verified numbers to provide the effectiveness of a free trial offer, it often results in higher sales and profits. How many free trial offers have you accepted during the past year?

Gift Merchandise It doesn't have to be Christmastime to receive a gift from a marketer. Of course, the free gift automatically comes with a purchase of a product or service. Interestingly, people still believe that they are getting something free, or at least at a special price. For example, the perception of receiving a free computer when they buy a new car has more appeal than just lowering the purchase price of the automobile. The reason is that the value of the computer is recognized, but the realistic number for buying a new car is uncertain, especially with a sales person.

Self-Liquidating Premiums This promotion allows you to purchase special items, called premiums, at very low or substantially reduced costs, but only if you first buy the brand running the promotion. Just send in your money with proof of purchase, and the company will ship the merchandise directly to your home address. It is called a self-liquidating premium because the premium item is being sold at its actual cost, and the brand sponsoring the promotion does not make any money from its sale. The rationale presented to the customer is that the opportunity to buy the merchandise at this exceptionally low price is made possible only through them and no one else.

Psychological Rewards

Loyalty Programs The most popular successful psychological reward strategy is a loyalty program. The more frequently you return to a store, the more money you spend online, or the more services you use, the greater the personal reward for you. These rewards are measured in points, visits, or other forms of loyalty. Airline loyalty programs have become so popular that the points earned from flying are almost the same as money. The only problem is the relationship of the earned rewards to their redemption value. For example, how many miles are required to receive a free ticket for travel on American Airlines, British Airways, or Qantas? Each airline has a different reward chart and procedure. This can easily be a competitive advantage or a strong reason to prefer an airline.

Point reward systems are everywhere, especially at the retail level. Walgreens drug stores has an extensive loyalty program, as well as Outback Steak House and the local ice cream store. Who wouldn't want a free cone on every fourth visit? Loyalty programs are essential in most consumer businesses. But, the challenge is planning and promoting an effective reward system. Points are another form of money. So, the relationship between points and profits must always be balanced.

Figure 9.4 highlights the three main reasons for emphasizing a customer loyalty program. First, loyalty programs discourage competitors. People will remain with the same brand as long as they know they are being rewarded for doing so. For example, how many times did you book the same airlines just so you could accumulate more miles? Or, shop at a retail store because they offered extra discounts or points for merchandise? Second, loyalty programs maintain a very solid and predictable sales base, which results in a consistent cash flow and guaranteed level of profitability. Third, loyalty programs provide excellent opportunities for

Figure 9.4 Benefits of Loyalty Programs

growth and expansion. When people are already loyal brand customers, they can be encouraged to try new products and services from the same company. Or if their satisfaction level is high, perhaps these same customers will be using the brand more frequently or sharing their good experiences with others.

Exclusive Experiences   There are some things money can't buy, and this type of promotion takes advantage of that perception, especially among the higher-income and luxury segments. While you can buy an expensive Rolex watch, you might not be able to have dinner with your favorite movie star or a private party with a sports hero. Making this type of arrangement takes more than a pile of cash and may not always be possible. But, corporations who are involved with entertainment companies, such as MGM and ABC television or football teams in the NFL, can make most anything happen.

Upwardly mobile buyers are also easily lured by promotions that feature new experiences. It provides them with a "talking point" with their associates at work, neighbors, and other people in their close circle of friends. Once again, making and spending money can cause diminishing returns in personal satisfaction. Receiving an experience, as a reward for purchasing a brand, really fits into the lifestyle of individuals who want to showcase their income and success.

People want more than just material things. They want something that they have never encountered before or want to try as an adventure. Activities and events that stimulate their minds and stir emotions are top of the list, along with learning a new skill, like painting, singing, gardening, kayaking, or kickboxing. Also, any experience that can be shared with others, such as family or friends, is attractive.

Millennials are the most responsive group because they love to discover new things, experiment with technology, and share everything on social media. They are also part of an emerging culture that would rather rent than own products and services, as evidenced by the growing popularity of Uber, Lyft, and other upstarts. Experiences of every kind are the magnets that attract potential buyers. But, the offers have to be perceived as more exotic, exciting, and entertaining than alternatives.

The motivational aspect of unique or exceptional experiences provides three psychological benefits for customers and potential buyers. As shown in Figure 9.5, they are emotional, excitement, and exclusivity. The first is the emotional response to the offer, as well as the initial emotional attachment to the brand. Some people, as you have observed, become almost obsessed with a particular brand and frequently become product ambassadors by praising the brand with its benefits on social media. The second component of the motivation value of experience is the excitement created by learning and then responding to the offer. Again, a loyal customer will be getting something that few people will ever be able to have or

Figure 9.5 Motivational Value of Experiences

become involved with. Exclusivity is the last motivational value, which makes the entire experience very special.

Here are several examples involving experiences and psychological motivational factors.

Membership Clubs   Joining a club has requirements. If membership is perceived as valuable, then customers will participate. In some cases, such as owning a Jeep vehicle, membership is automatic. This entitles its members to participate in a variety of company-sponsored activities and events.

Special Recognition   Everyone likes to be praised for their achievements or accomplishments. Brands can honor their customers for what they have done or contributed to the betterment of society. This form of recognition is a small but powerful way of building and boosting customer relationships.

Limited Editions   You have one, but no one else can get one. The appeal of exclusivity has its place in marketing and sales promotion. By creating a limited edition of a product or service, the brand has created demand for an item that can only be acquired by an immediate purchase.

Targeted Interactions

This cluster of sales promotion tactics includes brand sampling, free software downloads, games and puzzles, sweepstakes and contests, and product demonstrations. The value and benefit of each of these tactics are connected to intentional attempts to directly engage people in either a physical or an online environment. While there are many differences among the tactics, interaction with a live person is the preferred method of involvement. Let's take a look at these promotions.

Brand Sampling   If you are walking by a bakery, chocolate store, or movie theatre with popcorn, the aroma quickly gets your attention. And after tasting a sample, well, you might be ready to buy a few pounds or kilos. The product frequently sells itself, or at least makes someone aware of its taste and characteristics.

Sampling has been around for a long time, but it is just as effective as it was 100 years ago. But today, we have the Internet and new sampling methods, such as free downloads of music, games, or information. Another popular variation is a 30-day "trial period" and a free subscription or viewing. Digital technology and mobile marketing have increased the possibilities of sampling and interacting with potential purchasers on a regular basis.

The reason why sampling is such an effective strategy is simple. There is more than one sale involved. If the shopper likes the product and purchases it, this can lead to brand loyalty that translates into many sales over multiple months or years. In marketing terms, this is known as the "lifetime customer value," which can be calculated using specific numbers and financial value.

The financial value and benefits from sampling can be easily estimated. The calculation is a progression of percentages, as shown in Figure 9.6, a hypothetical example. If a free sample of a product is given to 1000 shoppers in a retail store, then brand name awareness is instantly increased among everyone who received the sample. But, what if 300 of those people actually decided to purchase the promoted brand on that same day, perhaps motivated by a coupon or other incentive offer? And, what if 100 of these same people continued to purchase that same brand on a regular basis? Finally, what if the other 200 people did not buy the product again or only purchased it occasionally? It's time for you to do the math. Just decide the retail purchase price of the product multiplied by the initial purchasers who became brand loyal for a year.

There are many different kinds of sampling distribution methods, including in-store, home delivery, postal mail, package inserts, in-media, and street teams. While all can be effective, the exact method depends upon the amount of money allocated to the promotion, amount of time required, quantities budgeted for sampling, number of shoppers or people involved, and other cost variables. In-store sampling is perhaps the most effective way because it is provided in the same location where a consumer can immediately purchase the product or service.

Other sample methods are more expensive, such as home delivery and postal mail, while in-media distribution is a novel but specialized application. Package inserts are simply small samples of a product placed in a normal package. In-media samples are those small pieces of paper inserted into the sides of magazines that

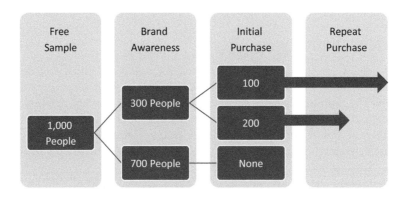

Figure 9.6 Sampling Payout Calculations

release an aroma through micro-encapsulation, also known as "scratch and sniff." Amazingly, nearly every scent can be reproduced through this process, from the smell of hot buttered popcorn to leather jackets.

Many brands use a street team as a micro-strategy, which is a very flexible, low-cost method to guarantee exposure to a brand. They are easy to organize and quick to launch. There are no rules or requirements. There are no formats. The street team can contain any number of people, but two or three per team is best. The number of teams depends on the budget as well as the task required. Adequate coverage of a target demographic group is the primary purpose of a team.

Red Bull and Monster are examples of national companies that use street teams. Perhaps you have seen one of their sponsored vehicles with an oversized reproduction of an energy drink, and a swarm of young people who are wearing t-shirts with the logo of Red Bull or Monster. Free hats, bags, and other fun merchandise are frequently distributed from the branded vehicle.

But, is it an efficient marketing communication strategy? Not really. The cost per person contacted is relatively high compared with other options. Street teams can selectively appear in nearly any public setting, from parking lots to music concerts and from office buildings, schools, and factories to city parks, shopping centers, and other places with plenty of people. Still, street teams are popular and frequently used to promote many products and services. It makes the most sense to go to this option when introducing a new brand, emphasizing a competitive advantage, or basically to gain exposure among highly desirable "influencers."

Free Software Downloads   Are you giving away nothing for something? In a certain way, yes. Software is not like a product that has a permanent value. Offer a product for free, and the profit from that unsold item has been eliminated. But, software has a fixed cost for development. So, it can be sold again and again and again. Total profit is a cumulative effect, based on individual sales, whenever they occur. The value of the free download, if connected to a future purchase, is similar to product sampling.

Games and Puzzles   Online gamification is more than just entertainment when it involves brands. Games and puzzles are an innovative way to engage consumers and to generate many return visits to a website. The content can be created for a brand through a software development company. Participation in a game can include competitive events with prize rewards or recognition on the website. Usually, the games are offered free, but registration with a name and email is frequently required. This provides companies with valuable information for future emails and promotion programs.

Why do people like game and puzzles? There are many reasons. And, you already know most of them. But, the lure of participating is always contagious. There are other companies, which are not connected with any brand, that leverage the data obtained from people who visit their websites. This can be selling digital display advertising within the game or puzzle, or selling information collected from the participants, especially names, phone numbers, and emails.

Sweepstakes and Contests   Another way to gather plenty of names and email address is to promote a sweepstake or contest.

What's the difference? In a sweepstake, everyone has an equal chance to win. This is because the winners are selected at random. Even if you enter multiple times, the odds of winning are about the same as for a single entry. It all depends on how many total entries are received, but it is always possible that you have the winning entry. Good for your dreaming and business, too.

In a contest, a certain level of skill is required to perform a task or to create something. Judges are involved to ensure a professional evaluation of the task. This could involve drawing, writing, or just solving a problem. It doesn't make any difference what the contest is about as long as a substantial amount of entries are received. This is a great way to gather information and data about people that can be used for future promotions and marketing communication programs.

Ironically, the most important reason for a sweepstake or contest is the opportunity for data base input. This type of sales promotion program, among other things, allows collection of the names, emails, and a variety of other information about customers and prospective buyers. This benefit, which is shown in Figure 9.7, provides a new source of data for future email marketing, social media, and IMC campaigns. It can also be combined with reports that indicate responsiveness, especially when people voluntarily opt in or have to register during a limited time period.

Product Demonstrations   The best method is a live demonstration with a product presenter or sales representative. This provides an opportunity to engage a shopper and to focus their undivided attention on the brand. It encourages a shopper to ask questions as well as helping a demonstrator to move closer toward a final sale. When tasting or experiencing a product is not feasible, demonstrate how it works or when it is used. This is usually a live action event but can also be shown with video on a portable screen. Live demonstrations have the advantage of a realistic simulation of product usage with the opportunity for shoppers to ask questions and try a few things for themselves. Video is better when a consistent message is preferred, along with a smooth, error-free demonstration. Also, videotape presentations are much less expensive than live presenters and available for viewing on a continuous

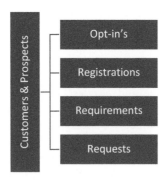

Figure 9.7 Opportunities for Data Base Input

basis. Product demonstrations are perfect for introducing a new product, gathering feedback from shoppers, or trying to stimulate immediate sales.

While television commercials and videos on YouTube are excellent ways to demonstrate the features and benefits of a brand, there is no effective feedback mechanism. While the number of viewers can be recorded, there is little opportunity for remarketing or contacting the individual. Online chat sessions can be an extremely effective way to encourage and engage viewers after a video demonstration on a brand's website. Although these can be automated responses to frequently asked questions, the value of live personal interaction is still the most effective.

Summary

Sales promotion is a short-term IMC strategy that stimulates immediate interest in a product or service. Financial and other incentives are offered, such as coupons, free samples, sweepstake prizes, cash back, experiences, bonus awards, or merchandise to specific target audiences to motivate a purchase decision. People respond to the perceived value, time limit for the offer, desirability of the brand, program complexity, and the number of requirements involved. The most important part of any promotion is the limited amount of time. It requires consumers to act immediately or lose the opportunity. The result is that a greater number of people will respond to an offer. Promotion offers can originate from three different sources: a manufacturer, a wholesaler, or a retailer. Manufacturers can provide incentives to any channel intermediary. Wholesalers, brokers, agents, or licensed representatives can offer similar incentives to retailers.

The cost of a sales promotion program is complex, since it involves the direct expenses of the offer as well as the associated costs. These include advertising support for the program, retail display materials, channel incentives, administrative expenses, and agency development fees.

Promotions also require extensive planning and coordination with distribution channel members, company sales associates, media resources, contracted suppliers, and internal management.

Measurement of sales promotion effectiveness depends on a combination of factors, such as increases in store traffic, website visits, social media posts, telephone inquiries, email requests, and the number of incremental units of the product or service sold during the promotional period.

Discussion Questions

1. Why are digital coupons more effective than paper coupons?
2. What are the advantages and disadvantages of a price reduction strategy?
3. Are BOGOs better than discounts? How often should they be offered to existing customers?
4. How appealing are coupon codes for online shopping? Do they attract new buyers?

5. Are live product demonstrations in a retail store a waste of time and money?
6. Is promoting a sweepstake better than a contest for attracting new customers?
7. What are the most appealing characteristics for a loyalty reward program? Give an example.
8. Do you think that product sampling is a good option for a new brand? What are the benefits?
9. Do sales promotion programs need advertising support in legacy media? Or social media?
10. What are the challenges in writing an objective for a sales promotion program or activity?

Chapter Assignments

1. Estimate the coupon redemption rate needed to achieve a 100,000 unit increase in Coke sales.
2. Plan a sales promotion event that stimulates 1000 visits to a website during a music concert.
3. Recommend a sweepstake promotion for a brand that features exciting prizes or experiences.
4. Make a list of five self-liquidating premiums for a local automotive dealer's marketing event.
5. Calculate the lifetime value of a new customer from a sampling program for a chocolate bar.

Continuity Case Study

The agency came over to the Athena office very early that day. They showed Adriana proprietary software that creates digital coupons. This was a great way to get people to try Athena for the first time. If consumers downloaded this mobile app, they would be able to receive notifications of special prices, deals, and featured promotional menus. Adriana liked the idea but knew that Martin was strongly opposed to any form of couponing. He believed that it eroded profit margins and projected an image of lower quality. Two years ago, one of the largest restaurant owners had tried couponing in their market but had had plenty of problems with its implementation.

After the coupon demonstration, Adriana asked the agency for their opinion on three different sales promotion programs: sweepstakes, sampling, and owner loyalty. There wasn't enough money in the budget to fund all of them, but enough for only one in the IMC plan. Tony suggested an idea for a "Win a Family Trip to Greece" sweepstake. He said that the trip would be very inexpensive and easy to promote. The creative director thought of imitating McDonald's with a "happy meal" for children. Adriana liked the sweepstake. She felt it reinforced the brand's positioning and had the potential to increase traffic.

1. What are the dangers of using paper coupons? Are digital coupons better?
2. Has Adriana thought of all the requirements for a sweepstake program?

3. Which of the two promotion ideas has the greatest sales potential?
4. How could a sampling or owner loyalty program be implemented?
5. What other promotional strategies could be recommended for Athena?

IMC Plan Development

Step One:
> Select the most relevant and appealing sales promotion strategies for your brand.

Step Two:
> Write an objective for each promotion along with the key performance metrics.

Step Three:
> Estimate the number of people who might respond to each promotional offer.

Step Four:
> Calculate the cost of planning, implementing, and managing every program.

Step Five:
> Determine the launch date for your promotion with a time frame for completion.

Chapter 10

Public Relations Strategies

Earned Media Coverage and Building Lasting Relationships

Learning Objectives

1. To be able to identify, interact, and build relationships with stakeholders
2. To recognize and understand the most important functions of public relations (PR)
3. To maximize content creation and distribution for companies and brands
4. To support Integrated Marketing Communication (IMC) strategies with PR programs, events, and activities.
5. To calculate earned media value using both financial and perceptual metrics

---

Introduction

Most of the time, companies have to pay for media exposure, but with PR, there is no cost. There is only one problem. Companies cannot control the content. The information, both good and bad, is a decision made by media publishers. So, any brand news could be distributed, or not. Publishers have absolutely no obligation to include facts, stories, or descriptions of products or services. That is the challenge of PR. Get what you can for free, but expect nothing.

There are also many different stakeholders or publics involved, such as the community, government, employees, suppliers, labor unions, educational institutions, industry leaders, and international companies. Each one is very important for building a positive and continuing relationship. This chapter briefly describes

DOI: 10.4324/9780367443382-10

the importance of communicating with these stakeholders and especially, building relationship. It is a very important, but often overlooked, pathway for IMC. After you learn more about publicity, then you will realize why so many corporations have a department dedicated to PR.

Value of Public Relations

Publicity is a word that is frequently used but not always understood. It can be considered good or bad, desired or avoided, and positive or negative. Publicity gets people talking and stimulates conversations as well as promoting people, products, and services. Publicity is simply exposure in any form of media. But, there is much more involved with publicity than a single event or popular activity. Public relations is a complex and ongoing series of events, circumstances, media exposure opportunities, and communication challenges.

Definition of Public Relations

Exactly what is public relations? We hear those words every day. Everyone is always talking about good PR and getting favorable press coverage. So, what is this process all about? Here is a simple definition that will help you to better understand this essential business function. Public relations is the strategic communication process that identifies, interacts, and builds mutually beneficial relationships among people, companies, and organizations. The ultimate goal of PR activity is to influence opinions, attitudes, beliefs, and images about a brand, business, organization, or social issue.

Here is why PR is so important to large corporations, small businesses, entrepreneurs, and non-profit organizations. First, PR activities are considered to be a form of earned media coverage. You do not have to pay the media, like advertising, to deliver a message. Second, the opportunity for leveraging PR is always available. The growing need for content is a challenge for most media platforms. So, PR is there to provide a steady flow of information. And third, PR requires a minimum amount of preparation. Press releases and digital news distribution can be prepared quickly and distributed immediately. But, it is extremely important to be accurate, clear, and transparent with any information released through media channels.

However, there is a downside. The final content that will be published or appears in multiple forms of digital media cannot be controlled. A media company is never obligated to use information that is received from a company or organization. And if it does, anything can be modified or changed. This can range from selecting portions to just using a few facts. And, there is always the possibility of negative or unfavorable comments. These include articles or blogs about a company, its products, or its management. So, there is a big trade-off: no cost versus no control.

IMC involves strategic planning to inform, persuade, and motivate individuals to purchase a product or service. However, there is an important distinction between the functions and activities of PR and marketing management. PR involves forming, or changing, attitudes among diverse groups of people, while

IMC focuses on promoting a brand and stimulating sales. This distinction is reflected in the official definition from the Public Relations Society of America: "Public relations is a strategic communication process that builds mutually beneficial relationships between organizations and their publics."

Earned Media Benefits

Every time there is information or news about a company, brand, person, or activity involving an organization that appears in any form of media, it is classified as earned media. This means that the financial value is based on the estimated cost of obtaining the same of exposure through paid advertising in any legacy or social media. As a result, you can quickly understand the value of earned media. But, receiving free publicity isn't easy. Competitors are trying just as hard as you would to get media coverage at no cost to them. Plus, the publications and media distribution networks are more concerned with the content that their readers, viewers, or listeners want to enjoy and definitely not the automatic promotion or coverage of a company or consumer brand.

Public Relations Agencies

As you learned in Chapter 2, there are thousands of small advertising agencies and digital marketing companies that develop creative ideas, purchase media, arrange sales promotion programs, and engage in other IMC activities. Although not as well known, there is an equal number of PR companies that provide a variety of services. And if you can't afford a PR agency, there are plenty of high-quality, professional individuals who are consultants in this field. As consultants, they perform essential PR services and usually have extensive contacts or relationships with traditional media, government officials, community leaders, and other influential people and organizations. Since their overhead is much lower, so is the price for their services. If you are a small business or entrepreneur, this can be very important. Another possibility is that an independent PR representative has a limited number of clients, so each one gets personal attention.

Building Stakeholder Relationships

The most important function of PR is to identify, contact, communicate, and form connections and relationships with groups that interact with or influence public attitudes or the overall perception and image of a company. While most of these groups are external to the organization, each one has a unique relationship with the company. As shown in Figure 10.1, these eight essential groups include media sources, industry members, professional associations, suppliers, employees, community, customers, and government. The challenge for a PR manager or department is to develop the most effective way to build a relationship of trust, confidence, and comfort among members within each of these essential groups, or stakeholders.

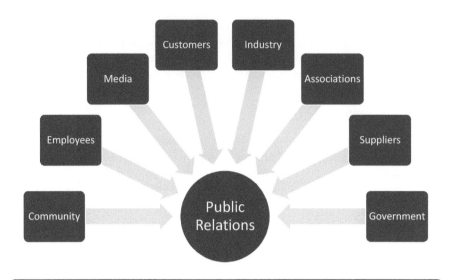

Figure 10.1 Identifying Relationship Groups

Customers

Customer relations can be handled through the PR department or the marketing department. It is the responsibility of a brand to listen to its customers before, during, and after making a purchase. When something is wrong with a product, or it is not working correctly, the reason must be determined and a reasonable solution provided. That is the only way to ensure customer satisfaction and maintain customer loyalty. While this is the responsibility of marketing, the difficulty is that customers often find and ask a PR department for assistance. What should be done? This is always a challenge, since the customer is always right.

Media Sources

Media relations are the foundation of publicity. But, there are many thousands of different media companies out there and millions of separate individuals involved. The publications or media sources that best serve your customer base or industry are the ones you are most concerned about influencing as well as building long-term relationships with over the years. While the top choices are easy to identify, there are many peripheral possibilities and others essential to corporate growth. For example, many companies target financial publications to influence their audience and boost the favorable perception of their stock as an investment opportunity.

Industry Members

What your competitors think of your company reflects on your reputation in the industry. That might not seem very important, but when it comes to making industry policy decisions, such as collaborating for favorable laws and government regulations, lack of respect can be a substantial negative factor in exclusion from the process. This also includes a company's external image for invitations to speak at conferences, educational seminars, and media interviews. So while competition will always be there, it is important to project a positive and progressive image.

Professional Associations

Every industry has one, or more, professional associations that provide services to its individual members as well as companies that support the organizations. Each association performs the function of being a unified voice of the industry both for lobbying purposes and for gaining public confidence. Companies that actively participate always have plenty of opportunities to recruit talented new employees and experienced managers. Plus, members learn from each other by sharing their best practices and networking with other executives with similar positions, titles, and responsibilities.

Suppliers

Businesses that provide products and services to another company have a relevant image. Do they pay promptly? How honest are they? Are their contracts fair or misleading? Suppliers want to work with companies that value their support services and recognize their contribution to the overall process of business management and marketing. While profitability is an essential requirement, the people that a company does business with can be more desirable and rewarding.

Employees

Employee communications includes a wide array of PR methods, such as the company magazine, newsletter, and other publication distribution methods with employees working in offices, plants, or warehouses. This is important not only to build a sense of contribution and belonging to a company but also to have a direct channel for messaging to employees so that they hear news announcements about the company and its activities before this information is released to the mass media. The worst thing that can happen is that employees find out what is happening from watching the local news on television or reading about it in a newspaper. Employees are a valuable asset for a company and should always be treated that way.

Community

Factory plants, warehouses, offices, and other facilities are an important and very visible part of the fabric of a local community. They provide employment, pay taxes, and contribute to the overall economic development and success of a geographic area. It is important to maintain a strong relationship with people in a specific geographic area. While not everyone in that community is an employee, there is a great amount of daily interaction with local business owners, retail store sales staff, and government officials. Community relations are very similar, but externally focused with an emphasis on getting the right messages out to selected individuals, groups, or organizations. The goal here is being an active and helpful member of the local business and living environment.

Government

Government relations is just another word for lobbying. The objective of lobbying is to get favorable legislation passed that helps the company to grow and become financially successful. This can be at the federal, state, or even local level. The specific need of each company will be different depending on the industry, the issues involved, and the importance of the situation: for example, new regulations on pollution control, increased taxes on profits, accounting practices, worker safety, reporting procedures, or tariffs on imported products. Lobbying requires plenty of personal contact and persistence along with frequent travel schedules. In addition, PR experts publish information and research reports to persuade government officials to either change or modify their positions. This can also involve attending public hearings, committee meetings, or other forums where an industry or company statement of opinion can be expressed.

Functions of Public Relations

The functions of a PR department at a corporation, as well as the services that can be provided by a PR agency, are shown in Figure 10.2. These functions include news releases, press conferences, company spokesperson, crisis management, executive speechwriting, content development, company website, social media management, community activities, sponsored events, internal publications, and corporate advertising. The PR manager will use an assortment of different communication methods for specific purposes. This can be a function of the task required, the amount of time available, the authorized budget, or the message involved.

Typically, the word "public" means the general audience, which includes nearly everyone. But, the professionals use this word to describe precisely which

Figure 10.2 Functions of Public Relations

public they want to reach with their message. Sound familiar? It is the same concept in a target market for advertising and sales promotion programs. Each public, stakeholder, or audience has a distinct profile, perspective, and passion. Communicating with them requires not only the right message but also the right timing and presentation of content. But, PR is more than just providing information and relevant content to these different publics. It is the continuing process of building and maintaining relationships as well as strengthening them over time. PR must also be viewed as a long-term strategy essential for the sustainability of a company, brand, or organization.

News Releases

In our digital world, the concept of a press release, or the more frequently used term "news release," has dramatically changed. A press release is longer just a single piece of printed paper, because the modern delivery method is now digital. No surprise here. However, there are thousands of press releases sent out every day by email, but there is a major difference between printed paper and digital documents. Keywords. Yes, the inclusion of keywords is essential. And, these are the same keywords that could be used for searching on Google or Bing. Pick the right keywords, and good things begin to happen. But finding the keywords is a combination of logic, skill, and imagination. Begin with a simple search and then, think about the other possibilities. Then, if you know how to use AdWords, Google can provide a short list for free. Other options include the keywords that competitors have used or that repeatedly appear in media.

Keywords are being constantly monitored by web crawlers, or search bots, which search the Internet to discover new content from either new or existing websites. This is part of the process of indexing information contained in the digital universe. Why is this important for a press release? Most media companies use software that involves web crawlers or spiders. If the keywords appear, the PR content is "flagged" and saved for review. If not, the press release is electronically skipped or more likely, deleted. So, no one will ever respond or even know that your information existed. Your publicity opportunity has been eliminated by technology, not people, because certain keywords were not used.

The digital media environment is also causing a major change in delivering PR content to news sources and publications. Enter the video press release. The format might be different, but the information is the same. How long? Or, how short? If it is going to be channeled through social media, then the shorter the overall length, the better. The attention span of journalists is limited, as is the amount of time available to review submissions. Then, consider the number of competitive PR agencies, each putting out digital media content for its clients. Getting noticed is difficult. Getting published is even more difficult.

Press Conferences

Press conferences, which are now called media conferences, are a strong tradition within PR. While it is important to share brand and company information with the media, it is essential to plan for it to be controlled and managed. The normal press conference, going back to the days of a newspaper-dominated world, is designed to give everyone in the media an equal opportunity to hear the news or announcement from a designated spokesperson, but at the same time. This means that media competitors are allowed equal access to the information, but what is published can be remarkably different, even when it comes from the same source. Although media representatives and journalists like to ask as many questions as possible, there is always a flexible, but limited, time period. Again, the rules of the event are arranged by a single individual, who is responsible for managing the flow and interaction at the press conference.

Who should attend? Typically, press conferences are an "invitation only" event, requiring a reservation. This ensures that the PR manager fills the room with the most important media. The selection criteria are the size of their daily audience or readership, their editorial reputation, or their relevance to the topic. Above all, the power to influence others is the most desirable characteristic. And, having a list of the expected attendees helps to prepare response strategies based on their previous interactions or history of reporting about the company.

Announcements are very important for a company but not so much for the media. Still, most magazines and newspapers, especially digital publications, need a continuous flow of content to fill their pages. And as more broadcast media companies maintain online versions with video, images, and text, there are countless opportunities to get excellent media coverage about people, events, activities, and brands. The topics will range from the hiring of new executive and managerial employees to the plans for building a new factory or distribution center. The receptivity of the media to these announcements is greatest among local publications or magazines that only feature news about a particular industry, such as automotive, real estate, fast food chains, construction, or banks. Digital newsletters are the best media source for distributing announcements, since their value is based on delivering recent news and information to their readers as fast as possible, especially before the same content is published by online competitors.

Company Spokesperson

Legally and financially, a corporation is a person. And with PR, it is the same. One voice speaks for all. In a corporation, that unifying voice could be a CEO, President, or Vice President, but most likely it will be the designed PR manager, and perhaps at a higher level, such as a Director of Corporate Communications. This is for two reasons. Individuals with professional training or experience with media relations are much more comfortable and effective in dealing with news reporters, journalists, or extremely unhappy groups of consumers. How you answer a question is often more important than what you say. So, the real skill of a PR specialist is to provide a satisfactory response without creating any misunderstandings, misinterpretations, or unwanted misrepresentations.

The second reason is that a "single source" eliminates the problems and conflicts associated with obtaining different answers and information from more than one person or company representative. There is an extremely good chance that the answers will not be the same and quite frequently, they may be conflicting. This situation would make any crisis, or situation, much worse and also instill a lack of trust and confidence in the company. The most important responsibility of the official spokesperson is always to deliver accurate, concise, and uncensored information to the media as well as to any other public. This requires preparation, practice, and professional abilities. The challenge demands a well-crafted message with answers to potential questions and a realistic description of the planned solution.

Crisis Management

PR is in the business of image management. It can come in many forms, such as crisis management, corporate advertising, advocacy promotions, and even philanthropy. The difference is the required speed of response and seriousness of the issues involved. Crisis management is at the top. Action must be taken immediately but still with great caution and accuracy. The perception of what the company does depends on how it communicates and handles the issues. Then, there are advocacy promotions. If a company wants to support a particular charity or social issue, it allocates financial funds and resources for that purpose. Participating in the cause also enables members of the company to actively get involved with the community and provides plenty of exposure opportunities through traditional media as well as a wide range of social media platforms. Philanthropy is a direct use of corporate money to impact individuals and non-profit organizations based on the goals established by those governing the funds. This can range from supporting cultural and social change to educational technology, environmental protection, and international charity.

Speechwriting

This is never easy. The writer has to completely understand the purpose and intent of the communication before the first word is ever created. Like any good storyteller, the speechwriter must begin with a strong introduction. Just like the headline of an advertisement, the initial sentence has to immediately capture the reader's, or listener's, attention. In fact, nearly every message involved with any form of IMC follows that same pattern of engagement. Next, the speechwriter has to develop the main idea and slowly guide everyone through the content. Best practices for preparing a successful speech usually include a conceptual outline, identifying the number of key points, or providing a preview of the final outcome. In the body of the speech, the words, phrases, and verbal imagery must be carefully crafted to support the intent or purpose of the speech as well as delivering interesting and relevant information to the targeted audience. And finally, the conclusion has to be dramatic, memorable, and impactful. Just as with advertising messages, a specific response, either psychological or physical, is expected and encouraged.

Knowing who is listening is also extremely important. Recognizing and reflecting the pre-existing attitudes of an audience most certainly creates greater empathy with the speaker, even if the speechwriter's message is designed to change or modify beliefs and opinions.

Content Development

Online publications are hungry for content. Professional writers and journalism cost money, which encourages media sources to use free content submitted by brand users or companies. PR departments can take advantage of this opportunity by frequently distributing short articles or interesting facts that are picked up by online publications. Prior to the Internet, there was a lot of personal contact and interaction between publicity generators and the media. Stories had to be presented in writing, but usually a visit to the publication's office was required to receive acceptable, but that was not always a guarantee of success. However, there is a big downside to the online world. It is too easy to just email content. And as a result, media publications receive hundreds of possible articles each day, which require time to read and evaluate. Who gets through, and what gets published online? That is the required skill of a PR manager. Content might be king, but a royal messenger will always be needed.

Not all documents sent to the media have to be press releases. There are plenty of opportunities to deliver information that is informative, educational, and helpful. This could be something unknown about the company or industry, such as popular trends, scientific or medical discoveries, or statistics involving product category usage rates or total consumption. These types of content stories are designed more for maintaining relationships with individual members of the media rather than expecting specific coverage. The content of these factual items has a different purpose, which is to demonstrate the knowledge, expertise, and leadership of the company.

This is a long-term strategy that builds a "good source" reputation when journalists are looking for quick answers or need help with understanding a situation, topic, product category, or company.

In Figure 10.3, there are three distribution opportunity pathways for media content: social media, featured stories, and information requests. With social media, there is an expectation of multiple postings and continual interaction. For example, information about a brand or company might be posted, then responses from customers, and a series of shared content with family, friends, and associates. With featured stories, there is the initial publication, extended coverage,

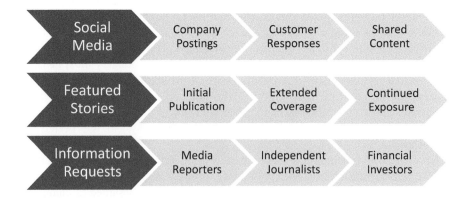

Figure 10.3 Content Distribution Opportunities

and ultimately, continued exposures of the content over time. With information requests, there are spontaneous and unanticipated inquiries made by media reporters, independent journalists, and financial investors, which require a professional response. This information or content must also be accurate, honest, and helpful to the individual who made the request, or there is no value.

Company Website

Corporate websites and brand websites are often the same. If they are designed correctly, you can quickly reach one through the other. While the marketing and advertising managers are responsible for the content of their "brand pages" or functional links to a separate website, corporate communications decides the look and feel of the homepage. The corporate website must reflect the image. Blogs are different. There can be personal blogs coming from a company, such as one from the President or CEO, or a PR blog. As you would expect, this digital media outlet is a perfect location for displaying and explaining a wide range of subjects and news information. It is very much a direct connection to the many publics that can be involved with a company or brand. While a basic website design is not changed very often, it still must contain timely updates of featured information and new perspectives of activity within the company.

Like it or not, social media are an important part of everyday life, especially for Millennials. But the use of social media is gaining popularity with all age groups. As increasing numbers are sharing their thoughts, photos, and videos, the need for companies and brands to be part of the process is essential. This is definitely not an easy task, since companies are unwanted participants in the communication. Their content is full of brand images and messages, usually perceived as an unwanted intrusion into space reserved for private and public interactions. Brands have to be presented as part of the fabric of everyday life. Their relevance gives customers meanings, but the source of the social media must be from the users, not the producers. While this is more a marketing challenge, PR involvement is always helpful. First, the participation must be slow, subtle, and regular to earn the trust and respect of the audience. Second, comments or posts should always be based on company relevance, not promotion. And third, always contribute but never criticize. The responsible use of social media for publicity is a more comprehensive and valuable approach to reach influential publics.

While most companies now have a full-time social media manager, that person is most likely in the marketing or advertising department. This makes internal coordination between the social media manager and the PR department very important. Neither should be posting without sharing the same information with the other, and in many cases, approvals are needed before releasing information to the public. Larger companies are now hiring separate social media managers for IMC and PR, but smaller companies and entrepreneurs must do everything themselves. Using scheduling platforms, such as Hootsuite and Sprout, makes it easier.

Community Activities

Whenever a company has a manufacturing facility, large warehouse, distribution center, or executive office within a community, active PR is required. Since there may be hundreds, or maybe thousands, of employees who live and work within a small geographic area, the PR department is compelled to be a good corporate citizen and participate in most of the local activities within the community. These can be civic events, charity fund-raisers, school programs, or any other relevant possibility. Tax revenues from the company already support the local government, but there are always requests for financial contributions or providing services at no cost to community-based functions.

Sponsored Events

Facts about what is happening when, and the purpose of the event, need to be communicated in a simple, concise, and helpful way. While these facts can be found on the Internet from other sources, the PR department must be the first to publish the information to ensure that it is correct and complete. The type of event doesn't matter, either a brand-oriented or a company-sponsored event, but there must be a single source at the company to contact to find more details or ask questions. This includes the individual's name, contact information, and job title.

Company executives and managers often give speeches or participate in panels at private workshops and seminars. These can involve a number of different industry organizations or associations, but most are national and held only several times a year. However, there are many local seminars that also attract high attendances when corporate experts are participating or speaking. The opportunity for the PR department is to promote their company in a leadership role. Photos, articles, and videos of a company's involvement in a seminar, especially with one of its executives or senior managers, are an excellent tool for this purpose. The options are endless but most certainly include internal company newsletters, trade publications, and immediate distribution through social media channels.

Information about the company, or the brand, is always available at consumer shows and exhibits, but is usually inexpensive and simple. This is primarily due to the cost of printing a large number of pieces that are easily thrown away by the end of the day. Still, it is a brief, but necessary, part of the PR exposure methods for building awareness of the company, not its brands. The marketing department handles the task of specific product and service brochures, but even those are rapidly diminishing in popularity with the increased use of mobile technology.

Internal Communications

The initial distribution of information about changes or major events within a company should be done among its employees. This is usually done through official emails but can also be in the form of written communications. It is essential that the people who work for an organization find out what is happening, either good or bad, before the information becomes news in a media source. Failure to share this simple communication can quickly lower morale and create unhappy employees, which is extremely damaging if they are interacting with customers.

Companies also create and distribute their own magazines, both online and printed for their employees. This is another way to distribute important information about the plans, activities, and focus of the company. A company publication also builds a feeling of unity, teamwork, and participation in a greater entity. The goal is to generate pride and enthusiasm for the company by describing and displaying the accomplishments of its products, people, and organization.

Corporate Advertising

Corporate advertising is very different from brand advertising. The subject or content of corporate advertising includes the philosophy of the company, its mission statement, and anything else that helps people understand what the company does and what it believes. The focal point is usually the products that it makes and sells or services provided. This is very intentional, planned, and carefully researched before being prepared for advertising or publicity. This advertising is designed to promote the company as a brand but might have radically different target audiences or influential publics. This results in a compilation of different media vehicles, including legacy publications, as well as a variety of digital websites and platforms.

In Figure 10.4, the relationship between media access and communication effectiveness is illustrated. This includes the nature of specialized audiences, diffused coverage, and variable content. If you consider the demographic, geographic, and psychographic composition of the nine different publics discussed in this chapter, the complexity of reaching a specialized audience becomes a real challenge. Then, there is the distribution and re-distribution of information through a wide spectrum of media platforms, especially when it involves Facebook, Instagram, or WhatsApp, where sharing can quickly become viral and geometrically expand instantly. And finally, variable content results in different levels of interest, priorities, and acceptance among the many competitive media channels. For example, as soon as one media resource publishes a news story or information, the other might immediately respond or choose not to include the content in their distribution system. It all depends on the importance and relevance.

Public Relations and IMC Strategies

PR is not always connected with the activities of brand advertising or IMC, yet it has a powerful and pervasive influence over consumer and stakeholder perceptions. The importance of earned media value is magnified by the level of awareness of a brand as well as its existing image. PR activities can contribute to

Figure 10.4 Media Access and Effectiveness

Figure 10.5 Public Relations and IMC Strategies

improving both awareness and image without the extremely large expenditures of money required for traditional legacy advertising media. While social media are frequently used to generate interest in a product or service, this represents only one part of a PR strategy for a brand.

Let's take a quick review of six important communication activities that involve PR and IMC. As shown in Figure 10.5, these include brand announcements, new product introductions, industry trade shows, brand questions and recalls, publicity for promotions, and sponsored events. Each of these activities has a different purpose and combination of skills needed to successfully support a brand and its relationship with customers.

Brand Announcements

The media appeal or attractiveness of the information about a brand is typically very low. Most publications and online media resources think that it is more about an attempt to get massive amounts of free exposure. But, there are exceptions. At one end, there are innovative and useful improvement or product features, and at the other end, mundane and unimportant product facts.

It comes down to how the information is presented and the value to the reader or viewer. For example, a mobile app that helps people to find empty parking places in a crowed city building has enough appeal to include during a morning television program, or a video doorbell camera to improve home security might also qualify. The final determinant is the perceived appeal of the product or the impact that it could have on people in a community.

New Product Introductions

Since the official launch date for the new brand is established many months in advance, there is plenty of time for the PR staff to prepare their materials. These include planned involvement in social media campaigns, promotional events, industry activities, and exclusive launch events. While a substantial amount of money from the IMC budget will be invested in advertising, publicity still is needed. Media coverage, either free or paid, earned or controlled, contributes to brand name awareness and positive attitudes among the target audience.

If you own a small company, or are planning to start a business, prepare to be a one-person PR department. The methods to get free publicity are the same, but the resources to do it are limited. This is still a much less expensive and easier way to generate awareness than advertising, but are there are no guarantees about what will be accepted for publicity or publication by the media. Just remember that PR can be an effective IMC strategy for any company or brand, regardless of budgets, product categories, industries, or marketing ability.

Industry Trade Show Activities

This is another collaborative effort between the marketing communication department and PR. The objective is to obtain as much pre-show publicity as possible for new products or announcements about the corporation or exhibitor. This can definitely increase the number of people visiting the company's display booth as well as making them interested in learning more about the new product or service. In many situations, an external PR agency is hired to personally contact or interact with media representatives during this period, since the trade show is only once a year. So, an exceptional amount of publicity is needed to maximize this type of event.

Product Recalls

It is never a good situation when the media publish reports on a product defect or recall. The responsibility of the PR department is to minimize the negative and quickly reassure existing customers. This is a very challenging and complicated situation that requires not only a professional but also one who is exceptionally cautious about the legal implications. The basic rule is to be honest, transparent, and open to questions. Most likely, there will be a series of media releases, press conferences, and the utilization of other channels of communication to answer related questions.

Publicity for Promotions

This can range from sweepstakes to rebates or can include any of the short-term marketing strategies for immediately stimulating sales. This typically does not have much appeal to the media, unless there is an unexpected part of the story or circumstance. For example, an offer to give a free taco to everyone in America during a World Series game most certainly qualified as an interesting piece of news that was quickly published. The "free taco" offer was dramatic, exciting, and sensational. And, the publicity from newspapers, television, and multiple websites automatically accelerated the rapid sharing of information through social media.

Sponsored Events

While this activity might be managed by the advertising or sales promotion department, the publicity potential of the event is excellent for the PR manager. Letting people know when and where the event is happening is the key to success.

This can be done with social media, but there are plenty of other ways to communicate the essential information. In either situation, the brand name and company should always be prominently displayed in any form of printed or digital messaging. Attendance is driven by the number of people who ultimately attend. This is where PR is extremely well prepared for attracting the most responsive audience.

Summary

PR is the formation and maintenance of relationships with a variety of different organizations, groups, and individuals. These publics include local community, government, company employees, suppliers, labor unions, financial publications, educational institutions, industry leaders, and international companies. The objective of this form of IMC strategy is to form opinions, change attitudes, and improve perceptions.

Publicity is measured by the media value that is earned through the exposure of a company, brand, or individual to a targeted audience. This is called earned media. The value of this earned media exposure is calculated from the actual cost of the media if the same amount of space or time had been used for advertising. Thus, the major benefit of PR is the financial value of free media coverage in digital media as well as in television, radio, newspapers, and magazines.

There is also the perceived media value that eventually influences surveys and opinion polls.

The PR department in a corporation, or small business, is responsible for distributing written and video press releases, arranging press conferences, speechwriting, communicating with employees, interacting with the community, attending trade shows, and managing crisis situations. The PR department also supports marketing management with publicity, online activity, and new product introductions.

Discussion Questions

1. Why is it important to build and maintain relationships with stakeholders?
2. How can you persuade a media journalist to write a content story about your company?
3. Should a small business owner or entrepreneur join an industry association?
4. What is the importance of using keywords in the writing of a press release?
5. Who is the best spokesperson for a company during a crisis situation or emergency?
6. Is it more effective to participate in a charity event or a local community activity?
7. What is the function of corporate advertising? Who is the preferred target audience?
8. Why should a PR agency be involved in planning a trade show?
9. How can publicity contribute to the successful launch of a new product or service?
10. Should PR managers depend on influential bloggers to promote a brand?

Chapter Assignments

1. Explore the website for the Public Relations Society of America (www.prsa .org).
2. Discover more about how to distribute news releases to media sources (www .prweb.com).
3. Take a closer look at the largest PR company in the world (www.edelman.com).
4. Outline a crisis management response plan for a major product recall with a national brand.
5. Estimate the media exposure value for a published content article in a national magazine.

Continuity Case Study

Martin read an article in the *Wall Street Journal* that praised the value of "free" media coverage. He was impressed with the ability of PR companies to get brands exposed without cost. While the "earned media" phenomenon was not new, the explosive growth of the Internet was creating an enormous demand for more content. Advertorials and "native advertising" were increasingly popular. Could this be used for Athena? Martin was curious. He wanted to know more. Martin also sent an email to Adriana and asked her to estimate the value of the publicity. This type of brand exposure, he believed, was worth much more than the amount of money that Athena had been spending on advertising.

Adriana remembered a documentary about the health benefits of eating yogurt. It was based on a popular book written by a biological chemist, who frequently appeared on the morning television talk shows. Adriana was impressed. She though he could do something similar talking about Greek food and the Mediterranean diet. She also asked a local yogurt company for a tour of its manufacturing plant. Perhaps, these ideas could lead to an excellent publicity opportunity or event. Adriana was not sure what to do next, but she wanted to try to extend her IMC activities.

1. How can Athena generate publicity for its restaurants?
2. Should Adriana hire a PR agency?
3. What other services can the PR agency provide?
4. Can the concept of earned media work for Athena?
5. Which publics are the most important to Athena?

IMC Plan Development

Step One:
    Identify the most important stakeholders involved with your product or service.
Step Two:
    Draft a written press release along with a script for a short video about your brand.

Step Three:

Create an "elevator pitch" that can be used at industry trade shows or exhibits.

Step Four:

Make a list of relevant publications and media distribution for a publicity campaign.

Step Five:

Select a community event or cause that can be part of your sponsorship strategy.

Chapter 11

Brand Visibility Strategies

Displaying a Physical Presence and Using Personal Contact

Learning Objectives

1. To become more aware of brand visibility opportunities
2. To evaluate the potential value of product placement proposals
3. To analyze and compare sponsorship and licensing arrangements
4. To understand the differences between advertising and brand visibility
5. To explore and understand the use of retail marketing materials

Introduction

Beyond advertising and digital media, there is another IMC dimension. It is finding new and innovative ways to insert brands and product images into everyday life. This includes featuring national or local brands in movies, television programs, music videos, and even video games, or allowing other companies to use your name or logo on products and services with a special licensing arrangement. Other creative uses are event sponsorships, prize awards, and paying a lot of money to have a sports or entertainment center be identified with your brand name. There is also the retail marketing environment with attractive packages, signs, and displays. Certainly, there are plenty of excellent opportunities to promote a brand without advertising or promotions.

DOI: 10.4324/9780367443382-11

Definition of Brand Visibility

While advertising, sales promotion, and public relations are very different IMC strategies, brand visibility has characteristics that are similar to all three. But, there are several important aspects that are unique. Here is why. There is no traditional media advertising involved, especially when competing companies purchase pages or media time for their brand messages. But, brand visibility influence can easily be incorporated into most of the content for viewable programs, movies, publication, or even games. There is no direct attempt to motivate the purchase of a product or service through financial incentives, but brand visibility can immediately change measurable awareness and favorable attitudes. And finally, customers and potential buyers are continually exposed to brands through unintentional involvement.

Brand visibility is defined as "any event, activity, or method that exposes individuals or groups to a brand name, logo, theme line, or image that requires a payment for participation, but requires either the exclusion of competitors or the ownership of exclusive intellectual properties." The money paid for participating in a brand visibility program depends on the amount and type of exposure. It can vary from a few hundred dollars to several million dollars per year.

Brand Visibility Categories

In this chapter, the following eight categories of brand visibility will be discussed, as shown in Figure 11.1: product placement, venue identification, event sponsorships, featured prizes, licensing rights, brand logo merchandise, product packaging, and retail display material. Each category has its own requirements, challenges, and opportunities. While most brand visibility activities are intended to be long-term strategies, others require shorter time frames.

Product Placement

The next time you are watching a feature length movie, just count all the brands and products that are displayed and incorporated into the story. It might be what the actors or actresses are drinking, wearing, or driving. Not too many things aren't on the list of possibilities. But, this did not happen by accident. It is part of

Figure 11.1 Categories of Brand Visibility

a mutually beneficial arrangement, most commonly called product placement. Essentially, a company pays for the opportunity to have a brand included in the filming or written into a script, screenplay, or action scene. Eventually, these become produced and distributed as motion pictures, television shows, live stage performances, musical recordings, and video games.

The practice of product placement evolved from the movie industry, where the need to assemble props, products, and people at specific locations was a major activity. However, a few very smart entrepreneurs began to work with production companies to substitute specific brands for generic products. The individuals who made the arrangements, of course, received a fee from the manufacturer of the brand. The real boost to the product placement industry came in 1982, when Reese's Peanut Butter Cups were part of a famous scene in the movie *ET*. Suddenly, advertisers began to recognize the promotional value of including a brand name in an entertainment production. In the movie *The Italian Job*, an electrifying car chase scene involved the Mini Cooper, a very small English car that was being reintroduced around the world. The surprising speed and maneuverability of these automobiles were demonstrated as an important part of the film. In addition, the company was able to negotiate for the use of promotional materials featuring photos taken during the production of the movie.

However, a manufacturer must use caution when contracting for product placement. The subject matter and content must be compatible with the brand image and the company's reputation. If the placement is arranged in a controversial situation, it potentially could have a negative impact. This is a particular sensitive area with marketing organizations that depend heavily on dealers, distributors, or franchisees for generating their sales and profits. If there is any negative publicity with the entertainment or the people involved, then the product placement is not a positive image or awareness-generating activity or event.

And, what might a company pay? It is all negotiable. But, the company does have to go out and find new entertainment programs and films for product placement. There are companies that specialize in it. Although some of the placement fees might be $50,000, $100,000, or even up to $250,000, there are plenty of reasons to hire them. Basically, these involve their connections and associations within Hollywood. First, the placement fee will be much lower than a television commercial. Second, the amount of exposure can be very large. As long as the featured brand is prominently displayed or adequately included, millions and millions of people can see it. Third, there is an indirect association with the actors and actresses. While there are no endorsements involved, the exposure of the brand in this context can be a boost to its image. Fourth, a product placement opens up a variety of opportunities for other sales promotions events, activities, and materials.

Is it worth the money? This depends on many factors. First, the amount of time that the brand is clearly visible on the screen. This could be anywhere from a few seconds to an extended period of time. Second, the number of times the brand appeared. Once. Twice. Or, many different times in multiple scenes. Third, the size of the image. Did the camera take a close-up shot of the brand, show some of its features, or make it a prominent part of the filming? Fourth, the person using the brand. Famous or recognizable? A superstar? Controversial? The importance of individuals using or engaged with the brand determines its value. And finally,

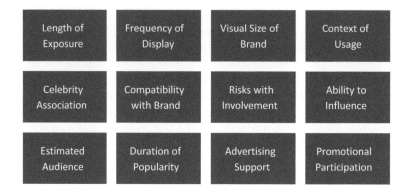

Length of Exposure	Frequency of Display	Visual Size of Brand	Context of Usage
Celebrity Association	Compatibility with Brand	Risks with Involvement	Ability to Influence
Estimated Audience	Duration of Popularity	Advertising Support	Promotional Participation

Figure 11.2 Product Placement Criteria

fifth, the anticipated size of the audience who will be viewing the movie or video production. The greater the number of people watching, the more desirable the situation. True, but this means higher prices, too.

Looking for how to evaluate a product placement opportunity? Look at Figure 11.2 for the criteria that should be used for that purpose. And, here is a quick and simple way to compare the costs and benefits. Start with an advertising pricing model. This method uses a calculation called impressions, which uses the total number of people exposed to an advertisement. If it is a film shown at a movie theatre, then the number of tickets sold is the estimating factor for the audience size; if it is a television show, the ratings or number of people actually viewing the program at that day and time. If it is a newspaper or magazine, the impressions are the circulation. If it is a website, it is the number of visitors or number of social media posts. If it is a video game, it is simply the number of boxes or packages sold with the game. There is always a way to determine the people involved and the value of the exposure being received for the brand.

To summarize, there are three strong reasons to use product placement as a brand visibility strategy. First, the cost is much lower than traditional advertising. Second, product placement provides a very subtle, but highly effective, way to influence brand perception. Third, a greater number of people will be exposed to the brand more frequently over a longer period of time.

Venue Identification

Corporations are constantly trying to find different ways of impressing their name and brands upon the public. One of the methods is venue identification. This promotion strategy involves a long-term commitment and a substantial amount of funds. In what is called naming rights, a company or organization pays the owners of a building, structure, or physical area for legal authorization to officially identify the property using its brand name. These rights can include displaying the company or brand name and logo in signs, displays, and any printed or digital material. This can be very important when the rights include promotional material, tickets, brochures, and multiple forms of IMC.

The first professional sports stadium to use a brand was Wrigley Field, home of the World Champion Chicago Cubs. The owner of a famous chewing gum company, William Wrigley, believed that it was an excellent promotional idea and since he owned the team, changed the name to Wrigley Field, the same name that exists today. That was way back in 1926. Since then, more than 83 professional sports teams, such as football, basketball, baseball, and hockey, have sold naming rights to their stadiums. It has been estimated that the combined value of these venues is about $4 billion. Surprisingly, banks lead the way. Today, there are 10 professional sports complexes in North America that have the name of a financial institution. The same venues are frequently used for other events, such as musical concerts, conventions, and entertainment performances. Great for the promoters and even better for the owners of the property. However, the biggest winners are the companies who secured the venue identification rights. The economic value has a tremendous payback for brands and corporations. Why? Because every time an event occurs, and the stadium or venue name is mentioned in the media, exposure and awareness increase. Every time the name of the stadium is printed on a ticket, poster, or display, or included in a website, blog, or social media page, exposure and awareness increase. And every time the results of a professional sports game are covered in television, radio, magazines, newspapers, or digital media, exposure and awareness increase. That most certainly explains the financial benefits of paying millions for naming rights.

In the future, there might be the possibility of extending venue identification programs to other types of buildings and structures. These could even be famous bridges, landmarks, harbors, expressways, or even sections of a metropolitan area. For example, the city of San Diego was seriously considering changing the name of one of its airports for increased city revenue. Who knows, some day you might be flying to Apple International Airport in California, crossing the Citicorp Bridge in New York, or driving down to Florida on the Sunkist Turnpike!

Brand Packaging

Let's start with the basics. Although packaging is part of the product or value proposition in the marketing mix, brand package represents another point of contact or interaction with potential buyers. The design of the package, particularly the colors and graphics, can influence a consumer during the final stages of the decision-making progress. As a result, the visual appearance of the package must be appealing to the target group while being compatible with the other forms of marketing communication. The package for a brand is part of its image. It sends a message to shoppers about the personality of the brand. Since many consumers do not make a final selection of products until they enter a store, the appeal of a package can influence the selection of a brand. In a certain way, a brand's packaging is similar to advertising. Its primary responsibility is getting the shopper's attention, but then, packaging also has the ability to stimulate immediate sales, just as in a sales promotion program. If the consumer is interested enough to pick up the product and examine it more carefully, then the package design has been very successful.

There are two different strategies that involve a brand's packaging and its appearance in advertising. The first strategy is that a visual image of the package should be used as often as possible in an advertising campaign. This means always including a picture of the package in television, magazine, and newspaper advertising as well as other forms of digital media and marketing communication. While this might not be pleasing to art directors and creative directors, it is an important part of IMC.

The package for a brand can be displayed indirectly, such as subtly incorporating it into the main illustration of a print advertisement, or directly, by having it featured in a separate section or highlighted in a rectangular box. For television, the package could be displayed several times during the commercial and most importantly, included in the final frames. In either of these situations, the purpose is to make a mental connection or memory file between the advertising images and viewing the package in a retail environment. If a certain level of "familiarity" can be established, then the probability of a purchase has been increased.

As part of some sales promotion programs, the packaging of the brand will be temporarily changed. This is done to call more attention to both the brand and information about the promotion. Even if a consumer is familiar with the product, a new visual look that highlights a special offer will always attract more interest. For example, the package could now include promotional copy, call-outs, and graphics that describe a sweepstake, a contest, a money-saving coupon, or an exciting premium. However, it is very important to ensure that the promotion of the brand does not interfere with the brand's image. Consistency of message delivery is essential in packaging as well as in advertising. This is one of the basic rules of IMC.

Event Sponsorship

There are three general types of sponsorship: exclusive, shared, and fractional sponsorship. Exclusive sponsorship, where there is only one company involved, is the most expensive but also extremely valuable. This sponsorship provides a company with the maximum amount of media coverage and hopefully, a positive association with the event among existing and potential customers. Shared sponsorship occurs with two to five sponsors, but there are no specific rules. While this type of sponsorship reduces the cost of participation, it also dilutes the value of being involved. However, if the event is large enough, there are plenty of promotional opportunities for everyone. In a fractional sponsorship, there is usually only one brand allowed in each product category. Depending on the size and nature of the event, there might be 10 to 15 different brands involved.

If you are uncertain about the value of the sponsorship, then take a closer look at Figure 11.3, which will provide you with several important guidelines. These require an examination and analysis of a number of variables, including the audience profile, financial benefits received, compatibility with the brand, total cost involved, preparation required, and the timing or duration of the event being considered. While there is no precise formula, the variables must be prioritized according to their importance and then used to make a final decision.

Event organizers sell a sponsorship "package" based on the amount of money required and the promotional benefits that have been arranged. Entry sponsorship is available at all levels of marketing, from national and regional sponsorship to local and community sponsorship. For example, the local bank or automotive

| Audience Profile | Benefits Received | Compatibility with Brand |
| Total Costs Involved | Preparation Required | Timing & Duration |

Figure 11.3 Event Sponsorship Evaluation

dealer might sponsor a minor league sports team. However, this is usually done more to appeal to customer loyalty and support than to support advertising and promotional programs. For example, the "A" package would include having a brand name and logo featured in the promotional advertising, inserted in press releases, and displayed on programs, materials, and signage at the event. In addition, the "A" package might provide the sponsor with a quantity of free admission tickets, access to restricted areas at the end, or a private reception with celebrities, officials, performers, or notable people during the event. These extra benefits of sponsorship can be extremely useful for companies that want to bring important clients or potential customers to interact in an informal, social environment.

So, what is a "B" sponsorship package? Less compared to the "A" package, but still beneficial.

Featured Prizes

Let other people advertising money work for you. There are many opportunities for brands to be offered as prizes or incentives in sweepstakes, contests, and other promotions. Not yours. But, promotions featuring your brand in another company's IMC activities. Pretty good use of your funds. Just give them the prize at no cost, and they will incorporate it into their programs and activities. That means millions of people will be seeing your product or service in national or local advertising. It saves them money but gives you extra exposure and awareness. All for the cost of what you make, not at the retail price, but at a special low rate as the producing company.

This could mean thousands of dollars of free advertising coverage. The value received can be calculated in the same way as product placement. First, estimate the number of people who will be exposed through the advertising, media, or audience coverage. Second, find out the price for advertising on any of these three message delivery options. And third, compare and analyze the numbers to determine the value of the offer, especially when you know the demographic profile of the media or the quality of the programs.

Typically, national advertising involves a heavy use of television commercials. But, it can also include plenty of direct mail, newspaper advertising, or digital promotions through social media.

At the local level, radio stations really like to offer prizes. Just "call in to win" programs are in every city in America. Just be sure to pick a station with a large audience, or you will be giving away free items without getting much back in return.

There are not very many restrictions on the type of products or services offered as prizes or sales incentives by brands. It can be something simple and inexpensive, or exotic and different. The most desired brands are ones that have an appealing life style value or have high-quality price points. The choices for charities, non-profits, or other organizations might not offer the coverage and media value that are possible with corporate promotions, but they still have a strong psychological influence among target consumer groups and existing customers.

Licensing Rights

A similar way to get extensive media coverage is licensing rights, which is when a promotional organization enters into a contractual agreement with a payment of cash in exchange for the rights to use a brand name, logo, or promotional message for a limited period of time. However, in this instance, the message and graphics are displayed on an individual, team, equipment, or object that is participating in a competitive event. For example, the United States Postal Service sponsored a world-famous bicycle professional in the Tour de France and another in a NASCAR racing series. Photographs were often on the sports pages of major newspapers in America, alongside plenty of television coverage.

Figure 11.4 shows eight different ways to take advantage of selling or leasing the intellectual property rights of a brand: the name, theme line, images, characters, activities, services, merchandise, and products. We have all purchased many of these items, from a Disney's licensed version of a Mickey Mouse coffee cup or shirt to an NFL jersey from your favorite team. It is an amazing way to extend the financial power of a brand as well as media exposure value around the world.

In addition to the media exposure, this type of sponsorship includes an important provision for the development of future advertising and sales promotion materials. If the individual or team is fortunate enough to win, then the value of the sponsorship increases. To capitalize on the drama, advertisers actually print or prepare materials before the event is concluded. If a victory results, the materials are distributed to dealers, franchisees, and retail stores. If not, then the promotional materials are destroyed. It is a very inexpensive way to capitalize on free media exposure.

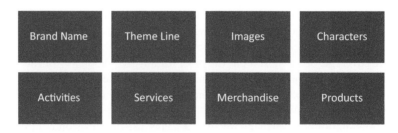

Figure 11.4 Licensing Opportunities

Logo Merchandise

According to the Advertising Specialty Institute, companies, organizations, and individuals spent over $15 billion in 2010 to purchase items to promote the brand name or logo. Simply put, logo merchandise is any item that has an advertiser's name, theme line, logo, symbol, icon, phrase, or contact information printed on its surface. A list compiled by the Institute included more than 650,000 different types of items that could be used as advertising specialties. For example, the most frequently used items include t-shirts, coffee mugs, pens, baseball hats, umbrellas, note pads, drinking cups, key chains, and calendars.

Typically, advertising specialties are given away free to consumers or businesses as part of a marketing communication program. National advertisers often use a number of items during the introduction of a new advertising theme or campaign. Local businesses like to use specialty items to keep their name in front of existing customers: for example, a monthly calendar with an address and telephone number or an inexpensive ball point pen distributed by a bank.

However, there are many brand names that actually sell merchandise with their logo imprinted as part of a marketing strategy to build consumer loyalty. These products are offered online, in catalogs, and are sometimes sold at events, exhibits, and other locations. The benefit is that "identifying" with a particular brand is a matter of personal pride and association with a life style image. For example, the original sports utility vehicle, Jeep, has a wide assortment of clothing, equipment, and other merchandise, including a working miniature version of a Jeep for children.

Retail Displays

As illustrated in Figure 11.5, retail marketing environments include a wide range of methods, such as exterior signage, aisle and wall displays, promotional material, shelve extenders, mobile app notifications, interactive touch screens, video viewing monitors, and store beacons. National manufacturers of brands often help with the design of these materials or pay a portion of the production or installation costs. And as you might have noticed, there has been a major shift from traditional printed materials to more digitally oriented categories. Previously, the entire purpose was to attract attention with large sizes and bright colors, while today, it is all about the process of interacting with customers. This is the impact of technology on marketing communication.

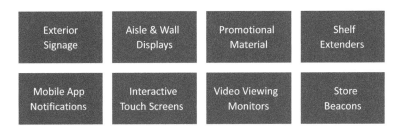

Figure 11.5 Retail Marketing Environments

When we began with the topic of artificial intelligence in Chapter 1, the possibility of facial recognition was discussed, along with the use of mobile apps to send text messages to customers This is part of the new future of advertising and sales promotion in retail store environments. Along with predictive analytics and behavioral psychology, brands will have the ability to personalize and customize brand messages to well-defined target audiences and individuals.

Summary

Brand visibility is a long-term IMC strategy that is designed to increase awareness and a positive image for a product or service. These strategies include product placement, venue identification, brand packaging, retail displays, event sponsorship, featured prizes, logo merchandise, and licensing rights. Most arrangements have long-term financial commitments or investments, while others are low cost and immediate. The brand positioning, competitor environment, and target market are the primary factors that determine the desirability of a brand visibility program.

The financial value of visibility proposals is evaluated using a comparison of the equivalent cost of media. Other methods are awareness research surveys and advertising models to measure consumer perception over time. The overall benefits from brand visibility projects or activities are the exposure value, minus the cost of implementation, plus increases in sales or market share.

As always, brand visibility must be leveraged with other IMC strategies and coordinated to maximize the effects of extended exposure, word-of-mouth discussions, and media publicity.

Discussion Questions

1. Why is brand visibility more important when compared with advertising?
2. Is product placement worth the money paid for exposure? If so, why?
3. Would you ever consider having your brand included in a video game?
4. Is it a good idea to pay several million dollars to have a brand name on a football stadium?
5. When should you not agree to have your product or service offered as a sweepstake prize?
6. How important is a package design for retail marketing and brand advertising?
7. What is an advertising specialty, and why is this type of brand visibility so popular?
8. Why should you consider licensing your brand name for clothing products?
9. Is it more effective to sponsor a music concert or a sporting event? Why?
10. How can digital technology be utilized for developing brand visibility strategies?

Chapter Assignments

1. Select a TV show you have seen recently and list the number of brands that were involved.
2. Your favorite sports team will change the name of its stadium. Which brand would you pick?
3. A pizza fast food chain is giving a big prize for its 10th anniversary. What could it be?
4. Recommend a list of items that can be licensed for a new Marvel Comics adventure movie.
5. Suggest three potential food sponsors for an international Grand Prix automotive race.

Continuity Case Study

Everyone in the conference room was excited. Athena Restaurants was going to be in a Hollywood movie. The only question was which one. The first choice was an action thriller starring Vin Diesel as a rogue FBI agent fighting terrorists in Europe. This was being independently produced and distributed. The next was a romantic comedy with Emma Stone and Melissa McCarthy that was scheduled as a Netflix series. And the third was an animation from Pixar about a young boy traveling to Mars to search for his lost dog. In this film, Cameron Diaz would be the voice of his mother, and Anne Hathaway would play his sister, who goes with him. This was part of a full-day "brainstorming" session on brand visibility. Adriana wanted to exploring licensing characters based on Greek mythology, beginning with Athena. She was convinced that this could get young children involved with the brand, possibly through their YouTube channel. Anthony was very supportive. He particularly liked action heroes, like Zeus, who would be perfect for a Saturday morning television series.

Several other possibilities were discussed. First was sponsoring Greek Independence Day on March 25. This was a popular event in many cities but not necessarily as big as other ethnic holidays. Second, a venue identification opportunity was available. The National Football League had just authorized a team for Las Vegas. It had not yet signed a contract for naming its new stadium. Third, co-promotions with other companies were considered. While a lot of names were suggested, there was no consensus. Adriana wanted to begin planning for next year, so getting started was very important. She knew that a long lead time was needed to coordinate the advertising and promotional activities for any decision that was made.

1. Which of the product placement opportunities should be accepted?
2. What do you think of licensing Greek mythology characters for children?
3. Does it make any sense to further investigate the stadium naming idea?
4. Can the company effectively leverage Greek Independence Day?
5. Which companies are good partners for a co-promotion with Athena?

IMC Plan Development

Step One:

Make a list of the movies and television shows that could be good choices for product placement.

Step Two:

Select merchandising items that are relevant for licensing and using your brand name and logo.

Step Three:

Create a concept for a new video game that will prominently feature your brand in its content.

Step Four:

Choose a clothing company that could use your product or service for its grand prize in a contest.

Step Five:

Propose a venue that might be interesting in negotiating with your brand for naming rights.

Chapter 12

B2B Communication Strategies

Retaining Customers and Discovering New Buyers

Learning Objectives

1. Understand the function and value of business-to-business (B2B) communication programs
2. Recognize the potential of using inbound marketing to attract new customers
3. Identity and recognize the most appropriate vertical media options for advertising
4. Evaluate the importance of annual trade shows for selling products and services
5. Select financial and psychological incentives for B2B promotions

Introduction

IMC isn't just for reaching and interacting with the general population of consumers. There is another level, which is equally important, but relatively hidden, and most frequently called B2B communication. This occurs between the producers of products and services and the channels of distribution, or marketing intermediaries. Manufacturers of consumer products always need to motivate wholesalers and retailers to select their brand as part of the value-added process in the chain of distribution. Manufacturers of industrial products and services want to sell what

DOI: 10.4324/9780367443382-12

they have to corporations, small businesses, and entrepreneurs. This can range from simple office supplies, equipment, and accounting systems to logo design, advertising campaign, and social media marketing. After reading this chapter, you will be able to better understand the challenges involved with B2B marketing and the IMC communication pathways that are available.

B2B Marketing Categories

B2B and consumer marketing have many things in common when it involves IMC. B2B communication utilizes the same IMC pathways to reach customers and potential buyers. These six pathways are advertising, sales promotion, public relations, brand visibility, digital platforms, and personal contact. However, the budgets are lower, the target audiences are different, and the channels are more specialized.

Figure 12.1 lists the eight most frequently used strategies for B2B marketing communication: inbound marketing, vertical media, horizontal media, industry trade shows, co-op advertising, merchandising support, online catalogs, and virtual showrooms.

Inbound Marketing

Inbound marketing is the reverse approach to traditional marketing. The assumption is that online search enables B2B companies to find the products and services they need without the assistance of a sales person. So, in the age of online search, B2B shoppers can always find you. That sounds impossible, but it's true. So, how do B2B shoppers become B2B customers? There are six essential inbound marketing methods, which are shown in Figure 12.2. These are complimentary consulting, industry reports, trending topics, free webinars, video tutorials, and data infograms. Inbound marketing is the reverse of consumer marketing, where manufacturers are aggressively pursuing customers with extensive advertising and sales promotion. Inbound marketing is more passive. Techniques such as industry reports and free webinars are the lure that attracts potential buyers to visit a company's website. The information provided is an important step toward establishing trust and building a relationship.

Figure 12.1 B2B Communication Strategies

Figure 12.2 Inbound Marketing Techniques

The largest and most successful inbound marketing company is Hubspot. It was the pioneer of inbound marketing and has earned a reputation for providing small and mid-size business with the tools needed for successfully attracting new customers. The Hubspot website describes the company as a "business-oriented growth model that attracts visitors, engages leads, and delights customers." They have multiple packages, including comprehensive Customer Relationship Management software and automated business resources that are designed for internal growth and customer retention as well as expansion. This includes tracking leads and contact along with providing customer support. There is a famous case study about Hubspot that is used in business school for evaluating the types of programs that best fit each company's goals. Hubspot's own marketing strategies includes simple but valuable information to attract new clients, such as free webinars, industry reports, and data infograms. If you are not familiar with the products and services of Hubspot, then go to www.hubspot.com and explore its many valuable features and options.

Complimentary Consulting   The offer is real. Free consulting for an hour or another limited amount of time. The situation provides the individual who is searching for a product or service with valuable and useful information. It also enables the user to evaluate the quality and desirability of the company involved. The benefit to the company making the offer is an authentic sales lead and potential customer. It also indicates the seriousness of the person and the nature of their intentions. Questions are answered, and data is collected. So, complimentary consulting is a win-win proposition.

Industry Reports   Industry reports, white papers, and statistical summaries are used to promote the knowledge, experience, and professionalism of the company offering these documents. This is usually excellent research information that saves time, money, and the challenge of understanding a market. These documents are free to download but require the completion of a short registration form that asks for the name, email, and business profile of the prospect. The information from the registration form can be used for follow-up communication, building a relationship, and even combined with future outbound marketing strategies.

Trending Topics   What's hot? And, what's not? Whenever a subject, famous person, sports story, or news event suddenly appears in social media with a dramatic increase in popularity, it instantly becomes a trending topic. Typically, there is a rapid expansion in the number of people talking about this trending topic across multiple social media platforms, but the frequency of appearance and duration only last for a very short period of time. Prominently featuring these topics in a brand website acts like a magnet by quickly attracting attention and stimulating interest in learning more about it. This becomes a very powerful and effective inbound marketing opportunity for B2B companies that are monitoring social media. Each platform has its own algorithm based on the unique number of users, frequency of engagement with the trending topic, and length of time that a topic has maintained a high level of interest. For example, Twitter uses hashtags for trending topics, while Google analyzes the search volume for keywords or phrases. The strategy of utilizing trending topics for inbound marketing can clearly demonstrate the ability of a B2B company to recognize, understand, and react to the information needs of a customer group.

Free Webinars   Webinars and podcasts are perhaps the single best way to identify a prospect and maintain a relationship with a B2B customer. Since they have already demonstrated a strong interest in a topic, the opportunity for converting them to a sale is there. If they are willing to watch or listen for an extended period of time, there is plenty of time to include a persuasive offer. However, there is the cost of preparing and promoting a webinar. This involves extensive use of social media as well as other forms of IMC. The content has to be fresh, the speaker must be engaging, and the length of the webinar must be appropriate to the topic. The most common format is 60 minutes, including a short pause for a question and answer period.

Video Tutorials   Video is powerful force for attracting potential buyers. Just like a magnet, video tutorials appeal to people who want to learn, know, and understand more about their market, their customers, and how to generate more revenue. Their appeal is very similar to a webinar but offered in a more flexible and convenient form. The videos can cover a wide range of topics and can be as specific or general as desired. However, it is best to keep the videos short, concise, and focused on a topic of interest.

Video tutorials can be downloaded directly from a company's website or be contained in a YouTube channel. Even if a contact or sales lead is not immediately provided, there is always excellent data collected on the number of views for each video tutorial and potential customers.

Data Infograms   What better way is there to communicate content? Infograms can summarize complex content, especially numerical information, and visually display the results. This method is a great way to distribute key points or useful research information and at the same time, connect your company to the source of the visual display. How about making your own Infogram today? It's fast, simple, and free. If you want to give it a go and get started, just go to www.infogram.com and register for the basic package. It allows you to make up to 10 projects using more than 37 interactive displays, including tree maps, stacked bars, and even those lofty word clouds. If you are not familiar with all the impressive graphic possibilities, click on the example menu tab at the top and then view the featured examples of chart types on the left side of the page. This service is also great for small businesses, entrepreneurs, and consultants who want to impress clients with data visualization.

Vertical Media

Every industry and market segment has multiple publications dedicated to covering important and highly relevant topics, companies, people, and technology. This information is available online through a subscription or in a printed version. The website for the publication is updated daily, so that the most essential news is always available. Perhaps the most valuable aspect of these vertical publications is the industry summary reports and analysis. While the content varies by industry, most B2B media publications contain comprehensive information based on extensive quantitative marketing research. Vertical media are definitely the most effective way to reach a combination of existing customers and potential buyers.

How do you know which publications to use for advertising to a particular industry or market segment? Your best resource is a media information service called SRDS (Standard Rate and Data). It does not sell media but rather, provides details about the costs and number of people who are reached by each publication. This includes more than 4700 different magazines that focus on specialized industries. There are over 190 separate categories or market classifications for using vertical media. For example, there are multiple publications with websites that reach the B2B customers in the following industries and market segments: automotive, banking, brewing, clothing, cosmetics, engineering, farm equipment, home furnishings, hotels, insurance, light fixtures, meat processing, motorcycles, paint, petroleum, pets, railroads, restaurants, robotics, shopping centers, sporting goods, telecommunication, tobacco, toys, woodworking, and welding. In addition, there are sub-specializations for each industry, including regional publications and publications that involve intermediaries in a channel of product distribution.

Here are just a few of the possibilities: *Automotive News*, *Southern Tire Dealer*, *Hardware Marketing News*, *Midwestern Furniture Retailer*, and *Hotel Management Digest*.

After the available publications are identified, the process used to select the best ones for advertising to customers and potential buyers in a specific market segment is the same as for consumer publications. The publication with the largest circulation is the best, but the cost-per-thousand (CPM) might be exceptionally high. This is usually acceptable, but alternative vertical media choices should also be evaluated from both a coverage and a cost perspective. Typically, more than one publication should be included in a B2B media plan, but the majority of the advertising money will be placed with the publication with the largest audience numbers.

Horizontal Media

Horizonal media represent publications that have a more general rather than specific appeal. For example, the topic of management is important to every business. So, there are online and printed publications that reach that market. The information about the type and number of horizontal media choices can be found through SRDS. This company has been providing B2B advertising cost information to agencies and advertisers for more than 100 years. Its services now include media research, including keywords, audience metrics, and even video media kits. Essentially, everything you need for planning a B2B advertising campaign is available through SRDS. Here is a link to its media planning page: https://next.srds.com/media-buyer-solutions/business-publication-media

Industry Trade Shows

Historically, it's called a trade show, but a more modern description is an industry exhibition or business opportunity event. Trade shows have been around for a long time. And, there is a very good reason. For most medium and small companies, it is extremely expensive to have a sales force that is required to contact every existing customer and at the same time, search for new potential buyers. A trade show provides the opportunity for manufacturers to display products and services to thousands of wholesalers and retailers—in a single location and at the same time!

There are four primary reasons for participating in an industry trade show. As shown in Figure 12.3, these reasons are new product introductions, brand visibility and market presence, maintaining relationships with customers, and identifying and attracting potential buyers. Trade shows are organized by either independent organizations or professional associations. There are more than 20,000 professional associations and non-profit organizations in the United States. While you can find most of them online, the single best source is the *Encyclopedia of Association*. This publication identifies and lists them all in a convenient form. Until COVID-19, preparing and participating in a trade show was the most important marketing activity for a B2B company. However, nearly every industry still had a virtual online trade show or exhibition.

Trade shows are not for the public. Registration is required, and attendance is limited to manufacturers, wholesalers, retailers, and other channel intermediaries. Why do we even need trade shows? Let's look at the numbers. Manufacturers do not have enough sales people to visit every possible buyer for its products or services. And, channel intermediaries, especially retailers, do not have the time, money, or resources to explore everything that is available for purchase. Thus, a trade show aggregates buyers and sellers for an annual B2B shopping mart. There

Figure 12.3 Industry Trade Shows

are more than 33,000 trade shows worldwide. Some are very large, international events, while others are smaller and more regionally focused. They include about 600 to 700 different categories of specialization. The value of a trade show varies by industry and its perceived importance.

The largest trade show in the United States is the Consumer Electronics Show (CES), which is held annually in Las Vegas, Nevada during the first weeks of January. This international event attracts more than 110,000 attendees. It is not open to the public. The products and services displayed are available only for B2B companies, wholesalers, and other channel intermediaries. Typically, exhibiting companies have booth locations along with presentations in large meeting rooms or auditoriums. In 2020, there were more than 4400 exhibitors from around the world.

The CES is a preview of the new products and services that will become available later in the year. This gives wholesalers and retailers the opportunity to inspect and evaluate new items before placing orders, even up to nine months in advance for Christmas and the holiday sales period. This industry event is especially important for the entertainment, media distribution, and advertising industries. Everything from emerging new technologies to advanced digital innovations is displayed. And, a demand for products and services that no one knew they ever needed is instantly created and ready for brand marketing and communication.

Virtual Display Exhibits

The world has changed, and now, digital has taken over the structure of trade shows. More industries are moving toward virtual shows and exhibits for B2B marketing communication. Figure 12.4 indicates the six most important characteristics or advantages of a virtual trade. These advantages include physical convenience, continuous access, guided site tours, brand comparisons, live chat interaction, and online ordering. First, the physical convenience is amazing. You can experience every booth, display, and product demonstration without leaving your home or office. No walking around. No crowds or confusion. No missed opportunities because you didn't find what you were looking for. But, there are also disadvantages. No sight-seeing, shopping, entertainment, or exploring the culture and life style of an exciting city. Second, a virtual trade show is open 24 hours a day during the official exhibit period. Explore and discover products and services no matter what time of day or night. And, even enjoy a midnight

Figure 12.4 Virtual Display Exhibits

snack from your home refrigerator! Third, you can enjoy a guided tour of the exhibit with pre-recorded videos from presenters or digital avatars. Fourth, brand comparisons are easy to complete without a sales person to influence your decision. Fifth, there is always live chat to answer specific questions or request more information. And sixth, online ordering in this B2B situation can also be a seamless experience.

If you have never gone to a virtual trade show, here is what to expect. Each participant must register and pay the attendance fee. Most likely, you will be given access to a digital app to download to your smartphone. Then, you can begin your journey down the virtual aisles. Stop at a booth and check in. Leave a message or make a request. Go to the main auditorium for a keynote speech or presentation on a topic of interest. Arrange a personal meeting or discussion with a company representative in a private Zoom meeting room. Interact with other attendees in the virtual trade show by posting your reaction to speech on Twitter or posting your review of a B2B company in Facebook.

Trade shows will continue to exist and even thrive with the growing popularity of virtual conferences. While there is no substitute for face-to-face contact, these real-time versions might be the next best thing. You don't need to shake hands, keep your social distance, or worry about picking up and examining products. Everything is the same as a physical trade show, only it exists through a digitally connected environment. Think of the advantages. meetings, and a strict time schedule. It is a small price to pay for remaining healthy and safe. Still, there is the inevitable fact that virtual conferences are extremely cost-efficient and highly productive.

Co-op Advertising

Co-operative (co-op) advertising is when a manufacturer, or channel intermediary, offers to pay a portion of the cost for local advertising. This can range anywhere from a basic 50/50 split to a sliding scale based on the value of the product or service being purchased. The primary purpose of co-op advertising is to reduce the marketing expense of the retailer, which increases profitability. But, there are restrictions. The retailer can only use pre-approved creative materials from the manufacturer. This ensures brand integrity, copyright protection, and a consistent advertising message. Creative formats and templates can be downloaded for either an advertising agency or an individual business owner. Thus, co-operative advertising is a mutually beneficial arrangement for both a retailer and a manufacturer or supplier. Plus, it maintains a seamless delivery of brand messages as part of an IMC Plan.

Merchandising Support

Signs, posters, counter placards, shelf extenders, aisle displays, wall postings, sales markers, and video screens are always needed for promotions at retail stores. Each of these items is a subtle reminder or method to capture the attention of a shopper and motivate a purchase. Since it is not always practical, or economical, for individual stores to produce their own promotional material for merchandising a brand, these materials are often provided at no cost, or at a minimum price, to retailers by a manufacturer or producer. Sometimes, wholesalers or channel members will provide funds for the purchase of these materials or subsidize them with a large initial order.

B2B Incentive Strategies

While the financial and psychological incentives used in B2B promotion campaigns are similar to consumer incentives, there is a significant difference. Most of the incentives designed for a B2B promotion are connected to the quantity purchased or flexible payment arrangements. There are multiple options, but the most frequently used incentive strategies are shown in Figure 12.5.

There are two kinds of B2B incentive: financial and psychological. Financial incentives include volume discounts, price concessions, free product gratuity, buy-back arrangements, discontinued model allowances, and performance bonuses. The psychological incentives include sales award recognition, trips and experiences, VIP event invitations, first option on new products, advisory panel memberships, and publicity in trade media.

Financial Incentives

Since successful businesses are always focused on maintaining or increasing sales, profit, and market share, it is not surprising that financial incentives are the best motivation. This includes any action that either reduces costs or increases income. And, cost reduction to a wholesaler, retailer, or broker can quickly be translated into profits. Income statements and balance sheets often reflect the impact of effective financial incentives for B2B marketing strategies.

Volume Discounts Volume discounts are available in every industry. Volume discounts are a very strong inducement, since they result in a sizable reduction in the selling price. The amount of the discount is usually based on the total number

Figure 12.5 B2B Incentive Strategies

of units ordered at the same time. The advantage to a manufacturer is the rapid elimination of inventory and a favorable increase in cash flow.

Wholesalers, or retailers, who benefit from a volume discount can immediately lower their selling price for that brand to attract more customers. The result is that the "pipeline" that brings products from manufacturers to consumers is filled and ready to be responsive to new demand.

Price Concessions   This promotional strategy is a flexible discount. The amount of reduction is not based on the published purchase price but is a negotiable amount. The seller has a range of selling prices that are acceptable, depending on many other factors. However, the buyer always wants to get the lowest price possible. That rarely happens. If it did, there would be little, if any, profit for the seller. When buyers and sellers begin to negotiate, both sides have to agree to a final purchase price.

Price concessions are not immediately offered. There has to be some reluctance, or resistance, from the potential buyers. Then, depending on the situation, a concession will be proposed for the purpose of ensuring a final sale. Concessions are essentially a compromise in the final price.

Free Extra Quantity   Any extra amount of a product or service, delivered without an invoice, can also be included with a promotion program. The quantity and requirements have a limited time period. For example, if a wholesaler or retailer purchases 40 cases of a snack bar brand, they can get an extra 5 cases without cost. This provides an excellent opportunity to reduce their retail selling profit, which benefits the consumer, or retain the extra quantity and sell it at the regular price.

This technique moves inventory faster through the channel of distribution. It is often used as part of a "push" strategy, where manufacturers incentivize wholesaler, and retailer, to order larger quantities of a brand. Having more items on a store shelf is a strong motivation to lower the retail selling price for consumers. Another promotion technique is the "pull strategy," where advertising and social media are used to stimulate the demand for products and services.

Buy-Back Arrangements   In many industries, retailers are allowed to return any unused or unsold stock for either a full or a partial credit. This policy was created to minimize the perceived risk of ordering or agreeing to sell a new line of items or brand. Unsold inventory represents zero profit. By enabling the distribution channel to return products, a more stable and predictable selling environment is maintained.

For example, in grocery stores, unsold magazines at the end of the month can be returned to the publisher for a credit. There are many stipulations about the details of a buy-back arrangement. Ultimately, these arrangements help smaller retailers who have a lower volume or profit margin.

Discontinued Model Allowances   Whenever a new model of a product or service is introduced, the wholesale selling price drops immediately. It is not that the item is any less valuable or beneficial, but the manufacturer wants to reduce its inventory as soon as possible. For example, in the automotive industry, dealers are given a 2% reduction in the price of the previous year's model. The reduction in the price also gives the dealer the opportunity to pass the saving on to their customers. But, this is not a requirement. The extra amount of money might be needed to pay for the cost of maintaining the inventory, which is based on the interest charged to the dealer for holding each car.

Whenever a product line, or item, from any industry is discontinued, the wholesale selling price will be decreased even more. This situation usually results from poor sales, below average profitability, lack of customer demand, brand improvement, or new technologies. The amount of the price reductions will depend on the need to liquidate items in the distribution system.

Sales Award Competition   The best salespeople earn additional money, gifts, and vacations as a reward for selling the greatest number of products or services. Ironically, this incentive motivates them to achieve specific sales goals by the end of a week, month, or year. While financial rewards for individual performance are always the preferred method, exotic vacations and experiences are also very exciting and stimulating. For others, winning a competition is the strongest motivating force.

Performance Bonuses   These cash payments for performance, known as "spiffs," are given to sales people when they have been able to sell a particular product, model, or service. This type of bonus program is designed to focus their attention on individual items, which might be more profitable or have been more difficult to liquidate. The time frame for these performance bonuses is typically very short, but the rewards can be substantial, depending on the industry.

Special Accommodations   Business clients and customers can negotiate for more than financial benefits. These special accommodations can be either business related or a personal request. For example, a business accommodation might be a delayed billing cycle, transformation preferences, or a flexible shipment delivery schedule. The personal requests are more involved and precarious. These can involve a variety of activities, experiences, or products: for example, very expensive tickets to attend a sporting event or popular performance, VIP room access, or a private dinner with a celebrity. Ethical issues exist when the action becomes more of a bribe rather than a favor or friendly gesture from a manufacturer to a customer, supplier, or media representative.

Psychological Incentives

There is more to incentives than just financial offers. This is especially true for B2B marketing communication. Just look at the situation. After the top performers receive a lot of extra money, additional funds will not be as attractive. What is more effective is a package of psychological incentives, such as trips and experiences, special recognition, VIP invitation events, first option on new products, advisory panel memberships, and publicity in trade media. Sometimes, free merchandise is substituted for money, such as letting a salesperson select products of equal value from an incentive catalog. Or, the financial incentive could be applied to an experience, such as a trip to Europe, Asia, or South America. In these cases, money is exchanged for items.

Successful people like to be recognized. This is an important psychological incentive, but a B2B company must find the right method to acknowledge the accomplishments of the recipient. It could be a simple award, like a certificate or trophy, or a more formal recognition dinner with invited guests and entertainment. Additional psychological incentives include VIP invitations to special events, such as sports, concerts, or art exhibits, based on the strategy of the promotion.

The honor of being selected to a prestigious advisory panel is an excellent psychological incentive as well as giving the opportunity to be featured in trade publications with interviews, photographs, and occasionally, video clips. Media exposure builds a reputation, which in turn, propels a dealer, distributor, or retail store owner into another level of potential achievement.

There are other incentives that involve the marketing of B2B products and services. For example, when a new model is introduced, the dealers, distributors, or retail stores that have previously demonstrated their sales proficiency have the right to a larger allotment of the new model. This group are frequently offered an option to increase their initial supply of the product. The rationale is that a larger inventory provides a competitive advantage and opportunity for market share.

International Considerations

With the Internet, every business can be global. But, there are a few simple but important things to remember. The most important considerations are culture, language, currency, and time zones.

These aspects of international business must be incorporated into an IMC plan. Culture is more than just the way people in another country do business; rather, it is the development of a deep understanding of the meaning of customs, traditions, and beliefs. This involves researching the country and discovering as much as possible about what is important in life, the family, and the degree of individualism. Language has to include accurate translations and the correct interpretation of idioms. And, the importance of dialects and accents within the same language must be known and applied in a proper way.

Contract prices and purchase agreements between companies in different countries can be disrupted by fluctuations in currency exchange rates. This can be a significant factor in estimating the sales and profit potential for international clients. There are multiple ways to protect the amount of money paid for a product or service, such as hedging, which ensures that prices will be equalized even if the currency exchange rates go up or down. This is a very complicated topic, especially when it involves transfer payments among divisions of the same company. Courses on international business provide a comprehensive description of this process.

And finally, the impact of time zones on global business is enormous. Even with modern digital communication systems, the time of day can limit the amount of contact time among individuals. For example, in the United States, there are 4 time zones, but there is a difference of 5 hours between New York and London, 6 hours between Miami and Milan, and more than 12 hours between Los Angeles and Melbourne, Austria. Fortunately, emails can be sent overnight and responded to in the morning. However, the office hours and availability of people in different cities and time zones is a difficult variable to coordinate and control. It is just one more aspect of global business that has an impact on the utilization of IMC.

Summary

B2B marketing communication is similar to consumer marketing, but it uses different channels and pathways for advertising media, sales promotion, and publicity. Specific vertical publications are available for brand message communication, including targeted media to reach wholesalers and retailers. Inbound marketing is also frequently used by industrial companies to attract shoppers for business products and services to their website. These inbound marketing methods include complimentary consulting, industry reports, trending topics, free webinars, video tutorials, and data infograms. Financial and psychological incentives are used by consumer brands to motivate marketing intermediaries to purchase and inventory larger quantities of items. Volume discounts, price concessions, free product gratuity, buy-back arrangements, discontinued model allowance, and merchandise rewards are examples of financial incentives. Sales award recognition, trips and experiences, VIP event invitations, first option on new products, advisory panel memberships, and publicity in trade media are examples of psychological incentives. The external feedback from store visits, sales people, competitors, customers, employees, and journalists is used to evaluate the success of a B2B program.

Discussion Questions

1. Which of the inbound marketing strategies is the most likely to attract potential customers?
2. What is the purpose and value of an industry trade fair, exhibition, or conference?
3. Are virtual trade fairs as effective as physical events? Explain the advantages and disadvantages.
4. Why is it important to join an industry association? How can you find out which one to join?
5. How does a co-op advertising program help local retailers with their marketing strategies?
6. What types of merchandising materials are most helpful for service-oriented businesses?
7. Select an industry and determine the most effective type of sales incentive to offer retailers.
8. What is the relationship between manufacturers and retailers involving brand messages?
9. Which is a better motivator for field sales members, cash or psychological incentives?
10. Do manufacturers need to advertise to wholesalers and retailers? What are their options?

Chapter Assignments

1. Evaluate the methods used by Hubspot to attract new B2B customers (www. hubspot.com).
2. Search on Google to find a vertical medium for a specific industry or B2B market segment.
3. Explore the idea of creating a virtual product display room (www.eventman-agerlog.com).
4. Locate and utilize the publication *Encyclopedia of Associations* for a product or service.
5. Identify the total number of wholesalers or retailers involved in a specific industry.

IMC Plan Development

Step One:
　　Select an inbound marketing strategy that focuses on attracting marketing intermediaries.

Step Two:
　　Locate the website for the most relevant industry trade show for your product or service.

Step Three:
　　Identify all the trade associations that might be important for publicity and promotions.

Step Four:
　　Analyze and recommend the most cost-efficient vertical business media publications.

Step Five:
　　Develop a financial and psychological incentive program for wholesalers and retailers.

Further Reading

Chapter 1

Campbell, C., Plangger, K., Sands, S., & Kietzmann, J. (2021). Preparing for an era of deepfakes and AI-generated ads: A framework for understanding responses to manipulated advertising. *Journal of Advertising*, 1–17. https://doi.org/10.1080/00913367.2021.1909515

Hurwitz, J., et al. (2019). *Augmented intelligence: The business power of human-machine collaboration*. Auerbach Publishers, Incorporated.

Issitt, M. L. (2020). *Robotics & artificial intelligence*. Grey House Publishing.

Kietzmann, J., Pachen, J., & Treene, E. (2018). Artificial intelligence in advertising: How marketers can leverage artificial intelligence along the consumer journey. *Journal of Advertising Research*, 58(3), 263–267. https://doi.org/10.2501/JAR-2018-035

Loureiro, S. M. C., Guerreiro, J., & Tussyadiah, I. (2021). Artificial intelligence in business: State of the art and future research agenda. *Journal of Business Research*, 129, 911–926, https://doi.org/10.1016/j.jbusres.2020.11.001

Marr, B. (2019). *Artificial intelligence in practice: How 50 successful companies used artificial intelligence to solve problems* (1st edition). Wiley.

Naidoo, J. (2018). Artificial intelligence in business communication: A snapshot. *International Journal of Business Communication*. https://doi.org/10.1177/2329488418819139

Rodgers, S. (2021). Themed issue introduction: Promises and perils of artificial intelligence and advertising. *Journal of Advertising*, 50(1), 1–10. https://doi.org/10.1080/00913367.2020.1868233

Ruiz-Real, J., Uribe-Toril, J., Torres, J. A., & Pablo, J. D. (2021). Artificial intelligence in business and economics research: Trends and future. *Journal of Business Economics and Management*, 22(1), 98–117.

Vakratsas, D., & Wang, X. (2021). Artificial intelligence in advertising creativity. *Journal of Advertising*, 50(1), 39–51. https://doi.org/10.1080/00913367.2020.1843090

Chapter 2

Barbas, S. (2015). *Laws of image: Privacy and publicity in America*. Stanford Law Books. https://doi.org/10.1515/9780804796712

Bruhn, M., & Schnebelen, S. (2017). Integrated marketing communication – From an instrumental to a customer-centric perspective. *European Journal of*

Marketing, 51(3), 464–489. http://dx.doi.org.library.capella.edu/10.1108/EJM -08-2015-0591

Laurie, S., & Mortimer, K. (2019). How to achieve true integration: The impact of integrated marketing communication on the client/agency relationship. *Journal of Marketing Management, 35*(3–4), 231–252.

Manser Payne, E. (2017). Omni-channel marketing, integrated marketing communications and consumer engagement. *Journal of Research in Interactive Marketing, 11*(2), 185–197. https://doi.org/10.1108/JRIM-08-2016-0091

Mullin, R., & Cummins, J. (2008). *Sales promotion: How to create, implement & integrate campaigns that really work.* Kogan Page.

Porcu, L., Del Barrio-Garcia, S., & Kitchen, P. J. (2017). Measuring integrated marketing communication by taking a broad organisational approach: The firm-wide IMC scale. *European Journal of Marketing, 51*(3), 692–718.

Schultz, D. (2016a). Flipping the value creation model. *Journal of Creating Value, 2*(2), 155–159. https://doi.org/10.1177/2394964316673165

Schultz, D. (2016b). The future of advertising or whatever we're going to call it. *Journal of Advertising, 45*(3), 276–285. https://doi.org/10.1080/00913367 .2016.1185061

Schultz, D. E., & Block, M. P. (2015). Beyond brand loyalty: Brand sustainability. *Journal of Marketing Communications, 21*(5), 340–355. https://doi.org/10 .1080/13527266.2013.821227

Sinha, S. K., & Verma, P. (2019). The link between sales promotion's benefits and consumers' perception: A comparative study between rural and urban consumers. *Global Business Review, 20*(2), 498–514. https://doi.org/10.1177 /0972150918825398

Valos, M. J., Haji Habibi, F., Casidy, R., Driesener, C. B., & Maplestone, V. L. (2016). Exploring the integration of social media within integrated marketing communication frameworks: Perspectives of services marketers. *Marketing Intelligence & Planning, 34*(1), 19–40. http://dx.doi.org.library.capella.edu/10 .1108/MIP-09-2014-0169

Chapter 3

Bode, C., & Geiger, I. (2020). Not just another internal service provider: How a firm's marketing research function influences uses of market research information. *European Journal of Marketing, 54*(2), 385–419. https://doi.org /10.1108/EJM-07-2019-0580

Dwivedi, Y. K., Ismagilova, E., Hughes, D. L., Carlson, J., Filieri, R., Jacobson, J., Jain, V., Karjaluoto, H., Kefi, H., Krishen, A. S., Kumar, V., Rahman, M. M., Raman, R., Rauschnabel, P. A., Rowley, J., Salo, J., Tran, G. A., & Wang, Y. (2021). Setting the future of digital and social media marketing research: Perspectives and research propositions. *International Journal of Information Management, 59*, 102168. https://doi.org/10.1016/j.ijinfomgt.2020.102168

Grewal, D., Herhausen, D., Ludwig, S., & Villarroel Ordenes, F. (2021). The future of digital communication research: Considering dynamics and multimodality. *Journal of Retailing.* https://doi.org/10.1016/j.jretai.2021.01.007

Lin, H., & Bruning, P. F. (2020). Sponsorship in focus: A typology of sponsorship contexts and research agenda. *Marketing Intelligence & Planning, 39*(2), 213–233. https://doi.org/10.1108/MIP-04-2020-0169

Plumeyer, A., Kottemann, P., Böger, D., & Decker, R. (2019). Measuring brand image: A systematic review, practical guidance, and future research directions. *Review of Managerial Science*, 13(2), 227–265. https://doi.org/10.1007/s11846-017-0251-2

Pratap, C. M. (2021). Online marketing research - Roles in generating customer insights. *Studies in Business and Economics (Romania)*, 16(1), 147–161. https://doi.org/10.2478/sbe-2021-0012

Raciti, M. M. (2021). Can an index approach improve social marketing competitor analysis? *Social Marketing Quarterly*, 27(3), 213–229. https://doi.org/10.1177/15245004211031872

Rezaei, S. (2021). Beyond explicit measures in marketing research: Methods, theoretical models, and applications. *Journal of Retailing and Consumer Services*, 61, 102545. https://doi.org/10.1016/j.jretconser.2021.102545

Robertson, J., Ferreira, C., & Paschen, J. (2021). Reading between the lines: Understanding customer experience with disruptive technology through online reviews. *Australasian Marketing Journal*, 29(3), 215–224. https://doi.org/10.1177/1839334921999487

Sheth, J. (2021). New areas of research in marketing strategy, consumer behavior, and marketing analytics: The future is bright. *Journal of Marketing Theory and Practice*, 29(1), 3–12. https://doi.org/10.1080/10696679.2020.1860679

Chapter 4

Del Barrio-García, S., Kamakura, W. A., & Luque-Martínez, T. (2019). A longitudinal cross-product analysis of media-budget allocations: How economic and technological disruptions affected media choices across industries. *Journal of Interactive Marketing*, 45, 1–15. https://doi.org/10.1016/j.intmar.2018.05.004

Johnson, B. (2019). WHOSE AD SPENDING IS UP? THE BIG FANG THEORY; Facebook, Amazon, Netflix and Alphabet's Google are pouring billions into their ad budgets. *Advertising Age*, 90(13), 9.

Johnson, B. (2020). WORLD'S LARGEST ADVERTISERS 2020; prime time: Amazon vaults into top spot, displacing procter & gamble. *Advertising Age*, 91(19), 28.

Johnson, B. (2021). After the storm, ad spending is on the rebound; the 200 biggest U.S. advertisers last year cut spending 6.2% but marketing budgets are rising amid a resurgent economy. *Advertising Age*, 92(10), 14.

Katz, H. E. (2017). *The media handbook: A complete guide to advertising media selection, planning, research, and buying* (6th ed.). Routledge.

Kolsarici, C., Vakratsas, D., & Naik, P. A. (2020). The anatomy of the advertising budget decision: How analytics and heuristics drive sales performance. *Journal of Marketing Research*, 57(3), 468–488. https://doi.org/10.1177/002224372090757

Schultz, E. J., Neff, J., & Pasquarelli, A. (2020). Six things that keep CMO's up all night; the top planning, messaging and media challenges on the minds of marketing leaders heading into 2021. *Advertising Age*, 91(17), 14.

Shi, H., Grewal, R., & Sridhar, H. (2021). Organizational herding in advertising spending disclosures: Evidence and mechanisms. *Journal of Marketing Research*, 58(3), 515–538. https://doi.org/10.1177/0022243720978954

Vartanov, S. A. (2020). The economic theory of advertising: The directions of formation. *Upravlencheskoe konsul'tirovanie*, *8*, 157–174. https://doi.org/10.22394/1726-1139-2020-8-157-174

Wang, X., Li, F., & Jia, F. (2020). Optimal advertising budget allocation across markets with different goals and various constraints. *Complexity (New York, N.Y.)*, *2020*, 1–12. https://doi.org/10.1155/2020/6162056

Chapter 5

Gajanova, L., Nadanyiova, M., & Moravcikova, D. (2019). The use of demographic and psychographic segmentation to creating marketing strategy of brand loyalty. *Scientific Annals of Economics and Business*, *66*(1), 65–84. https://doi.org/10.2478/saeb-2019-0005

Horvat, S., & Došen, Đ. O. (2020). Managing private labels based on psychographic consumer segments: Emerging European market perspective. *Organizations and Markets in Emerging Economies*, *11*(2). https://doi.org/10.15388/omee.2020.11.42

Hou, J. (2020). Online shopping patronage: Do demographics and psychographics really matter? *Journal of Marketing Development and Competitiveness*, *14*(5), 9–19. https://doi.org/10.33423/jmdc.v14i5.3981

Huang, Y., Liu, H., Li, W., Wang, Z., Hu, X., & Wang, W. (2020). Lifestyles in amazon: Evidence from online reviews enhanced recommender system. *International Journal of Market Research*, *62*(6), 689–706. https://doi.org/10.1177/1470785319844146

Jaiswal, D., Kaushal, V., Singh, P. K., & Biswas, A. (2020). Green market segmentation and consumer profiling: A cluster approach to an emerging consumer market. *Benchmarking: An International Journal*, *28*(3), 792–812. https://doi.org/10.1108/BIJ-05-2020-0247

Lavelle-Hill, R., Goulding, J., Smith, G., Clarke, D. D., & Bibby, P. A. (2020). Psychological and demographic predictors of plastic bag consumption in transaction data. *Journal of Environmental Psychology*, *72*, 101473. https://doi.org/10.1016/j.jenvp.2020.101473

Scheuffelen, S., Kemper, J., & Brettel, M. (2019). How do human attitudes and values predict online marketing responsiveness: Comparing consumer segmentation bases toward brand purchase and marketing response. *Journal of Advertising Research*, *59*(2), 142–157. https://doi.org/10.2501/JAR-2019-021

Tan, P. J., Tanusondjaja, A., Corsi, A., Lockshin, L., Villani, C., & Bogomolova, S. (2021). Behavioural and psychographic characteristics of supermarket catalogue users. *Journal of Retailing and Consumer Services*, *60*, 102469. https://doi.org/10.1016/j.jretconser.2021.102469

von Behren, S., Bönisch, L., Vallée, J., & Vortisch, P. (2021). Classifying car owners in latent psychographic profiles. *Transportation Research Record*, *2675*(7), 142–152. https://doi.org/10.1177/0361198121994839

Chapter 6

Bellman, S., Nenycz-Thiel, M., Kennedy, R., Hartnett, N., & Varan, D. (2019). Best measures of attention to creative tactics in TV advertising: When do attention-getting devices capture or reduce attention? *Journal of Advertising Research, 59*(3), 295–311. https://doi.org/10.2501/JAR-2019-002

Benoit, I. D., & Miller, E. G. (2019). When does creativity matter: The impact of consumption motive and claim set-size. *The Journal of Consumer Marketing, 36*(4), 449–460. https://doi.org/10.1108/JCM-03-2018-2624

Lee, P. Y., & Lau, K. W. (2018). A new triadic creative role for advertising industry: A study of creatives' role identity in the rise of social media advertising. *Creative Industries Journal, 11*(2), 137–157. https://doi.org/10.1080/17510694.2018.1434362

Madleňák, A. (2021). Geolocation services and marketing communication from a global point of view. https://doi.org/10.1051/shsconf/20219202040

Modig, E., Dahlén, M., & Colliander, J. (2014). Consumer-perceived signals of 'creative' versus 'efficient' advertising: Investigating the roles of expense and effort. *International Journal of Advertising, 33*(1), 137–154. https://doi.org/10.2501/IJA-33-1-137-154

Parker, J., Koslow, S., Ang, L., & Tevi, A. (2021). How does consumer insight support the leap to a creative idea?: Inside the creative process: Shifting the advertising appeal from functional to emotional. *Journal of Advertising Research, 61*(1), 30–43. https://doi.org/10.2501/JAR-2020-012

Pritchard, M. (2021). Commentary: "Half my digital advertising is wasted...". *Journal of Marketing, 85*(1), 26–29. https://doi.org/10.1177/0022242920971195

Pryshchenko, S. V. (2019). creative technologies in advertising design. *Creativity Studies, 12*(1), 146–165. https://doi.org/10.3846/cs.2019.8403

Rosengren, S., Eisend, M., Koslow, S., & Dahlen, M. (2020). A meta-analysis of when and how advertising creativity works. *Journal of Marketing, 84*(6), 39–56. https://doi.org/10.1177/0022242920929288

Till, B. D., & Baack, D. W. (2005). RECALL AND PERSUASION: Does creative advertising matter? *Journal of Advertising, 34*(3), 47–57. https://doi.org/10.1080/00913367.2005.10639201

Turnbull, S., & Wheeler, C. (2017). The advertising creative process: A study of UK agencies. *Journal of Marketing Communications, 23*(2), 176–194. https://doi.org/10.1080/13527266.2014.1000361

Zhou, S., Luo, J., Yu, T., Li, D., Yin, Y., & Tang, X. (2020). Towards a neural model of creative evaluation in advertising: An electrophysiological study. *Scientific Reports, 10*(1), 21958–21958. https://doi.org/10.1038/s41598-020-79044-0

Chapter 7

Croxen-John, D., & van Tonder, J. (2020). *E-commerce website optimization: Why 95% of your website visitors don't buy, and what you can do about it.* Kogan Page, Limited.

Dovzhik, V., Dovzhik, G., & Fedyanina, T. (2019). Using e-marketing on the example of detailed targeting technology. *E-Management, 2*(3), 29–37. https://doi.org/10.26425/2658-3445-2019-3-29-37

Kühnel, J., Ebner, M., & Ebner, M. (2020). Chatbots for brand representation in comparison with traditional websites. *International Journal of Interactive Mobile Technologies, 14*(18), 18–33. https://doi.org/10.3991/ijim.v14i18.13433

Levin, A. (2020). *Influencer marketing for brands: What YouTube and Instagram can teach you about the future of digital advertising* (1st 2020. ed.). Apress.

Li, J., Luo, X., Lu, X., & Moriguchi, T. (2021). The double-edged effects of E-commerce cart retargeting: Does retargeting too early backfire? *Journal of Marketing, 85*(4), 123–140. https://doi.org/10.1177/0022242920959043

Liu, M., Yue, W., Qiu, L., & Li, J. (2020). An effective budget management framework for real-time bidding in online advertising. *IEEE Access, 8,* 131107–131118. https://doi.org/10.1109/ACCESS.2020.2970463

Mukherjee, K., & Banerjee, N. (2019). Social networking sites and customers' attitude towards advertisements. *Journal of Research in Interactive Marketing, 13*(4), 477–491. https://doi.org/10.1108/JRIM-06-2018-0081

Schultz, C. D. (2018). The impact of ad positioning in search engine advertising: A multifaceted decision problem. *Electronic Commerce Research,* 1–24. https://doi.org/10.1007/s10660-018-9313-z

Silva, S. C., Duarte, P. A. O., & Almeida, S. R. (2020). How companies evaluate the ROI of social media marketing programmes: Insights from B2B and B2C. *The Journal of Business & Industrial Marketing, 35*(12), 2097–2110. https://doi.org/10.1108/JBIM-06-2019-0291

Tunuguntla, S., & Hoban, P. R. (2021). A near-optimal bidding strategy for real-time display advertising auctions. *Journal of Marketing Research, 58*(1), 1–21. https://doi.org/10.1177/0022243720968547

Chapter 8

Bellman, S., Beal, V., Wooley, B., & Varan, D. (2020). Viewing time as a cross-media metric: Comparing viewing time for video advertising on television and online. *Journal of Business Research, 120,* 103–113. https://doi.org/10.1016/j.jbusres.2020.07.034

Bruce, N. I., Becker, M., & Reinartz, W. (2020). Communicating brands in television advertising. *Journal of Marketing Research, 57*(2), 236–256. https://doi.org/10.1177/0022243719892576

Findley, F., Johnson, K., Crang, D., & Stewart, D. W. (2020). Effectiveness and efficiency of TV's brand-building power: A historical review: Why the persuasion rating point (PRP) is a more accurate metric than the GRP. *Journal of Advertising Research, 60*(4), 361. https://doi.org/10.2501/JAR-2020-011

Laming, D. (2020). Recall of advertisements after various lapses of time. *Psychological Research.* https://doi.org/10.1007/s00426-020-01408-y

Lesscher, L., Lobschat, L., & Verhoef, P. C. (2021). Do offline and online go hand in hand? Cross-channel and synergy effects of direct mailing and display advertising. *International Journal of Research in Marketing, 38*(3), 678–697. https://doi.org/10.1016/j.ijresmar.2020.11.003

Quirino, F. G. S., Ribeiro, L. M. P., Assis, L. B., & Silva, A. F. (2020). 200 million in action: The cordial man and the film analysis of world cup television advertisements. *Soccer and Society, 21*(2), 180–195. https://doi.org/10.1080/14660970.2018.1544556

Varan, D., Nenycz-Thiel, M., Kennedy, R., & Bellman, S. (2020). The effects of commercial length on advertising impact: What short advertisements can and cannot deliver. *Journal of Advertising Research, 60*(1), 54–70. https://doi.org/10.2501/JAR-2019-036

Vyas, R., & Parmar, G. (2019). A study on role of television advertisement on cosmetic purchase among youth. *Global Journal of Research in Management, 9*(1), 29.

Weibel, D., di Francesco, R., Kopf, R., Fahrni, S., Brunner, A., Kronenberg, P., Lobmaier, J. S., Reber, T. P., Mast, F. W., & Wissmath, B. (2019). TV vs. YouTube: TV advertisements capture more visual attention, create more positive emotions and have a stronger impact on implicit long-term memory. *Frontiers in Psychology, 10*, 626–626. https://doi.org/10.3389/fpsyg.2019 .00626

Wolf, H. G., VII, & Donato, P. (2019). Six-second advertisements on television: Best practices for capturing visual attention. *Journal of Advertising Research, 59*(2), 196–207. https://doi.org/10.2501/JAR-2019-012

Chapter 9

Bandyopadhyay, N., Sivakumaran, B., Patro, S., & Kumar, R. S. (2021). Immediate or delayed! Whether various types of consumer sales promotions drive impulse buying?: An empirical investigation. *Journal of Retailing and Consumer Services, 61*, 102532. https://doi.org/10.1016/j.jretconser.2021 .102532

Fam, K., Brito, P. Q., Gadekar, M., Richard, J. E., Jargal, U., & Liu, W. (2019). Consumer attitude towards sales promotion techniques: A multi-country study. *Asia Pacific Journal of Marketing and Logistics, 31*(2), 437–463. https://doi .org/10.1108/APJML-01-2018-0005

Gorji, M., & Siami, S. (2020). How sales promotion display affects customer shopping intentions in retails. *International Journal of Retail & Distribution Management.* https://doi.org/10.1108/IJRDM-12-2019-0407

Jin, S. V., & Muqaddam, A. (2019). Product placement 2.0: "Do brands need influencers, or do influencers need brands?". *The Journal of Brand Management, 26*(5), 522–537. https://doi.org/10.1057/s41262-019-00151-z

Kaveh, A., Nazari, M., van der Rest, J.-P., & Mira, S. A. (2020). Customer engagement in sales promotion. *Marketing Intelligence & Planning, 39*(3), 424–437. https://doi.org/10.1108/MIP-11-2019-0582

Peng, L., Zhang, W., Wang, X., & Liang, S. (2019). Moderating effects of time pressure on the relationship between perceived value and purchase intention in social E-commerce sales promotion: Considering the impact of product involvement. *Information & Management, 56*(2), 317–328. https://doi.org/10 .1016/j.im.2018.11.007

Russell, C. A. (2019). Expanding the agenda of research on product placement: A commercial intertext. *Journal of Advertising, 48*(1), 38–48. https://doi.org/10 .1080/00913367.2019.1579690

Sinha, S. K., & Verma, P. (2018). Impact of sales promotion's benefits on brand equity: An empirical investigation. *Global Business Review, 19*(6), 1663–1680. https://doi.org/10.1177/0972150918794977

Sinha, S. K., & Verma, P. (2019). The link between sales promotion's benefits and consumers perception: A comparative study between rural and urban consumers. *Global Business Review, 20*(2), 498–514. https://doi.org/10.1177 /0972150918825398

Yang, B., & Mattila, A. S. (2020). How rational thinking style affects sales promotion effectiveness. *International Journal of Hospitality Management*, *84*, 102335. https://doi.org/10.1016/j.ijhm.2019.102335

Chapter 10

Davies, C., & Hobbs, M. (2020). Irresistible possibilities: Examining the uses and consequences of social media influencers for contemporary public relations. *Public Relations Review*, *46*(5). https://doi.org/10.1016/j.pubrev.2020.101983

Hurst, B., & Johnston, K. A. (2021). The social imperative in public relations: Utilities of social impact, social license and engagement. *Public Relations Review*, *47*(2). https://doi.org/10.1016/j.pubrev.2021.102039

Knight, W. M., & Sweetser, K. D. (2021). Mind the gap: Understanding public relations competence in the eyes of practitioners and the dominant coalition. *Public Relations Review*, *47*(2), 102037. https://doi.org/10.1016/j.pubrev.2021.102037

Lee, Y., & Kim, K. H. (2020). De-motivating employees' negative communication behaviors on anonymous social media: The role of public relations. *Public Relations Review*, *46*(4), 101955. https://doi.org/10.1016/j.pubrev.2020.101955

Marsh, C. (2021). Echoes and shadows: Situating social licenses to operate within the six R's of public relations. *Public Relations Review*, *47*(1), 102015. https://doi.org/10.1016/j.pubrev.2021.102015

Mehta, A. M., Liu, B. F., Tyquin, E., & Tam, L. (2021). A process view of crisis misinformation: How public relations professionals detect, manage, and evaluate crisis misinformation. *Public Relations Review*, *47*(2), 102040. https://doi.org/10.1016/j.pubrev.2021.102040

Topić, M., Cunha, M. J., Reigstad, A., Jelen-Sanchez, A., & Moreno, Á. (2020). Women in public relations (1982–2019). *Journal of Communication Management (London, England)*. https://doi.org/10.1108/JCOM-11-2019-0143

Tsetsura, K., & Vergara, L. (2021). The U.S. capability framework for public relations and communication management: Results of a national three-stage study. *Public Relations Review*, *47*(2), 102016. https://doi.org/10.1016/j.pubrev.2021.102016

Xu, J. (2020). Does the medium matter? A meta-analysis on using social media vs. traditional media in crisis communication. *Public Relations Review*, *46*(4), 101947. https://doi.org/10.1016/j.pubrev.2020.101947

Zabolotna, A., & Yu, S. M. (2020). Developing corporate communication with stakeholders of IT-enterprise in the foreign market. *Bìznes Ìnform (Multilingual Ed.)*, *11*(514), 411–417. https://doi.org/10.32983/2222-4459-2020-11-411-417

Chapter 11

Baker, K. (2019). *Axios: Pittsburgh's heinz field highlights the skyrocketing cost of NFL stadium naming rights*. Newstex.

Colucci, M., Montaguti, E., & Lago, U. (2008). Managing brand extension via licensing: An investigation into the high-end fashion industry. *International*

Journal of Research in Marketing, 25(2), 129–137. https://doi.org/10.1016/j .ijresmar.2008.01.002

DelVecchio, D., Henard, D. H., & Freling, T. H. (2006). The effect of sales promotion on post-promotion brand preference: A meta-analysis. *Journal of Retailing*, 82(3), 203–213. https://doi.org/10.1016/j.jretai.2005.10.001

Hofer, K. M. (2015). International brand promotion standardization and performance. *Management Research Review*, 38(7), 685–702. https://doi.org /10.1108/MRR-06-2013-0136

Jayachandran, S., Kaufman, P., Kumar, V., & Hewett, K. (2013). Brand licensing: What drives royalty rates? *Journal of Marketing*, 77(5), 108–122. https://doi .org/10.1509/jm.11.0145

Kim, C., & Takashima, K. (2019). Effects of retail organisation design on improving private label merchandising. *European Journal of Marketing*, 53(12), 2582–2603. https://doi.org/10.1108/EJM-03-2018-0194

Kpossa, M. R., & Lick, E. (2020). Visual merchandising of pastries in foodscapes: The influence of plate colours on consumers' flavour expectations and perceptions. *Journal of Retailing and Consumer Services*, 52, 101684. https:// doi.org/10.1016

Kwak, D. H., Kwon, Y., & Lim, C. (2015). Licensing a sports brand: Effects of team brand cue, identification, and performance priming on multidimensional values and purchase intentions. *The Journal of Product & Brand Management*, 24(3), 198–210. https://doi.org/10.1108/JPBM-05-2014-0579

Martin, D. S., Bourdeau, B. L., & Stephan, J. (2020). Measuring the effectiveness of facility naming rights sponsorships. *Journal of Business Research*, 110, 51–64. https://doi.org/10.1016/j.jbusres.2019.12.036

Roggeveen, A. L., Grewal, D., Karsberg, J., Noble, S. M., Nordfält, J., Patrick, V. M., Schweiger, E., Soysal, G., Dillard, A., Cooper, N., & Olson, R. (2021). Forging meaningful consumer-brand relationships through creative merchandise offerings and innovative merchandising strategies. *Journal of Retailing*, 97(1), 81–98. https://doi.org/10.1016/j.jretai.2020.11.006

Chapter 12

Bag, S., Gupta, S., Kumar, A., & Sivarajah, U. (2021). An integrated artificial intelligence framework for knowledge creation and B2B marketing rational decision making for improving firm performance. *Industrial Marketing Management*, 92(92), 178–189. https://doi.org/10.1016/j.indmarman.2020.12 .001

Chang, Y., Wang, X., Su, L., & Cui, A. P. (2020). B2B brand orientation, relationship commitment, and buyer-supplier relational performance. *The Journal of Business & Industrial Marketing*, 36(2), 324–336. https://doi.org /10.1108/JBIM-10-2019-0454

Fraccastoro, S., Gabrielsson, M., & Pullins, E. B. (2021). The integrated use of social media, digital, and traditional communication tools in the B2B sales process of international SMEs. *International Business Review*, 30(4), 101776. https://doi.org/10.1016/j.ibusrev.2020.101776

Kim, K. H., & Moon, H. (2021). Innovative digital marketing management in B2B markets. *Industrial Marketing Management*, 95, 1–4. https://doi.org/10 .1016/j.indmarman.2021.01.016

Mora Cortez, R., Højbjerg Clarke, A., & Freytag, P. V. (2021). B2B market segmentation: A systematic review and research agenda. *Journal of Business Research*, *126*, 415–428. https://doi.org/10.1016/j.jbusres.2020.12.070

Paschen, J., Paschen, U., Pala, E., & Kietzmann, J. (2021). Artificial intelligence (AI) and value co-creation in B2B sales: Activities, actors and resources. *Australasian Marketing Journal*, *29*(3), 243–251. https://doi.org/10.1016/j.ausmj.2020.06.004

Swani, K., Brown, B. P., & Mudambi, S. M. (2020). The untapped potential of B2B advertising: A literature review and future agenda. *Industrial Marketing Management*, *89*, 581–593. https://doi.org/10.1016/j.indmarman.2019.05.010

Tanner, J. F. (2021). The state of business to business marketing research. *Journal of Marketing Theory and Practice*, *29*(1), 92–100. https://doi.org/10.1080/10696679.2020.1860682

Yaghtin, S., Safarzadeh, H., & Karimi Zand, M. (2020). Planning a goal-oriented B2B content marketing strategy. *Marketing Intelligence & Planning*. https://doi.org/10.1108/MIP-11-2019-0559

Yoon, Y. L., Yoon, Y., Nam, H., & Choi, J. (2021). Buyer-supplier matching in online B2B marketplace: An empirical study of small- and medium-sized enterprises (SMEs). *Industrial Marketing Management*, *93*, 90–100. https://doi.org/10.1016/j.indmarman.2020.12.010

Index